Style Manual

An official guide to the form and style of Federal Government publishing | **2016**

Keeping America Informed | OFFICIAL

Names: United States. Government Publishing Office, author.
Title: Style manual : an official guide to the form and style of federal government publications / U.S. Government Publishing Office.
Other titles: Official guide to the form and style of federal government publications | Also known as: GPO style manual

ISBN 978-1986408059

Previous printings of the GPO STYLE MANUAL: 1894, 1898, 1900, 1903, 1908, 1909, 1911, 1912, 1914, 1917, 1922, 1923, 1924, 1926, 1928, 1929, 1933, 1934, 1935, 1937, 1939, 1945, 1953, 1959, 1962, 1967, 1973, 1984, 2000, 2008

EXTRACT FROM THE PUBLIC PRINTING LAW

(TITLE 44, U.S.C.)

§ 1105. Form and style of work for departments

The Director of the Government Publishing Office shall determine the form and style in which the printing or binding ordered by a department is executed, and the material and the size of type used, having proper regard to economy, workmanship, and the purposes for which the work is needed.

(Pub. L. 90–620, Oct. 22, 1968, 82 Stat. 1261; Pub. L. 113–235, div. H, title I, § 1301(c)(1), Dec. 16, 2014, 128 Stat. 2537.)

Historical and Revision Notes

Based on 44 U.S. Code, 1964 ed., § 216 (Jan. 12, 1895, ch. 23, § 51, 28 Stat. 608).

Amendments

2014—Pub. L. 113–235 substituted "Director of the Government Publishing Office" for "Public Printer".

About This Manual

The GPO STYLE MANUAL, as it is popularly known, is issued under the authority of section 1105 of title 44 of the U.S. Code, which requires the Director of the GPO to "determine the form and style in which the printing . . . ordered by a department is executed, . . . having proper regard to economy, workmanship, and the purposes for which the work is needed." The MANUAL is prepared by the GPO Style Board, composed of proofreading, printing, and Government documents specialists from within GPO, where all congressional publications and many other key Government documents are prepared.

The first GPO STYLE MANUAL appeared in 1894. It was developed originally as a printer's stylebook to standardize word and type treatment, and it remains so today. Through successive editions, however, the MANUAL has come to be widely recognized by writers and editors both within and outside the Federal Government as one of the most useful resources in the editorial arsenal. And now in the 21st century, writers and editors are using the MANUAL in the preparation of the informational content of Government publications that appear in digital formats.

Writers and editors whose disciplines have taught them aspects of style different from those found in the GPO STYLE MANUAL will appreciate the difficulty of establishing a single standard. Users of this MANUAL should consider it instead as a general guide. Its rules cannot be regarded as rigid, for the printed word assumes many shapes and variations in final presentation, and usage changes over time as language evolves. Periodically the MANUAL is updated, as this edition has been, to eliminate obsolete standards, update form and usage, and adjust the guidance for document preparation and appearance to current custom.

Comments and suggestions from users of the GPO STYLE MANUAL are welcomed. All such correspondence may be emailed to the GPO Style Board at gpostyle@gpo.gov.

A digital version of this Manual appears on GPO's **govinfo** at https://www.govinfo.gov/gpo-style-manual. Revisions and updates are made to the online version of this Manual periodically. Accordingly, that document rather than the printed edition should be consulted as the most up-to-date version available.

For the purposes of the GPO Style Manual, examples provided throughout both the printed and digital versions are to be given the same weight as the enumerated rules.

Acknowledgments

The GPO Style Board would like to thank the following people for assistance in the production of this edition of the GPO Style Manual:

Special thanks go to Michael M. Shelton, Program Analyst, Office of Policy, National Park Service, and Member of the U.S. Board on Geographic Names, for his wealth of knowledge, special consultation, and research during the entire revision process of this Manual. He has, indeed, been a true friend to the Board.

M. Michael Abramson, past Chair of the GPO Style Board, who acted as an adviser to the present Style Board.

Elizabeth Appel, Bureau of Indian Affairs, U.S. Department of the Interior, for advice on the issue of capitalization of "Tribe" and "Tribal."

Douglas Caldwell, Geospatial Research Laboratory, U.S. Army Engineer Research and Development Center and Jacqueline Nolan, Geography and Map Division, Library of Congress, for information on acronyms and cartographic names.

The offices of Indiana Senators Dan Coats and Joe Donnelly and Indiana Governor Mike Pence for information regarding the demonym "Hoosier."

Rachel R. Creviston, Chief of Staff, Office of the Secretary of the Senate; Matthew P. McGowan, Senate Committee on Rules and Administration; and Corey Plank, Lead Cartographer—Remote Sensing, Bureau of Land Management, for consulting on the issue regarding compass directional abbreviations.

Linda Crown, Administrative Specialist, Office of Weights and Measures, National Institute of Standards and Technology, for information on terms of measures.

Robert W. Dahl, Cadastral Surveyor, U.S. Department of the Interior, Bureau of Land Management, Minerals & Realty Management Directorate, Division of Lands, Realty & Cadastral Survey (WO-350), for his contribution of the Principal Meridians and Base Lines of the United States tables, Chapter 18.

Cynthia L. Etkin, Program Planning Specialist, Office of the Superintendent of Documents, Government Publishing Office, for her assistance in the production of this MANUAL.

Dean Gardei, Brand and Web Manager, Government Publishing Office, for the design of the cover and title page.

Solange A. Garvey, Foreign Affairs Officer and Leo Dillon, Office of the Geographer and Global Issues, U.S. Department of State; and Trent Palmer, Executive Secretary for Foreign Names, U.S. Board on Geographic Names, for information on foreign countries and terms.

Jeremy Gelb, IT Specialist, Government Publishing Office, for technical assistance in the production of this MANUAL.

Christine Jones, Editorial Team Lead, Information Design and Publishing Staff, National Center for Health Statistics, Centers for Disease Control and Prevention, for information on medical eponyms.

Library Services & Content Management Staff, including Patricia A. Duplantis, Systems Librarian; Laurie B. Hall, Chief and Acting Superintendent of Documents; James M. Mauldin, Manager, Office of Archival Management; and Kelly M. Seifert, Strategic Communications Coordinator, for their feedback and support.

Christine McMahon, Program Planner, Programs, Strategy and Technology, Government Publishing Office, for her contribution in updating the GPO's Digital Information Initiatives.

James Moore, Gibbs & Cox, Inc., for information regarding technical abbreviations.

Kirk Petri and Jon Quandt, Lead Program Planners, Programs, Strategy and Technology, and John Foley and Jiang (John) Zheng, IT Specialists, Information Technology, Government Publishing Office, for their contributions in updating the information technology acronyms and initialisms section in the abbreviations and letter symbols chapter.

Kathleen Swiatek, IT Specialist, IT Product Support, for Bill language assistance.

Marcia Thompson, Chief, Congressional Record Index Office, Government Publishing Office, for revisions to the pages relating to the Congressional Record Index.

Louis Yost, Executive Secretary and Jennifer Runyon, Staff, U.S. Board on Geographic Names, for help on a variety of names and geographic issues.

Employees of the Production Planning and Control Division, Government Publishing Office, for their contributions during the preproduction/production process.

Employees of the Proof and Copy Markup Section, Government Publishing Office, for their constant contributions to the GPO STYLE MANUAL.

Current users who have contributed many ideas and suggestions that were incorporated into this edition of the GPO STYLE MANUAL.

GPO's Digital Information Initiatives

In the digital age, GPO is responsible for providing public access to the digital versions of many of the official documents it prints, as well as—to the greatest extent possible—the digital versions of Government publications that are not printed but are otherwise made available on other Federal websites. GPO recognizes that a Federal author today often begins the content creation process at a computer, and frequently publishes the final document to the web without creating a print version that will make its way to a user's hands or a library's shelves.

GPO Access

To accommodate this transition in Federal publishing strategies while preserving GPO's core responsibility for ensuring public access to Government publications, Congress enacted Public Law 103-40, the Government Printing Office Electronic Information Access Enhancement Act of 1993, which required GPO to establish access to key Government publications in digital format and provide a system of storage to ensure permanent public access to the information they contain. Opened to the public in 1994, the resulting website, *GPO Access*, was GPO's entrance into the digital age. In 2003, the National Archives and Records Administration formally recognized GPO as an affiliate archive for the digital content on the *GPO Access* site. *GPO Access* operated for 15 years before it was retired following the introduction of GPO's Federal Digital System (FDsys).

Federal Digital System (FDsys)

To meet continued public demand for access to digital Government publications, provide for an increased range of search and retrieval options, and ensure the preservation of official Government information content in the 21st century, GPO embarked on the construction of a more comprehensive online capability, called the Federal Digital System, or FDsys, available at www.fdsys.gov.

FDsys was launched as a beta website in 2009 and permanently replaced *GPO Access* in 2011. FDsys provides free access to hundreds of thousands of official Federal Government publications in digital format from all three branches of the Federal Government, including congressional bills, the Congressional Record, the Federal Register, the Compilation of Presidential Documents, the U.S. Code, the Code of Federal Regulations, and opinions from more than 100 Federal courts. In 2016, GPO reached a milestone of two billion retrievals of digital Government information from FDsys (the equivalent of nine retrievals per second over seven years of operation).

govinfo beta website

In February 2016, GPO launched the next generation of digital public access, **govinfo** (at www.govinfo.gov) as a public beta website to eventually replace the FDsys public website. **govinfo** is a redesign of FDsys featuring a modern, easy-to-use look and feel that syncs with the need of today's Government information users for quick and effective digital access across a variety of digital platforms. It was developed with a focus on implementing feedback from users and improving overall search and access to FDsys content. The redesigned, mobile-friendly website incorporates state-of-the-art innovative technologies and includes several new features for an overall enhanced user experience. **govinfo** is the new front door to accessing the same official, preserved content that GPO has made available through *GPO Access* and FDsys for more than two decades.

The key new features of **govinfo** include the capability to link related content, new ways to browse content, a new open-source search engine, enhancements to the search filters, and more options for sharing pages and content on social media.

Digital preservation

Content in FDsys and **govinfo** is preserved to ensure permanent availability in electronic form. As a preservation repository, GPO follows archival system standards to ensure long-term preservation and access to digital content. GPO's digital stewardship vision is to operate a standards-based preservation repository and to implement user-friendly, responsive, and innovative technologies to ensure that all archived content information can be obtained, rendered, used, and understood by the designated community into the future.

In 2015, GPO began pursuing certification of its flagship system as a Trustworthy Digital Repository for Government information under ISO 16363: Audit and Certification of Trustworthy Digital Repositories.

Authentication of digital documents

The increasing use of documents in digital format poses a special challenge in verifying authenticity, because digital technology makes such documents easy to alter or copy in unauthorized or illegitimate ways. GPO assures users that the publications available from GPO websites are as official and authentic as publications that have been printed by GPO for many years. GPO digital systems operate with established trust relationships between all parties in digital transactions. A visible digital signature, viewed as the GPO Seal of Authenticity signified by an eagle, verifies document integrity and authenticity on GPO online Federal documents. The visible digital signature on PDF documents on FDsys and **govinfo** signifies a guarantee that the information in the document is official, authentic, and secure.

XML bulk data repository

Since the launch of FDsys, GPO has worked with partners in the legislative and executive branches to expand the availability of Government information content in support of an open and transparent government. One such effort involves making content available in machine-readable Extensible Markup Language (XML) format for bulk download. The effort began in 2009 and has grown to nine collections now available through GPO's bulk data repository at www.gpo.gov/fdsys/bulkdata. The repository features data collections including text, summary, and status information for bills introduced in the House of Representatives and the Senate, the annual official and unofficial digital versions of the Code of Federal Regulations, the Federal Register, the U.S. Government Manual, and the Public Papers of the Presidents of the United States.

Information available on GPO's XML bulk data repository helps maximize the ways this data can be used or repurposed by users. Making information available in XML permits data to be reused and repurposed for mobile web applications, data mashups, and other analytical tools by third-party providers, contributing to efforts supporting openness and transparency in government.

Catalog of U.S. Government Publications (CGP)

GPO is responsible for creating a catalog and index for all public documents published by the Federal Government that are not confidential in character. This work serves libraries and the public nationwide and enables people to locate desired Government publications in all formats. The public interface for accessing these cataloging records is the Catalog of U.S. Government Publications (CGP), which is available in digital format at http://catalog.gpo.gov. Using the CGP, anyone can freely access descriptive information for historical and current Government publications as well as digital links to their full content. Print versions of U.S. Government publications may be found by contacting a Federal depository library: https://catalog.gpo.gov/fdlpdir/FDLPdir.jsp.

Ben's Guide to the U.S. Government

Ben's Guide, available at http://bensguide.gpo.gov, provides learning tools for K–12 students, parents, and educators. The site provides age-specific explanations about how the Federal Government works, explains the use of the primary source materials available on FDsys and **govinfo**, and explains GPO's role in the Federal Government.

Online U.S. Government Bookstore

Government information users may also locate and order publications available for sale in both print and digital—including eBook—formats through GPO's Publication and Information Sales Program. Orders may be placed online securely at https://bookstore.gpo.gov.

Applicability of the GPO Style Manual to digital publications

The rules of grammar, spelling, punctuation, and related matters, as stated in this Manual, will serve well when preparing documents for digital access. Most of the documents on FDsys and **govinfo** are derived from databases used in the printing of Government publications. As the availability of Government publications in digital formats continues to grow, the rules as stated in this Manual will continue to be GPO's standard for all document preparation, whether for conventional printing or digital access.

Contents

1. Advice to Authors and Editors

The GPO Style Manual is intended to facilitate the production of Government publications. Careful observance of the following suggestions will aid in expediting your publication and reduce costs.

1.1. Making changes after submission of copy delays the production of the publication and adds to the expense of the work; therefore, copy must be carefully edited before being submitted to the Government Publishing Office.

1.2. Legible copy, not faint reproductions, must be furnished.

1.3. Copy should be on one side only with each sheet numbered consecutively. If both sides of copy are to be used, a duplicate set of copy must be furnished.

1.4. To avoid unnecessary expense, it is advisable to have each page begin with a new paragraph.

1.5. Proper names, signatures, figures, foreign words, and technical terms should be written plainly.

1.6. Chemical symbols, such as Al, Cl, Tl are sometimes mistaken for A1, C1, T1. Editors must indicate whether the second character is a letter or a figure.

1.7. Footnote reference marks in text and tables should be arranged consecutively from left to right across each page of copy.

1.8. Photographs, drawings, and legends being used for illustrations should be placed in the manuscript where they are to appear in the publication. They should be on individual sheets, as they are handled separately during typesetting.

1.9. If a publication is composed of several parts, a scheme of the desired arrangement must accompany the first installment of copy.

1.10. To reduce the possibility of costly blank pages, avoid use of new odd pages and halftitles whenever possible. Generally these refinements should be limited to quality bookwork.

1.11. Samples should be furnished if possible. They should be plainly marked showing the desired type, size of type page, illustrations if any, paper, trim, lettering, and binding.

1.12. In looseleaf or perforated-on-fold work, indicate folio sequence, including blank pages, by circling in blue. Begin with first text page (title). Do not folio separate covers or dividers.

1.13. Indicate on copy if separate or self-cover. When reverse printing in whole or in part is required, indicate if solid or tone.

1.14. Avoid use of oversize fold-ins wherever possible. This can be done by splitting a would-be fold-in and arranging the material to appear as facing pages in the text. Where fold-ins are numerous and cannot be split, consider folding and inserting these into an envelope pasted to the inside back cover.

1.15. Every effort should be made to keep complete jobs of over 4 pages to signatures (folded units) of 8, 12, 16, 24, or 32 pages. Where possible, avoid having more than two blank pages at the end.

1.16. Indicate alternative choice of paper on the requisition. Where possible, confine choice of paper to general use items carried in inventory as shown in the GPO Paper Catalogue (https://www.gpo.gov/pdfs/customers/GPOPaperCatalogue0614.pdf).

1.17. If nonstandard trim sizes and/or type areas are used, indicate head and back margins. Otherwise, GPO will determine the margins.

1.18. Customers should submit copy for running heads and indicate the numbering sequence for folios, including the preliminary pages.

1.19. Corrections should be made on first proofs returned, as later proofs are intended for verification only. All corrections must be indicated on the "R" (revise) set of proofs, and only that set should be returned to GPO.

1.20. Corrections should be marked in the margins of a proof opposite the indicated errors, not by writing over the print or between the lines. All queries on proofs must be answered or no change will be made.

1.21. The following GPO publications relate to material included in this MANUAL.

Government Paper Specification Standards

The purpose of these standards is to achieve compliance with relevant statutes regarding printing papers; address environmental, workplace safety, and paper longevity issues; and achieve maximum savings in the Government's paper purchases. 2011 (https://www.gpo.gov/pdfs/customers/sfas/vol12/vol_12.pdf).

GPO Paper Samples

This publication is a supplement to Government Paper Specification Standards. It includes samples of papers used by GPO. Used as a planning aid and guide in selecting an adequate grade, weight, and color of paper for a job of printing. 2011.

1.22. Corrections made to proofs should be indicated as follows:

Mark	Meaning
⊙	Insert period
	Insert comma
:	Insert colon
;	Insert semicolon
?	Insert question mark
!	Insert exclamation mark
=/	Insert hyphen
	Insert apostrophe
	Insert quotation marks
	Insert 1-en dash
	Insert 1-em dash
#	Insert space
ld>	Insert ( ) points of space
shill	Insert shilling
∨	Superior
∧	Inferior
(/)	Parentheses
[/]	Brackets
□	Indent 1 em
□□	Indent 2 ems
¶	Paragraph
no ¶	No paragraph
tr	Transpose[1]—used in margin
	Transpose[2]—used in text
sp	Spell out
ital	Italic—used in margin
	Italic—used in text
b.f.	Boldface—used in margin
	Boldface—used in text
s.c.	Small caps—used in margin
	Small caps—used in text

Mark	Meaning
rom.	Roman type
caps.	Caps—used in margin
	Caps—used in text
c+sc	Caps & small caps—used in margin
	Caps & small caps—used in text
l.c.	Lowercase—used in margin
/	Used in text to show deletion or substitution
	Delete
	Delete and close up
w.f.	Wrong font
	Close up
	Move right
	Move left
	Move up
	Move down
‖	Align vertically
=	Align horizontally
	Center horizontally
	Center vertically
eq.#	Equalize space—used in margin
	Equalize space—used in text
....	Let it stand—used in text
stet.	Let it stand—used in margin
⊗	Letter(s) not clear
run over	Carry over to next line
run back	Carry back to preceding line
out, see copy	Something omitted—see copy
S/?	Question to author to delete[3]
∧	Caret—General indicator used to mark position of error.

[1] In lieu of the traditional mark "tr" used to indicate letter or number transpositions, the striking out of the incorrect letters or numbers and the placement of the correct matter in the margin of the proof is the preferred method of indicating transposition corrections.

[2] Corrections involving more than two characters should be marked by striking out the entire word or number and placing the correct form in the margin. This mark should be reserved to show transposition of words.

[3] The form of any query carried should be such that an answer may be given simply by crossing out the complete query if a negative decision is made or the right-hand (question mark) portion to indicate an affirmative answer.

TYPOGRAPHICAL ERRORS

It does not appear that the earliest printers had any method of correcting errors before the form was on the press/ The learned The learned correctors of the first two centuries of printing were notproofreaders in our sense/ they where rather what we should term office editors Their labors were chiefly to see that the proof corresponded to the copy, but that the printed page was correct in its latinity that the words were there, and that the sense was right. They cared but little about orthography, bad letters or purely printers errors, and when the text seemed to them wrong they consulted fresh authorities or altered it on their own responsibility. Good proofs in the modern sense, were impossible until professional readers were employed men who had first a printer's education, and then spent many years in the correction of proof. The orthography of English, which for the past century has undergone little change, was very fluctuating until after the publication of Johnson's Dictionary, and capitals, which have been used with considerable regularity for the past 80 years, were previously used on the miss or hit plan. The approach to regularity, so far as we have, may be attributed to the growth of a class of professional proofreaders, and it is to them that we owe the correctness of modern printing. More er ors have been found in the Bible than in any other one work. For many generations it was frequently the case that Bibles were brought out stealthily, from fear of governmental interference. They were frequently printed from imperfect texts, and were often modified to meet the views of those who publised themThe story is related that a certain woman in Germany, who was the wife of a Printer, and had become disgusted with the continual assertions of the superiority of man over woman which she had heard, hurried into the composing room while her husband was at supper and altered a sentence in the Bible, which he was printing, so that it read Narr instead of Herr, thus making the verse read "And he shall be thy fool" instead of "and he shall be thy lord." The word not was omitted by Barker, the king's printer in England in 1632, in printing the seventh commandment He was fined £3,000 on this account.

Note.—The system of marking proofs can be made easier by the use of an imaginary vertical line through the center of the type area. The placement of corrections in the left-hand margin for those errors found in the left-hand portion of the proof and in the right-hand margin for right-side errors prevents overcrowding of marks and facilitates corrections.

2. General Instructions

Job planning

2.1. New publications are evaluated by application specialists who review their requirements and design the necessary formats. Each format is made to conform exactly to the copy's specifications for page dimensions, line length, indentions, typefaces, etc. Upon completion, sample pages are produced and submitted to the customer. At this time, customer agencies are requested to indicate precise details of any style changes because this set of pages serves as a guide for the copy preparer, the beginning of actual production.

2.2. Changes in the needs of the library community have led to a move toward uniform treatment of the component parts of publications. In developing standards to guide publishers of Government documents, consideration has been given to the changing needs of those who seek to produce, reference, index, abstract, store, search, and retrieve data. Certain identifying elements will be printed on all publications in accordance with this MANUAL and with standards developed by the American National Standards Institute (ANSI).

Publications such as books and pamphlets should contain:

(a) Title and other title information;
(b) Name of department issuing or creating the publication;
(c) Name of author(s) and editor(s) (department or individual);
(d) Date of issuance;
(e) Availability (publisher, printer, or other source and address);
(f) Superintendent of Documents classification and stock numbers, if applicable; and
(g) International Standard Book Number (ISBN).

(See ANSI Standard Z39.15, Title Leaves of a Book.)

Reports of a scientific or technical nature should contain:

(a) Title and other title information;
(b) Report number;
(c) Author(s);
(d) Performing organization;
(e) Sponsoring department;
(f) Date of issuance;
(g) Type of report and period covered;
(h) Availability (publisher, printer, or other source and address); and
(i) Superintendent of Documents classification and stock numbers if applicable.

(See ANSI/NISO Standard Z39.18—2005 (R2010), Scientific and Technical Reports—Preparation, Presentation, and Preservation.)

Journals, magazines, periodicals, and similar publications should contain:

(a) Title and other title information;
(b) Volume and issue numbers;
(c) Date of issue;
(d) Publishing or sponsoring department;
(e) Availability (publisher, printer, or other source and address);
(f) International Standard Serial Number; and
(g) Superintendent of Documents classification and stock numbers if applicable.

(See ANSI Standard Z39.1, American Standard Reference Data and Arrangement of Periodicals.)

Federal Aviation Administration ← *Sponsoring organization*

Report number → DOT/FAA/AM–08/6

Availability statement → Office of Aerospace Medicine
Washington, DC 20591

Title → **Use of Weather Information by General Aviation Pilots, Part I, Quantitative: Reported Use and Value of Providers and Products**

Author → William R. Knecht

Performing organization name and address → Civil Aerospace Medical Institute
Oklahoma City, OK 73125

Date → March 2008

Type of report → Final Report

Notes:

(1) This sample report cover is reduced in size.

(2) In this sample, items are justified left. Other cover designs and typefaces are acceptable.

(3) This sample page was prepared according to the guidelines of the American National Standards Institute, www.ansi.org. Users of ANSI standards are cautioned that all standards are reviewed periodically and subject to revision.

Makeup

2.3. The design and makeup of a publication is the responsibility of the publisher. However, when the following elements occur in Government publications, they generally appear in the sequence listed below. The designation "new odd page" generally refers to bookwork and is not required in most pamphlet- and magazine-type publications.

(a) *False title* (frontispiece, if any, on back).

(b) *Frontispiece*, faces title page.

(c) *Title page* (new odd page).

(d) *Back of title*, blank, but frequently carries such useful bibliographic information as list of board members, congressional resolution authorizing publication, note of editions and printings, GPO imprint if departmental imprint appears on title page, sales notice, etc.

(e) *Letter of transmittal* (new odd page).

(f) *Foreword* (new odd page), differs from a preface in that it is an introductory note written as an endorsement by a person other than the author. An introduction differs from a foreword or a preface in that it is the initial part of the text; if the book is divided into chapters, it should be the first chapter.

(g) *Preface* (new odd page), by author.

(h) *Acknowledgments* (new odd page), if not part of preface.

(i) *Contents* (new odd page), immediately followed by list of illustrations and list of tables, as parts of contents.

(j) *Halftitle*, new odd page preceding first page of text.

(k) *Text*, begins with page 1 (if halftitle is used, begins with p. 3).

(l) *Glossary* (new odd page).

(m) *Bibliography* (new odd page).

(n) *Appendix* (new odd page).

(o) *Index* (new odd page).

2.4. Preliminary pages use small-cap Roman numerals. Pages in the back of the book (index, etc.), use lowercase Roman numerals.

2.5. Booklets of 32 pages or less can be printed more economically with a self-cover. A table of contents, title page, foreword, preface, etc., is not usually necessary with so few pages. If some of this preliminary matter is necessary, it is more practical to combine them (e.g., contents on cover; or contents, title, and foreword on cover 2).

2.6. Widow lines (lines less than full width of measure) at top of pages are to be avoided, if possible, but are permitted if absolutely necessary to maintain uniform makeup and page depth. Rewording to fill the line is a preferred alternative.

2.7. Paragraphs may start on the last line of a page whenever necessary. If it is found necessary to make a short page, the facing page should be of approximate equal depth.

2.8. A blank space or sink of 6 picas should be placed at the head of each new odd or even page of 46-pica or greater depth; pages with a depth of from 36 to 45 picas, inclusive, will carry a 5-pica sink; pages less than 36 picas, 4 picas.

2.9. When centered top folios are used, the folio on a new page is set 2 points smaller than the top folios, centered at the bottom, and enclosed in parentheses.

2.10. When running heads with top folios are used, running heads are included in overall page depth. However, first pages of chapters and other pages with bottom folios do not include the folios as part of the overall page depth.

2.11. Jobs that have bottom folios will align them in the margin, including those on preliminary pages. If at all possible, avoid use of running heads in conjunction with bottom folios.

2.12. Contents, list of illustrations, preface, or any other matter that makes a page in itself will retain normal 6-pica sink.

2.13. Footnote references are repeated in boxheads or in continued lines over tables, unless special orders are given not to do so.

2.14. When a table continues, its headnote is repeated without the word *Continued.*

2.15. A landscape or broadside table that continues from an even to an odd page must be positioned to read through the center (gutter) of the publication when its size is not sufficient to fill both pages.

2.16. A broadside table of less than page width will center on the page.

2.17. Centerheads, whether in boldface, caps, caps and small caps, small caps, or italic, should have more space above than below. Uniform spacing should be maintained throughout the page.

2.18. In making up a page of two or more columns, text preceding a page-width illustration will be divided equally into the appropriate number of columns above the illustration.

2.19. All backstrips should read down (from top to bottom).

Copy preparation

2.20. At the beginning of each job the proper formats must be plainly marked. New Odd or New Page, Preliminary, Cover, Title, or Back Title should also be plainly indicated.

2.21. Copy preparers must mark those things not readily understood when reading the manuscript. They must also mark the correct element identifier code for each data element, as well as indicate other matters of style necessary to give the publication good typographic appearance.

2.22. Preparers must indicate the proper subformat at the beginning of each extension, verify folios, and plainly indicate references, footnotes, cut-ins, etc.

2.23. Quoted or extract matter and lists should be set smaller than text with space above and below. Quotation marks at the beginning and end of paragraphs should be omitted. If the same type size is used, quoted matter should be indented 2 ems on both sides with space top and bottom, and initial and closing quotes should be omitted.

2.24. In congressional hearings, the name of the interrogator or witness who continues speaking is repeated following a head set in boldface, a paragraph enclosed in parentheses, or a paragraph enclosed in brackets.

In a head set in boldface, the title "Mr." is not used, and "the Honorable" preceding a name is shortened to "Hon." Street addresses are also deleted. Example: "Statement of Hon. John P. Blank, Member, American Bar Association, Washington, DC".

2.25. Paragraph or section numbers (or letters) followed by figures or letters in parentheses will close up, as "section 7(B)(1)(*a*)," "paragraph 23(*a*)," "paragraph b(*7*)," "paragraph (*a*)(2)"; *but* "section 9(a) (*1*) and (*2*)", "section 7 *a* and *b*". In case of an unavoidable break, division will be made after elements in parentheses, and no hyphen is used.

Capitalization

2.26. The customer should indicate use of capital and lowercase letters.

Datelines, addresses, and signatures

2.27. Copy preparers must mark caps, small caps, italic, abbreviations, indentions, and line breaks where necessary. (For more detailed instructions, see Chapter 16 "Datelines, Addresses, and Signatures.")

Decimals and common fractions

2.28. In figure columns containing both decimals and common fractions, such decimals and/or fractions will not be aligned. The columns will be set flush right.

"Et cetera," "etc.," and "and so forth"

2.29. In printing a speaker's language, the words *and so forth* or *et cetera* are preferred, but in "FIC & punc." matter *etc.* is acceptable. If a quoted extract is set in type smaller than that of the preceding text and the speaker has summed up the remainder of the quotation with the words *and so forth* or *et cetera*, these words should be placed at the beginning of the next line, flush and lowercase, and an em dash should be used at the end of the extract.

Folioing and stamping copy

2.30. Folios should be placed in the upper right corner, preferably half an inch from the top.

Headings

2.31. The element identifier codes to be used for all headings must be marked. Caps, caps and small caps, small caps, caps and lowercase, sentence case, or italic must be prepared. (See rule 3.53.)

Pickup

2.32. The jacket number of a job from which matter is to be picked up must be indicated. New matter and pickup matter should conform in style.

Sidenotes and cut-in notes

2.33. Sidenotes and cut-in notes are set each line flush left and ragged right, unless otherwise prepared, and are always set solid. Sidenotes are usually set in 6 point, 4½ picas wide. Footnotes to sidenotes and text should be set 21½ picas.

SEC. 920. Abuse of the rule.

An alleged violation of the rule relating to admission to the floor presents a question of privilege (III, 2624, 2625; VI, 579), but not a higher question of privilege than an election case (III, 2626). In one case where an ex-Member was abusing the privilege . . . .

Signs, symbols, etc.

2.34. All signs, symbols, dashes, superiors, etc., must be clearly marked. Names of Greek letters must be indicated, as they are frequently mistaken for italic letters or symbols.

2.35. Some typesetting systems produce characters that look the same as figures. A lowercase l resembles a figure 1 and a capital O looks like a figure 0. Questionable characters will be printed as figures unless otherwise marked.

Letters illustrating shape and form

2.36. Use the same font for text and capital letters that convey shape and form, e.g., U-shape(d), A-frame, T-bone, and I-beam.

2.37. Plurals are formed by adding an apostrophe and the letter *s* to letters illustrating shape and form, such as T's and Y's. *Golf tee(s)* should be spelled, as shape is not indicated.

2.38. A capital letter is used in *U-boat*, *V–8*, and other expressions which have no reference to shape or form.

Fol. lit. and FIC & punc.

2.39. After submittal to GPO, manuscript copy is stamped "Fol. lit." or "FIC & punc." The difference between these two typesetting instructions is explained thus:

Copy is followed when stamped "Fol. lit." (follow literally). Copy authorized to be marked "Fol. lit." must be thoroughly prepared by the requisitioning agency as to capitalization, punctuation (including compounding), abbreviations, signs, symbols, figures, and italic. Such copy, including even obvious errors, will be followed. The lack of preparation on copy so designated will, in itself, constitute preparation. "Fol. lit." does not include size and style of type or spacing.

Obvious errors are corrected in copy marked "FIC & punc." (follow, including capitalization and punctuation).

2.40. Bill copy will be followed as supplied and treated as "FIC & punc." (See rule 2.39.) This data is transmitted to the GPO with formatting codes in place, requiring minimal copy preparation.

2.41. Copy preparer's instructions, which accompany each job, are written to cover the general style and certain peculiarities or deviations from style. These instructions must be followed.

Abbreviations

2.42. In marking abbreviations to be spelled, preparers must show what the spelled form should be, unless the abbreviations are common. An unfamiliar abbreviation, with spelled-out form unavailable, will not be changed.

Type composition

2.43. Operators and revisers must study carefully the rules governing composition.

2.44. In correcting pickup matter, the operator must indicate plainly on the proof what portion, if any, was actually reset.

2.45. Every precaution must be taken to prevent the soiling of proofs, as it is necessary for the reviser to see clearly every mark on the margin of a proof after it has been corrected.

2.46. Queries intended for the author are not to be corrected. Such queries, however, are not to be carried on jobs going directly to press.

Leading and spacing

2.47. Spacing of text is governed by the leading, narrow spacing being more desirable in solid than in leaded matter.

2.48. Solid matter (text) is defined as those lines set without horizontal space between them. Leaded text is defined as lines separated by 1 or 2 points of space.

2.49. A single justified word space will be used between sentences (key one space when typing). This applies to all types of composition.

2.50. Center or flush heads set in caps, caps and small caps, small caps, or boldface are keyed with regular justified spaces between words.

2.51. Centerheads are set apart from the text by the use of spacing. More space is always inserted above a heading than below. In 10-point type, the spacing would be 10 points over and 8 points under a heading; in 8- and 6-point type, the spacing would be 8 points above and 6 points below.

2.52. Unless otherwise marked, flush heads are separated from text by 4 points of space above and 2 points of space below in solid matter, and by 6 points of space above and 4 points of space below in leaded matter.

2.53. Full-measure numbered or lettered paragraphs and quoted extracts are not separated by space from adjoining matter.

2.54. Extracts that are set off from the text by smaller type or are indented on both sides or indented 3 ems on the left side (courtwork only) are separated by 6 points of space in leaded matter and by 4 points of space in solid matter.

2.55. Extracts set solid in leaded matter are separated from the text by 6 points.

2.56. Flush lines following extracts are separated by 6 points of space in leaded matter and by 4 points in solid matter.

2.57. Footnotes and legends are leaded if the text is leaded, and are solid if the text is solid.

2.58. Leaderwork is separated from text by 4 points above and 4 points below.

Indents

2.59. In measures less than 30 picas, the paragraph indent is 1 em. Paragraph indents in cut-in matter are 3 ems, overs are 2 ems. Datelines and signatures are indented in multiples of 2 ems. Addresses are set flush left.

2.60. In measures 30 picas or wider, the paragraph indent is 2 ems. Paragraph indents in cut-in matter are 6 ems, overs are 4 ems. Datelines and signatures are indented in multiples of 2 ems. Addresses are set flush left.

2.61. In measures less than 30 picas, overruns in hanging indents are 1 em more than the first line. To avoid conflict with an indent that follows, such as a subentry or paragraph, the overrun indent is made 1 em more than the following line.

2.62. In measures 30 picas or wider, overruns in hanging indents are 2 ems more than the first line. To avoid conflict with an indent that follows, such as a subentry or paragraph, the overrun indent is made 2 ems more than the following line.

2.63. Indents of matter set in smaller type should be the same, in points, as that of adjoining main-text indented matter.

2.64. Two-line centerheads are centered, but heads of three or more lines are set with a hanging indent.

2.65. Overs in flush heads are indented 2 ems in measures less than 30 picas, and 3 ems in wider measures.

Legends for illustrations

2.66. It is preferred that legends and explanatory data consisting of one or two lines are set centered, while those with more than two lines are set with a hanging indent. Legends are set full measure regardless of the width of the illustration. Paragraph style is acceptable.

2.67. Legend lines for illustrations that appear broad or turn page (landscape) should be printed to read up; an even-page legend should be on the inside margin and an odd-page legend on the outside margin.

2.68. Unless otherwise indicated, legends for illustrations are set in 8-point roman, sentence case.

2.69. Periods are used after legends and explanatory remarks beneath illustrations. However, legends without descriptive language do not use a period. (See rule 8.116.)

2.70. At the beginning of a legend or standing alone, *Figure* preceding the identifying number or letter is set in caps and small caps and is not abbreviated.

FIGURE 5, *not* FIG. 5 FIGURE A, *not* FIG. A

2.71. If a chart carries both a legend and footnotes, the legend is placed above the chart.

2.72. Letter symbols used in legends for illustrations are set in lowercase italic without periods.

Proofreading

2.73. All special instructions, layouts, and style sheets must be included with the first installment of each job.

2.74. If the proofreader detects inconsistent or erroneous statements, it is their responsibility to query them.

2.75. All queries appearing on the copy must be carried to the author's set of proofs.

2.76. Proofs that are illegible or are in any manner defective must be called to the attention of the deskperson.

2.77. The manner in which correction marks are made on a proof is of considerable importance. Straggling, unsymmetrical characters, disconnected marks placed in the margin above or below the lines to which they relate, irregular lines leading from an incorrect letter or word to a correction, large marks, marks made with a blunt pencil, indistinct marks, and frequent use of the eraser to obliterate marks hastily or incorrectly made are faults to be avoided. The transposition mark should not be used in little-known words or in figures. It is better to cancel the letters or figures and write them in the margin in the order in which they are to appear.

2.78. In reading proof of wide tables, the proofreader should place the correction as near as possible to the error.

2.79. To assure proper placement of footnotes, the proofreader and reviser must draw a ring around footnote references on the proofs, then check off each corresponding footnote number.

2.80. Proofreaders must not make important changes in indents or tables without consulting the referee.

2.81. Follow the marks of the copy preparer, as they are in a position to know more about the peculiarities of a job than one who reads but a small portion of it.

2.82. Any proposed deviation from the prepared manuscript must be queried to the referee.

2.83. All instructions on copy must be carried on proof by readers.

2.84. Folios of copy must be run by the proofreader and marked on the proof.

2.85. All instructions, comments, and extraneous notes on both copy and proofs that are not intended to be set as part of the text must be circled.

Revising galley proofs

2.86. The importance of revising proofs cannot be overemphasized. Although a reviser is not expected to read proof, it is not enough to follow the marks found on the proof. The reviser should detect errors and inconsistencies and must see that all corrections have been properly made and that words or lines have not been transposed or eliminated in making the corrections.

2.87. A reviser must not remodel the punctuation of the proofreaders or make any important changes. If an important change should be made, the reviser must submit the proposed change to the supervisor for a decision.

2.88. In the body of the work, new pages must be properly indicated on the proof. (For new-page information, see rule 2.3 "Makeup.")

2.89. All instructions and queries on proofs must be transferred to the revised set of proofs.

Revising page proofs

2.90. Page revising requires great diligence and care. The reviser must see that the rules governing the instructions of previous workers have been followed.

2.91. The reviser is responsible for marking all bleed and off-center pages.

2.92. A blank page must be indicated at the bottom of the preceding page.

2.93. Special care must be exercised in revising corrected matter. If it appears that a correction has not been made, the reviser should carefully examine each line on the page to see if the correction was inserted in the wrong place.

2.94. The following rules must be carefully observed:

(a) See that the proof is clean and clear; request another if necessary.

(b) Verify that the galley proofs are in order and that the data on the galleys runs in properly to facilitate continuous makeup.

(c) Make sure that different sets of proofs of the same job are correctly marked in series ("R," "2R," "3R," etc.); where a sheet is stamped "Another proof," carry the same designating "R" on the corresponding clean proof. Advance the "R," "2R," "3R," etc., on each set of page proofs returned from the originating office.

(d) Run the page folios, make sure they are consecutive and that the running heads, if used, are correct. Check connection pages. Verify correct sequence for footnote references and placement. It is imperative that footnotes appear or begin on the same page as their reference, unless style dictates that all footnotes are to appear together in one location.

(e) Watch for dropouts, doublets, and transpositions.

(f) Legend lines of full-page illustrations that appear broad should be printed to read up—the even-page legend on the binding or inside margin and the odd-page legend on the outside margin.

(g) If a footnote is eliminated, do not renumber the footnotes; change footnote to read "Footnote eliminated."

2.95. If a footnote is added in proof, use the preceding number with a superior letter added, as ^{15a}.

2.96. If a table (with or without footnotes) ends a page that has footnotes to the text, the text footnotes fall at the bottom of the page, with a 50-point rule above them. (See rule 13.76.)

Press revising

2.97. Press revising calls for the exercise of utmost care. The press reviser must be thoroughly familiar with the style and makeup of Government publications. They are required to OK all forms that go to press—bookwork, covers, jobwork, etc.—and must see that all queries are answered. Knowledge of the bindery operations required to complete a book or job and familiarity with all types of imposition, folds, etc., is helpful. The reviser must be capable of ascertaining the proper head, back, and side margins for all work, to ensure proper trimming of the completed job.

2.98. Although speed is essential when forms reach the press reviser, accuracy is still paramount and must not be sacrificed.

Signature marks, etc.

2.99. Unless otherwise indicated, signature marks are set in 6-point lowercase and indented 3 ems.

2.100. Figures indicating the year should follow the jacket number in signature marks:

125–327—16——4
116–529—16—pt. 5——3
116–529—16—vol. 1——3

2.101. When the allmark (○) and signature or the imprint and signature appear on same page, the signature line is placed below the allmark or imprint. (See rule 2.113.)

2.102. The allmark is placed below the page, bulletin, or circular number but above the signature line, if both appear on the same page.

2.103. Imprints and signature lines appearing on short pages of text are placed at the bottom of the page.

2.104. On a congressional job reprinted because of a change, the House and Senate have approved the following styles:

House of Representatives:	Senate:
★17–234—16——2	17–235—16——2 ★(Star Print)

2.105. The following forms are used for signature marks in House and Senate documents and reports printed on session jackets:

H. Doc. 73, 16–1——2
S. Doc. 57, 16–2, pt. 1——2
H. Rept. 120, 16–2——8
S. Doc. 57, 16–1——2
S. Doc. 57, 16–2, vol. 1——2
S. Rept. 100, 16–2——9

2.106. In a document or report printed on other than a session jacket, use the jacket number, year, and signature number only, omitting the document or report number. (See rule 2.100.)

2.107. For pasters or foldouts, the jacket number, the year, and the page to be faced by the paster or foldout are used as follows (note punctuation):

12–344——16 (Face p. 10)

2.108. On a paster or foldout facing an even page, the marks are placed on the lower right-hand side; on a paster or foldout facing an odd page, the marks are placed on the lower left-hand side.

2.109. If more than one paster or foldout faces the same page, they are numbered as follows:

12–344——16 (Face p. 19) No. 1
12–344——16 (Face p. 19) No. 2

2.110. When a paster or foldout follows the text, the allmark is placed on the last page of the text and never on the paster or foldout.

Imprints

2.111. Unless otherwise stipulated, the GPO imprint must appear on all printed matter, with the exception of certain classified work.

2.112. The full GPO imprint is used on the title page of a congressional speech.

2.113. The imprint and allmark are not used together on any page; if one is used, the other is omitted.

2.114. The imprint is not used on a halftitle or on any page of a cover, with the exception of congressional hearings.

2.115. If there is a title page, the imprint is placed on the title page; but if there is no title page, or if the title page is entirely an illustration, the imprint is placed on the last page of the text 4 ems from flush right and below the bottom folio.

2.116. The GPO logo is used only on GPO publications. If it is printed on page II, the full imprint is used on the title page; if it is printed on the title page, use the half imprint only, thus—Washington : 2016.

Imprint variations

2.117. This is one style of an imprint that can appear on the title page.

For sale by the Superintendent of Documents, U.S. Government Publishing Office
•Internet: bookstore.gpo.gov•Phone: Toll Free 866–512–1800
•DC area 202–512–1800•Fax: 202–512–2104
•Mail: Stop SSOP, Washington, DC 20402–0001
•www.govinfo.gov

2.118. In the event that a title page is not used, the imprint is printed on the last page and positioned flush left below the text.

For sale by the Superintendent of Documents, U.S. Government Publishing Office
•Internet: bookstore.gpo.gov•Phone: toll free 866–512–1800
• DC area 202–512–1800•Fax: 202–512–2250
•Mail: Stop SSOP, Washington, DC 20402–0001
•www.govinfo.gov

2.119. Outside-purchase publications are identified by the GPO logo at the beginning of the imprint line. These lines are positioned 4 ems from the right margin.

GPO U.S. GOVERNMENT PUBLISHING OFFICE: 2016—456–789

2.120. Publications purchased outside that are reprinted by the GPO use an em dash in lieu of the GPO logo.

—U.S. GOVERNMENT PUBLISHING OFFICE: 2016—456–789

2.121. Jobs set on outside purchase but printed by the GPO use an asterisk in lieu of the GPO logo.

*U.S. GOVERNMENT PUBLISHING OFFICE: 2016—456–789

2.122. Publications produced from camera copy supplied to the GPO are identified by *cc* printed at the end of the line.

U.S. GOVERNMENT PUBLISHING OFFICE: 2016—123–456–cc

Reprints

2.123. To aid bibliographic identification of reprints or revisions, the dates of the original edition and of reprint or revision should be supplied by the author on the title page or in some other suitable place. Thus:

First edition July 2000
Reprinted July 2005
First printed June 2000
Revised June 2005

Original edition May 2000
Reprinted May 2005
Revised July 2007

2.124. The year in the imprint on cover, title page, or elsewhere is not changed from that in the original print, nor are the signatures changed, unless other revisions are necessary.

Sales notices

2.125. The use of sales notices is discouraged.

2.126. If there is a cover but no title page, the sales notice is printed on the cover. Unless otherwise indicated, if there is a title page, with or without a cover, the sales notice is printed at the bottom of the title page below a cross rule. If there is no cover or title page, any sales notice is printed at the end of the text, below the imprint, and the two are separated by a cross rule.

Franking

2.127. The franking (mailing) privilege on covers for Government publications should be at least 1⅛ inches from the trim.

Bibliographies or references

2.128. There are many styles available to bibliographers, for there are many classes of documents.

A Government bulletin citation, according to one authority, would be treated as follows:

> Author's name (if the article is signed); title of article (in quotation marks); the publication (usually in italic), with correct references to volume, number, series, pages, date, and publisher (U.S. Govt. Pub. Off.).

Therefore the example would read:

U.S. Department of the Interior, "Highlights in history of forest and related natural resource conservation," *Conservation Bulletin*, No. 41 (serial number not italic), Washington, U.S. Dept. of the Interior (*or* U.S. Govt. Pub. Off.), 1997. 1 p. (*or* p. 1).

Another Government periodical citation would read as follows:

Kirwan, Patrick S., "New Qualified Plug-in Electric Drive Motor Vehicle Credit," *Internal Revenue Bulletin*, No. 2009-48, pp. 713–717 (November 30, 2009), Internal Revenue Service.

Clarity may be maintained by capitalizing each word in book titles, with only the first word in the title of articles.

Other examples are:

Preston W. Slosson, *The Great Crusade And After: 1914–1928* (New York: Macmillan, 1930)

Edward B. Rosa, "The economic importance of the scientific work of the government," *J. Wash. Acad. Sci.* 10, 342 (1920)

or:

Preston W. Slosson, The Great Crusade and After: 1914–1928 (New York: Macmillan, 1930)

Edward B. Rosa, "The Economic Importance of the Scientific Work of the Government," J. Wash. Acad. Sci. 10, 342 (1920)

Note in this that the principal words in both book titles and titles of articles are capitalized. Consistency is more important in bibliographic style than the style itself.

The science of bibliography is covered in many texts, and the following references are available for study:

The Chicago Manual of Style, University of Chicago Press, Chicago, 2010 (www.chicagomanualofstyle.org/home.html).

Words Into Type, Prentice-Hall, New York, 1974.

3. Capitalization Rules

(See also Chapter 4 "Capitalization Examples" and Chapter 9 "Abbreviations and Letter Symbols")

3.1. It is impossible to give rules that will cover every conceivable problem in capitalization, but, by considering the purpose to be served and the underlying principles, it is possible to attain a considerable degree of uniformity. The list of approved forms given in chapter 4 will serve as a guide. Obviously such a list cannot be complete. The correct usage with respect to any term not included can be determined by analogy or by application of the rules.

Historic or documentary accuracy

3.2. Where historic, documentary, technical, or scientific accuracy is required, capitalization and other features of style of the original text should be followed.

Proper names

3.3. Proper names are capitalized.

Rome	John Macadam	Italy
Brussels	Macadam family	Anglo-Saxon

Derivatives of proper names

3.4. Derivatives of proper names used with a proper meaning are capitalized.

Roman (of Rome)	Johannean	Italian

3.5. Derivatives of proper names used with acquired independent common meaning, or no longer identified with such names, are set lowercased. Since this depends upon general and long-continued usage, a more definite and all-inclusive rule cannot be formulated in advance.

roman (type)	macadam (crushed rock)	italicize
brussels sprouts	watt (electric unit)	anglicize
venetian blinds	plaster of paris	pasteurize

Common nouns and adjectives in proper names

3.6. A common noun or adjective forming an essential part of a proper name is capitalized; the common noun used alone as a substitute for the name of a place or thing is not capitalized.

Massachusetts Avenue; the avenue
Washington Monument; the monument
Statue of Liberty; the statue
Hoover Dam; the dam
Boston Light; the light
Modoc National Forest; the national forest
Panama Canal; the canal
Soldiers' Home in Holyoke; the soldiers' home
Johnson House (hotel); Johnson house (residence)
Crow Reservation; the reservation
Cape of Good Hope; the cape
Jersey City
Washington City
but city of Washington; the city
Cook County; the county
Great Lakes; the lakes
Lake of the Woods; the lake
North Platte River; the river
Lower California
but lower Mississippi
Charles the First; Charles I
Seventeenth Census; the 1960 census

3.7. If a common noun or adjective forming an essential part of a name becomes separated from the rest of the name by an intervening common noun or adjective, the entire expression is no longer a proper noun and is therefore not capitalized.

Union Station: union passenger station
Eastern States: eastern farming States
United States popularly elected government

3.8. A common noun used alone as a well-known short form of a specific proper name is capitalized.

the Capitol building in Washington, DC; *but* State capitol building
the Channel (English Channel)
the Chunnel (tunnel below English Channel)
the District (District of Columbia)

3.9. The plural form of a common noun capitalized as part of a proper name is also capitalized.

Seventh and I Streets
Lakes Erie and Ontario
Potomac and James Rivers
State and Treasury Departments
British, French, and United States Governments
Presidents Washington and Adams

3.10. A common noun used with a date, number, or letter, merely to denote time or sequence, or for the purpose of reference, record, or temporary convenience, does not form a proper name and is therefore not capitalized. (See also rule 3.39.)

abstract B	figure 7	room A722
amendment 5	first district (not congressional)	rule 8
apartment 2	flight 007	schedule K
appendix C	graph 8	section 3
article 1	group 7	signature 4
book II	mile 7.5	spring 1926
chapter III	page 2	station 27
chart B	paragraph 4	table 4
class I	part I	title IV
collection 6	phase 3	volume X
column 2	plate IV	ward 2
drawing 6	region 3	
exhibit D		

3.11. The following terms are lowercased, even with a name or number.

aqueduct	irrigation project	shipway
breakwater	jetty	slip
buoy	levee	spillway
chute	lock	turnpike
dike	pier	watershed
dock	reclamation project	weir
drydock	ship canal	wharf

Definite article in proper place names

3.12. To achieve greater distinction or to adhere to the authorized form, the word *the* (or its equivalent in a foreign language) is capitalized when used as a part of an official name or title. When such name or title is used adjectively, *the* is not capitalized, nor is *the* supplied at any time when not in copy.

> *British Consul* v. *The Mermaid* (title of legal case)
> The Dalles (OR); The Weirs (NH); *but* the Dalles region; the Weirs streets
> The Hague; *but* the Hague Court; the Second Hague Conference
> El Salvador; Las Cruces; L'Esterel
> The National Mall; The Mall (Washington, DC only)
> The Gambia

but the Congo, the Sudan, the Netherlands

3.13. Rule 3.12 does not apply in references to newspapers, periodicals, vessels, airships, trains, firm names, etc.

the Washington Post	the U-3
the Times	the *Los Angeles*
the Atlantic Monthly	the Hotel Roanoke
the *Mermaid*	the National Photo Co.

Particles in names of persons

3.14. In foreign names such particles as *d'*, *da*, *de*, *della*, *den*, *du*, *van*, and *von* are capitalized unless preceded by a forename or title. Individual usage, if ascertainable, should be followed.

> Da Ponte; Cardinal da Ponte
> Den Uyl; Johannes den Uyl; Prime Minister den Uyl
> Du Pont; E.I. du Pont de Nemours & Co.
> Van Rensselaer; Stephen van Rensselaer
> Von Braun; Dr. Wernher von Braun

but d'Orbigny; Alcide d'Orbigny; de la Madrid; Miguel de la Madrid

3.15. In anglicized names such particles are usually capitalized, even if preceded by a forename or title, but individual usage, if ascertainable, should be followed.

> Justice Van Devanter; Reginald De Koven
> Thomas De Quincey; William De Morgan
> Henry van Dyke (his usage)
> Samuel F. Du Pont (his usage); Irénée du Pont

3.16. If copy is not clear as to the form of such a name (for example, *La Forge* or *Laforge*), the two-word form should be used.

3.17. In names set in capitals, *de, von*, etc., are also capitalized.

Names of organized bodies

3.18. The full names of existing or proposed organized bodies and their shortened names are capitalized; other substitutes, which are most often regarded as common nouns, are capitalized only in certain specified instances to indicate preeminence or distinction.

National governmental units:

U.S. Congress: 114th Congress; the Congress; Congress; the Senate; the House; Committee of the Whole, the Committee; *but* committee (all other congressional committees)

Department of Agriculture: the Department; Division of Publications, the Division; similarly all major departmental units; *but* legislative, executive, and judicial departments

Bureau of the Census: the Census Bureau, the Bureau; *but* the agency

Environmental Protection Agency: the Agency

Geological Survey: the Survey

Government Publishing Office: the Publishing Office, the Office

American Embassy, British Embassy: the Embassy; *but* the consulate; the consulate general

Treasury of the United States: General Treasury; National Treasury; Public Treasury; the Treasury; Treasury notes; New York Subtreasury, the subtreasury

Department of Defense: Military Establishment; Armed Forces; All-Volunteer Forces; *but* armed services

U.S. Army: the Army; All-Volunteer Army; the Infantry; 81st Regiment; Army Establishment; the Army Band; Army officer; Regular Army officer; Reserve officer; Volunteer officer; *but* army shoe; Grant's army; Robinson's brigade; the brigade; the corps; the regiment; infantryman

U.S. Navy: the Navy; the Marine Corps; Navy (Naval) Establishment; Navy officer; *but* naval shipyard; naval officer; naval station

U.S. Air Force: the Air Force

U.S. Coast Guard: the Coast Guard

French Ministry of Foreign Affairs; the Ministry; French Army; British Navy

American Indian and Alaska Native federally recognized entities:

Shawnee Tribe, the Tribe; Cherokee Nation, the Nation; Alturas Indian Rancheria, the Rancheria; Cahuilla Band of Indians, the Band; Takotna Village, the Village; Akiak Native Community, the Community

International organizations:

United Nations: the Council; the Assembly; the Secretariat

Permanent Court of Arbitration: the Court; the Tribunal (only in the proceedings of a specific arbitration tribunal)
Hague Peace Conference of 1907: the Hague Conference; the Peace Conference; the Conference

Common-noun substitutes:

Virginia General Assembly: the assembly
California State Highway Commission: Highway Commission of California; the highway commission; the commission
Montgomery County Board of Health: the Board of Health, Montgomery County; the board of health; the board
Common Council of the City of Pittsburgh: the common council; the council
Buffalo Consumers' League: the consumers' league; the league
Republican Party: the party
Southern Railroad Co.: the Southern Railroad; Southern Co.; Southern Road; the railroad company; the company
Riggs National Bank: the Riggs Bank; the bank
Metropolitan Club: the club
Yale School of Law: Yale University School of Law; School of Law, Yale University; school of law

3.19. The names of members and adherents of organized bodies are capitalized to distinguish them from the same words used merely in a descriptive sense.

a Representative (U.S.)	a Shriner	a Boy Scout
a Republican	a Socialist	a Knight (K.C., K.P., etc.)
an Elk	an Odd Fellow	
a Federalist	a Democrat	

Names of countries, domains, and administrative divisions

3.20. The official designations of countries, national domains, and their principal administrative divisions are capitalized only if used as part of proper names, as proper names, or as proper adjectives. (See Chapter 17, Principal Foreign Countries table.)

United States: the Republic; the Nation; the Union; the Government; also Federal, Federal Government; *but* republic (when not referring specifically to one such entity); republican (in general sense); a nation devoted to peace

New York State: the State, a State (a definite political subdivision of first rank); State of Veracruz; Balkan States; six States of Australia; State rights; *but* state (referring to a federal government, the body politic); foreign states; church and state; statehood; state's evidence

Territory: territory of American Samoa, Guam, Virgin Islands; Yukon, Northwest Territories; the Territory(ies), Territorial

Dominion of Canada: the Dominion; but dominion (in general sense)

Ontario Province, Province of Ontario: the Province, Provincial; but province, provincial (in general sense)

3.21. The similar designations *commonwealth, confederation (federal), government, nation (national), powers, republic,* etc., are capitalized only if used as part of proper names, as proper names, or as proper adjectives.

British Commonwealth, Commonwealth of Virginia: the Commonwealth; *but* a commonwealth government (general sense)

Swiss Confederation: the Confederation; the Federal Council; the Federal Government; *but* confederation, federal (in general sense)

French Government: the Government; French and Italian Governments: the Governments; *but* government (in general sense); the Churchill government; European governments

Cherokee Nation: the Nation; *but* Greek nation; American nations

National Government (of any specific nation); *but* national customs

Allied Powers, Allies (in World Wars I and II); *but* our allies, weaker allies; Central Powers (in World War I); *but* the powers; European powers

Republic of South Africa: the Republic; *but* republic (in general sense)

Names of regions, localities, and geographic features

3.22. A descriptive term used to denote a definite region, locality, or geographic feature is a proper name and is therefore capitalized; also for temporary distinction a coined name of a region is capitalized.

the North Atlantic States	the Continental Divide
the Gulf States	Deep South
the Central States	Midsouth
the Pacific Coast States	the Far East
the Lake States	Far Eastern
East North Central States	the East
Eastern North Central States	Middle East
Far Western States	Middle Eastern
Eastern United States	Mideast
the West	Mideastern (Asia)
the Midwest	Near East (Balkans, etc.)
the Middle West	the Promised Land
the Far West	the Continent (continental Europe)
the Eastern Shore (Chesapeake Bay)	the Western Hemisphere
the Badlands (SD and NE)	the North Pole

the North and South Poles
the Temperate Zone
the Torrid Zone
the East Side
Lower East Side (sections of a city)

Western Europe, Central Europe)
(political entities)
but
lower 48 (States)
the Northeast corridor

3.23. A descriptive term used to denote direction or position is not a proper name and is therefore not capitalized.

north; south; east; west
northerly; northern; northward
eastern; oriental; occidental
east Pennsylvania
southern California
northern Virginia; *but* Northern Virginia (D.C. suburbs)
west Florida; *but* West Florida (1763–1819)
eastern region; western region
north-central region
east coast; eastern seaboard
northern Italy
southern France
but East Germany; West Germany (former political entities)

Names of calendar divisions

3.24. The names of calendar divisions are capitalized.

January; February; March; etc.
Monday; Tuesday; Wednesday; etc.
but spring; summer; autumn (fall); winter

Names of holidays, etc.

3.25. The names of holidays and ecclesiastic feast and fast days are capitalized.

April Fools' Day
Arbor Day
Armed Forces Day
Birthday of Martin Luther King, Jr.
Christmas Day, Eve
Columbus Day
Father's Day
Feast of the Passover; the Passover
Flag Day

Fourth of July; the Fourth
Halloween
Hanukkah
Inauguration Day (Federal)
Independence Day
Labor Day
Lincoln's Birthday
Memorial Day (also
Decoration Day)

Mother's Day
New Year's Day, Eve
Patriot Day
Presidents Day
Ramadan
Rosh Hashanah
St. Valentine's Day
Thanksgiving Day
Veterans Day
Washington's Birthday
Yom Kippur
but election day, primary day

Trade names and trademarks

3.26. Trade names, variety names, and names of market grades and brands are capitalized. Some trade names have come into usage as generic terms (e.g., cellophane, thermos, and aspirin); when reference is being made to the formal company or specific product name, capitalization should be used. (See Chapter 4 "Capitalization Examples" trade names and trademarks.)

Choice lamb (market grade)
Red Radiance rose (variety)
Xerox (the company)
but photocopy (the process)

Scientific names

3.27. The name of a phylum, class, order, family, or genus is capitalized. The name of a species is not capitalized, even if derived from a proper name. (See rule 11.9.)

Arthropoda (phylum), Crustacea (class), Hypoparia (order), Agnostidae (family), *Agnostus* (genus)
Agnostus canadensis; Aconitum wilsonii; Epigaea repens (genus and species)

3.28. In scientific descriptions coined terms derived from proper names are not capitalized.

aviculoid
menodontine

3.29. Any plural formed by adding *s* to a Latin generic name is capitalized.

Rhynchonellas
Spirifers

3.30. In soil science the 12 soil orders are capitalized.

Alfisols
Andisols
Aridisols
Entisols
Gelisols
Histosols
Inceptisols
Mollisols
Oxisols
Spodosols
Ultisols
Vertisols

3.31. Capitalize the names of the celestial bodies as well as the planets.

Sun	Mars	Alpha Centauri
Moon	the Big Dipper	Orion
Saturn	Ceres	the Milky Way
Earth	Kepler-1647b	*but* the moons of Jupiter

3.32. In general, names of diseases, viruses, and syndromes are not capitalized. An exception is when the disease is named for the person who discovered it or the geographic location where the disease occurred.

Alzheimer('s) disease	Hodgkin lymphoma
cancer	Lyme disease
diabetes	measles
Down syndrome	Parkinson('s) disease
Ebola virus	West Nile virus
group A strep infection; hepatitis C; herpes B virus	Zika virus

Historical or political events

3.33. Names of historical or political events used as a proper name are capitalized.

Battle of Bunker Hill	Holocaust, the	Renaissance
Christian Era	Middle Ages	the American
Cold War	New Deal	Revolution; the
D-Day	New Federalism	Revolution
Dust Bowl	New Frontier	V-E Day
Fall of Rome	Prohibition	War of 1812
Great Depression	Restoration	War on Poverty
Great Society	Reformation	

but Korean war; Vietnam war; Gulf war

Personification

3.34. A vivid personification is capitalized.

The Chair recognizes the gentlewoman from New York;
but I spoke with the chair yesterday.
For Nature wields her scepter mercilessly.
All of a sudden,
Time stood still.

Religious terms

3.35. Words denoting the Deity except *who, whose,* and *whom;* names for the Bible and other sacred writings and their parts; names of confessions of faith and of religious bodies and their adherents; and words specifically denoting Satan are all capitalized.

Heavenly Father; the Almighty; Lord; Thee; Thou; He; Him; *but* himself; You, Your; Thy, Thine; [God's] fatherhood
Mass; Communion
Divine Father; *but* divine providence; divine guidance; divine service
Son of Man; Jesus' sonship; the Messiah; *but* a messiah; messiahship; messianic; messianize; christology; christological
Bible, Holy Scriptures, Scriptures, Word; Koran; Talmud; *also* Biblical; Scriptural; Koranic; Talmudic
New Testament; Ten Commandments
Gospel (memoir of Christ); *but* gospel music
Apostles' Creed
Episcopal Church; an Episcopalian; Catholicism; a Protestant
Christian; *also* Christendom; Christianity; Christianize
Black Friars; Brother(s); King's Daughters; Daughter(s); Ursuline Sisters; Sister(s)
Satan; the Devil; *but* a devil; the devils; devil's advocate

Titles of persons

3.36. Civil, religious, military, and professional titles, as well as those of nobility, immediately preceding a name are capitalized.

President Obama	Dr. Bellinger
Queen Elizabeth II	Nurse Joyce Norton
Ambassador Acton	Professor Leverett
Lieutenant Fowler	Examiner Jones (law)
Chairman Williams	Vice-Presidential candidate Smith

but baseball player Harper; maintenance person Flow; foreperson Taylor

3.37. To indicate preeminence or distinction in certain specified instances, a common-noun title immediately following the name of a person or used alone as a substitute for it is capitalized.

Title of a head or assistant head of state:

Barack Obama, President of the United States: the President; the President-elect; the Executive; the Chief Magistrate; the Commander in Chief; ex-President Bush; former President Reagan; *similarly* the Vice President; the Vice-President-elect; ex-Vice-President Cheney

Terry McAuliffe, Governor of Virginia: the Governor of Virginia; the Governor; *similarly* the Lieutenant Governor; *but* secretary of state of Idaho; attorney general of Maine

Title of a head or assistant head of an existing or a proposed National governmental unit:

John Kerry, Secretary of State: the Secretary; *similarly* the Acting Secretary; the Under Secretary; the Assistant Secretary; the Director; the Chief or Assistant Chief; the Chief Clerk; *but* Secretaries of the military departments; secretaryship

Titles of the military:

General of the Army(ies): United States only; Supreme Allied Commander; General Joseph F. Dunford, Jr., Chairman, Joint Chiefs of Staff; Joint Chiefs of Staff; Chief of Staff, U.S. Air Force; the Chief of Staff; *but* the commanding general; general (military title standing alone not capitalized)

Titles of members of diplomatic corps:

Walter S. Gifford, Ambassador Extraordinary and Plenipotentiary: the American Ambassador; the British Ambassador; the Ambassador; the Senior Ambassador; Her Excellency; *similarly* the Envoy Extraordinary and Minister Plenipotentiary; the Envoy; the Minister; the Chargé d'Affaires; the Chargé; Ambassador at Large; Minister Without Portfolio; *but* the consul general; the consul; the attaché

Title of a ruler or prince:

Elizabeth II, Queen of the United Kingdom of Great Britain and Northern Ireland: the Queen; the Crown; Her Most Gracious Majesty; Her Majesty; *similarly* the Emperor; the Sultan

Charles, Prince of Wales: the Prince; His Royal Highness

Titles not capitalized:

Charles F. Hughes, rear admiral, U.S. Navy: the rear admiral

Steven Knapp, president of The George Washington University: the president

C.H. Eckles, professor of dairy husbandry: the professor

Barbara Prophet, chairwoman of the committee; the chairman; the chairperson; the chair

3.38. In formal lists of delegates and representatives of governments, all titles and descriptive designations immediately following the names should be capitalized if any one is capitalized.

3.39. A title in the second person is capitalized.

Your Excellency	Mr. Chairman	*but* not conversational salutations
Your Highness	Madam Chairman	my dear General
Your Honor	Mr. Secretary	my dear sir

Titles of publications, papers, documents, acts, laws, etc.

3.40. In the full or short English titles of periodicals, series of publications, annual reports, historic documents, and works of art, the first word and all important words are capitalized.

Statutes at Large; Revised Statutes; District Code; Bancroft's History; Journal (House or Senate) (short titles); *but* the code; the statutes
Atlantic Charter; Balfour Declaration; *but* British white paper
Chicago's American; *but* Chicago American Publishing Co.
Reader's Digest; *but* New York Times Magazine; Newsweek magazine
Monograph 55; Research Paper 123; Bulletin 420; Circular A; Article 15: Uniform Code of Military Justice; Senate Document 70; House Resolution 45; Presidential Proclamation No. 24; Executive Order No. 24; Royal Decree No. 24; Public Law 89–1; Private and Union Calendars; Calendar No. 80; Calendar Wednesday; Committee Print No. 32, committee print; *but* Senate bill 416; House bill 61; Congressional Record
Annual Report of the Government Publishing Office, 2015; *but* seventh annual report, 19th annual report
Declaration of Independence; the Declaration
Constitution (United States or with name of country); constitutional; *but* New York State constitution: first amendment, 12th amendment
Kellogg-Briand Pact; North Atlantic Pact; Atlantic Pact; Treaty of Versailles; Jay Treaty; *but* treaty of peace, the treaty (descriptive designations); treaty of 1919
United States v. *Four Hundred Twenty-two Casks of Wine* (law)
American Gothic, Nighthawks (paintings)

3.41. All principal words are capitalized in titles of addresses, albums, articles, books, captions, chapter and part headings, editorials, essays, headings, headlines, motion pictures and plays (including television and radio programs), papers, short poems, reports, songs, subheadings, subjects, and themes. The foregoing are also quoted.

3.42. In the short or popular titles of acts (Federal, State, or foreign) the first word and all important words are capitalized.

Revenue Act; Walsh-Healey Act; Freedom of Information Act; Classification Act; *but* the act; Harrison narcotic law; Harrison narcotic bill; interstate commerce law; sunset law

3.43. The capitalization of the titles of books, etc., written in a foreign language is to conform to the national practice in that language.

First words

3.44. The first word following a comma or a colon that introduces a complete sentence or a direct quotation is capitalized. (See also rule 3.45)

The question is, Shall the bill pass?
He asked, "And where are you going?"
The following question came up for discussion: What policy should be adopted?
His only rule was this: Chickens are not allowed past the front parlor.

3.45. The first word following a colon, an exclamation point, or a question mark is not capitalized if the matter following is merely a supplementary remark making the meaning clearer.

Revolutions are not made: they come.
Intelligence is not replaced by mechanism: even the televox must be guided by its master's voice.
But two months dead! nay, not so much; not two.
What is this? Your knees to me? to your corrected son?

3.46. The first word of a fragmentary quotation is not capitalized.

She objected "to the phraseology, not to the ideas."
"The President," he said, "will veto the bill."

3.47. The first word of a line of poetry is capitalized.

Lives of great men all remind us
We can make our lives sublime.

3.48. The first word of a run-in list following a colon is not capitalized. (For lists that are not run in, see rule 8.28.)

There are three primary pigment colors: magenta, yellow, and cyan.
The vote was as follows: in the affirmative, 23; in the negative, 11; not voting, 3.
His goals were these: (1) learn Spanish, (2) see the Grand Canyon, and (3) climb Mt. Everest.

3.49. The first word following *Whereas* in resolutions, contracts, etc., is not capitalized; the first word following an enacting or resolving clause is capitalized.

Whereas the Constitution provides . . . ; and
Whereas, moreover, . . . : Therefore be it
Whereas the Senate provided for the . . . : Now, therefore, be it
Resolved, That . . . ; and be it further
Resolved (jointly), That . . .

Resolved by the House of Representatives (the Senate concurring), That . . . .
(Concurrent resolution, Federal Government.)
Resolved by the Senate of Oklahoma (the House of Representatives concurring therein), That . . . . (Concurrent resolution, using name of State.)
Resolved by the senate (the house of representatives concurring therein), That . . . .
(Concurrent resolution, not using name of State.)
Resolved by the Assembly and Senate of the State of California (jointly), That . . . .
(Joint resolution, using name of State.)
Resolved by the Washington Board of Trade, That . . .
Provided, That . . .
Provided further, That . . .
Provided, however, That . . .
And provided further, That . . .
Ordered, That . . .
Be it enacted, That . . .

Centerheads and sideheads

3.50. Unless otherwise marked, centerheads are set in capitals, and sideheads are set in sentence case. In centerheads making two lines, wordbreaks should be avoided. The first line should be centered and set as full as possible.

3.51. In heads set in caps, a small-cap *c* or *ac,* if available, is used in such names as *McLean* or *MacLeod*; otherwise a lowercase *c* or *ac* is used. In heads set in small caps, a thin space is used after the *c* or the *ac.*

3.52. In such names as *LeRoy, DeHostis, LaFollette,* etc. (one-word forms only), set in caps, the second letter of the particle is made a small cap, if available; otherwise lowercase is used. In heads set in small caps, a thin space is used.

3.53. In matter set in caps and small caps or caps and lowercase, capitalize all principal words, including parts of compounds which would be capitalized standing alone. The articles *a, an,* and *the;* the prepositions *at, by, for, in, of, on, per, to,* and *up;* the conjunctions *and, as, but, if, or,* and *nor;* and the second element of a compound numeral are not capitalized. (See also rule 8.133.)

World en Route to All-Out War
Curfew To Be Set for 10 o'Clock (To capitalized in an infinitive verb)
Man Hit With 2-Inch Pipe
No-Par-Value Stock for Sale

Yankees May Be Winners in Zig-Zag Race
Ex-Senator Is To Be Admitted
Notice of Filing and Order on Exemption From Requirements
but Building on Twenty-first Street (if spelled)
One Hundred Twenty-three Years (if spelled)
Only One-tenth of Shipping Was Idle
Many 35-Millimeter Films in Production
Built-Up Stockpiles Are Necessary (*Up* is an adverb here)
The Per Diem Was Increased (*Per Diem* is used as a noun here); Lower Taxes per Person (*per* is a preposition here)

3.54. If a normally lowercased short word is used in juxtaposition with a capitalized word of like significance, it should also be capitalized.

Buildings On and Near the National Mall

3.55. In a heading set in caps and lowercase or in caps and small caps, a normally lowercased last word, if it is the only lowercased word in the heading, should also be capitalized.

All Returns Are In

3.56. Verbs and the first element of an infinitive are capitalized.

Controls To Be Applied
but Aid Sent to Disaster Area (*to* is a preposition here)

3.57. In matter set in caps and small caps, such abbreviations as *etc., et al.,* and *p.m.* are set in small caps; in matter set in caps and lowercase, these abbreviations are set in lowercase.

PLANES, GUNS, SHIPS, ETC.
Planes, Guns, Ships, etc.
JAMES BROS. ET AL.
James, Nelson, et al.
IN RE THE 8 P.M. MEETING
In re the 8 p.m. Meeting

3.58. Paragraph series letters in parentheses appearing in heads set in caps, caps and small caps, small caps, or in caps and lowercase are to be set as in copy.

SECTION 1.580(f)(1)

Addresses, salutations, and signatures

3.59. The first word and all principal words in addresses, salutations, and signatures are capitalized. See Chapter 16 "Datelines, Addresses, and Signatures."

Interjections

3.60. The interjection "O" is always capitalized. Other interjections within a sentence are not capitalized.

Sail on, O Ship of State!
For lo! the days are hastening on.
But, oh, how fortunate!

4. Capitalization Examples

A

A-bomb
abstract B, 1, etc.
Academy:
  Air Force; the Academy
  Andover; the academy
  Coast Guard; the Academy
  Merchant Marine; the Academy
  Military; the Academy
  National Academy of Sciences; the Academy of Sciences; the academy
  Naval; the Academy
  but service academies
accord, Paris peace (*see* Agreement)
accords, Helsinki
Act (Federal, State, or foreign), short or popular title or with number; the act:
  Affordable Care
  Appropriations
  Classification
  Clear Skies
  Economy
  Flood Control
  Military Selective Service
  No Child Left Behind
  Organic Act of Virgin Islands
  Panama Canal
  PATRIOT
  Revenue
  Sarbanes-Oxley
  Stockpiling
  Tariff
  Trademark
  Walsh-Healey Act; *but* Walsh-Healey law (or bill)
act, labor-management relations
Acting, if part of capitalized title
Active Duty
Adjutant General, the (*see* The)
Administration, with name; capitalized standing alone if Federal unit:
  Farmers Home
  Food and Drug
  Maritime
  Transportation Security
  but Obama administration; administration bill, policy, etc.
Administrative Law Judge Davis; Judge Davis; an administrative law judge
Admiralty, British, etc.
Admiralty, Lord of the
Adobe Acrobat Reader
Adviser, Legal (Department of State)
Africa:
  east
  East Coast
  north
  South
  South-West (Territory of)
  West Coast
African American (noun)
African-American (adjective)
Agency, if part of name; capitalized standing alone if referring to Federal unit:
  Central Intelligence; the Agency
Agent Orange
Age(s):
  Age of Discovery
  Dark Ages
  Elizabethan Age
  Golden Age (of Pericles only)
  Middle Ages
  but atomic age; Cambrian age; copper age; ice age; missile age; rocket age; space age; stone age; etc.
Agreement, with name; the agreement:
  General Agreement on Tariffs and Trade (GATT); the general agreement

International Coffee Agreement; the coffee agreement
North American Free-Trade Agreement (NAFTA)
Status of Forces; *but* status-of-forces agreements
United States-Canada Free-Trade Agreement; the free-trade agreement
but the Geneva agreement; the Potsdam agreement; Paris peace agreement

Air Force:
Air National Guard (*see* National)
Base (with name); Air Force base (*see* Base; Station)
Civil Air Patrol; Civil Patrol; the patrol
Command (*see* Command)
One (Presidential plane)
Reserve
Reserve Officers' Training Corps

Airport: LaGuardia; Reagan National; the airport

Alaska Native:
the Native; *but* Ohio native, a native of Alaska, etc.

Al Jazeera

Alliance, Farmers', etc.; the alliance

alliances and coalitions (*see also* powers):
Allied Powers; the powers (World Wars I and II)
Atlantic alliance
Axis, the; Axis Powers; the powers
Benelux (Belgium, Netherlands, Luxembourg)
Big Four (European); of the Pacific
Big Three
Central Powers; the powers (World War I)
Coalition of the Willing
European Economic Community
Fritalux (France, Italy, Benelux countries)
North Atlantic Treaty Organization (*see* Organization)
Western Powers

Allied (World Wars I and II):
armies
Governments
Nations
peoples
Powers; the powers; *but* European powers
Supreme Allied Commander

Allies, the (World Wars I and II); *also* members of Western bloc (political entity); *but* our allies; weaker allies, etc.

al-Qaida

Alzheimer('s) disease

Ambassador:
British, etc.; the Ambassador; the Senior Ambassador; His Excellency
Extraordinary and Plenipotentiary; the Ambassador; Ambassador at Large; an ambassador

amendment:
Baker amendment
Social Security Amendments of 1983; 1983 amendments; the Social Security amendments; the amendments
to the Constitution (U.S.); *but* First Amendment, 14th Amendment, etc.; the Amendment

American:
Federation of Labor and Congress of Industrial Organizations (AFL–CIO); the federation
Gold Star Mothers, Inc.; Gold Star Mothers; a Mother
Legion (*see* Legion)
National Red Cross; the Red Cross
War Mothers; a Mother

AmeriCorps Program

Amtrak (National Railroad Passenger Corporation)

Ancient Free and Accepted Masons; a Mason; a Freemason

Annex, if part of name of building; the annex
Antarctic Ocean (*see* Arctic; Ocean)
appendix 1, A, II, etc.; the appendix; *but* Appendix II (when part of title); Appendix II:[1] Education Directory
appropriation bill (*see also* bill):
  deficiency
  Department of Agriculture
  for any governmental unit
  independent offices
aquaculture; acquiculture
Arab States
Arabic numerals
Arboretum, National; the Arboretum
Archipelago, Philippine, etc.; the archipelago
Architect of the Capitol; the Architect
Archivist of the United States; the Archivist
Arctic:
  Circle
  currents
  Ocean
  zone
  but subarctic
arctic (descriptive adjective):
  clothing
  conditions
  fox
  grass
  night
  seas
Area, if part of name; the area:
  Cape Hatteras Recreational
  White Pass Recreation; etc.
  but area 2; free trade area; Metropolitan Washington area; bay area; nonsmoking area
Arlington:
  Memorial Amphitheater; the Memorial Amphitheater; the amphitheater
  Memorial Bridge (*see* Bridge)
  National Cemetery (*see* Cemetery)
Arm, Infantry, etc. (military); the arm
Armed Forces (synonym for overall Military Establishment):
  British
  Retirement Home (AFRH)
  of the United States
armed services
armistice
Armory, Springfield, etc.; the armory
Army, American or foreign, if part of name; capitalized standing alone only if referring to U.S. Army:
  Active; Active-Duty
  Adjutant General, the
  All-Volunteer
  Band (*see* Band)
  branches; Gordon Highlanders; Royal Guards; etc.
  Brigade, 1st, etc.; the brigade; Robinson's brigade
  Command (*see* Command)
  Command and General Staff College (*see* College)
  Company A; A Company; the company
  Confederate (referring to Southern Confederacy); the Confederates
  Continental; Continentals
  Corps, Reserve (*see* Corps)
  District of Washington (military); the district
  Division, 1st, etc.; the division
  Engineers (the Corps of Engineers); the Engineers; *but* Army engineer
  Establishment
  Field Establishment
  Field Forces (*see* Forces)
  Finance Department; the Department
  1st, etc.
  General of the Army; *but* the general
  General Staff; the Staff
  Headquarters, 1st Regiment

[1] The colon is preferred; a dash is permissible; *but* a comma is too weak.

Headquarters of the; the headquarters
Regiment, 1st, etc.; the regiment
Regular Army officer; a Regular
Revolutionary (American, British, French, etc.)
service
Surgeon General, the (*see* Surgeon General)
Volunteer; the Volunteers; a Volunteer
army:
Lee's army; *but* Clark's 5th Army
mobile
mule, shoe, etc.
of occupation; occupation army
Red
Arsenal, Rock Island, etc.; the arsenal
article 15; *but* Article 15, when part of title: Article 15: Uniform Code of Military Justice
Articles:
of Confederation (U.S.)
of Impeachment; the articles
Asian American (noun)
Asian-American (adjective)
Assembly (*see* United Nations)
Assembly of New York; the assembly (*see also* Legislative Assembly)
Assistant, if part of capitalized title; the assistant
assistant, Presidential (*see* Presidential)
Assistant Secretary (*see* Secretary)
Associate Justice (*see* Supreme Court)
Association, if part of name; capitalized standing alone if referring to Federal unit:
American Association for the Advancement of Science; the association
Federal National Mortgage (Fannie Mae); the Association
Young Women's Christian; the association
Astrophysical Observatory (*see* Observatory)
Atlantic (*see also* Pacific):
Charter (*see* Charter)
coast
Coast States
community
Destroyer Flotilla; the destroyer flotilla; the flotilla
Fleet (*see* Fleet)
mid-Atlantic
North
seaboard
slope
South
time, standard time (*see* time)
but cisatlantic; transatlantic
Attorney General (U.S. or foreign country); *but* attorney general of Maine, etc.
attorney, U.S.
Authority, capitalized standing alone if referring to Federal unit:
National Shipping; the Authority
Port Authority of New York and New Jersey; the port authority; the authority
Tennessee Valley; the Authority
Auto Train (Amtrak)
autumn
Avenue, Constitution, etc.; the avenue
Award:
Academy
Distinguished Service
Merit
Mother of the Year
the award (*see also* decorations, etc.)
Axis, the (*see* alliances)
Ayatollah; an ayatollah

B

baby boomer
Badlands (SD and NE)
Balkan States (*see* States)

Baltic States (*see* States)
Band, if part of name; the band:
  Army, Marine, Navy
Bank, if part of name; the bank; capitalized standing alone if referring to international bank:
  Export-Import Bank of the United States; Ex-Im Bank; the Bank
  Farm Loan Bank of Dallas; Dallas Farm Loan Bank; farm loan bank; farm loan bank at Dallas
  Farmers & Mechanics, etc.
  Federal Land Bank of Louisville; Louisville Federal Land Bank; land bank at Louisville; Federal land bank
  Federal Reserve Bank of New York; Richmond Federal Reserve Bank; *but* Reserve bank at Richmond; Federal Reserve bank; Reserve bank; Reserve city
  First National, etc.
  German Central; the Bank
  International Bank for Reconstruction and Development; the Bank
  but blood bank, central reserve, soil bank
Bar, if part of name; Maryland (State) Bar Association; Maryland (State) bar; the State bar; the bar association
Barracks, if part of name; the barracks:
  Carlisle
  Disciplinary (Leavenworth)
  Marine (District of Columbia)
  but A barracks; barracks A; etc.
Base, Andrews Air Force; Air Force base; the base (*see also* Naval); *but* Sandia Base
Basin (*see* geographic terms)
Battery, the (New York City)
Battle, if part of name; the battle:
  of Gettysburg; *but* battle at Gettysburg; etc.
  of Fallujah; of the Marne; of the Wilderness; of Waterloo; etc.
battlefield, Bull Run, etc.
battleground, Manassas, etc.
Bay, San Francisco Bay area; the bay area
Belt, if part of name; the belt:
  Bible
  Farm
  Rust
  Sun
  but money belt
Beltway, capitalized with name; the beltway
Bench (*see* Supreme Bench)
Benelux (*see* alliances)
Bible; Biblical; Scriptures; Ten Commandments; etc. (*see also* book)
bicentennial
bill, Kiess; Senate bill 217; House bill 31 (*see also* appropriation bill)
Bill of Rights (historic document); *but* GI bill of rights
Bizonia; bizonal; bizone
Black (African American)
Black Caucus (*see* Congressional)
bloc (*see* Western)
block (grants)
Bluegrass region, etc.
Bluetooth
B'nai B'rith
Board, if part of name; capitalized standing alone only if referring to Federal or international board:
  Employees' Compensation Appeals
  Federal Reserve (*see* Federal)
  Military Production and Supply (NATO)
  National Labor Relations
  of Directors (Federal unit); *but* board of directors (nongovernmental)
  of Health of Montgomery County; Montgomery County Board of Health; the board of health; the board
  of Regents (Smithsonian)
  of Visitors (Military and Naval Academies)

on Geographic Names
Railroad Retirement
Boko Haram
bond:
Government
savings
series EE
Treasury
book:
books of the Bible
First Book of Samuel; etc.
Good Book (synonym for Bible)
book 1, I, etc.; *but* Book 1, when part of title: Book 1: The Golden Legend
Boolean:
logic
operator
search
border, United States-Mexican
Borough, if part of name: Borough of the Bronx; the borough
Botanic Garden (National); the garden (not Botanical Gardens)
Bowl, Dust, Rose, Super, etc.; the bowl
Boy Scouts (the organization); a Boy Scout; a Scout; Scouting; Eagle Scout; Explorer Scout
Branch, if part of name; capitalized standing alone only if referring to a Federal unit:
Accounts
Public Buildings
but executive, judicial, or legislative branch
Bridge, if part of name; the bridge:
Arlington Memorial; Memorial;
Francis Scott Key; Key
but Baltimore & Ohio Railroad bridge
Brother(s) (adherent of religious order)
budget:
department
estimate
Federal
message
performance-type
President's
Budget of the United States Government, the Budget (publication)
Building, if part of name; the building:
Capitol (*see* Capitol Building)
Colorado
House (or Senate) Office
Investment
Russell Senate Office
Cannon House Office
Pentagon
the National Archives; the Archives
Treasury; Treasury Annex
Bulletin 420; Farmers' Bulletin No. 420
Bureau, if part of name; capitalized standing alone if referring to Federal or international unit:
of Customs (name changed to U.S. Customs and Border Protection)
of Engraving and Printing
of Indian Affairs

C

C–SPAN
Cabinet, American or foreign, if part of name or standing alone (*see also* foreign cabinets):
British Cabinet; the Cabinet
the President's Cabinet; the Cabinet; Cabinet officer, member
Calendar, if part of name; the calendar:
Consent; etc.
House
No. 99; Calendars Nos. 1 and 2
of Bills and Resolutions
Private
Senate
Unanimous Consent
Union
Wednesday (legislative)
Cambrian age (*see* Ages)

Camp Lejeune; David, etc.; the camp
Canal, with name; the canal:
  Cross-Florida Barge
  Isthmian
  Panama
Cape (*see* geographic terms)
Capital, Capital City, National Capital (Washington, DC); *but* the capital (State)
Capitol Building (with State name); the capitol
Capitol, the (Washington, DC):
  Architect of
  Building
  caucus room
  Chamber
  Cloakroom
  dome
  Grounds
  Halls (House and Senate)
  Halls of Congress
  Hill; the Hill
  Police (*see* Police)
  Power Plant
  Prayer Room
  Press Gallery, etc.
  rotunda
  Senate wing
  stationery room
  Statuary Hall
  the well (House or Senate)
  west front
catch-22
Caucasian (*see* White)
caucus: Republican; *but* Congressional Black Caucus (incorporated name); Sun Belt Caucus
CD
Cemetery, if part of name: Arlington National; the cemetery
Census:
  Twenty-third Decennial (title); Twenty-third (title); the census
  2000 census
  2000 Census of Agriculture; the census of agriculture; the census
  the 23d and subsequent decennial censuses
Center, if part of name; the Center (Federal); the center (non-Federal):
  Agricultural Research, etc.; the Center (Federal)
  Kennedy Center for the Performing Arts; the Kennedy Center; the Center (Federal)
  the Lincoln Center; the center (non-Federal)
central Asia, etc.
Central America
Central Europe
Central States
central time (*see* time)
century, first, 21st, etc.
Chairman, Chairwoman, Chair:
  of the Board of Directors; the Chairman (Federal); *but* chairman of the board of directors (non-Federal)
  of the Committee of the Whole House; the Chairman
  of the Federal Trade Commission; the Chairman
  Vice
chairman, chairwoman, chair (congressional):
  of the Appropriations Committee
  of the Subcommittee on Banking
  but Chairman Rogers, Chairwoman Capito
Chair, the, if personified
Chamber of Commerce; the chamber:
  of Ada; Ada Chamber of Commerce; the chamber of commerce
  of the United States; U.S. Chamber of Commerce; the chamber of commerce; national chamber
Chamber, the (Senate or House)

channel 3 (TV); the channel
Chaplain (House or Senate); *but* Navy chaplain
chapter 5, II, etc.; *but* Chapter 5, when part of title: Chapter 5: Research and Development; Washington chapter, Red Cross
Chargé d'Affaires, British, etc.; the Chargé d'Affaires; the Chargé
chart 2, A, II, etc.; *but* Chart 2, when part of legend: Chart 2.—Army strength
Charter, capitalized with name; the charter:
  Atlantic
  United Nations
cheese: Camembert, Cheddar, Parmesan, Provolone, Roquefort, etc.
Chief, if referring to head of Federal unit; the Chief:
  Clerk
  Forester (*see* Forester)
  Intelligence Office
  Judge
  Justice (U.S. Supreme Court); *but* chief justice (of a State)
  Magistrate (the President)
  of Division of Publications
  of Engineers (Army)
  of Naval Operations
  of Staff
Christian; Christendom; Christianity; Christianize; *but* christen
church and state
church calendar:
  Christmas
  Easter
  Lent
  Pentecost (Whitsuntide)
Church, if part of name of organization or building
Circle, if part of name; the circle:
  Arctic
  Logan
  but great circle
Circular 420
cities, sections of, official or popular names:
  East Side
  French Quarter (New Orleans)
  Latin Quarter (Paris)
  North End
  Northwest Washington, etc. (District of Columbia); the Northwest; *but* northwest (directional)
  the Loop (Chicago)
City, if part of corporate or popular name; the city:
  Kansas City; the two Kansas Citys
  Mexico City
  New York City; *but* city of New York
  Twin Cities
  Washington City; *but* city of Washington
  Windy City (Chicago)
  but Reserve city (*see* Bank)
civil action No. 46
civil defense
Civil War (*see* War)
Clan, if part of tribal name; Clan MacArthur; the clan
class 2, A, II, etc.; *but* Class 2 when part of title: Class 2: Leather Products
Clerk, the, of the House of Representatives; of the Supreme Court of the United States
clerk, the, of the Senate
client
client-server
cloud computing; the cloud
coal sizes: pea, barley, buckwheat, stove, etc.
coalition; coalition force; coalition members, etc.
coast: Atlantic, east, gulf, west, etc.
Coast Guard, U.S.; the Coast Guard; Coastguardsman Smith; *but* a coastguardsman; a guardsman; Reserve
Coastal Plain (Atlantic and Gulf)

Code (in shortened title of a publication); the code:
District
Federal Criminal
Internal Revenue (*also* Tax Code)
International (signal)
of Federal Regulations
Penal; Criminal; etc.
Pennsylvania State
Radio
Television
Uniform Code of Military Justice
United States
ZIP Code (copyrighted)
but civil code; flag code; Morse code
codel (congressional delegation)
collection, Brady, etc.; the collection
collector of customs
College, if part of name; the college:
Armed Forces Staff
Command and General Staff
Gettysburg
National War
of Bishops
but electoral college
college degrees: bachelor of arts, master's, etc.
Colonials (American Colonial Army); *but* colonial times, etc.
Colonies, the:
Thirteen
Thirteen American
Thirteen Original
but 13 separate Colonies
colonists, the
Command, capitalize with name; the command:
Air Force Materiel
Army
Central (CENCOM)
Naval Space
Zone of Interior
Commandant, the (Coast Guard or Marine Corps only)
Commandos, the; Commando raid; a commando
Commission (if part of name; capitalized standing alone if referring to Federal or international commission):
International Boundary, United States and Canada
of Fine Arts
Public Buildings
Commissioner, if referring to Federal or international commission; the Commissioner:
Land Bank; *but* land bank commissioner loans
of Customs and Border Protection
U.S. (International Boundary Commission, etc.)
but a U.S. commissioner
Committee (or Subcommittee) (if part of name; the Committee, if referring to international or noncongressional Federal committee or to the Committee of the Whole, the Committee of the Whole House, or the Committee of the Whole House on the state of the Union):
American Medical Association Committee on Education; the committee on education; the committee
Appropriations, etc.; the committee; Subcommittee on Appropriations; the subcommittee; subcommittee of the Appropriations Committee
Democratic National; the national committee; the committee; Democratic national committeeman
Democratic policy committee; the committee
Joint Committee on Printing; the Joint Committee; the committee; *but* a joint committee

of Defense Ministers (NATO); the
Committee (*see also* Organization, North Atlantic Treaty)
of One Hundred, etc.; the committee
on Finance; the committee
President's Advisory Committee on Management; the Committee
Republican National; the national committee; the committee; Republican national committeeman
Republican policy committee; the committee
Senate policy committee
Subcommittee on Immigration; the subcommittee
but Baker committee
ad hoc committee
conference committee
Committee Print No. 32; Committee Prints Nos. 8 and 9; committee print
Common Cause
Common Core State Standards Initiative; Common Core
Commonwealth:
British Commonwealth; the Commonwealth
of Australia
of Kentucky
of Massachusetts
of Pennsylvania
of Virginia
Communist Party; a Communist
compact, U.S. marine fisheries, etc.; the compact
Company, if part of name; capitalized standing alone if referring to unit of Federal Government:
Procter & Gamble Co.; the company
Comptroller of the Currency; the Comptroller
Comptroller General (U.S.); the Comptroller
Comsat
Concor
Confederacy (of the South)
Confederate:
Army
flag
Government
soldier
States
Confederation, Articles of
Conference, if referring to governmental (U.S.) or international conference:
Bretton Woods; the Conference
Judicial Conference of the United States; U.S. Judicial Conference; Judicial Conference; the Conference
Tenth Annual Conference of the United Methodist Churches; the conference
Congress (convention), if part of name; capitalized standing alone if referring to international congress:
of Industrial Organizations
of Parents and Teachers, National; the congress
Congress (legislature), if referring to national congress:
of Bolivia, etc.; the Congress
of the United States; First, Second, 10th, 103d, etc.; the Congress; Library of
Congressional:
Black Caucus; the Black Caucus; the caucus
Directory, the directory
District, First, 10th, etc.; the First District; the congressional district; the district
Medal of Honor (*see* decorations)
but congressional action, committee, etc.
Congressman; Congresswoman; Congressman at Large; Member of Congress; Member; membership
Conservative Party; a Conservative

Constitution, with name of country; capitalized standing alone when referring to a specific national constitution; *but* New York State Constitution; the constitution
constitutional
consul, British, general, etc.
consulate, British, etc.
Consumer Price Index (official title); the price index; the index; *but* a consumers' price index (descriptive)
Continent, only if following name; North American Continent; the continent; *but* the Continent (continental Europe)
Continental:
  Army; the Army
  Congress; the Congress
  Divide (*see* Divide)
  Outer Continental Shelf
  Shelf; the shelf; a continental shelf
continental Europe, United States, etc.
Continentals (Revolutionary soldiers)
Convention, governmental (U.S.), international, or national political; the convention:
  89th National Convention of the American Legion
  Constitutional (United States, 1787); the Convention
  Democratic National; Democratic
  Genocide (international)
  on International Civil Aviation
  Republican National; Republican
  Universal Postal Union; Postal Union *also* International Postal; Warsaw
copper age (*see* Ages)
Corporation, if part of name; the Corporation, if referring to unit of Federal Government:
  Commodity Credit
  Federal Deposit Insurance
  National Railroad Passenger (Amtrak)
  Rand Corp.; the corporation
  Saint Lawrence Seaway Development (American)
  St. Lawrence Seaway Management (Canadian)
  Union Carbide Corp.; the corporation
  Virgin Islands
Corps, if part of name; the corps, all other uses:
  Adjutant General's
  Army Reserve
  Chemical
  Finance
  Foreign Service Officer (*see* Foreign Service)
  Job
  Judge Advocate General's
  Marine (*see* Marine Corps)
  Medical
  Military Police
  Nurse
  of Cadets (West Point)
  of Engineers; Army Engineers; the Engineers; *but* Army engineer; the corps
  Ordnance
  Peace; Peace Corpsman; the corpsman
  Quartermaster
  Reserve Officers' Training (ROTC)
  VII Corps, etc.
  Signal
  Transportation
  Youth
  but diplomatic corps
corpsman; hospital corpsman
corridor, Northeast
Council, if part of name; capitalized standing alone if referring to Federal or international unit (*see also* United Nations):
  Boston City; the council
  Her Majesty's Privy Council; the Privy Council; the Council

National Security; the Council
of Foreign Ministers (NATO); the Council
of the Organization of American States; the Council
Philadelphia City; the council
counsel; general counsel
County, Prince George's; county of Prince George's; County Kilkenny, etc.; Loudoun and Fairfax Counties; the county
country
Court (of law) capitalized if part of name; capitalized standing alone if referring to the Supreme Court of the United States, to the Court of Impeachment (U.S. Senate), or to an international court:
Circuit Court of the United States for the Tenth Circuit; Circuit Court for the Tenth Circuit; the circuit court; the court; the tenth circuit
Court of Appeals for the State of North Carolina, etc.; the Tenth Circuit Court of Appeals; the court of appeals; the court
Court of Claims; the court
Court of Impeachment, the Senate; the Court
District Court of the United States for the Eastern District of Missouri; the district court; the court
International Court of Justice; the Court
Permanent Court of Arbitration; the Court
Superior Court of the District of Columbia; the superior court; the court
Supreme Court of the United States (*see* Supreme Court)
Supreme Court of Virginia, etc.; the supreme court; the court
Tax Court; the court
U.S. Court of Appeals for the District of Columbia; the court
Covenant, League of Nations; the covenant
Creed, Apostles'; the Creed
Crown, if referring to a ruler; *but* crown colony, lands, etc.
Current, if part of name; the current:
Humboldt
Japan
North Equatorial
customhouse; customs official
czar; czarist

D

D-Day
Dalai Lama
Dalles, The; *but* the Dalles region
Dark Ages (*see* Ages)
Daughters of the American Revolution; a Daughter
daylight saving time
Declaration, capitalized with name:
of Independence; the Declaration
of Panama; the declaration
decorations, medals, etc., awarded by United States or any foreign national government; the medal, the cross, the ribbon (*see also* Award):
Air Medal
Bronze Star Medal
Commendation Ribbon
Congressional Medal of Honor
Croix de Guerre
Distinguished Flying Cross
Distinguished Service Cross
Distinguished Service Medal
Good Conduct Medal
Legion of Merit
Medal for Merit
Medal of Freedom
Medal of Honor

Purple Heart
Silver Star Medal
Soldier's Medal
Victoria Cross
Victory Medal
but oakleaf cluster
also Carnegie Medal; Olympic Gold Medal; Mother of the Year ; *but* gold medal

Decree (*see* Executive); Royal Decree
Deep South
Defense Establishment (*see* Establishment)
Deity, words denoting, capitalized
Delegate (U.S. Congress)
Delegates, Virginia House of
delegate (to a conference); the delegate; the delegation
Delta, Mississippi River; the delta
Democratic Party; a Democrat
Department, if part of name; capitalized standing alone if referring to a Federal or international unit:

of Agriculture
of the Treasury
of Veterans Affairs
Yale University Department of Economics; the department of economics; the department

Department of New York, American Legion
department:

executive
judicial
legislative

Depot, if part of name; the depot (*see also* Station)
Depression, Great
Deputy, if part of capitalized title; *but* the deputy

derivatives of proper names:

alaska seal (fur)
angora wool
angstrom unit
argyle wool
artesian well
astrakhan fabric
babbitt metal
benday process
bologna
bordeaux
bourbon whiskey
bowie knife
braille
brazil nut
brazilwood
brewer's yeast
bristolboard
brussel sprouts
brussels carpet
bunsen burner
burley tobacco
canada balsam (microscopy)
carlsbad twins (petrography)
cashmere shawl
castile soap
cesarean section
chantilly lace
chesterfield coat
china clay
chinese blue
collins (drink)
congo red
cordovan leather
coulomb
curie
degaussing apparatus
delftware
derby hat
diesel engine, dieselize
dixie cup
dotted swiss
epsom salt
fedora hat
frankfurter
french chalk
french dressing
french-fried potatoes
fuller's earth
gargantuan
gauss
georgette crepe
german silver
gilbert
glauber salt
gothic type
graham cracker
herculean task
hessian fly
holland cloth
hoolamite detector
hudson seal (fur)
india ink
india rubber
italic type
jamaica ginger
japan varnish
jersey fabric
johnin test
joule
knickerbocker
kraft paper
lambert
leghorn hat
levant leather
levantine silk
lilliputian
logan tent
london purple
lyonnaise potatoes
macadamized road
mach (no period) number
madras cloth
maginot line (nonliteral)
manila paper
maraschino cherry
mason jar
maxwell
melba toast
mercerized fabric
merino sheep
molotov cocktail
morocco leather
morris chair
murphy bed
navy blue
nelson, half nelson, etc.
neon light
newton
nissen hut
norfolk jacket
oriental rug
oxford shoe
panama hat
parianware
paris green
parkerhouse roll
pasteurized milk
persian lamb
petri dish
pharisaic
philistine
photostat
pitman arm
pitot tube
plaster of paris
prussian blue

quisling
quixotic idea
quonset hut
rembert wheel
roentgen
roman candle
roman cement
roman type
russia leather
russian bath
rutherford
sanforize
saratoga chips
scotch plaid, *but*
Scotch tape
(trademark)
shanghai
siamese twins
spanish omelet
stillson wrench
surah silk
swiss cheese
timothy grass
turkey red
turkish towel
utopia, utopian
vandyke collar
vaseline
venetian blind
venturi tube
victoria (carriage)
vienna bread
virginia reel
wedgwoodware
wheatstone bridge
wilton rug
zeppelin

dial-up
Diet, Japanese (legislative body)
diplomatic corps (*see also* Corps; service)
Director, if referring to head of Federal or international unit; the Director:
District Director of Internal Revenue
of the Government Publishing Office
of the Fish and Wildlife Service
of National Intelligence
of the Mint
Office of Management and Budget
but director, board of directors (nongovernmental)
Director General of Foreign Service; the Director General; the Director
diseases and related terms (see rule 3.32):
AIDS (acquired immunodeficiency syndrome)
Alzheimer('s) disease
autism, autism spectrum disorder (ASD)
cerebral palsy
Down syndrome
Ebola virus
German measles
HIV (human immunodeficiency virus)
Hodgkin: lymphoma; disease
Lyme disease
Marfan syndrome
Ménierè's disease
myasthenia gravis
Parkinson('s) disease
post-traumatic stress disorder (PTSD)
spina bifida
Zika virus
Distinguished Service Medal, etc. (*see* decorations)
District, if part of name; the district:
Alexandria School District No. 4; school district No. 4
Congressional (with number)
Federal (*see* Federal)
Los Angeles Water; the water district
but customs district No. 2; first assembly district; public utility district
District of Columbia; the District:
Anacostia Flats; the flats
Arlington Memorial Bridge; the Memorial Bridge; the bridge
Children's Hospital; the hospital
District jail; the jail; DC jail
Ellipse, the
Mall, The National; The Mall
Mayor (when pertaining to the District of Columbia only)
Metropolitan Police; Metropolitan police officer; the police
police court
Public Library; the library
Reflecting Pool; the pool
Tidal Basin; the basin
Washington Channel; the channel
Divide, Continental (Rocky Mountains); the divide
Divine Father; *but* divine guidance, divine providence, divine service
Division, Army, if part of name: 1st Cavalry Division; 1st Air Cavalry Division; the division
Division, if referring to Federal governmental unit; the Division:
Buick Motor Division; the division; a division of General Motors

Passport; the Division
but Trinity River division (reclamation); the division
Dixie
docket No. 66; dockets Nos. 76 and 77
Doctrine, Monroe; the doctrine; *but* Truman, Eisenhower doctrine
doctrine, fairness
Document, if part of name; the document:
Document No. 130
Document Numbered One Hundred Thirty
draconian
drawing II, A, 3, etc.; *but* Drawing 2 when part of title: Drawing 2.—Hydroelectric Power Development
dumpster
Dust Bowl (*see* Bowl)

E

Earth (planet)
East:
Coast (Africa)
Middle, Mideast (Asia)
Near (Balkans)
Side of New York
South Central States
the East (section of United States)
east:
Africa
coast (U.S.)
Pennsylvania
Eastern:
Gulf States
Middle, Mideastern (Asia)
North Central States
Shore (Chesapeake Bay)
States
United States
eastern:
France
seaboard
Wisconsin
easterner
Ebola virus
eBook
EE bond
electoral college; the electors
Elizabethan Age (*see* Ages)
email (lowercase within a sentence)
Email (uppercase "E" to start a sentence)
Emancipation Proclamation (*see* Proclamation)
Embassy, British, etc.; the Embassy
Emperor, Japanese, etc.; the Emperor
Empire, Roman; the empire
Engine Company, Bethesda; engine company No. 6; No. 6 engine company; the company
Engineer officer, etc. (of Engineer Corps); the Engineers
Engineers, Chief of (Army)
Engineers, Corps of (*see* Corps)
Envoy Extraordinary and Minister Plenipotentiary; the Envoy; the Minister
Equator, the; equatorial
Establishment, if part of name; the establishment:
Army
Army Field
Defense
Federal
Military
Naval
Naval Establishments Regs
Navy
Postal
Regular
Reserve
Shore
but civil establishment; legislative establishment
Estate, Girard (a foundation); the estate
estate, third (the commons); fourth (the press); tax; etc.

Eurodollar, euro
Excellency, His, Her; Their Excellencies
Exchange, New York Stock; the stock exchange; the exchange
Executive (President of United States):
  Chief
  Decree No. 100; Decree 100; *but* Executive decree; direction
  Mansion; the mansion; the White House
  Office; the Office
  Order No. 34; Order 34; *but* Executive order
  power
executive:
  agreement
  branch
  communication
  department
  document
  paper
  privilege
exhibit 2, A, II, etc.; *but* Exhibit 2, when part of title: Exhibit 2: Capital Expenditures, 1935–49
Expedition, Byrd; Lewis and Clark; the expedition
Exposition, California-Pacific International, etc.; the exposition

F

Fair Deal
Fair, World's, etc.; the fair; Texas State Fair
fall (season)
Falls, Niagara; the falls
Far East, Far Eastern; Far West (U.S.); *but* far western
Farm, if part of name; the farm:
  Johnson Farm; *but* Johnson's farm
  San Diego Farm
  Wild Tiger Farm
Fascist; fascism
Father of our Country (Washington)
FDsys
Fed, the (no period)
Federal (synonym for United States or other sovereign power):
  Depository Library Program *but* Federal depository library, libraries
  Digital System
  District (Mexico)
  Establishment
  Government (of any national government)
  grand jury; the grand jury
  land bank (*see* Bank)
  Register (publication); the Register
  Reserve Board, the Board; *also* Federal Reserve System, the System; Federal Reserve Board Regulation W, *but* Federal regulation W
  but a federal form of government
federally
fellow, fellowship (academic)
Field, Wrigley, Frank Wiley, etc.; the field
figure 2, A, II, etc. (illustration); *but* Figure 2, when part of legend: Figure 2.—Market scenes
firewall
firm names:
  ACDelco
  Amazon
  America Online (AOL)
  Apple
  Bausch & Lomb Inc.
  BP
  Bristol-Myers Squibb
  Carson, Pirie, Scott & Co.
  Coldwell Banker
  Colgate-Palmolive Co.
  Comcast
  DIRECTV
  Dow Jones & Co., Inc.
  Dun & Bradstreet
  eBay
  E.I. du Pont de Nemours & Co.
  Facebook

FedEx
GlaxoSmithKline
Google
Hamilton Beach/Proctor Silex, Inc.
Hartmarx Corp.
Hewlett-Packard
Houghton Mifflin Co.
Ingersoll-Rand Co.
Intel Corp.
J.C. Penney Co., Inc.
Johns-Manville Corp.
Kennecott Exploration Co.
Kmart
Libbey-Owens-Ford Co.
LinkedIn
Macmillan Co.
Merck & Co., Inc.
Merrill Lynch
Microsoft
Pfizer Inc.
Phelps Dodge Corp.
PricewaterhouseCoopers
Procter & Gamble Co.
Rand McNally & Co.
Rolls-Royce
Sun Microsystems
3M
Twitter
Underwriters Laboratories, Inc.
Walmart
Wal-Mart Stores, Inc.
Weyerhaeuser Co.
Xerox Corp.
YouTube

First Family (Presidential)
First Lady (wife of President)
First World War (*see* War)
flag code
flag, U.S.:
Old Flag, Old Glory
Stars and Stripes
Star-Spangled Banner

flags, foreign:
Tricolor (French)
Union Jack (British)
United Nations

Fleet, if part of name; the fleet:
Atlantic
Channel
Grand
High Seas
Marine Force
Naval Reserve
Pacific
6th Fleet, etc.
U.S.

flex fuel
floor (House or Senate)
flyway; Canadian flyway, etc.
Force(s), if part of name; the force(s):
Active Forces
Active-Duty
Air (*see also* Air Force)
All-Volunteer
Armed Forces (synonym for overall U.S. Military Establishment)
Army Field Forces; the Field Forces
Fleet Marine
Navy Battle (*see* Navy)
Navy Scouting (*see* Navy)
Rapid Deployment
Task Force 70; the task force; *but* task force report
United Nations Emergency; the Emergency Force; the Force; *but* United Nations police force

foreign cabinets:
Minister of Foreign Affairs; Foreign Minister; the Minister
Ministry of Foreign Affairs; the Ministry
Office of Foreign Missions; the Office
Minister Plenipotentiary
Premier
Prime Minister

Foreign Legion (French); the legion

Foreign Service; the Service:
officer
Officer Corps; the corps
Reserve officer; the Reserve officer
Reserve Officer Corps; the Reserve Corps; the corps
Staff officer; the Staff officer
Staff Officer Corps; the Staff Corps; the corps
Forest, if part of name; the national forest; the forest:
Angeles National
Black
Coconino and Prescott National Forests
but State and National forests (*see* System)
Forester (Chief of Forest Service); the Chief; *also* Chief Forester
form 2, A, II, etc.; *but* Form 2, when part of title: Form 1040: Individual Income Tax Return; *but* withholding tax form
Fort McHenry, etc.; the fort
Foundation, if part of name; capitalized standing alone if referring to Federal unit:
Chemical; the foundation
Ford; the foundation
National Science; the Foundation
Russell Sage; the foundation
Founding Fathers; Founders/Founder (of this Nation, Country)
four freedoms
Framers (of the U.S. Constitution; of the Bill of Rights)
free world
Frisco (for San Francisco; no apostrophe)
Fritalux (*see* alliances)
Fund, if part of name; capitalized standing alone if referring to international or United Nations fund:
Democracy (United Nations); the Fund
International Monetary; the Fund
but civil service retirement fund; highway trust fund; mutual security fund; national service life insurance fund; revolving fund

G

Gadsden Purchase
Gallery of Art, National (*see* National)
Gallup Poll; the poll
Gambia, The
GAO (Government Accountability Office)
Geiger counter
General Order No. 14; General Orders No. 14; a general order
General Schedule
Generation X
gentile
Geographer, the (State Department)
geographic terms (terms, such as those listed below,[2] are capitalized if part of name; are lowercased in general sense (rivers of Virginia and Maryland)):

Archipelago
Area
Arroyo
Atoll
Bank
Bar
Basin, Upper (Lower) Colorado River, etc. (legal entity); *but* Hansen flood-control basin; Missouri River basin (drainage); upper Colorado River storage project
Bay
Bayou
Beach
Bench
Bend
Bight
Bluff
Bog
Borough (boro)
Bottom
Branch (stream)
Brook
Butte
Canal; the canal (Panama)
Canyon
Cape
Cascade
Cave
Cavern
Channel; *but* Mississippi River channel(s)
Cirque
Coulee
Cove
Crag
Crater
Creek
Crossroads
Current (ocean feature)
Cut
Cutoff
Dam
Delta
Desert
Divide
Dome (not geologic)
Draw (stream)
Dune
Escarpment
Estuary
Falls
Fault
Flat(s)
Floodway
Ford
Forest

[2] List compiled with cooperation of the U.S. Board on Geographic Names.

Fork (stream)	Palisades
Gap	Park
Geyser	Pass
Glacier	Passage
Glen	Peak
Gorge	Peninsula
Gulch	Plain
Gulf	Plateau
Gut	Point
Harbor	Pond
Head	Pool
Hill	Port (water body)
Hogback	Prairie
Hollow	Range (mountain)
Hook	Rapids
Horn	Ravine
Hot Spring	Reef
Icefield	Reservoir
Ice Shelf	Ridge
Inlet	River
Island	Roads (anchorage)
Isle	Rock
Islet	Run (stream)
Keys (Florida only)	Sea
Knob	Seaway
Lagoon	Shoal
Lake	Sink
Landing	Slough
Ledge	Sound
Lowland	Spit
Marsh	Spring
Massif	Spur
Mesa	Strait
Monument	Stream
Moraine	Summit
Mound	Swamp
Mount	Terrace
Mountain	Thoroughfare
Narrows	Trench
Neck	Trough
Needle	Valley
Notch	Volcano
Oasis	Wash
Ocean	Waterway
Oxbow	Woods

Geological Survey (*see* Survey)
GI bill of rights
Girl Scouts (organization); a Girl Scout; a Scout; Scouting
G-man
Gold Star Mothers (*see* American)
Golden Age (*see* Ages)
Golden Rule
Gospel, if referring to the first four books of the New Testament; *but* gospel music
Government:
  British, etc.; the Government
  department, officials, -owned, publications, etc. (U.S. Government)
  National and State Governments
  Printing Office (historical)
  Publishing Office (*see* Office)
  U.S.; National; Federal; Tribal
Government information product
government:
  Churchill
  Communist
  District (of Columbia)
  European governments
  Federal, State, and municipal governments
  insular; island
  local
  military
  seat of
  State
  State and Provincial governments
  Territorial
governmental
Governor:
  of Louisiana, etc.; the Governor; a Governor; State Governor(s); Governors' conference
  of Puerto Rico; the Governor
  of the Federal Reserve Board; the Governor
Governor General of Canada; the Governor General
govinfo (always bold)
grand jury (*see* Federal)
Grange, the (National)
grant, Pell
graph 2, A, II, etc.; *but* Graph 2, when part of title: Graph 2.—Production levels
Great:
  Basin
  Depression
  Divide
  Lakes; the lakes; lake(s) traffic
  Plains; *but* southern Great Plains

Seal (any nation)
Society
War (*see* War)
White Way (New York City)
great circle (navigation)
Greater Los Angeles, Greater New York
gross national product (GNP)
Group:
G8 (Group of 8) (representatives of the eight leading industrial nations)
Helsinki Monitoring; the group
Military Advisory Group; the group
Standing (*see* Organization)
World Bank
group 2, II, A, etc.; *but* Group 2, when part of title: Group II: List of Counties by States
Guard, National (*see* National)
guardsman (*see* Coast Guard; National Guard)
Gulf:
Coast States; *but* gulf coast
of Mexico; the gulf
States
Stream; the stream

H

Hague, The
Hall (U.S. Senate or House)
Halls of Congress
H-bomb; H-hour
Headquarters:
Alaskan Command; the command headquarters
4th Regiment Headquarters; regimental headquarters
32d Division Headquarters; the division headquarters
hearing examiner
Heaven (religious); heaven (place)
Heimlich maneuver
hell (place)
Hells (no apostrophe) Canyon
Hemisphere, Eastern; Western; etc.; the hemisphere
Hezbollah
High Church
High Commissioner
High Court (*see* Supreme Court)
high definition
High School, if part of name: Western; the high school
Highway No. 40; Route 40; State Route 9; the highway
Hill (the Capitol)
Hispanic
Holocaust, the (World War II); a holocaust
Holy Scriptures; Holy Writ (Bible)
home page
Hoosier
Hospice, if part of name
Hospital, if part of name; the hospital:
Howard University
St. Elizabeths (no apostrophe)
but naval (marine or Army) hospital
hospital corpsman (*see* corpsman)
House, if part of name:
Blair
Johnson house (private residence)
of Representatives; the House (U.S.)
Office Building (*see* Building)
Ohio (State); the house
but both Houses; lower (or upper) House (Congress)
House of Representatives (U.S.), titles of officers standing alone capitalized:
Chairman (Committee of the Whole)
Chaplain
Clerk; *but* legislative clerk, etc.
Doorkeeper
Official Reporter(s) of Debates
Parliamentarian
Postmaster
post office
Sergeant at Arms

Speaker pro tempore
Speaker; speakership
HUD (Department of Housing and Urban Development)
Hudson's Bay Co.
Hurricane Andrew, Katrina, Rita, etc.

I

ice age (*see* Ages)
imam
Independent Party; an Independent
Indians (*see* 3.18):
Absentee Shawnee
Alaska (*see* Native)
Eastern (or Lower) Band of Cherokee; the Band
Five Civilized Tribes; the Tribes
Native Americans
Shawnee Tribe; the Tribe
Six Nations (Iroquois Confederacy)
Tribe (if federally recognized)
Initiative, Caribbean Basin; *but* strategic defense initiative
Inquisition, Spanish; the Inquisition
inspector general
Institute, if part of name; capitalized standing alone if referring to Federal or international organization:
National Cancer; the Cancer Institute; the Institute
National Institutes of Health; the Institutes
of International Law; the Institute
Woman's; the institute
Institution, if part of name; capitalized standing alone if referring to Federal unit:
Brookings; the institution
Carnegie; the institution
Smithsonian; the Institution
insular government; island government
intercoastal waterway (*see* waterway)
interdepartmental
interface
International Court of Justice; the Court
international:
banks (*see* Bank)
boundary
dateline
law
Morse code (*see* Code)
internet (lowercase within a sentence)
Internet (uppercase "I" to start a sentence)
Internet of Things
Interstate 95; I–95; the interstate
Intracoastal Waterway; the waterway (*see also* waterway)
intranet
intrastate
Irish potato
Iron Curtain; the curtain
Islam; Islamic
Isthmian Canal (*see* Canal)
Isthmus of Panama; the isthmus

J

Japan Current (*see* Current)
Java (computer language)
Jersey cattle
Job Corps
Joint Chiefs of Staff; Chiefs of Staff
Joint Committee on Printing (*see* Committee)
Journal clerk; the clerk
Journal (House or Senate)
Judge Advocate General, the
judge; chief judge; circuit judge; district judge; *but* Judge Judy
judiciary, the
Justice; Justice Alito, etc.

K

kaffiyeh (Arabic headdress)
King of Thailand, etc.; the King
Koran, the; Koranic
Krugerrand

L

Laboratory, if part of name; capitalized standing alone if referring to Federal unit: Forest Products; the Laboratory; *but* laboratory (non-Federal)
Lake: Erie, of the Woods, Great Salt; the lake
Lane, if part of name: Maiden; the lane
Latino, Latina
Latter-day Saints
law, copyright law; Ohm's, etc.
League, Urban; the league
Legion:
  American; the Legion; a Legionnaire
  French Foreign; the legion
Legislative Assembly, if part of name: of New York; of Puerto Rico, etc.; the legislative assembly; the assembly
legislative branch, clerk, session, etc.
Legislature:
  National Legislature (U.S. Congress); the Legislature
  Ohio Legislature; Legislature of Ohio; the State legislature; the legislature
Letters Patent No. 378,964; *but* patent No. 378,964; letters patent
Liberal Party; a Liberal
Libertarian Party; a Libertarian
Liberty Bell
Librarian of Congress; the Librarian
Library:
  Army; the library
  Harry S. Truman; the library
  of Congress; the Library
  Hillsborough Public; the library
Lieutenant Governor of Idaho, etc.; the Lieutenant Governor
Light, if part of name; the light:
  Boston
  Buffalo South Pier Light 2; *but* light No. 2; light 2
  but Massachusetts Bay lights
Lighthouse (*see* Light Station)
Lightship, if part of name; the lightship:
  Grays Reef
  North Manitou Shoal
Light Station, if part of name; the light station; the station:
  Minots Ledge
  Watch Hill
Line(s), if part of name; the line(s):
  Greyhound (bus)
  Holland America (cruises)
  Maginot (fortification)
line:
  Mason-Dixon line *or* Mason and Dixon's line
  State
listserv
Local:
  Columbia Typographical Union, Local 101
  International Brotherhood of Electrical Workers Local 180; *but* local No. 180
local time, local standard time (*see* time)
locator service
Loop, the (*see* cities)
Louisiana Purchase
Low Church
Lower, if part of name:
  California (Mexico)
  Colorado River Basin
  Egypt
  Peninsula (of Michigan)
lower:
  48 (States)
  House of Congress
  Mississippi

M

Madam:
  Chair
  Chairman
  Chairwoman
Magna Carta
Majesty, His, Her, Your; Their Majesties

Majority Leader McConnell; Majority Leader McCarthy; *but* the majority leader (U.S. Congress)
Mall, The National; The Mall (District of Columbia)
Mansion, Executive (*see* Executive)
map 3, A, II, etc.; *but* Map 2, when part of title: Map 2.—Railroads of Middle Atlantic States
mariculture
Marine Corps; the corps:
  Marines (the corps); *but* marines (individuals)
  Reserve; the Reserve
  also a marine; a woman marine; the women marines (individuals); soldiers, sailors, coastguardsmen, and marines
Maritime Provinces (Canada) (*see* Province)
Marshal (*see* Supreme Court)
marshal (U.S.)
medals (*see* decorations)
Medicaid
MediCal
Medicare Act; Medicare plan
Medicare Plus
Medicare Program
Medigap
Member, if referring to Senator, Representative, Delegate, or Resident Commissioner of U.S. Congress; *also* Member at Large; Member of Parliament, etc.; *but* membership; member of U.S. congressional committee
Memorial:
  Jefferson
  Lincoln
  Vietnam
  WWII
  Korean
  Franklin D. Roosevelt etc.; the memorial
Merchant Marine Reserve; the Reserve; *but* U.S. merchant marine; the merchant marine
Metroliner
Metropolitan Washington, etc.; *but* Washington metropolitan area
midcontinent region
Middle Ages (*see* Ages)
Middle Atlantic States
Middle East; Mideast; Mideastern; Middle Eastern (Asia)
Midwest (section of United States); Midwestern States; *but* midwestern farmers, etc.
Military Academy (*see* Academy)
Military Establishment (*see* Establishment)
milkshed, Ohio, etc. (region)
millennials
millennium
Minister Plenipotentiary; the Minister; Minister Without Portfolio (*see also* foreign cabinets)
Ministry (*see* foreign cabinets)
Minority Leader Reid; Minority Leader Pelosi; *but* the minority leader (U.S. Congress)
Mint, Philadelphia, etc.; the mint
minutemen (colonial)
missiles: capitalize such missile names as Hellfire, Sparrow, Tomahawk, Scud, Trident, etc.; *but* cruise missile, air-to-air missile, surface-to-air missile, etc.
Mission, if part of name; the mission:
  Gospel
  but diplomatic mission; military mission; Jones mission
Monument:
  Bunker Hill; the monument
  Grounds; the grounds (Washington Monument)
  National (*see* National)
  Washington; the monument (District of Columbia)

Mountain States
mountain time, mountain standard time (*see* time)
Moving Pictures Experts Group (MPEG)
Mr. Chairman; Mr. Secretary; etc.
Mujahedeen
mullah
Museum, capitalize with name; the museum:
  Field
  National
  National Air and Space; the Air Museum
  National Museum of African American History and Culture
National Museum of the American Indian

N

Nation (synonym for United States); *but* a nation; nationwide; *also* French nation, Balkan nations
nation, in general, standing alone
National, in conjunction with capitalized name:
  Academy of Sciences (*see* Academy)
  Archives and Records Administration; the National Archives; the Archives
  Capital (Washington); the Capital; *but* national capital area
  Endowment for the Arts; the Endowment
  Gallery of Art; the National Gallery; the gallery
  Grange; the Grange
  Guard, Ohio, etc.; Air National; the National Guard; the Guard; a guardsman; Reserve; *but* a National Guard man; National Guardsman
  Legislature (*see* Legislature)
  Muir Woods National Monument, etc.; the national monument; the monument
  Museum (*see* Museum)
  Park Service
  Park, Yellowstone, etc.; Yellowstone Park; the national park; the park
  Treasury; the Treasury
  War College
  Woman's Party
  Zoological Park (*see* Zoological)
national:
  agency check (NAC)
  anthem, customs, spirit, etc.
  British, Mexican, etc.
  defense agencies
  stockpile
  water policy
Native: Alaska; American; *but* Ohio native, etc.
Naval, if part of name:
  Academy (*see* Academy)
  Air Station (NAS) Patuxent River; Pensacola; etc.
  Base Guam; the naval base
  Observatory (*see* Observatory)
  Reserve; the Reserve; a reservist
  Reserve Force; the force
  Reserve officer; a Reserve officer
  Shipyard (if preceding or following name): Brooklyn Naval Shipyard; Naval Shipyard, Brooklyn; *but* the naval shipyard
  Volunteer Naval Reserve
  War College; the War College; the college
naval, in general sense:
  command (*see* Command)
  expenditures, maneuvers, officer, service, stores, etc.
  petroleum reserves; *but* Naval Petroleum Reserve No. 2 (Buena Vista Hills Naval Reserve); reserve No. 2
navel orange
Navy, American or foreign, if part of name; capitalized standing alone only if referring to U.S. Navy:
  Admiral of the; the admiral

Battle Force; the Battle Force; the force
Establishment; the establishment
Hospital Corps; hospital corpsman; the corps
Regular
Seabees (construction battalion); a Seabee
navy yard
Nazi; Nazism
Near East (Balkans, etc.)
network
New Deal; anti-New Deal
New England States
New Federalism
New Frontier
New World; *but* new world order
North:
Atlantic
Atlantic States
Atlantic Treaty (*see* Treaty)
Atlantic Treaty Organization (NATO) (*see* Organization)
Equatorial Current (*see* Current)
Korea
Pole
Slope (Alaska)
Star (Polaris)
the North (section of United States)
north:
Africa
Ohio, Virginia, etc.
north-central region, etc.
Northeast corridor
northern Ohio
Northern States
northerner
Northwest Pacific
Northwest Territory (1799)
Northwest, the (section of the United States)
Northwest Washington (*see* cities)
Northwestern:
States
United States
numbers capitalized if spelled out as part of a name:
Air Force One (Presidential plane)
Charles the First
Committee of One Hundred
Twenty-third Census (*see* Census)

O

Observatory, capitalized with name:
Astrophysical; the Observatory
Lick; the observatory (nongovernmental)
Naval; the Observatory
Occident, the; occidental
Ocean, if part of name; the ocean:
Antarctic
Arctic
Atlantic
North Atlantic, etc.
Pacific
Southern
South Pacific, etc.
Southwest Pacific, etc.
Oceanographer (the Hydrographer), Navy
Office, if referring to unit of Federal Government; the Office:
Executive
Foreign and Commonwealth (U.K.)
Government Printing; the Printing Office (historical)
Government Publishing; the Publishing Office; the Office
Naval Oceanographic
of Chief of Naval Operations
of General Counsel
of Management and Budget
of Personnel Management
of the Secretary (Defense); Secretary's Office
Patent and Trademark
but New York regional office (including branch, division, or section therein); the regional office; the office

officer:
  Army
  Marine; *but* naval and marine officers
  Navy; Navy and Marine officers
  Regular Army; Regular; a Regular
  Reserve
Old Dominion (Virginia)
Old South
Old World
Olympic Games; Olympiad; XXXI Olympic Games
ombudsman, Maryland (State)
online
Operation Iraqi Freedom, Desert Storm
Order of Business No. 56 (congressional calendar)
Ordnance:
  Corps (*see* Corps)
  Department; the Department
Organization, if part of name; capitalized standing alone if referring to international unit:
  International Labour (ILO)
  North Atlantic Treaty (NATO):
    Chiefs of Staff
    Committee of Defense Ministers
    Council
    Council of Foreign Ministers
    Defense Committee
    Military Committee
    Pact
    Regional Planning Group; the Group
    Standing Group; the Group
  of American States (OAS)
  United Nations Educational, Scientific, and Cultural (UNESCO)
  but nongovernmental organization (NGO)
Orient, the; oriental (objects)
Osama bin Laden
Outer Continental Shelf (*see* Continental)

P

Pacific (*see also* Atlantic):
  Basin
  coast
  Coast States
  Northwest
  rim
  seaboard
  slope
  South
  States
  time, Pacific standard time (*see* time)
  but cispacific; transpacific
pan-American games; *but* Pan American Day
Pan American Union (renamed; *see* Organization of American States)
Panel, the Federal Service Impasses (Federal), etc.; the Panel
Panhandle of Texas; Texas Panhandle; the panhandle; etc.
papers, Woodrow Wilson, etc.; the papers; *but* white paper
Parish, Caddo, etc.; *but* parish of Caddo (Louisiana civil division); the parish
Park, Fairmount, etc.; the park (*see also* National)
Park Police, U.S.; park policeman
Park Service
Park, Zoological (*see* Zoological)
Parkway, George Washington Memorial; the memorial parkway; the parkway
Parliament, Houses of; the Parliament
Parliamentarian (U.S. Senate or House)
part 2, A, II, etc.; *but* Part 2, when part of title: Part 2: Iron and Steel Industry
Party, if part of name; the party
Pass, Brenner, capitalized if part of name; the pass
patent (*see* Letters Patent)
Peninsula Upper (Lower) (Michigan); the peninsula
Penitentiary, United States; the penitentiary
petrodollar
phase 2; phase I

Philippines, Republic of the
Pilgrim Fathers (1620); the Pilgrims; a Pilgrim
Place, if part of name: Jefferson Place; the place
Plains (Great Plains), the
plan:
  controlled materials
  5-year
  Marshall (European Recovery Program)
Planetarium, Fels, Hayden; the planetarium
plant, United States Steel, etc.
plate 2, A, II, etc.; *but* Plate 2, when part of title: Plate 2.—Rural Structures
Plaza, Union Station (Washington, DC); the plaza
Pledge of Allegiance; the pledge
Pole: North, South; the pole; subpolar
Pole Star (Polaris); polar star
Police, if part of name; the police:
  Capitol
  Park, U.S.
  White House
political action committee (PAC)
political parties and adherents (*see* specific political party)
Pool, Northwest Power, etc.; the pool
Pope; *but* papal, patriarch, pontiff, primate
Port, if part of name; Port of Norfolk; Norfolk Port; the port (*see* Authority)
Post Office, Chicago, etc.; the post office
P.O. Box (with number); *but* post office box (in general sense)
Postmaster General
PostScript; *but* a postscript
Powers, if part of name; the powers (*see also* alliances):
  Allied (World Wars I and II)
  Axis (World War II)
  Western
  but European powers
precinct; first, 10th precinct
Premier (*see* foreign cabinets)
Preserve, Sullys Hill, National Game
Presidency (office of the head of Government)
President:
  of the United States; the Executive; the Chief Magistrate; the Commander in Chief; the President-elect; ex-President; former President; *also* preceding name
  of any other country; the President of Federal or international unit
  but president of the Norfolk Southern Railway; president of the Federal Reserve Bank of New York
Presidential assistant, authority, order, proclamation, candidate, election, timber, year, etc.
Prime Minister (*see* foreign cabinets)
Prison, New Jersey State; the prison
Privy Council, Her Majesty's (*see* Council)
Prize, Nobel, Pulitzer, etc.; the prize
Proclamation, Emancipation; Presidential Proclamation No. 24; Proclamation No. 24; the proclamation; *but* Presidential proclamation
Program, if part of name:
  European Recovery
  Fulbright
  Mutual Defense Assistance
  but universal military training; government bailout
Progressive Party; a Progressive
Project:
  Gutenberg
  Manhattan
  Vote Smart
Proposition 13
Prosecutor; Special Prosecutor (Federal)
Province, Provincial, if referring to an administrative subdivision: Ontario Province; Province of Ontario; Maritime Provinces (Canada); the Province

Proving Ground, Aberdeen, etc.; the proving ground
Public Law; Public Law 110–161, etc.
Public Printer; the Government Printer; the Printer (historical)
public utility district (*see* District)
Pueblo, Santa Clara; the pueblo (place); the Pueblo (Tribe)
Purchase, Gadsden, Louisiana, etc.
Puritan; puritanical
Pyrrhic victory

Q

Quad Cities (Davenport, Rock Island, Moline, East Moline, and Bettendorf)
query
queue

R

Radio Free Europe/Radio Liberty
Railroad, Alaska; the railroad
Ranch, King, etc.; the ranch
Range, Cascade, etc. (mountains); the range
Rebellion, if part of name; the rebellion:
- Boxer
- Whisky

Reconstruction period (post-Civil War)
Red army
Red Cross, American, American National
Reds, the; a Red (political)
Reformatory, Michigan; the reformatory
Refuge, Blackwater National Wildlife, etc.; Blackwater Refuge; the refuge
region, north-central, etc.; first region, 10th region; region 7; midcontinent
Regular Army, Navy; a Regular (*see also* officer)
regulation:
- greenhouse gas
- W (*see also* Federal Reserve Board)
- *but* Veterans Entitlements Regulations

religious terms:
- Baha'i
- Baptist
- Brahman
- Buddhist
- Catholic; Catholicism; *but* catholic (universal)
- Christian
- Christian Science
- Evangelical United Brethren
- Hindu; Hinduism
- Islam; Islamic
- Jewish
- Latter-day Saints
- Muslim: Shiite; Sunni
- New Thought
- Protestant; Protestantism
- Scientology
- Seventh-day Adventists
- Seventh Day Baptists
- Sikh
- Zoroastrian

Renaissance, the (era)
Report, if part of name (with date or number); the annual report; the report:
- 2015 Report of the Chief of the Forest Service
- 9/11 Commission Report
- Annual Report of the Secretary of Defense for the year ended September 30, 2015
- President's Economic Report; the Economic Report
- Railroad Retirement Board Annual Report, 2015; *but* annual report of the Railroad Retirement Board
- Report No. 31
- United States Reports (publication)

Reporter, the (U.S. Supreme Court)
Representative; Representative at Large (U.S. Congress); U.N.
Republic, capitalized if part of name; capitalized standing alone if referring to a specific government:
- Czech

French
Irish
of Bosnia and Herzegovina
of Panama
of the Philippines
Slovak
also the American Republics; South American Republics; the Latin American Republics; the Republics
Republican Party; a Republican
Reservation (forest, military, or Indian), if part of name; the reservation:
Hill Military
Standing Rock
Reserve, if part of name; the Reserve (*see also* Air Force; Army Corps; Coast Guard; Foreign Service; Marine Corps; Merchant Marine; Naval; National Guard):
Active
Air Force
Army
bank (*see* Bank)
Board, Federal (*see* Federal)
city (*see* Bank)
components
Enlisted
Establishment
Inactive
Naval
officer
Officers' Training Corps
Ready
Retired
Standby
Strategic
Reserves, the; reservist
Resolution, with number; the resolution:
House Joint Resolution 3
Senate Concurrent Resolution 18
War Powers Resolution (short title)
but Tonkin resolution
Revised Statutes (U.S.); Supplement to the Revised Statutes; the statutes; Statutes at Large (U.S.)
Revolution, Revolutionary (if referring to the American, French, or English Revolution) (*see also* War)
rim; the Pacific rim
Road, if part of name: Benning; the road
Roman numerals, common nouns used with, not capitalized:
book II; chapter II; part II; etc.
but Book II: Modern Types (complete heading); Part XI: Early Thought (complete heading)
Route 66, State Route 9 (highways)
rule 21; rule XXI; *but* Rule 21, when part of title: Rule 21: Renewal of Motion
Rules:
of the House of Representatives; *but* rules of the House; House rule X
Standing Rules of the Senate (publication); *but* rules of the Senate
also Commission rules

S

Sabbath; Sabbath Day
savings bond (*see* bond)
schedule 2, A, II, etc.; *but* Schedule 2, when part of title; Schedule 2: Open and Prepay Stations
School, if part of name; the school:
any school of U.S. Armed Forces
Hayes
Pawnee Indian
Public School 13; P.S. 13
school district (*see* District)
Scriptures; Holy Scriptures (the Bible)
Seabees (*see* Navy)
seaboard, Atlantic, eastern, etc.
seasons:
autumn (fall)
spring
summer
winter

seaway (*see* geographic terms; Corporation)
Second World War (*see* War)
Secretariat (*see* United Nations)
Secretaries of the Army and the Navy; *but* Secretaries of the military departments; secretaryship
Secretary, head of national governmental unit:
  of Defense; of State; etc.; the Secretary
  of State for Foreign Affairs (British); for the Commonwealth, etc.; the Secretary
  of the Smithsonian Institution; the Secretary
  also the Assistant Secretary; the Executive Secretary
Secretary General; the Secretary General:
  Organization of American States
  United Nations
section 2, A, II, etc.; *but* Section 2, when part of title: Section 2: Test Construction Theory
Selective Service (*see* Service; System)
Senate (U.S.), titles of officers standing alone capitalized:
  Chaplain
  Chief Clerk
  Doorkeeper
  Official Reporter(s)
  Parliamentarian
  Postmaster
  President of the
  President pro tempore
  Presiding Officer
  Secretary
  Sergeant at Arms
Senate, Ohio (State); the senate
Senator (U.S. Congress); *but* lowercased if referring to a State senator, unless preceding a name
senatorial
Sergeant at Arms (U.S. Senate or House)
Sermon on the Mount
server
Service, if referring to Federal unit; the Service:
  Extension
  Federal Mediation and Conciliation
  Fish and Wildlife
  Foreign (*see* Foreign Service)
  Forest
  Internal Revenue
  Marshals
  National Park
  Natural Resources Conservation
  Postal
  Secret (Homeland Security)
  Selective (*see also* System); *but* selective service, in general sense; selective service classification 1–A, 4–F, etc.
  Senior Executive
service:
  airmail
  Army
  city delivery
  consular
  customs
  diplomatic
  employment (State)
  extension (State)
  general delivery
  naval
  Navy
  parcel post
  postal field
  rural free delivery; rural delivery; free delivery
  special delivery
  star route
Shelf, Continental (*see* Continental)
ship of state (unless personified)
Sister(s) (adherent of religious order)
Six Nations (*see* Indians)
Smithsonian Institution (*see* Institution)

Social Security Administration (U.S.), application, check, number, pension, trust fund, system, etc.
Socialist Party; a Socialist
Society, if part of name; the society:
  American Cancer Society, Inc.
  of the Cincinnati
soil bank
soil orders (see rule 3.30)
Soldiers' Home; the soldiers' home; (*see* Armed Forces Retirement Home)
Solicitor for the Department of Labor, etc.; the Solicitor
Solicitor General (Department of Justice)
Son of Man (Christ)
Sons of the American Revolution (organization); a Son; a Real Son
South:
  American Republics (*see* Republic)
  American States
  Atlantic
  Atlantic States
  Deep South (U.S.)
  Korea
  Midsouth (U.S.)
  Pacific
  Pole
  the South (section of United States); Southland
Southeast Asia
southern California, southeastern California, etc.
Southern States
Southern United States
southerner
Southwest, the (section of United States)
space shuttle; the shuttle
space station
spam (email)
Spanish-American War (*see* War)
Speaker of the House of Representatives; the Speaker
special agent
specialist
Special Order No. 12; Special Orders, No. 12; a special order
Spirit of '76 (painting); *but* spirit of '76 (in general sense)
Sputnik
Square, Lafayette, etc.; the square
Staff, Foreign Service (*see* Foreign Service); Air (U.K.)
standard time (*see* time)
Star of Bethlehem
Star-Spangled Banner (*see* flag)
State:
  Champion
  government
  legislature (*see* Legislature)
  line, Iowa; Ohio-Indiana, etc.
  New York
  of Israel
  of Maryland
  of the Union Message/Address
  of Veracruz
  out-of-State (adjective); *but* out-of-stater
  prison
  Vatican City
state:
  church and
  of the art: state-of-the-art technology
  welfare
  also downstate, instate, multistate, statehood, statehouse, stateside, statewide, substate, tristate, upstate
State's attorney
state's evidence
states' rights (international)
States:
  Arab
  Balkan
  Baltic
  East North Central
  East South Central

Eastern; *but* eastern industrial States
Eastern Gulf
Eastern North Central, etc.
Far Western
Gulf; Gulf Coast
Lake
Latin American
lower 48
Middle
Middle Atlantic
Middle Western
Midwestern
Mountain
New England
North Atlantic
Northwestern, etc.
Organization of American
Pacific
Pacific Coast
rights (U.S.)
South American
South Atlantic
Southern
the six States of Australia; a foreign state
Thirteen Original; original 13 States
Western; *but* western Gulf; western farming States

Station, if part of name; the station; not capitalized if referring to surveying or similar work:
Grand Central
Naval Air Engineering
television station WSYR–TV
Union; Union Depot; the depot
WAMU station; station WMAL; radio station WSM; broadcasting station WJSV

station 9; substation A
Statue of Liberty; the statue
Statutes at Large (U.S.) (*see also* Revised Statutes)
Stealth: bomber, fighter
Stockpile, Strategic National
stone age (*see* Ages)
storage facility
Stream, Gulf (*see* Gulf; geographic terms)
Street, if part of name; the street:
I Street (not Eye Street)
110th Street
U Street (not You Street)

subcommittee (*see* Committee)
subtropical, subtropic(s) (*see* tropical)
summit meeting; Earth summit
Sun; a sun
Super Bowl
Superfund; the fund
Superintendent, if referring to head of Federal unit; the Superintendent:
of Documents (Government Publishing Office)
of the Naval (or Military) Academy

Supplement to the Revised Statutes (*see* Revised Statutes)
Supreme Bench; the Bench; *also* High Bench; High Tribunal
Supreme Court (U.S.); the Court; *also* High Court; titles of officers standing alone capitalized:
Associate Justice
Chief Justice
Clerk
Marshal
Reporter
but Ohio Supreme Court; the supreme court

Surgeon General, the (Air Force, Army, Navy, and Public Health Service)
Survey, if part of name of Federal unit; the Survey: Geodetic; Geological
System, if referring to Federal unit; the System:
Federal Home Loan Bank; the System
Federal Reserve; the System
National Forest; the System
National Highway; Interstate Highway; the System

National Park; the System
National Trails; the System
National Wild and Scenic Rivers; the System
Regional Metro System; Metro system
Selective Service (*see also* Service)
State and National forests
but Amtrak railway system; Amtrak system; the system
also Federal land bank system

T

table 2, II, A, etc.; *but* Table 2, when part of title: Table 2: Degrees of Land Deterioration
task force (*see* Force)
Team, USAREUR Technical Assistance, etc.; the team
television station (*see* Station)
Telnet
Ten Commandments
Territorial, if referring to a political subdivision
Territory:
Northwest (1799); the territory
Trust Territory of the Pacific Islands; Pacific Islands Trust Territory; the trust territory; the territory
Yukon, Northwest Territories; the Territory(ies), Territorial (Canada)
but territory of: American Samoa, Guam, Virgin Islands
The, part of name, capitalized:
The Dalles; The Gambia; The Hague; The Weirs; *but* the Dalles Dam; the Dalles region; the Hague Conference; the Weirs streets
but the Adjutant General; the National Archives; the Archives; the Times; the Mermaid
Third World
Thirteen American Colonies, etc. (*see* Colonies)
Thirteen Original States
Thruway, New York State; the thruway
time:
Alaska, Alaska standard
Atlantic, Atlantic standard
central, central standard
eastern, eastern daylight, eastern daylight saving (no *s*), eastern standard
Greenwich mean time (GMT)
Hawaii-Aleutian standard
local, local standard
mountain, mountain standard
Pacific, Pacific standard
universal
title 2, II, A, etc.; *but* Title 2, when part of title: Title 2: General Provisions
Tomb:
Grant's; the tomb
of the Unknowns; of the Unknown Soldier; Unknown Soldier's Tomb; the tomb (*see also* Unknown Soldier)
Tower, Eiffel, etc.; the tower
Township, Union; township of Union
trade names and trademarks:

Blu-Ray	MasterCard
Coca-Cola	TiVo
Dr Pepper	U-Haul
Hersheypark	UNIX
iPhone	VISA
iPod	Yahoo!
iTunes	ZIP Code (Postal)

Trade Representative (U.S.)
transatlantic; transpacific; trans-Siberian, etc.; *but* Transjordan; Trans-Alaska
Treasurer, Assistant, of the United States; the Assistant Treasurer; *but* assistant treasurer at New York, etc.
Treasurer of the United States; the Treasurer
Treasury notes; Treasurys
Treasury, of the United States; General; National; Public
Treaty, if part of name; the treaty:
Jay
North Atlantic; North Atlantic Defense

of Versailles
but treaty of 1919
triad
Tribe; Tribal (federally recognized) (*see* Indians)
Tribunal, standing alone capitalized only in minutes and official reports of a specific arbitration; *also* High Tribunal; the Tribunal (Supreme Court)
Tropic of Cancer, of Capricorn; the Tropics
tropical; neotropic, neotropical, sub-tropic(s), subtropical
Trust, Power, etc.
trust territory (*see* Territory)
Tunnel, Lincoln, etc.; the tunnel; *but* irrigation, railroad, etc., tunnel
Turnpike, Pennsylvania, etc.; the turnpike
Twin Cities (Minneapolis and St. Paul)

U

U-boat
Under Secretary, if referring to officer of Federal Government; the Under Secretary:
of Agriculture
of State
of the Treasury
Uniform Code of Military Justice (*see* Code)
Union (if part of proper name; capitalized standing alone if synonym for United States or if referring to international unit):
Columbia Typographical
European
Pan American (former name; *see* Organization of American States)
Station; *but* union passenger station; union freight station
Teamsters; the Teamsters; the union; *also* the Auto Workers, etc.
Universal Postal; the Postal Union
Woman's Christian Temperance
but a painters union; printers union
United Nations:
Charter; the charter
Educational, Scientific, and Cultural Organization (UNESCO) (*see* Organization)
Food and Agriculture Organization (FAO)
General Assembly; the Assembly
International Children's Emergency Fund (UNICEF)
International Court of Justice; the Court
Permanent Court of Arbitration (*see* Court)
Secretariat, the
Secretary General
Security Council; the Council
World Employment Conference
World Health Organization (WHO); the Organization
universal:
military training (*see* Program)
time (*see* time)
University, if part of name: Stanford; the university
Unknown Soldier; Unknown of World War II; World War II Unknown; Unknown of Korea; Korea Unknown; the Unknowns (*see also* Tomb)
Upper, if part of name:
Colorado River Basin
Egypt
Peninsula (of Michigan)
but upper House of Congress
U.S.S.R. (former Union of Soviet Socialist Republics)

V

Valley, Shenandoah, etc.; the valley; *but* the valleys of Virginia and Maryland
V–E Day; V–J Day; V-chip
veteran, World War II; Vietnam

Veterans Affairs, Department of (*see* Department)
Vice Chairman, etc. (same as Chairman)
vice consul, British, etc.
Vice President (same as President)
Voice of America; the Voice
volume 2, A, II, etc.; *but* Volume 2, when part of title; Volume 2: Five Rivers in America's Future

W

War, if part of formal name:
- Between the States
- Civil
- First World War; World War I; World War; Great War; Second World War; World War II
- for Independence (1776)
- French and Indian (1754–63)
- Mexican
- of 1812
- of the Rebellion; the rebellion
- on Crime
- on Drugs
- on Poverty
- on Terrorism, Global
- Revolutionary; of the Revolution; the Revolution
- Seven Years'
- Six-Day (Arab-Israeli)
- Spanish-American
- the two World Wars
- *also* post-World War II

war, descriptive or undeclared:
- cold, hot
- European
- French and Indian wars
- Indian
- Korean
- Persian Gulf; Gulf
- third world; world war III
- Vietnam
- with Mexico

War College, National (*see* College)
War Mothers (*see* American)
ward 1, 2, etc.; first, 11th, etc.
Washington's Farewell Address
water district (*see* District)
waterway, inland, intercoastal, etc.; *but* Intracoastal Waterway
web (lowercase within a sentence):
- #address
- #page
- site

Web (upper case "W" to start a sentence)
Week, Fire Prevention; etc.
Weirs, The; *but* the Weirs streets
welfare state
West:
- Bank (Jordan)
- Coast (Africa); *but* west coast (U.S.)
- End, etc. (section of city)
- Europe (political entity)
- Far West; Far Western States
- Florida (1763–1819)
- Middle (United States); Midwest
- South Central States, etc.
- the West (section of United States; *also* world political entity)

west, western Pennsylvania
Western:
- bloc
- civilization
- countries
- Europe(an) (political entity)
- Hemisphere; the hemisphere
- ideas
- Powers
- States
- United States
- World
- *but* far western; western farming States (U.S.)

westerner
Whip, Majority; Minority
Whisky Rebellion (*see* Rebellion)

White (*see* Caucasian)
White House:
  Blue Room
  East Room
  Oval Office
  Police (*see* Police)
  Red Room
  Rose Garden
  State Dining Room
white paper, British, etc.
Wi-Fi
Wilderness, capitalized with name; San Joaquin Wilderness, CA; the wilderness; *but* the Wilderness (Virginia battlefield)
Wood, if part of name:
  Belleau
  County
  Fort Leonard
World: New, Old, Third; *but* free world
World Bank; the Bank
World Series
World War (*see* War)
World War II veteran
world wide web, the web

X

x ray (note: no hyphen)

Y

year, calendar, fiscal
Your Excellency; Your Honor; Your Majesty; etc.
Youth Corps; the Corps

Z

Zika virus
ZIP Code number; ZIP+4
Zone, if part of name; the zone:
  British (in Germany)
  Canal (Panama)
  Eastern, Western (Germany)
  Frigid
  Hot (infectious area)
  of Interior (*see* Command)
  Temperate, Torrid; the zone
  U.S. Foreign Trade; Foreign Trade Zone; *but* the foreign trade zone, free trade zone
zone:
  Arctic
  eastern standard time
  no-fly
  polar
  tropical
Zoological Park (National); the zoo; the park

5. Spelling

(See also Chapter 7 "Compounding Examples" and Chapter 9 "Abbreviations and Letter Symbols")

5.1. GPO uses Webster's Third New International Dictionary as its guide for the spelling of words not appearing in the GPO STYLE MANUAL. Colloquial and dialect spellings are not used unless required by the subject matter or specially requested. The tendency of some producers of computer-assisted publications to rely on the limited capability of some spell-checking programs adds importance to this list.

Preferred and difficult spellings

5.2. In addition to indicating the preferred forms of words with variant spellings, the list also contains other words frequently misspelled or causing uncertainty.

A

abattoir
aberration
abetter
  abettor (law)
abridgment
absorb (take in)
  adsorb (adhesion)
abysmal
a cappella
accede (yield)
  exceed (surpass)
accepter
  acceptor (law)
accessory
accommodate
accordion
accouter
accursed
acetic (acid)
  ascetic (austere)
acknowledgment
acoustic
adapter
adjurer
adjuster
ad nauseam
adviser
  advisor (law)
adz
aegis
aesthetic
affect (influence, v.)
  effect (result, finish, n., v.)
afterward(s)
  afterword
aging
aid (n., v.)
aide
aide-de-camp
albumen (egg)
  albumin (chemistry)
align
allottee
all ready (prepared)
  already (previous)
all right
altogether (completely)
  all together (collectively)
aluminum
ambidextrous
amoeba
ampoule
analog
analogous
anemia
anesthetic
aneurysm
anomalous
anonymous
antediluvian
antibiotics (n.)
  antibiotic (adj.)
anyway (adv.)
anywise (adv.)
appall, -ed, -ing
appareled, -ing
aquatic
aqueduct
archaeology
arrester
artifact
artisan
ascendance, -ant
ascent (rise)
  assent (consent)
assassinate
athenaeum
attester
autogiro
awhile (for some time)
  a while (a short time)
ax
aye

B

backward
baloney (nonsense)
  bologna (sausage)
bandanna
bargainer
  bargainor (law)
baritone
bark (boat)
barreled, -ing
bastille
bathyscaph
battalion
bazaar (event)
  bizarre (strange or absurd)
behoove
beneficent

benefited, -ing
bettor (wagerer)
beveled, -ing
biased, -ing
blessed
bloc (group)
  block (grants)
blond(e)
bluing
born (birth)
  borne (carried)
bouillon (soup)
  bullion (metal)
boulder
bourgeoisie
breach (gap)
  breech (lower part)
brier
briquet, -ted, -ting
Britannia
broadax
bronco
brunet(te)
buccaneer
buncombe
bunion
bur
burned
bus, bused, buses, busing
butadiene

C

caffeine
calcareous
calcimine
caldron
calendar
calender (paper finish)
caliber
caliper
calk (spike)
  caulk (seal)
calligraphy
callus (n.)
  callous (adj.)
calorie
canceled, -ing
cancellation
candor
canister
cannot
canoeing
cantaloupe
canvas (cloth)
  canvass (solicit)
capital (city, money)
  capitol (building)
carabao (sing., pl.)
carat (gem weight)
  caret (omission mark)
  karat (gold weight)
carbureted, -ing
carburetor
Caribbean
caroled, -ing
carotene
carrot
cartilage
caster (roller)
  castor (oil)
casual (informal)
  causal (cause)
catalog, -ed, -ing
cataloger
catsup
caviar
caviled, -er, -ing
center
centipede
centrifugal
cesarean
chairmaned
chaise longue; lounge
chancellor
channeled, -ing
chaperon(e)
chautauqua
chauvinism
chiffonier
chile con carne
chili (pepper)
chiseled, -ing
chlorophyll
cigarette
citable
cite (quote)
  site (place)
clamor
climactic (climax)
  climatic (climate)
cocaine
coconut
cocoon
coleslaw
colloquy
colossal
combated, -ing
commenter
  commentor (law)
commingle
commiserate
complement (complete)
  compliment (praise)
confectionery
confidant(e)
  confident (sure)
confirmer
  confirmor (law)
conjurer
connecter
  connector (road)
connoisseur
consecrator
consensus
consignor
consulter
consummate
contradicter
control, -lable, -ling
converter
conveyor
cookie
cornetist
corollary
corvette
councilor (of council)
  counselor (adviser)
counseled, -ing
cozy
crawfish
creneled, -ing
crystaled, -ing
crystalline
crystallize
cudgeled, -ing
cyclopedia
czar

D

darndest
debarkation
decaffeinated
decalogue
defense
deliverer
  deliveror (law)
demagogue
demarcation
de minimis
dependent
descendant (n., adj.)
desecrater
desiccate
desuetude (suspended)
  destitute (bereft)
detractor
develop, -ment

device (contrivance)
 devise (convey)
dextrous (syllable division)
diaeresis
diaeretic
 diuretic (water pill)
diagramed, -ing
diagrammatic
dialed, -ing
dialogue
dialysis
diaphragm
diarrhea
dickey
dietitian
diffuser
dike
dilettante
dinghy (boat)
diphtheria
discreet (prudent)
 discrete (distinct)
disheveled, -ing
disc (computer)
dispatch
dissension
distention
distill, -ed, -ing, -ment
distributor
diverter
divorcee (masc., fem.)
doctoral
doctrinaire
doggerel
dossier
doweled, -ing
downward
dreadnought
dreamed
drought
dueled, -ing
duffelbag
dullness
dumbfound
dwelt
dyeing (coloring)
 dying (death)

E

eastward
ecstasy
edema
edgewise
electronics (n.)
 electronic (adj.)
eleemosynary
elicit (to draw)
 illicit (illegal)
embarrass
embed
embellish
emboweled, -ing
emboweler
emigrant (go from)
 immigrant (go into)
emigree
eminent (famous)
 imminent (soon)
emoji
employee
enameled, -ing
encage
encase
encave
enclasp
enclose
enclosure
encumber
encumbrance
encyclopedia
endorse, -ment
endwise
enfeeble
enforce, -ment
engraft
enroll, -ed, -ing, -ment
enshade
ensheathe
ensnare
ensure (guarantee)
 insure (protect)
entrench
entrepreneur
entrust
entwine
envelop (v.)
 envelope (n.)
enwrap
eon
epaulet, -ed, -ing
epiglottis
epilogue
equaled, -ing
erysipelas
escallop
escapable
esophagus
etiology
evacuee
evanescent
eviscerate
evocative
exhibitor
exhilarate
exonerate
exorbitant
expellant
exposé (n., exposure)
 expose (v., to lay open)
exsiccate
extant (in existence)
 extent (range)
extoll, -ed, -ing
eyeing
eyrie

F

fantasy
farther (distance)
 further (degree)
favor
fecal
feces
fetal
fetish
fetus
fiance(e)
fiber
fiche (microfiche)
filigree
finable
finagle
financier
fjord
flammable (*not* inflammable)
flection
fledgling
flextime
flier
flotage
flotation
fluorescent
focused, -ing
folderol
forbade
forbear (endurance)
 forebear (ancestor)
foresee
forgettable
forgo (relinquish)
 forego (precede)
format, formatted, formatting
forswear
fortissimo
forward (ahead)
 foreword (preface)
fricassee
fuchsia

fueler
fulfill, -ed, -ing, -ment
fulsome
fungus (n., adj.)
funneled, -ing
furor
fuse (all meanings)
fuselage
fusillade

G

gaiety
gaily
galosh
gamboled, -ing
garrote
gauge
gazetteer
gelatin
genealogy
generalissimo
germane
glamorous
glamour
glycerin
gobbledygook
goodbye
govinfo (always bold)
graveled, -ing
gray
grievous
groveled, -ing
gruesome
guarantee (n., v.)
  guaranty (n., law)
guerrilla (warfare)
  gorilla (ape)
guesstimate
guttural
gypsy

H

hallelujah
hara-kiri
harass
harebrained
healthful (for health)
healthy (with health)
heinous
hemoglobin
hemorrhage
hiccup
highfalutin
hijack
homeopath
homogeneity
homogeneous (mixed uniformly)
homogenous (of similar origin)
homologue
hors d'oeuvre
hypocrisy
hypotenuse

I

idiosyncrasy
idle (inactive)
  idol (statue)
idyll
imminent (soon)
  eminent (famous)
impaneled, -ing
impasse
imperiled, -ing
impostor
impresario
imprimatur
inculcate
indict (to accuse)
  indite (to compose)
inequity (unfairness)
  iniquity (sin)
inferable
infold
ingenious (skillful)
  ingenuous (simple)
innocuous
innuendo
inoculate
inquire, inquiry
install, -ed, -ing, -ment
installation
instill, -ed, -ing
insure (protect)
  ensure (guarantee)
intelligentsia
interceptor
interment (burial)
  internment (jail)
intern
intervener
  intervenor (law)
intransigent (n., adj.)
in vitro
in vivo
iridescent
italic

J

jalopy
jalousie
jerry-(built)
  jury-(rigged)
jeweled, -ing, -er
jewelry
judgeship
judgment
jujitsu
juxtaposition

K

karat
kerneled, -ing
kerosene
ketchup
kidnapped, -ing
kidnapper
kilogram
knapsack
kopek
kumquat

L

labeled, -ing
lacquer
landward
lath (wood)
  lathe (machine)
laureled
leukemia
leveled, -ing
leveler
liable (responsible)
  libel (legal)
liaison
libelant
libeled, -ing
libelee
libeler
license
licenser (issuer)
  licensor (grantor)
licorice
likable
lilliputian
linage (lines)
  lineage (descent)
liquefy
liquor
  liqueur
liter
livable
loath (reluctant)
  loathe (detest)
lodestar
lodestone
lodgment
logistics (n.)
  logistic (adj.)

louver
luster
lyonnaise

M

madam
Mafia
maim
maize (corn)
  maze (labyrinth)
maneuver
manifold
manikin (dwarf)
mannequin (model)
mantel (shelf)
  mantle (cloak)
marbleize
marijuana
marshaled, -ing
marshaler
marveled, -ing
marvelous
material (goods)
  materiel (military)
meager
medaled, -ing
medalist
medieval
meme
metaled, -ing
metalize
meteorology
  (weather)
  metrology
    (weights and
    measures)
meter
mil (1⁄1000 inch)
  mill (1⁄1000 dollar)
mileage
miliary
  (tuberculosis)
milieu
milk cow
millenary (1,000)
  millinery (hats)
millennium
minable
missilery
misspell
miter
mnemonic
moccasin
modeled, -ing
modeler
mold
mollusk
molt
moneys
monogramed, -ing
monologue
mortise
movable
mucilage
mucus (n.)
  mucous (adj.)
Muslim
mustache

N

naphtha
Navajo
Nazism
neophyte
niacin
nickel
niter
nonplused
northward
Novocain
  (trademark)
novocaine
  (anesthetic)

O

obbligato
obloquy
ocher
octet
offal
offense
omelet
ophthalmology
opossum
orangutan
orbited, -ing
ordinance (law)
  ordnance
    (military)
organdy
overseas or oversea

P

pajamas
palate (mouth)
  palette (colors)
  pallet (bed or
    freight)
paleontology
paneled, -ing
paraffin
paralleled, -ing
parallelepiped
parceled, -ing
partisan
pastime
patrol, -led, -ling
peccadillo
pedant (n.)
  pedantic (adj.)
peddler
penciled, -ing
pendant (n.)
  pendent (u.m.)
percent
peremptory
    (decisive)
  preemptory
    (preference)
perennial
periled, -ing
permittee
perquisite (privilege)
  prerequisite
    (requirement)
personal (individual)
  personnel (staff)
perspective (view)
  prospective
    (expected)
petaled, -ing
pharaoh
pharmacopeia
phoenix
phlegm
phony
phosphorus (n.)
  phosphorous (adj.)
photostated
pickax
picnicking
pipet
plaque
plastics (n.)
  plastic (adj.)
pledger
  pledgor (law)
plenitude
pliers
plow
poleax
pollination
pommeled, -ing
pontoon
porcelaneous
practice (n., v.)
precedence
  (priority)
  precedents (usage)
prerogative
pretense
preventive
principal (chief)
  principle
    (proposition)
privilege

proffer
programmatic
programmed, -mer,
 -ming
prologue
promissory
pronunciation
propel, -led, -ling
propellant (n.)
 propellent (adj.)
prophecy (n.)
 prophesy (v.)
ptomaine
pubic (anatomy)
pulmotor
pusillanimous

Q

quarreled, -ing
quartet
quaternary
questionnaire
queue

R

raccoon
racket (all meanings)
rapprochement
rarefy
rarity
ratable
rational (adj.)
 rationale (n.)
rattan
raveled, -ing
reconnaissance
reconnoiter
recyclable
referable
refuse
registrar
reinforce
relater
 relator (law)
remodeler
renaissance
reparable
repellant (n.)
 repellent (adj.)
requester
 requestor (law)
rescission
responder
 (electronics)
responser
 (electronics)
reveled, -er, -ing
rhyme, rhythmic
RIFing, RIFed, RIFs
rivaled, -ing
roweled, -ing
ruble

S

saccharin (n.)
 saccharine (adj.)
sacrilegious
salable
sandaled, -ing
savable
savanna
savior
 Saviour (Christ)
scalloped, -ing
schizophrenia
scion (horticulture)
scurrilous
seismology
selvage (edging)
 salvage (save)
sentineled, -ing
separate (v., adj.)
sepulcher
seriatim
settler
 settlor (law)
sewage (waste)
 sewerage (drain
 system)
sextet
Shakespearean
shellacking
shoveled, -ing
shriveled, -ing
sideward
signaled, -ing
siphon
site (place)
 cite (quote)
sizable
skeptic
skillful
skulduggery
sleight (deft)
 slight (meager)
smolder
sniveled, -ing
snorkel
soliloquy
sometime
 (formerly)
 some time (some
 time ago)
 some times (at
 times)
southward
spacious (space)
 specious
 (deceptive)
specter
spirituous (liquor)
spirochete
spoliation
stationary (fixed)
 stationery (paper)
statue (sculpture)
 stature (height)
 statute (law)
staunch
stenciled, -ing
stenciler
stifling
stratagem
stubbornness
stultify
stupefy
subpoena, -ed
subtlety
succor
sulfur (also
 derivatives)
 sulfanilamide
 sulfureted, -ing
supererogation
surfeit
surreptitious
surveillance
swiveled, -ing
sylvan
synonymous
syrup

T

taboo
tactician
tasseled, -ing
tattoo
taxied, -ing
technique
teetotaler
tercentenary
theater
therefor (for it)
 therefore (for that
 reason)
thiamine
thralldom
thrash (beat)
 thresh (grain)
threshold
tie, tied, tying
timber (wood)
 timbre (tone)
tinseled, -ing
titer
tonsillitis
tormenter

totaled, -ing
toward
toweled, -ing
toxemia
trafficking
trammeled, -ing
tranquilize(r)
tranquillity
transcendent
transferable
transferor
transferred
transonic
transponder
(electronics)
transshipment
traveled, -ing
traveler
travelogue
triptych
trolley
troop (soldiers)
troupe (actors)
troweled, -ing
tryptophan
tularemia
tunneled, -ing
tunneler
turquoise
typify
tyrannical
tyro

U

unctuous
unwieldy
upward
uremia
usable

V

vacillate
valance (drape)
valence
(chemistry)
veld
veranda
vermilion
vicissitude
victualed, -ing
victualer
vilify
villain
visa, -ed, -ing
vitamin
vitrify
volcanism
voluntarism
votable
vying

W

wainscoting
warranter
warrantor (law)
warranty
weeviled, -ing
welder
westward
whimsy
whiskey, -s
willful
withe
woeful
woolen
woolly
worshiped, -er, -ing

Anglicized and foreign words

5.3. Diacritical marks are not used with anglicized words.

A

abaca
aide memoire
a la carte
a la king
a la mode
angstrom
aperitif
applique
apropos
auto(s)-da-fe

B

blase
boutonniere
brassiere

C

cabana
cafe
cafeteria
caique
canape
cause celebre
chateau
cliche
cloisonne
comedienne
comme ci
comme ca
communique
confrere
consomme
cortege
coulee
coup de grace
coup d'etat
coupe
creme
crepe
crepe de chine
critique
critiquing

D

debacle
debris
debut
debutante
decollete
dejeuner
denouement
depot
dos-a-dos

E

eclair
eclat
ecru
elan
elite
entree
etude

F

facade
faience
faux pas
fete
fiance (masc., fem.)
frappe

G

garcon
glace
grille
gruyere

H

habitue

I

ingenue

J
jardiniere

L
laissez faire
litterateur

M
materiel
matinee
melange
melee
menage
mesalliance
metier
moire

N
naive
naivete
nee

O
opera bouffe
opera comique

P
papier mache
piece de resistance
pleiade
porte cochere
porte lumiere
portiere
pousse cafe
premiere
protege (masc., fem.)
puree

R
rale
recherche
regime
risque
role
rotisserie
roue

S
saute
seance
senor
smorgasbord
soiree
souffle
suede

T
table d'hote
tete-a-tete
tragedienne

V
vicuna
vis-a-vis

5.4. Foreign words carry the diacritical marks as an essential part of their spelling.

à l'américaine
attaché
béton
blessé
calèche
cañada
cañon
chargé
chargé d'affaires
congé
crédit foncier
crédit mobilier
curé
déjà vu
détente
doña
entrepôt
exposé
longéron
mañana
maté
mère
nacré
outré
passé (masc., fem.)
pâté
père
piña
précis
raisonné
résumé
touché

Plural forms

5.5. Nouns ending in *o* immediately preceded by a vowel add *s* to form the plural; nouns ending in *o* preceded by a consonant add *es* to form the plural, except as indicated in the following list.

albinos
armadillos
avocados
banjos
cantos
cascos
centos
didos
duodecimos
dynamos
escudos
falsettos
gauchos
ghettos
halos
indigos
infernos
juntos
kimonos
lassos
magnetos
mementos
merinos
mestizos
octavos
octodecimos
pianos
piccolos
pomelos
provisos
quartos
salvos
sextodecimos
sextos
siroccos
solos
tangelos
tobaccos
twos
tyros
virtuosos
zeros

5.6. When a noun is hyphenated with an adverb or preposition, the plural is formed on the noun.

comings-in	hangers-on	markers-up
fillers-in	listeners-in	passers-by
goings-on	lookers-on	swearers-in

5.7. When neither word is a noun, the plural is formed on the last word.

also-rans	go-betweens	run-ins
come-ons	higher-ups	tie-ins

5.8. In forming the plurals of compound terms, the significant word takes the plural form.

Significant word first:
- adjutants general
- aides-de-camp
- ambassadors at large
- attorneys at law
- attorneys general
- billets-doux
- bills of fare
- brothers-in-law
- chargés d'affaires
- chiefs of staff
- commanders in chief
- comptrollers general
- consuls general
- courts-martial
- crepes suzette
- daughters-in-law
- governors general
- grants-in-aid
- heirs at law
- inspectors general
- men-of-war
- ministers-designate
- mothers-in-law
- notaries public
- pilots-in-command
- postmasters general
- presidents-elect
- prisoners of war
- reductions in force
- rights-of-way
- secretaries general
- sergeants at arms
- sergeants major
- solicitors general
- surgeons general

Significant word in middle:
- assistant attorneys general
- assistant chiefs of staff
- assistant comptrollers general
- assistant surgeons general

Significant word last:
- assistant attorneys
- assistant commissioners
- assistant corporation counsels
- assistant directors
- assistant general counsels
- brigadier generals
- deputy judges
- deputy sheriffs
- general counsels
- judge advocates
- judge advocate generals
- lieutenant colonels
- major generals
- provost marshals
- provost marshal generals
- quartermaster generals

trade unions
under secretaries
vice chairmen
men employees
secretaries-treasurers
women aviators

Both words equally significant:
Bulletins Nos. 27 and 28 *not*
Bulletin Nos. 27 and 28 *but*
Bulletin No. 27 or 28
coats of arms
masters at arms
men buyers

No word significant in itself:
forget-me-nots
hand-me-downs
jack-in-the-pulpits
man-of-the-earths
pick-me-ups
will-o'-the-wisps

5.9. Nouns ending with *ful* form the plural by adding *s* at the end; if it is necessary to express the idea that more than one container was filled, the two elements of the solid compound are printed as separate words and the plural is formed by adding *s* to the noun.

five bucketfuls of the mixture (one bucket filled five times)
five buckets full of earth (separate buckets)
three cupfuls of flour (one cup filled three times)
three cups full of coffee (separate cups)

5.10. The following list comprises other words the plurals of which may cause difficulty.

addendum, addenda
adieu, adieus
agendum, agenda
alga, algae
alumnus, alumni (masc.); alumna, alumnae (fem.)
antenna, antennas (antennae, zoology)
appendix, appendixes
aquarium, aquariums
automaton, automatons
axis, axes
bandeau, bandeaux
basis, bases
bateau, bateaux
beau, beaus
cactus, cactuses
calix, calices
cargo, cargoes
chassis (singular and plural)
cherub, cherubs
cicatrix, cicatrices
Co., Cos.
coccus, cocci
consortium, consortia
corrigendum, corrigenda
crisis, crises
criterion, criteria
curriculum, curriculums, curricula
datum (singular), data (plural, but singular in collective sense)
desideratum, desiderata
dilettante, dilettanti
dogma, dogmas
ellipsis, ellipses
equilibrium, equilibriums (equilibria, scientific)
erratum, errata
executrix, executrices
flambeau, flambeaus

focus, focuses
folium, folia
formula, formulas
forum, forums
fungus, fungi
genius, geniuses
genus, genera
gladiolus (singular and plural)
helix, helices
hypothesis, hypotheses
index, indexes (indices, scientific)
insigne, insignia
italic (singular and plural)
Kansas Citys
lacuna, lacunae
larva, larvae
larynx, larynxes
lens, lenses
lira, lire
locus, loci
madam, mesdames
Marys
matrix, matrices
maximum, maximums, maxima
medium, mediums *or* media
memorandum, memorandums, memoranda
minimum, minimums, minima
minutia, minutiae
monsieur, messieurs
nucleus, nuclei
oasis, oases
octopus, octopuses
opus, opera
parenthesis, parentheses
phenomenon, phenomena
phylum, phyla
plateau, plateaus
podium, podiums
procès-verbal, procès-verbaux
radius, radii
radix, radixes
referendum, referendums
sanatorium, sanatoriums
sanitarium, sanitariums
septum, septa
sequela, sequelae
seraph, seraphs
seta, setae
ski, skis
stadium, stadiums
stimulus, stimuli
stratum, strata
stylus, styluses
syllabus, syllabuses
symposium, symposia
synopsis, synopses
tableau, tableaus
taxi, taxis
terminus, termini
testatrix, testatrices
thesaurus, thesauri
thesis, theses
thorax, thoraxes
vertebra, vertebras (vertebrae, zoology)
virtuoso, virtuosos
vortex, vortexes

Endings "ible" and "able"

5.11. The following words end in *ible*; other words in this class end in *able*.

abhorrible
accendible
accessible
addible
adducible
admissible
appetible
apprehensible
audible
avertible
bipartible
circumscriptible
coctible
coercible
cognoscible
cohesible
collapsible
collectible(s)
combustible
comestible
commonsensible
compactible
compatible
competible

compossible
comprehensible
compressible
conducible
conductible
confluxible
congestible
contemptible
controvertible
conversable (oral)
conversible (convertible)
convertible
convincible
corrigible
corrodible
corrosible
corruptible
credible
crucible
cullible
decoctible
deducible
deductible
defeasible
defectible
defensible
delible
deprehensible
depressible
descendible
destructible
diffrangible
diffusible
digestible
dimensible
discernible
discerpible
discerptible
discussible
dispersible
dissectible
distensible
distractible
divertible
divestible
divisible
docible
edible
educible
effectible
effervescible
eligible
eludible
erodible
evasible
eversible
evincible
exemptible
exhaustible
exigible
expansible
explosible
expressible
extensible
fallible
feasible
fencible
flexible
fluxible
forcible
frangible
fungible
fusible
gullible
horrible
ignitible
illegible
immersible
immiscible
impartible
impatible
impedible
imperceptible
impermissible
imperscriptible
impersuasible
implausible
impossible
imprescriptible
imputrescible
inaccessible
inadmissible
inapprehensible
inaudible
incircumscriptible
incoercible
incognoscrible
incombustible
incommiscible
incompatible
incomprehensible
incompressible
inconcussible
incontrovertible
inconvertible
inconvincible
incorrigible
incorrodible
incorruptible
incredible
indefeasible
indefectible
indefensible
indelible
indeprehensible
indestructible
indigestible
indiscernible
indivertible
indivisible
indocible
inducible
ineffervescible
ineligible
ineludible
inevasible
inexhaustible
inexpansible
inexpressible
infallible
infeasible
inflexible
infractible
infrangible
infusible
innascible
inscriptible
insensible
instructible
insubmergible
insuppressible
insusceptible
intactible
intangible
intelligible
interconvertible
interruptible
intervisible
invendible
invertible
invincible
invisible
irascible
irreducible
irrefrangible
irremissible
irreprehensible
irrepressible
irresistible
irresponsible
irreversible
legible
mandible
marcescible
miscible
negligible
nexible
omissible
ostensible
partible
passable (open)

passible (feeling)
perceptible
perfectible
permissible
persuasible
pervertible
plausible
possible
prehensible
prescriptible
producible
productible
protrusible
putrescible
receptible
redemptible
reducible
reflectible
reflexible
refrangible
remissible
renascible
rendible
reprehensible
repressible
reproducible
resistible
responsible
reversible
revertible
risible
runcible
sconcible
seducible
sensible
sponsible
suasible
subdivisible
submergible
submersible
subvertible
suggestible
supersensible
suppressible
susceptible
suspensible
tangible
tensible
terrible
thurible
traducible
transmissible
transvertible
tripartible
unadmissible
uncorruptible
unexhaustible
unexpressible
unintelligible
unresponsible
unsusceptible
vendible
vincible
visible
vitrescible

Endings "ise," "ize," and "yze"

5.12. A large number of words have the termination *ise, ize,* or *yze*. The letter *l* is followed by *yze* if the word expresses an idea of loosening or separating, as *analyze*; all other words of this class, except those ending with the suffix *wise* and those in the following list, end in *ize*.

advertise
advise
affranchise
apprise (to inform)
  apprize (to appraise)
arise
chastise
circumcise
comprise
compromise
demise
despise
devise
disenfranchise
disfranchise
disguise
emprise
enfranchise
enterprise
excise
exercise
exorcise
franchise
improvise
incise
merchandise
misadvise
mortise
premise
prise (to force)
  prize (to value)
reprise
revise
rise
supervise
surmise
surprise
televise

Endings "cede," "ceed," and "sede"

5.13. Only one word ends in *sede* (supersede); only three end in *ceed* (exceed, proceed, succeed); all other words of this class end in *cede* (precede, secede, etc.).

Doubled consonants

5.14. A single consonant following a single vowel and ending in a monosyllable or a final accented syllable is doubled before a suffix beginning with a vowel.

bag, bagging	red, reddish	*but*
format, formatting	rob, robbing	total, totaled, totaling
input, inputting	transfer, transferred	travel, traveled, traveling

5.15. If the accent in a derivative falls upon an earlier syllable than it does in the root word, the consonant is not doubled.

refer, reference	prefer, preference	infer, inference

Indefinite articles

5.16. The indefinite article *a* is used before a consonant and an aspirated *h*; *an* is used before a silent *h* and all vowels except *u* pronounced as in *visual* and *o* pronounced as in *one.*

a historic occasion	an herbseller	*but*
a hotel	an hour	an H-U-D directive
a human being	an honor	a HUD directive
a humble man	an onion	
a union	an oyster	

5.17. When a group of initials begins with *b, c, d, g, j, k, p, q, t, u, v, w, y,* or *z*, each having a consonant sound, the indefinite article *a* is used.

a BLS compilation	a GAO limitation	a WWW search
a CIO finding	a UFO sighting	

5.18. When a group of initials begins with *a, e, f, h, i, l, m, n, o, r, s,* or *x*, each having a vowel sound, the indefinite article *an* is used.

an AEC report	an NSC (en) proclamation
an FCC (ef) ruling	an RFC (ahr) loan

5.19. Use of the indefinite article *a* or *an* before a numerical expression is determined by the consonant or vowel sound of the beginning syllable.

an 11-year-old	an VIII (eight) classification
a onetime winner	a IV–F (four ef) category (military draft)
a III (three) group	a 4–H Club

Geographic names

5.20. The spelling of geographic names must conform to the decisions of the U.S. Board on Geographic Names (BGN) (http://geonames.usgs.gov). In the absence of such a decision, the U.S. Directory of Post Offices is to be used.

5.21. If the decisions or the rules of the BGN permit the use of either the local official form or the conventional English form, it is the prerogative of the originating office to select the form that is most suitable for the matter in hand; therefore, in marking copy or reading proof, it is required only to verify the spelling of the particular form used. GPO's preference is for the conventional English form. Copy will be followed as to accents, but these should be consistent throughout the entire job.

Nationalities, etc.

5.22. The table on Demonyms in Chapter 17 "Useful Tables" shows forms to be used for nouns and adjectives denoting nationality.

5.23. In designating the natives of the States, the following forms will be used.

Alabamian	Kentuckian	North Dakotan
Alaskan	Louisianian	Ohioan
Arizonan	Mainer	Oklahoman
Arkansan	Marylander	Oregonian
Californian	Massachusettsan	Pennsylvanian
Coloradan	Michiganian	Rhode Islander
Connecticuter	Minnesotan	South Carolinian
Delawarean	Mississippian	South Dakotan
Floridian	Missourian	Tennessean
Georgian	Montanan	Texan
Hawaii resident	Nebraskan	Utahn
Hoosier	Nevadan	Vermonter
(Indiana)	New Hampshirite	Virginian
Idahoan	New Jerseyan	Washingtonian
Illinoisan	New Mexican	West Virginian
Iowan	New Yorker	Wisconsinite
Kansan	North Carolinian	Wyomingite

5.24. Observe the following forms:

Alaska Native
Asian American
Black or African American
Hispanic or Latino
Native American or American Indian
Native Hawaiian
Pacific Islander
Puerto Rican
White

Native American words

5.25. Words, including Tribal and other proper names of Indian, Alaska Native, Hawaiian, and other groups, are to be followed literally as to spelling and the use of spaces, diacriticals, hyphens, etc.

Transliteration

5.26. In the spelling of nongeographic words transliterated from Chinese, Japanese, or any other language that does not have a Latin alphabet, copy is to be followed literally.

6. Compounding Rules

(See also Chapter 7 "Compounding Examples")

6.1. A compound word is a union of two or more words, either with or without a hyphen. It conveys a unit idea that is not as clearly or quickly conveyed by the component words in unconnected succession. The hyphen is a mark of punctuation that not only unites but also separates the component words; it facilitates understanding, aids readability, and ensures correct pronunciation. When compound words must be divided at the end of a line, such division should be made leaving prefixes and combining forms of more than one syllable intact.

6.2. In applying the rules in this chapter and in using the list of examples in the following chapter, "Compounding Examples," the fluid nature of our language should be kept in mind. Word forms constantly undergo modification. Although it is often the case that hyphenated compound words eventually lose their hyphen, many of them start out unhyphenated.

6.3. The rules, therefore, are somewhat flexible. Exceptions must necessarily be allowed. Current language trends continue to point to closing up certain words which, through either frequent use or widespread dissemination through modern media exposure, have become fixed in the reader's mind as units of thought. The tendency to merge two short words continues to be a natural progression toward better communication.

General rules

6.4. In general, omit the hyphen when words appear in regular order and the omission causes no ambiguity in sense or sound.

banking hours	eye opener	real estate
blood pressure	fellow citizen	rock candy
book value	living costs	training ship
census taker	palm oil	violin teacher
day laborer	patent right	

6.5. Words are usually combined to express a literal or nonliteral (figurative) unit idea that would not be as clearly expressed in unconnected succession.

afterglow	forget-me-not	right-of-way
bookkeeping	gentleman	whitewash
cupboard	newsprint	

6.6. A derivative of a compound retains the solid or hyphenated form of the original compound unless otherwise indicated.

coldbloodedness	outlawry	Y-shaped
footnoting	praiseworthiness	
ill-advisedly	railroader	

6.7. A hyphen is used to avoid doubling a vowel or tripling a consonant, except after the short prefixes *co, de, pre, pro,* and *re,* which are generally printed solid. (See also rules 6.29 and 6.32.)

cooperation	semi-independent	shell-like
deemphasis	brass-smith	hull-less
preexisting	Inverness-shire	*but*
anti-inflation	thimble-eye	co-occupant
micro-organism	ultra-atomic	cross section

Solid compounds

6.8. Print solid two nouns that form a third when the compound has only one primary accent, especially when the prefixed noun consists of only one syllable or when one of the elements loses its original accent.

airship	cupboard	footnote
bathroom	dressmaker	locksmith
bookseller	fishmonger	workman

6.9. Print solid a noun consisting of a short verb and an adverb as its second element, except when the use of the solid form would interfere with comprehension.

blowout	builddown	flareback
breakdown	cooldown	giveaway
hangover	runoff	*but*
holdup	setup	cut-in
makeready	showdown	phase-in
markoff	thowaway	run-in
pickup	tradeoff	sit-in

6.10. Compounds beginning with the following nouns are usually printed solid.

book
eye
horse
house
mill
play
school
shop
snow
way
wood
work

6.11. Compounds ending in the following are usually printed solid, especially when the prefixed word consists of one syllable.

berry
bird
blossom
board
boat
book
borne
bound
box
boy
brained
bug
bush
cam
craft
field
fish
flower
fly
girl
grower
headed
hearted
holder
hopper
house
keeper
keeping
land
light
like
line
load
maid
maker
making
man
master
mate
mill
mistress
monger
over
owner
  but #ownership
person
picker
picking
piece
plane
power
proof
roach
room
shop
site
skin
smith
stone
store
tail
tight
time (not clock)
ward
ware
water
way
wear
weed
wide
wise
woman
wood
work
worker
working
worm
worthy
writer

6.12. Print solid *any, every, no,* and *some* when combined with *body, thing,* and *where.* When *one* is the second element, print as two words if meaning a single or particular person or thing. To avoid mispronunciation, print *no one* as two words at all times.

anybody	everywhere	somebody
anything	everyone	something
anywhere	nobody	somewhere
anyone	nothing	someone
everybody	nowhere	
everything	no one	

but any one of us may stay; every one of the pilots is responsible; every body was accounted for

6.13. Print compound personal pronouns as one word.

herself	oneself	yourself
himself	ourselves	yourselves
itself	themselves	
myself	thyself	

6.14. Print as one word compass directions consisting of two points, but use a hyphen after the first point when three points are combined.

northeast	north-northeast
southwest	south-southwest

also north-south alignment

Unit modifiers

6.15. Print a hyphen between words, or abbreviations and words, combined to form a unit modifier immediately preceding the word modified, except as indicated in rule 6.16 and elsewhere throughout this chapter. This applies particularly to combinations in which one element is a present or past participle.

agreed-upon standards	Federal-State-local cooperation
Baltimore-Washington road	German-English descent
collective-bargaining talks	guided-missile program
contested-election case	hearing-impaired class
contract-bar rule	high-speed line
cost-of-living increase	large-scale project
drought-stricken area	law-abiding citizen
English-speaking nation	long-term loan
fire-tested material	line-item veto

long-term-payment loan
low-cost housing
lump-sum payment
most-favored-nation clause
multiple-purpose uses
no-par-value stock
one-on-one situation
part-time personnel
rust-resistant covering
service-connected disability
state-of-the-art technology
supply-side economics
tool-and-die maker
up-or-down vote
U.S.-owned property; U.S.-flagship
1-inch diameter; 2-inch-diameter pipe
a 4-percent increase, the 10-percent rise

but

4 percent citric acid
4 percent interest. (Note the absence of an article: *a, an,* or *the*. The word *of* is understood here.)

6.16. Where meaning is clear and readability is not aided, it is not necessary to use a hyphen to form a temporary or made compound. Restraint should be exercised in forming unnecessary combinations of words used in normal sequence.

atomic energy power
bituminous coal industry
child welfare plan
civil rights case
civil service examination
durable goods industry
flood control study
free enterprise system
ground water levels
high school student
elementary school grade
income tax form
interstate commerce law
land bank loan
land use program
life insurance company
mutual security funds
national defense appropriation
natural gas company
per capita expenditure
Portland cement plant
production credit loan
public at large
public utility plant
real estate tax
small businessman
Social Security pension
soil conservation measures
special delivery mail
parcel post delivery
speech correction class

but no-hyphen rule (readability aided); *not* no hyphen rule

6.17. Print without a hyphen a compound predicate (either adjective or noun) whose second element is a present participle.

The duties were price fixing.
The effects were far reaching.
The shale was oil bearing.
The area is used for beet raising.

6.18. Print without a hyphen a compound predicate adjective the second element of which is a past participle. Omit the hyphen in a predicate modifier of comparative or superlative degree.

The area is drought stricken.	This material is fire tested.
The paper is fine grained.	The cars are higher priced.
Moderately fine grained wood.	The reporters are better informed.

6.19. Print without a hyphen a two-word modifier the first element of which is a comparative or superlative.

better drained soil	*but*
best liked books	uppercrust society
higher level decision	lowercase, uppercase type
highest priced apartment	upperclassman
larger sized dress	bestseller (noun)
better paying job	lighter-than-air craft
lower income group	higher-than-market price

6.20. Do not use a hyphen in a two-word unit modifier the first element of which is an adverb ending in *ly*, nor use hyphens in a three-word unit modifier the first two elements of which are adverbs.

eagerly awaited moment	*but*
wholly owned subsidiary	ever-normal granary
unusually well preserved specimen	ever-rising flood
very well defined usage	still-new car
longer than usual lunch period	still-lingering doubt
not too distant future	well-known lawyer
most often heard phrase	well-kept secret

6.21. Proper nouns used as unit modifiers, either in their basic or derived form, retain their original form; but the hyphen is printed when combining forms.

Latin American countries	Seventh-day Adventists
North Carolina roads	*but*
a Mexican American	Minneapolis-St. Paul region
South American trade	North American-South American sphere
Spanish-American pride	French-English descent
Winston-Salem festival	Washington–Wilkes-Barre route *or* Washington/Wilkes-Barre route
African-American program	
Anglo-Saxon period	
Franco-Prussian War	

6.22. Do not confuse a modifier with the word it modifies.

elderly clothesman	well-trained schoolteacher
old-clothes man	elementary school teacher
competent shoemaker	preschool children (kindergarten)
wooden-shoe maker	pre-school children (before school)
field canning factory	rezoned wastesite
tomato-canning factory	hazardous-waste site
brave servicemen	
service men and women	*but*
light blue hat (weight)	common stockholder
light-blue hat (color)	stock ownership
average taxpayer	small businessman
income-tax payer	working men and women
American flagship (military)	steam powerplant site
American-flag ship	meat packinghouse owner

6.23. Where two or more hyphenated compounds have a common basic element but this element is omitted in all but the last term, the hyphens are retained.

2- to 3- and 4- to 5-ton trucks
2- by 4-inch boards, *but* boards 2 to 6 inches wide
8-, 10-, and 16-foot boards
6.4-, 3.1-, and 2-percent pay raises
moss- and ivy-covered walls, *not* moss and ivy-covered walls
long- and short-term money rates, *not* long and short-term money rates

but twofold or threefold, *not* two or threefold
goat, sheep, and calf skins, *not* goat, sheep, and calfskins
intrastate and intracity, *not* intra-state and -city
American owned and managed companies
preoperative and postoperative examination

6.24. Do not use a hyphen in a unit modifier consisting of a foreign phrase.

ante bellum days	ex officio member	per diem employee
bona fide transaction	per capita tax	prima facie evidence

6.25. Do not print a hyphen in a unit modifier containing a letter or a numeral as its second element.

abstract B pages	class II railroad	point 4 program
article 3 provisions	grade A milk	ward D beds

6.26. Do not use a hyphen in a unit modifier enclosed in quotation marks unless it is normally a hyphenated term, but quotation marks are not to be used in lieu of a hyphen.

"blue sky" law	*but*
"good neighbor" policy	right-to-work law
"tie-in" sale	line-item veto

6.27. Print combination color terms as separate words, but use a hyphen when such color terms are unit modifiers.

bluish green	bluish-green feathers
dark green	iron-gray sink
orange red	silver-gray body

6.28. Do not use a hyphen between independent adjectives preceding a noun.

big gray cat	a fine old southern gentleman

Prefixes, suffixes, and combining forms

6.29. Print solid combining forms and prefixes, except as indicated elsewhere.

*after*birth	*infra*red	*peri*patetic
*Anglo*mania	*inter*view	*plano*convex
*ante*date	*intra*spinal	*poly*nodal
*anti*slavery	*intro*vert	*post*script
*bi*weekly	*iso*metric	*pre*exist
*by*law	*macro*analysis	*pro*consul
*circum*navigation	*meso*thorax	*pseudo*scholastic
*cis*alpine	*meta*genesis	*re*enact
*co*operate	*micro*phone	*retro*spect
*contra*position	*mis*state	*semi*official
*counter*case	*mono*gram	*step*father
*de*energize	*multi*color	*sub*secretary
*demi*tasse	*neo*phyte	*super*market
*ex*communicate	*non*neutral	*thermo*couple
*extra*curricular	*off*set	*trans*onic
*fore*tell	*out*bake	*trans*ship
*heroi*comic	*over*active	*tri*color
*hyper*sensitive	*pan*cosmic	*ultra*violet
*hypo*acid	*para*centric	*un*necessary
*in*bound	*parti*coated	*under*flow

6.30. Print solid combining forms and suffixes, except as indicated elsewhere.

port*able*	geog*raphy*	inner*most*
cover*age*	man*hood*	partner*ship*
oper*ate*	self*ish*	lone*some*
plebis*cite*	meat*less*	home*stead*
twenty*fold*	out*let*	north*ward*
spoon*ful*	wave*like*	clock*wise*
kilo*gram*	procure*ment*	

6.31. Print solid words ending in *like*, but use a hyphen to avoid tripling a consonant or when the first element is a proper name.

lifelike	girllike	Scotland-like
lilylike	bell-like	McArtor-like

6.32. Use a hyphen or hyphens to prevent mispronunciation, to ensure a definite accent on each element of the compound, or to avoid ambiguity.

anti-hog-cholera serum	re-creation (create again)
co-occurrence	re-lay (lay again)
co-op	re-sign (sign again)
mid-decade	re-sorting (sort again)
multi-ply (several plies)	re-treat (treat again)
non-civil-service position	un-ionized
non-tumor-bearing tissue	un-uniformity
pre-midcourse review	
pre-position (before)	*but*
pro-choice	rereferred
pro-life	rereviewed
re-cover (cover again)	

6.33. Use a hyphen to join duplicated prefixes.

re-redirect	sub-subcommittee	super-superlative

6.34. Print with a hyphen the prefixes *ex*, *self*, and *quasi*.

ex-governor	quasi-argument
ex-serviceman	quasi-corporation
ex-son-in-law	quasi-young
ex-vice-president	
self-control	*but*
self-educated	selfhood
quasi-academic	selfsame

6.35. Unless usage demands otherwise, use a hyphen to join a prefix or combining form to a capitalized word. (The hyphen is retained in words of this class set in caps.)

anti-American
pro-British
un-American
non-Government
neo-Nazi
post-World War II
  or post-Second World War
non-Federal

but
nongovernmental
overanglicize
transatlantic

Numerical compounds

6.36. Print a hyphen between the elements of compound numbers from twenty-one to ninety-nine and in adjective compounds with a numerical first element.

twenty-one
twenty-first
6-footer
6-foot-11-inch man
24-inch ruler
3-week vacation
8-hour day
10-minute delay
20th-century progress
3-to-1 ratio
5-to-4 vote
.22-caliber cartridge
2-cent-per-pound tax
four-in-hand tie
three-and-twenty
two-sided question
multimillion-dollar fund
10-dollar-per-car tax
thirty- (30-) day period

but
one hundred twenty-one
100-odd
foursome
threescore
foursquare
$20 million airfield
second grade children

6.37. Print without a hyphen a modifier consisting of a possessive noun preceded by a numeral. (See also rule 8.14.)

1 month's layoff
1 week's pay
2 hours' work
3 weeks' vacation
1 minute's delay
but a 1-minute delay

6.38. Print a hyphen between the elements of a fraction, but omit it between the numerator and the denominator when the hyphen appears in either or in both.

one-thousandth	twenty-three thirtieths
two-thirds	twenty-one thirty-seconds
two one-thousandths	three-fourths of an inch

6.39. A unit modifier following and reading back to the word or words modified takes a hyphen and is printed in the singular.

motor, alternating-current, 3-phase, 60-cycle, 115-volt
glass jars: 5-gallon, 2-gallon, 1-quart
belts: 2-inch, $1\frac{1}{4}$-inch, $\frac{1}{2}$-inch, $\frac{1}{4}$-inch

Civil and military titles

6.40. Do not hyphenate a civil or military title denoting a single office, but print a double title with a hyphen.

ambassador at large	secretary-treasurer
assistant attorney general	sergeant at arms
commander in chief	treasurer-manager
comptroller general	under secretary
Congressman at Large	*but* under-secretaryship
major general	vice president
notary public	*but* vice-presidency
secretary general	

6.41. The adjectives *elect* and *designate,* as the last element of a title, require a hyphen.

President-elect (Federal)	ambassador-designate
Vice-President-elect (Federal)	minister-designate
Secretary of Housing and Urban Development-designate	

Scientific and technical terms

6.42. Do not print a hyphen in scientific terms (names of chemicals, diseases, animals, insects, plants) used as unit modifiers if no hyphen appears in their original form.

carbon monoxide poisoning
guinea pig raising
hog cholera serum
methyl bromide solution
stem rust control
equivalent uranium content
whooping cough remedy
but
Russian-olive plantings
Douglas-fir tree

6.43. Chemical elements used in combination with full-size figures use a hyphen; chemical symbols do not.

polonium-210
uranium-235
^{235}U
^{90}Sr
$^{234}U_{92}$

6.44. Note use of hyphens and closeup punctuation in chemical formulas.

9-nitroanthra(1,9,4,10)bis(1)oxathiazone-2,7-bisdioxide
Cr-Ni-Mo
2,4-D

6.45. Print a hyphen between the elements of technical or contrived compound units of measurement.

candela-hour
crop-year
horsepower-hour
light-year
passenger-mile
staff-hour
work-year
but kilowatthour

Improvised compounds

6.46. Print with a hyphen the elements of an improvised compound.

blue-pencil (v.)
18-year-old (n., u.m.)
know-it-all (n.)
know-how (n.)
lick-the-finger-and-test-the-wind economics
make-believe (n., u.m.)
one-man-one-vote principle
roll-on/roll-off ship
George "Pay-As-You-Go" Miller
stick-in-the-mud (n.)
let-George-do-it attitude
how-to-be-beautiful course
hard-and-fast rule
penny-wise and pound-foolish policy
first-come-first-served basis
but a basis of first come, first served

6.47. Use hyphens in a prepositional-phrase compound noun consisting of three or more words.

cat-o'-nine-tails	man-of-war	*but*
government-in-exile	mother-in-law	heir at law
grant-in-aid	mother-of-pearl	next of kin
jack-in-the-box	patent-in-fee	officer in charge

6.48. When the corresponding noun form is printed as separate words, the verb form is always hyphenated.

cold-shoulder	blue-pencil	cross-brace

6.49. Print a hyphen in a compound formed of repetitive or conflicting terms and in a compound naming the same thing under two aspects.

boogie-woogie	hanky-panky	young-old
comedy-ballet	murder-suicide	*but*
dead-alive	nitty-gritty	bowwow
devil-devil	pitter-patter	dillydally
even-stephen	razzle-dazzle	hubbub
farce-melodrama	walkie-talkie	nitwit
fiddle-faddle	willy-nilly	riffraff

6.50. Use a hyphen in a nonliteral compound expression containing an apostrophe in its first element.

asses'-eyes	bull's-eye	crow's-nest
ass's-foot	cat's-paw	

6.51. Use a hyphen to join a single capital letter to a noun or a participle.

H-bomb	C-section	*but*
I-beam	V-necked	x ray
T-shaped	S-iron	x raying
U-boat	T-square	S turns
C-chip	X-ed out	

6.52. Print idiomatic phrases without hyphens.

come by	insofar as	nowadays
inasmuch as	Monday week	

7. Compounding Examples

7.1. The following examples are based on the rules for compounding found in chapter 6. Obviously, this list or any other list of compound words could not possibly be a complete reference due to sheer volume. However, an analogy of the words listed with like prefixes and suffixes together with an application of the rules will result in easier handling of those compound words not listed.

7.2. In order to keep the list from becoming cumbersome, certain restrictions had to be adopted.

7.3. The listing of hyphenated compounds ending in *ed* was kept to a minimum. The rationale was to provide one or two examples under a keyword rather than needless repetition.

7.4. Similarly, many two-word forms which create no difficulty were omitted.

7.5. Care was exercised to achieve fuller coverage of solid compounds, particularly when the adopted form is different than that of Webster's Third New International Dictionary. This dictionary is GPO's guide for spelling with the exception of those words listed in rule 5.2. It is not GPO's guide to compounding.

7.6. A distinction exists between words used in a literal sense and a nonliteral sense. With few exceptions, one-word forms usually express a nonliteral interpretation, while two-word forms invariably convey a literal meaning. For example, a person may have an interesting *sideline* or hobby, but be forced to sit on the *side line* during periods of inactivity.

7.7. Distinction should also be made in the compounding of two words to form an adjective modifier and the use of the same words as a predicate adjective; e.g., "crystal-clear water," *but* "the spring water is crystal clear"; "fire-tested material," *but* "the material is fire tested."

7.8. Caution should be exercised when distinguishing whether a succession of words is being used as a compound or whether they simply appear together. Consider, for example, "We know *someone* should do it and who that *some one* ought to be."

7.9. Combining forms and prefixes are usually printed solid. For greater readability, the hyphen is sometimes used to avoid doubling a vowel (*anti-inflation, naso-orbital*); to facilitate a normally capitalized word (*mid-April, non-European*); to assure distinct pronunciation of each element of a compound or ready comprehension of intended meaning (*contra-ion, un-ionized*); or to join a combining form or prefix to a hyphenated compound (*equi-gram-molar, pro-mother-in-law*).

7.10. As nouns and adjectives, *holdup, calldown, layout, makeup,* and similar words should be printed solid. Their *er* derivatives, (*holder-up, caller-down, layer-out,* and *maker-up*) require hyphens. Such compounds as *run-in, run-on,* and *tie-in* resist quick comprehension when solid. They are therefore hyphenated.

7.11. Words spelled alike but pronounced differently, such as *tear-dimmed* and *tearsheet, wind tunnel* and *windup,* are listed under the same keyword.

7.12. Words printed flush in the following list combine with the words which follow to indicate solid or hyphenated compounds. A spacemark (#) appearing before an indented entry indicates a two-word form, but two-word forms appearing in the adjective position usually take a hyphen.

7.13. To indicate word function, several abbreviations have been appended. They are: *adv.*, adverb; *n.*, noun; *v.*, verb; *u.m.*, unit modifier; *pref.*, prefix; *c.f.*, combining form; and *conj.*, conjunction.

A

A
BC(s) (n.)
–B–C (u.m.)
-bomb
-day
-flat
-frame
-pole
-sharp

a
borning, etc.
foot
while (adv.)

abdomino (c.f.)
all one word

able
-bodied (u.m.)
-minded (u.m.)

about-face

above
-cited (u.m.)
deck
-found (u.m.)
-given (u.m.)
ground (u.m.)
-mentioned (u.m.)
-named (u.m.)
-said (u.m.)
-water (u.m.)
-written (u.m.)

absentminded
ace-high (u.m.)

acid
fast
-treat (v.)
works

ack-ack

acre
-foot
-inch

actino (c.f.)
all one word

addle
brain
head
pate

add-on (n., u.m.)

adeno (c.f.)
all one word

aero (c.f.)
-otitis
rest one word

afore
all one word

after (c.f.)
all one word

agar-agar

age
less
long
-old (u.m.)
-stricken (u.m.)
-weary (u.m.)

agribusiness

ague
-faced (u.m.)
-plagued (u.m.)
-sore (u.m.)

aide-de-camp

air
bag
base
bill
blast
-blasted (u.m.)
blown
brake
brush
burst
cargo
-clear (u.m.)
coach
-condition (all forms)
-cool (v.)
-cooled (u.m.)
course
crew
-dried (u.m.)
-driven (u.m.)
drome
drop
-dry (u.m., v.)
fare
-floated (u.m.)
flow
foil
-formed (u.m.)
frame
freight
gap
glow
hammer
head
hole
hose
lane
lift
#line (line for air)
line (aviation)
liner
link
locked
mail
mark (v.)
marker
mass
minded
park
path
photo
port (all meanings)
#raid
scoop
ship
show
sick
-slaked (u.m.)
sleeve
space
speed
stream
strike
strip
#time (radio and TV)
wave
woman
worthy

alder-leaved (u.m.)

ale
cup
-fed (u.m.)
glass

alkali#land

all
-absorbing (u.m.)
-aged (u.m.)
-American
-clear (n., u.m.)
-fired (u.m.)
-flotation (mining)
#fours
#in
-inclusive (u.m.)
mark (printing)
-out (u.m.)
-possessed (u.m.)
-round (u.m.)
spice
-star (u.m.)
time (u.m.)
wise

alleyway

allo (c.f.)
all one word

almsgiver

along
ship

shore
side
alpen
glow
stock
alpha
-cellulose
-iron
-naphthol
also-ran (n., u.m.)
alto
cumulus
relievo
stratus
amber
-clear (u.m.)
-colored (u.m.)
-tipped (u.m.)
ambi (c.f.)
all one word
amidships
amino
#acid
as prefix, all one word
ampere
-foot
-hour
meter
-minute
-second
amphi (pref.)
all one word
amylo (c.f.)
all one word
anchor
hold
#light
plate
angel
cake
-eyed (u.m.)
-faced (u.m.)
food
angio (c.f.)
all one word
angle
hook
meter
wing
worm
Anglo (c.f.)
-American, etc.
rest one word
anhydr(o) (c.f.)
all one word
ankle
bone
-deep (u.m.)
jack
ant
eater
hill
ante (pref.)
#bellum, etc.
-Christian, etc.
#mortem
mortem (nonliteral)
rest one word
antero (c.f.)
all one word
anthra (c.f.)
all one word
anthropo (c.f.)
all one word
anti (pref.)
-American, etc.
-choice
christ
god
-hog-cholera (u.m.)
-icer
-imperial
-inflation, etc.
-life
-missile-missile (u.m.)
missile
-New#Deal, etc.
personnel
trust, etc.
rest one word
antro (c.f.)
all one word
anvil
-faced (u.m.)
-headed (u.m.)
any
body
how
one
#one (one thing or one of a group)
place (adv.)
aorto (c.f.)
all one word
apo (pref.)
all one word
apple
cart
jack
#juice
sauce
-scented (u.m.)
April-fool (v.)
aqua
culture
lung
marine
meter
puncture
tint
tone
aquo (c.f.)
-ion
rest one word
arc
-over (n., u.m.)
-weld (v.)
arch (pref.)
band
bishop
duke
enemy
-Protestant
archeo (c.f.)
all one word
archi (pref.)
all one word
archo (c.f.)
all one word
areo (c.f.)
all one word
aristo (c.f.)
all one word
arithmo (c.f.)
all one word
arm
band
bone
chair
hole
lift
pit
plate
rack
rest
-shaped (u.m.)
armor
-clad (u.m.)
-piercing (u.m.)
plate
-plated (u.m.)
smith
arm's-length (u.m.)
arrow
head
-leaved (u.m.)
plate

-shaped (u.m.)
shot
-toothed (u.m.)
arseno (c.f.)
all one word
art-colored (u.m.)
arterio (c.f.)
all one word
arthro (c.f.)
all one word
artillery
man
woman
asbestos
-covered (u.m.)
-packed (u.m.)
ash
bin
can
-colored (u.m.)
-free (u.m.)
-gray (u.m.)
#heap
pan
pile
pit
tray
assembly
#line
man
#room
astro (c.f.)
all one word
attorney#at#law
audio
frequency
gram
meter
tape
visual
auri (c.f.)
-iodide
rest one word
authorship
auto (c.f.)
-logon
matic#backup
-objective
-observation
-omnibus
-ophthalmoscope
rest one word
awe
-bound (u.m.)
-filled (u.m.)
-inspired (u.m.)
some
ax
-adz
-grinding (u.m.)
hammer
head
-shaped (u.m.)
axletree
axo (c.f.)
all one word
azo (c.f.)
-orange
-orchil
-orseilline
rest one word

B

B-flat
baby
#boomer
face (n.)
#food
sit (v.)
sitter
back
ache
band
bite (v.)
biter
bone
breaker
cap
chain
charge
-country (u.m.)
cross
date
down (n., u.m.)
drop
face
feed
fill
fire
flap
flash
flow
-focus (v.)
furrow
ground
hand
haul
-in (n., u.m.)
lash
list (v.)
log
lotter
packer (n.)
paddle (v.)
pay
payment
pedal (v.)
plate
rest
road
run
saw
scatter
set
shift
slide
space
spin
spread
staff
stage
stairs
stamp
stay
stitch
stop
strap
-streeter
stretch (n.)
string
strip (book)
stroke
-swath (v.)
swept
swing
tack
talk
tender
tenter
-titrate (v.)
track (v.)
trail
up (n., u.m.)
wall
wash
water
backer
-down
-off
-up
bag
boy
-cheeked (u.m.)
girl
pipe
-shaped (u.m.)
baggage
man
#rack
#room
#train
bailout (n., u.m.)

bake
oven
pan
shop
bald
faced
head (n.)
ball
field
#game
-like
park (nonliteral)
#park (literal)
player
point (n., u.m.)
stock
ballot#box
band
aid
box
cutter
saw
stand
string
-tailed (u.m.)
wagon
width
bandy
ball
-legged (u.m.)
bangup (n., u.m.)
bank
book
note
#paper
side (stream)
bantamweight
bar
#bit
code
keeper
maid
post
tender
-wound (u.m.)
bare
-armed (u.m.)
back
bone
faced
foot
handed
legged
necked
worn
barge-laden (u.m.)
bark
cutter
peel
-tanned (u.m.)
barley
corn
mow
#water
barnstormer
barrel
head
-roll (v.)
-shaped (u.m.)
base
ball
ball#bat
line
#line (surveying)
-minded (u.m.)
basi (c.f.)
all one word
basketball
bas-relief
bat
blind
-eyed (u.m.)
fowl
wing
batch#file
bath
mat
robe
#towel
tub
batswing (cloth)
battercake
battle
ax
-fallen (u.m.)
front
ground
-scarred (u.m.)
ship
stead
wagon
baybolt
beach
comber
head
wagon
bead
flush
roll
beak
head
iron
-shaped (u.m.)
beam
filling
-making (u.m.)
bean
bag
cod
-fed (u.m.)
pole
pot
setter
-shaped (u.m.)
stalk
bear
baiting
herd
hide
hound
off (n., u.m.)
trap
beater
-out
-up
beauty
-blind (u.m.)
-clad (u.m.)
#shop
beaverpelt
bed
board
bug
chair
chamber
clothes
cord
cover
-fallen (u.m.)
fast
fellow
frame
lamp
linen
pad
pan
plate
post
quilt
rail
#rest
ridden
rock
sheet
sick
side
sore
space
spread
spring
stand

stead
straw
time
bee
bread
-eater
herd
hive
keeper
line
way
beechnut
beef
eater
#extract
-faced (u.m.)
head
steak
bees
wax
wing
beet
field
#sugar
beetle
-browed (u.m.)
head
stock
before
-cited (u.m.)
hand
-mentioned (u.m.)
-named (u.m.)
behindhand
bell
-bottomed (u.m.)
crank
-crowned (u.m.)
hanger
hop
mouthed
ringer
wether
belly
ache
band
buster
button
fed (u.m.)
pinch
belowstairs
belt
-driven (u.m.)
saw
bench
fellow
-hardened (u.m.)
made (u.m.)
mark (nonliteral)
#mark (surveying)
warmer
#warrant
bentwing (n., u.m.)
benzo (c.f.)
all one word
berry-brown (u.m.)
best
#man
seller (n.)
beta
-glucose
tron
between
decks
whiles
bi (pref.)
-iliac
rest one word
big
-eared (u.m.)
-eyed (u.m.)
head (ego)
horn (sheep)
-horned (u.m.)
-leaguer
mouthed
name (top rank)
(n., u.m.)
bill
back
beetle
broker
fold
head
hook
poster
sticker
billet
-doux
head
billingsgate
bio (c.f.)
-aeration
-osmosis
rest one word
birchbark
bird
bath
bander
cage
call
catcher
#dog (literal)
dog (nonliteral)
-eyed (u.m.)
-faced (u.m.)
life
lime
lore
mouthed
seed
shot
watcher
bird's
-eye
#nest (literal) (n.)
-nest (n., u.m., v.)
birth
bed
#date
day
mark
place
right
#year
biscuit-shaped
(u.m.)
bismuto (c.f.)
all one word
bit
coin
-mapped
stock
bitter
-ender
head
sweet
-tongued (u.m.)
black
ball (nonliteral)
-bordered (u.m.)
-eyed (u.m.)
guard
jack
leg
list
mail
mark
#market (n.)
-market (u.m., v.)
-marketer
out (n., u.m.)
plate (printing)
print
-robed (u.m.)
#sheep (all
meanings)
shirted
snake
strap (n.)
-tie (u.m.)
top

#widow
blast
hole
plate
blasto (c.f.)
all one word
bleach
ground
works
blear
eye
-eyed (u.m.)
-witted (u.m.)
blepharo (c.f.)
all one word
blight-resistant (u.m.)
blind
-bomb (v.)
-flying (u.m.)
fold
-loaded (u.m.)
#man
spot
stitch
story
blink-eyed (u.m.)
blithe-looking (u.m.)
blitzkrieg
block
buster
head
hole (v.)
ship
blood
-alcohol (u.m.)
bath
beat
curdling
-drenched (u.m.)
-giving (u.m.)
guilty
-hot (u.m.)
hound
letting
mobile
-red (u.m.)
ripe
shed
shot
spiller
spot
stain
stock
stream
sucker
thirsty
-warm (u.m.)
bloody
-nosed (u.m.)
-red (u.m.)
blossom
-bordered (u.m.)
-laden (u.m.)
blow
back
by (n., u.m.)
cock
down (n., u.m.)
gun
hard (n.)
hole
iron
lamp
off (n., u.m.)
out (n., u.m.)
pipe
spray
through (u.m.)
torch
tube
up (n., u.m.)
blue
-annealed (u.m.)
beard (n.)
blood
bonnet
book (nonliteral)
bottle
coat (n.)
-eyed (u.m.)
gill
grass
-gray (u.m.)
-green (u.m.)
-hot (u.m.)
jack
jacket
nose
-pencil (v.)
point (oyster)
print
stocking
streak (nonliteral)
tongue (n.)
blunder
buss
head
blunt
-edged (u.m.)
-spoken (u.m.)
boar
spear
staff
board
#foot
rack
walk
boat
builder
crew
head
hook
house
loader
owner
#people
setter
shop
side
swain
wright
yard
bob
cat
sled
stay
tail
white
bobby
pin
-soxer
body
bearer
bending
builder
-centered (u.m.)
guard
-mind
plate
bog
-eyed (u.m.)
land
man
trot (v.)
boil
down (n., u.m.)
off (n., u.m.)
out (n., u.m.)
over (n., u.m.)
boiler
-off
-out
plate
works
boiling#house
bold
face (printing)
-spirited (u.m.)

bolt
cutter
head
hole
-shaped (u.m.)
strake
bomb
drop
fall
shell
sight
thrower
-throwing (u.m.)
bone
ache
#ash
black
breaker
-bred (u.m.)
-dry (u.m.)
-eater
-hard (u.m.)
head
lace
meal
set
shaker
-white (u.m.)
boobytrap
boogie-woogie
book
binder
case
dealer
#end
fair
-fed (u.m.)
fold
-learned (u.m.)
-lined (u.m.)
list
lore
lover
mark
mobile
plate
rack
rest
sale
seller
shelf
stack
stall
stamp
stand
stitch
-stitching (u.m.)
-taught (u.m.)
wright
boom
town
truck
boondoggling
boot
black
hose
jack
lace
last
leg
lick
strap
bore
hole
safe
sight
bosom
-deep (u.m.)
-folded (u.m.)
-making (u.m.)
bottle
-fed (u.m.)
neck
-nosed (u.m.)
bottom#land
boughpot
bow
back
bent
grace
head
knot
legged
-necked (u.m.)
pin
shot
sprit
stave
string
wow
box
car
haul
head (printing)
truck
boxer
-off
-up
brachio (c.f.)
all one word
brachy (c.f.)
all one word
brain
cap
child
-cracked (u.m.)
pan
sick
-spun (u.m.)
storm
-tired (u.m.)
wash
brake
drum
head
meter
shoe
brandnew (u.m.)
brandy
-burnt (u.m.)
wine
brass
-armed (u.m.)
-bold (u.m.)
-smith
works
brave
hearted
-looking (u.m.)
-minded (u.m.)
brazen
-browed (u.m.)
face
bread
basket
crumb
earner
fruit
#knife
liner
plate
seller
stuff
#tray
winner
break
away (n., u.m.)
ax
back (n., u.m.)
bone (fever)
#circuit
down (n., u.m.)
-even (u.m.)
fast
fast#room
front
-in (n., u.m.)
neck
off (n., u.m.)
out (n., u.m.)
point

through (n., u.m.)
up (n., u.m.)
wind (n.)
breaker
-down
-off
-up
breast
band
beam
bone
-deep (u.m.)
-fed (u.m.)
feed
-high (u.m.)
hook
mark
piece
pin
plate
plow
rail
rope
work
breath
-blown (u.m.)
-tainted (u.m.)
taking
breech
block
cloth
loader
-loading (u.m.)
lock
pin
plug
sight
breeze
-borne (u.m.)
-lifted (u.m.)
-swept (u.m.)
way
bribe
-free (u.m.)
giver
taker
bric-a-brac
brick
bat
-built (u.m.)
-colored (u.m.)
kiln
layer
liner
mason
-red (u.m.)
setter
work
yard
bride
bed
bowl
cake
chamber
cup
groom
knot
lace
maiden
stake
bridge
builder
head
pot
tree
#wall
work
briefcase
bright
-colored (u.m.)
-eyed (u.m.)
brilliant
-cut (u.m.)
-green (u.m.)
brine-soaked (u.m.)
bringer-up
bristle
cone (u.m.)
-pointed (u.m.)
broad
acre
ax
band (n., u.m.)
-beamed (u.m.)
brim
cast
cloth
head
#jump
leaf (n.)
-leaved (u.m.)
loom
minded
-mouthed (u.m.)
share (n., v.)
sheet (n.)
side
sword
wife
woven
broken
-down (u.m.)
-legged (u.m.)
-mouthed (u.m.)
bromo (c.f.)
all one word
bronchio (c.f.)
all one word
broncho (c.f.)
all one word
broncobuster
bronze
-clad (u.m.)
-covered (u.m.)
-red (u.m.)
broom
#handle
-leaved (u.m.)
-making (u.m.)
stick
brother
hood
-in-law
brow
beat
point
post
brown
back
-eyed (u.m.)
out (n., u.m.)
print
brush
ball
#holder
off (n., u.m.)
-treat (v.)
#up
brusher
-off
-up
buck
eye
-eyed (u.m.)
horn
hound
passer
plate
pot
saw
shot
skinned
stall
stay
stove
tooth
wagon
wash
bucketshaped (u.m.)
buff
-tipped (u.m.)

ware
-yellow (u.m.)
bug
bear
bite
-eyed (u.m.)
build
down (n., u.m.)
up (n., u.m.)
built
-in (u.m.)
-up (u.m.)
bulb-tee (u.m.)
bulbo (c.f.)
all one word
bulk
head
-pile (v.)
weigh (v.)
bull
baiting
dog
doze
-faced (u.m.)
fight
frog
head
-mouthed (u.m.)
neck
nose
pen
ring
#terrier
toad
-voiced (u.m.)
whack
whip
bullet
head
maker
proof
bull's
-eye (nonliteral)
-foot
bumble
bee
foot
kite
bung
hole
start
burn
-in (n., u.m.)
out (n., u.m.)
up (n., u.m.)
burned-over (u.m.)
burner-off
burnt
-out (u.m.)
-up (u.m.)
bus
boy
#conductor
driver
fare
girl
line
load
bush
beater
buck
fighter
-grown (u.m.)
hammer
-leaguer
ranger
whacker
bustup (n., u.m.)
busy
body
-fingered (u.m.)
head
butt
-joint (v.)
saw
stock
strap
-weld (v.)
butter
ball
-colored (u.m.)
fat
fingers
head
milk
mouth
nut
print
-rigged (u.m.)
scotch
-smooth (u.m.)
-yellow (u.m.)
button
-eared (u.m.)
-headed (u.m.)
hold
hole
hook
mold
by
-and-by
-the-way (n., u.m.)
-your-leave (n., u.m.)
rest one word

C

C
-sharp
-star
-tube
cab
driver
fare
#owner
stand
cabbagehead
cabinet
maker
making
cable-laid (u.m.)
caco (c.f.)
all one word
cage#bird
cake
baker
bread
-eater
mixer
-mixing (u.m.)
pan
walk
calci (c.f.)
all one word
calk-weld (v.)
call
back (n., u.m.)
box
down (n., u.m.)
-in (n., u.m.)
note
-off (n., u.m.)
out (n., u.m.)
-over (n., u.m.)
up (n., u.m.)
camshaft
camel
back (rubber)
-backed (u.m.)
case
driver
-faced (u.m.)
camel's-hair (u.m.)
camp
fire
ground
stool
can
capper

not
#opener
canalside
candle
bomb
-foot
holder
-hour
lighter
lit
-meter
power
-shaped (u.m.)
stand
stick
wick
wright
candystick
cane
-backed (u.m.)
brake
crusher
cutter
#sugar
canker
-eaten (u.m.)
-mouthed (u.m.)
cannonball
canvas-covered (u.m.)
cap
-flash (v.)
nut
screw
sheaf
shore
car
barn
break
builder
fare
goose
hop
jacker
lot
-mile
owner
pool
port
sick
wash
carbo (c.f.)
all one word
carbol (c.f.)
all one word
carcino (c.f.)
all one word
card
case
-index (u.m., v.)
player
sharp
stock
cardio (c.f.)
-aortic
rest one word
care
free
giver
-laden (u.m.)
taker
-tired (u.m.)
worn
carpet
bagger
beater
#cleaner
-cleaning (u.m.)
-covered (u.m.)
fitter
layer
-smooth (u.m.)
-sweeping (u.m.)
weaver
-weaving (u.m.)
web
woven
carpo (c.f.)
-olecranal
rest one word
carriage-making (u.m.)
carrot
-colored (u.m.)
head (nonliteral)
juice
top (nonliteral)
carry
all (n., u.m.)
around (n., u.m.)
back (n., u.m.)
forward (n.)
-in (n., u.m.)
out (n., u.m.)
over (n., u.m.)
cart
load
wheel (coin)
whip
wright
case
bearer
finding
hammer
harden
load
mated
worker
caser-in
cashflow
cast
away (n., u.m.)
back (n., u.m.)
-by (u.m.)
off (n., u.m.)
out (n., u.m.)
-ridden (u.m.)
-weld (v.)
caster
-off
-out
castlebuilder (nonliteral)
cat
back
beam
bird
call
-eyed (u.m.)
face (n.)
fall
gut
head
hole
hook
-ion
like
nap
nip
-o'-nine-tails
stitch
walk
CAT scan
catch
all (n., u.m.)
-as-catch-can (u.m.)
cry
penny
plate
up (n., u.m.)
weight
word
cater
corner
wauling
cat's
-eye (nonliteral)
-paw (nonliteral)
cattle
#boat

feed
-raising (u.m.)
yak
cauliflower
-eared (u.m.)
#ware
causeway
cave
dweller
-dwelling (u.m.)
#fish
-in (n., u.m.)
cease-fire (n., u.m.)
cedar-colored (u.m.)
celi (c.f.)
all one word
celio (c.f.)
all one word
cell
cement
-covered (u.m.)
mason
-temper (v.)
census
#taker
-taking
center
#field (sports)
head (printing)
line
most
piece
-second
centi (c.f.)
all one word
centimeter-gram-second
centri (c.f.)
all one word
centro (c.f.)
all one word
cephalo (c.f.)
all one word
cerato (c.f.)
all one word
cerebro (c.f.)
-ocular
rest one word
certificate holder
cervico (c.f.)
-occipital
-orbicular
rest one word
cess
pipe
pit
pool
chaffcutter
chain
#belt
-driven (u.m.)
#gang
stitch
chair
fast
mender
person
-shaped (u.m.)
warmer
chalk
cutter
line
-white (u.m.)
chamber
maid
woman
changeover
chapfallen
chapelgoing
char
broiler
coal
pit
woman
charge
#book
off (n., u.m.)
out (n., u.m.)
chartbook
chattermark
cheapskate
check
bite
forger
hook
-in (n., u.m.)
list
mark
nut
off (n., u.m.)
out (n., u.m.)
passer (n.)
point
rack
rail
rein
ring
roll
rope
row
sheet
strap
string
up (n., u.m.)
washer
weigher
writer
checker
-in
-off
-out
-up
cheek
bone
strap
cheerleader
cheese
burger
cake
cloth
curd
cutter
head
lip
parer
plate
chemico (c.f.)
all one word
chemo (c.f.)
all one word
cherry
-colored (u.m.)
stone (nonliteral)
#stone (literal)
chestnut
-colored (u.m.)
-red (u.m.)
chicken
bill
-billed (u.m.)
#breast
breasted
#coop
#farm
feed
heart
pox
#yard
chief
#justice
-justiceship
#mate
child
bearing
bed
birth
care
crowing
hood
kind
life
-minded (u.m.)

ridden
#support
wife
chill-cast (u.m., v.)
chin
band
-bearded (u.m.)
-chin
cloth
cough
-high (u.m.)
rest
strap
china
-blue (u.m.)
#shop
ware
Chinatown
chipmunk
chiro (c.f.)
all one word
chisel
-cut (u.m.)
-edged (u.m.)
#maker
chitchat
chitter-chatter
chloro (c.f.)
all one word
chock
ablock
-full (u.m.)
chocolate
-brown (u.m.)
-coated (u.m.)
#maker
choir
boy
#master
choke
bore
chain
damp
out (n., u.m.)
point
strap
chole (c.f.)
all one word
chondro (c.f.)
-osseous
rest one word
chop
-chop
stick
chowchow
Christ
-given (u.m.)
-inspired (u.m.)
like
chromo (c.f.)
all one word
chrono (c.f.)
all one word
chuck
hole
plate
wagon
church
#choir
goer
like
work
yard
churn
-butted (u.m.)
milk
cigar
case
cutter
-shaped (u.m.)
cigarette
#holder
#maker
-making (u.m.)
cine (c.f.)
all one word
circuitbreaker
circum (pref.)
arctic, pacific, etc.
-Saturnal, etc.
rest one word
cirro (c.f.)
all one word
cis (pref.)
alpine
atlantic
-trans (u.m.)
rest one word
city
-born (u.m.)
-bred (u.m.)
folk
#man
scape
clam
bake
shell
clampdown (n., u.m.)
clap
net
trap
clasphook
class
book
-conscious (u.m.)
#consciousness
#day
work
claw
bar
-footed (u.m.)
hammer
hatchet
-tailed (u.m.)
clay
bank
-colored (u.m.)
pan
pit
works
clean
-cut (u.m.)
handed
out (n., u.m.)
-shaved (u.m.)
-smelling (u.m.)
up (n., u.m.)
clear
cole
-cut (u.m.)
cut (forestry) (n., v.)
-eyed (u.m.)
headed
-sighted (u.m.)
up (n., u.m.)
wing
clearinghouse
cleft
-footed (u.m.)
-graft (v.)
client/server
cliff
dweller
-dwelling (u.m.)
hanger
side
top
-worn (u.m.)
clinch-built (u.m.)
clink-clank
clinker-built (u.m.)
clip
-clop
-edged (u.m.)
sheet
clipper-built (u.m.)
cloak
-and-dagger (n., u.m.)

room
clock
case
face
-minded (u.m.)
setter
#speed
watcher
close
bred
-connected (u.m.)
cross
-cut (u.m.)
down (n.)
-fertilize (v.)
fisted
handed
-knit
minded
mouthed
out (n., u.m.)
up (n., u.m.)
closed
-circuit (u.m.)
#end
#shop
cloth-backed (u.m.)
clothes
bag
basket
brush
#closet
horse
pin
line
press
rack
#tree
cloud
base
burst
cap
-hidden (u.m.)
clover
bloom
leaf
seed
sick
club
#car
foot
hand
haul
mobile
ridden
room
root
-shaped (u.m.)
co (pref.)
-op
exist, operate, etc.
processor
rest one word
coach
-and-four
builder
whip
coal
bag
bed
bin
-black (u.m.)
breaker
#car
dealer
digger
-faced (u.m.)
hole
-laden (u.m.)
#loader
#mine
#oil
pit
rake
sack (astron. only)
shed
ship
#tar
#truck
yard
coastside
coat
hanger
rack
tailed
cob
head
meal
shed
web
cock
bill
brain
crow
eye
fight
head
pit
#robin
spur
sure
-tailed (u.m.)
up (n., u.m.)
cockleshell
cockscomb
cod
bank
fishing
head
#liver
piece
pitchings
smack
code
#name
-named (u.m.)
coffee
break
cake
-colored (u.m.)
-growing (u.m.)
pot
room
cofferdam
cogwheel
coin-operated (u.m.)
cold
blooded
-chisel (v.)
cuts
-draw (v.)
finch
-flow (v.)
-forge (v.)
frame
-hammer (v.)
-hammered (u.m.)
pack
-press (v.)
-roll (v.)
-rolled (u.m.)
-short (u.m.)
-shortness
-shoulder (v.)
type (printing)
#war
#wave
-work (v.)
cole
seed
slaw
coli (c.f.)
all one word
collar
bag
band
bone
colo (c.f.)
all one word
color
bearer

blind
#blindness
fast
-free (u.m.)
#line
type (printing) (n.)
-washed (u.m.)
comb-toothed (u.m.)
come
-along (tool)
back (n., u.m.)
-between (n.)
down (n.)
-off (n., u.m.)
-on (n., u.m.)
-out (n.)
-outer
uppance
comic#book
command
-line
#prompt
commander#in #chief
common
-carrier
#law
place
#sense (n.)
sense (u.m.)
weal
wealth
companionship
compressed#file
comptime
cone
-shaped (u.m.)
speaker
conference#room
Congressman#at #Large

contra (pref.)
-acting
-approach
-ion
rest one word
cook
book
off (n., u.m.)
out (n., u.m.)
shack
stove
coolheaded
cooped
-in (u.m.)
-up (u.m.)
cop
#out (v.)
out (n.)
copper
-bottomed (u.m.)
-colored (u.m.)
head
-headed (u.m.)
#mine
nose
plate
-plated (u.m.)
smith
works
copy
cat
cutter
desk
#editor
fitter
holding
reader
right
writer
coral
-beaded (u.m.)
-red (u.m.)

cork
-lined (u.m.)
screw
corn
bin
bread
cake
cob
cracker
crib
crusher
cutter
dodger
-fed (u.m.)
husk
loft
meal
#pone
stalk
starch
corner
bind
post
corpsmember
cost
#effective (n.)
-effectiveness
wise
costo (c.f.)
all one word
cotton
-clad (u.m.)
-covered (u.m.)
-growing (u.m.)
#mill
mouth (snake)
packer
picker, ing
seed
sick
countdown (n., u.m.)
counter
#check (banking)
#septum
-off
act, propaganda, top, etc.
as combining form, one word
country
-born (u.m.)
-bred (u.m.)
folk
people
side
wide
county
#seat
wide
court
bred
-martial
ship
cousin
hood
-in-law
cover
alls
let
side
up (n., u.m.)
cow
barn
bell
catcher
-eyed (u.m.)
gate
hand
herd
hide
hitch
lick
path
pen
#pony

pox
puncher
shed
sucker
crab
cake
catcher
eater
faced
hole
meat
stick
crack
down (n., u.m.)
#house
jaw
pot
-the-whip (n., u.m.)
up (n., u.m.)
cradle
side
#snatcher
song
cranio (c.f.)
all one word
crank
case
-driven (u.m.)
pin
pit
shaft
crapehanger
crashdive (v.)
crazy
bone
cat
cream
cake
-colored (u.m.)
creditworthiness
creek
bed
side
creep
hole
mouse
crepe#de#chine
crestfallen
crew
cut
member
cribstrap
crime
fighter
solver
wave
crisscross
crook
all one word
crooked
-foot (n.)
-legged (u.m.)
-nosed (u.m.)
crop
-bound (u.m.)
-haired (u.m.)
head
mark
-year
cross
-appeal
arm
band
bar
beam
bearer
bedded
belt
bench
-bidding
bill (bird)
#bill (legal)
bind
bolt
bond
bones
bred
breed
-bridge (v.)
-brush (v.)
-carve (v.)
-channel (u.m.)
-check
-claim
-compound (v.)
-connect (v.)
-country (u.m.)
-cultivate (v.)
current
-curve (math.) (n.)
cut
-date (v.)
-drain (v.)
-dye (v.)
-dyeing (n.)
-examine (v.)
-eye (n., u.m.)
-eyed (u.m.)
fall
feed
-fertile (u.m.)
-fertilize (v.)
-fiber (u.m.)
file
fire
flow
foot
-grained (u.m.)
hair
hand
hatch
haul
head
-immunity
-index (u.m.)
-interrogate (v.)
-interrogatory
-invite (v.)
legged
legs
-level (v.)
-license (v.)
lift (v.)
lock
lots
mark
member
patch
path
plow (v.)
-pollinate (v.)
-purpose (n.)
-question
rail
-reaction
-refer (v.)
-reference
road
row
-service
-shaft
-slide
-staff
-sterile
-stitch
-stone
-stratification
-sue (v.)
-surge (v.)
talk
tie
town
track
trail
tree
under (n., u.m.)
-vote
walk
web
wind
word

crow
bait
bar
foot
crowd
funding
sourcing
crownbar
crow's
-foot (nonliteral)
-nest (nonliteral)
crybaby
crypto (c.f.)
-Christian, etc.
rest one word
crystal
-clear (u.m.)
-girded (u.m.)
-smooth (u.m.)
cubbyhole
cumulo (c.f.)
all one word
cup
bearer
cake
ful
head
curb
side
stoner
cure-all (n., u.m.)
curly
head
locks (n.)
currycomb
cussword
custom
-built (u.m.)
-made (u.m.)
-tailored (u.m.)
cut
away (n., u.m.)
back (n., u.m.)
glass
-in (n., u.m.)
off (n., u.m.)
out (n., u.m.)
rate (u.m.)
throat
-toothed (u.m.)
-under (u.m.)
-up (n., u.m.)
cutter
-built (u.m.)
-down
head
-off
-out
-rigged (u.m.)
-up
cuttlebone
cyano (c.f.)
all one word
cyber
bullying
security
cyclecar
cyclo (c.f.)
-olefin
rest one word
cysto (c.f.)
all one word
cyto (c.f.)
all one word

D

D
-Day
-major
-plus-4-day
dairy
-fed (u.m.)
-made (u.m.)
daisy#chain
damp
proofing
-stained (u.m.)
damping-off (n., u.m.)
dancehall
danger#line
dare
-all (n., u.m.)
devil
say
dark
-eyed (u.m.)
horse (nonliteral)
room (n.)
-skinned (u.m.)
dash
plate
wheel
data
bank
base
set
date
lined
mark
daughter-in-law
dawn
-gray (u.m.)
streak
day
beam
bed
break
-bright (u.m.)
care
dream
-fly (aviation) (v.)
-flying (u.m.)
going
lighted
lit
long (u.m.)
mark
side
star
-to-day (u.m.)
worker
de (pref.)
-air
icer
-ink
-ion
centralize, energize, etc.
rest one word
dead
-alive
beat (n.)
born
-burn (v.)
#center
-cold (u.m.)
-dip (v.)
-drunk (u.m.)
-ender
eye (n.)
-eyed (u.m.)
fall
head
-heated (u.m.)
-heater
-heavy (u.m.)
latch
#load
lock
pan
-roast (v.)
weight (n., u.m.)
wood
death
bed
blow
day
-divided (u.m.)
-doom (v.)
#house
-struck (u.m.)

trap
watch
-weary (u.m.)
decision
#making (n.)
-making (u.m., v.)
deckhand
deep
-affected (u.m.)
-cut (u.m.)
-felt (u.m.)
-freeze (u.m., v.)
-frying (u.m.)
going
-grown (u.m.)
-laid (u.m.)
most
mouthed
-rooted (u.m.)
#sea
-seated (u.m.)
-set (u.m.)
-sunk (u.m.)
-voiced (u.m.)
water (u.m.)
deer
drive (n.)
-eyed (u.m.)
food
herd
horn
hound
meat
stalker
stand
tick
dehydr(o) (c.f.)
all one word
demi (pref.)
-Christian, etc.
-incognito
rest one word
dermato (c.f.)
all one word
desk
#room
top (n., u.m.)
dessert
#fork
#knife
spoon
deutero (c.f.)
all one word
devil
-devil
dog (a marine)
-inspired (u.m.)
-ridden (u.m.)
dew
beam
cap
-clad (u.m.)
claw
damp
-drenched (u.m.)
drop
fall
-fed (u.m.)
-laden (u.m.)
lap
point
dextro (c.f.)
all one word
di (pref.)
all one word
dia (pref.)
all one word
dialog#box
dial-up
diamond
back
-backed (u.m.)
-shaped (u.m.)
diazo (c.f.)
-oxide
rest one word
dice
cup
play
die
-away (u.m.)
back
case
-cast (u.m., v.)
caster
-cut (u.m., v.)
cutter
hard (n., u.m.)
head
#proof (philately) (n.)
setter
sinker
-square (u.m.)
stock
diesel
-driven (u.m.)
-electric (u.m.)
dillydally
dim
-lighted (u.m.)
lit
out (n., u.m.)
diner-out
ding
bat
dong
dining#room
dinitro (c.f.)
#spray
rest one word
dip
-dye (v.)
-grained (u.m.)
head
stick
dipper-in
direct
-connected (u.m.)
-indirect
direction-finding (u.m.)
dirt
-cheap (u.m.)
fast
-incrusted (u.m.)
plate
dirty
-faced (u.m.)
-minded (u.m.)
#work
dis (pref.)
all one word
disc drive
dish
cloth
#cover
pan
rack
rag
#towel
washer
disk
jockey
pack
plow
-shaped (u.m.)
ditch
bank
digger
rider
side
dive
-bomb (v.)
#bomber
do
-all (n., u.m.)
-gooder
-little (n., u.m.)
-nothing (n., u.m.)

dock
hand
head
side
worker
dog
bite
-bitten (u.m.)
breeder
cart
catcher
#days
-drawn (u.m.)
-ear (v.)
-eared (u.m.)
face (soldier)
-faced (u.m.)
fall
fight
#food
-headed (u.m.)
hole
leg
#owner
race
shore
sled
-tired (u.m.)
tooth
-toothed (u.m.)
trick
trot
watch
-weary (u.m.)
doll
face
-faced (u.m.)
dollyhead
donkey
back
-drawn (u.m.)
-eared (u.m.)
doomsday
door
bed
bell
case
check
frame
head
jamb
keeper
knob
knocker
mat
nail
#opener
plate
post
-shaped (u.m.)
sill
step
stop
dope
fiend
passer
pusher
sheet
dorsi (c.f.)
all one word
dorso (c.f.)
-occipital
rest one word
dot
-matrix
#pitch
double
-barrel (n., u.m.)
-barreled (u.m.)
-bitt (v.)
-breasted (u.m.)
-charge (v.)
check (n., v.)
checked (u.m., v.)
-chinned (u.m.)
-click
cross (nonliteral)
deal (v.)
-decker
dipper (nonliteral)
-duty (u.m.)
-dye (v.)
-edged (u.m.)
-ender
-entendre
handed
-headed (u.m.)
header
-jointed
-leaded (u.m.)
-quick (u.m.)
-sided
#space (v.)
#take
talk
tone (printing)
tree
-trouble
-up (u.m., v.)
#work
dough
boy
-colored (u.m.)
mixer
nut
down
beat
by
cast
check
coast
come
-covered (u.m.)
crier
cry
curved
cut
dale
draft
drag
face
fall
feed
filled
flow
fold
grade
gradient
growth
hanging
haul
hearted
hill
lead
load
lock (n.)
look
most
payment
pour
rate
right
river
rush
shore
side
sitting
slip
slope
-soft (u.m.)
spout
stage
stairs
state
stream
street
stroke
sun (adv., u.m.)
swing
take
throw

thrust
time
town
trampling
trend
trodden
turn
valley
weigh
weight
wind

draft
age (allowance)
#age
-exempt (u.m.)

drag
bar
bolt
net
pipe
rope
saw
staff
wire

dragger
-down
-in
-out
-up

dragon
-eyed (u.m.)
fly
#piece

drain
cleaner
pipe
plug
tile

drainage
#area
#basin
way

draw
-arch (n.)
arm
back
bar
beam
bench
bolt
bore
bridge
cut
down (n., u.m.)
file
gate
gear
glove
head
horse
knife
knot
link
loom
net
off (n., u.m.)
out (n., u.m.)
pin
plate
point
sheet
span
stop
string
tongs
tube

drawer
-down
-in
-off
-out

drawing
#board
#room

dream
-haunted (u.m.)
land
lore
world

dredge#net
dressup (n., u.m.)
dressing#room

drift
#boat
bolt
meter
-mining (u.m.)
#net
pin
wind

drill
case
-like
stock

drip
cock
-drip
-dry (u.m., v.)
sheet
stick

drive
away (n., u.m.)
belt
bolt
by (n., u.m.)
cap
head
-in (n., u.m.)
pipe
screw
#shaft
way

drop
away (n., u.m.)
bolt
cloth
-down
-forge (v.)
front
hammer
head
kick
leaf (n., u.m.)
leg
off (n., u.m.)
out (n., u.m.)
sonde
stitch

drug
-addicted (u.m.)
mixer
passer
pusher
seller
#user

drum
beat
fire
head
stick
-up (n., u.m.)

dry
-burnt (u.m.)
#cell
clean
-cure (v.)
dock
-dye (v.)
-farm (v.)
farming (n., u.m.)
gulch (nonliteral)
lot
-pack (u.m., v.)
-rotted (u.m.)
-salt (v.)
wash

duck
bill

-billed (u.m.)
bore
#breast
foot (tool)
-footed (u.m.)
pin
pond
walk
due
-in (n., u.m.)
out (n., u.m.)
duffelbag
dug
out (n.)
-up (u.m.)
dull
-edged (u.m.)
head
-looking (u.m.)
-witted (u.m.)
dumdum
dumb
bell
waiter
dump
car
cart
site
duo (c.f.)
all one word
dust
bag
bin
brush
cloth
-covered (u.m.)
fall
-gray (u.m.)
-laden (u.m.)
pan
storm
duty
bound
-free (u.m.)
dwelling#house
dye
mixer
stuff
works
dys (pref.)
all one word

E

E-minor
e
Book
-commerce
file
Government
Library
mail
eagle
#eye
-eyed (u.m.)
ear
ache
cap
drop
drum
flap
guard
hole
lap
lobe
mark
#muff
phone
-piercing (u.m.)
plug
ring
screw
shot
sore
splitting
tab
wax
wig
witness
earth
bank
born
-bred (u.m.)
fall
fast
-fed (u.m.)
fill
grubber
#house
kin
lit
mover
nut
quake
-shaking (u.m.)
slide
-stained (u.m.)
wall
east
bound
-central (u.m.)
going
-northeast
#side
-sider
-southeast
Eastertime
easy
going
mark (n.)
-rising (u.m.)
-spoken (u.m.)
eavesdrop
ebbtide
edge
#plane
shot
ways
wise
eel
cake
catcher
fare
pot
pout
skin
spear
egg
beater (all meanings)
cup
eater
fruit
head (nonliteral)
hot (n.)
nog
plant
-shaped (u.m.)
shell
-white (u.m.)
eight
-angled (u.m.)
#ball
fold
penny (nail)
-ply (u.m.)
score
-wheeler
elbowchair
elder
#brother
-leaved (u.m.)
electro (c.f.)
-optics
-osmosis
-ultrafiltration
rest one word
embryo (c.f.)
all one word
empty
handed
-looking (u.m.)
en
#banc

#gros
#route
encephalo (c.f.)
all one word
end
-all (n., u.m.)
bell
game
-measure (v.)
ender
-on
-up
endo (c.f.)
all one word
engine
#shop
-sized (u.m.)
work
#worker
#yard
entero (c.f.)
all one word
entry
#book
way
envelope
#holder
#maker
epi (pref.)
all one word
equi (c.f.)
-gram-molar
rest one word
ere
long
now
errorproof
erythro (c.f.)
all one word
even
glow
handed
minded
-numbered (u.m.)
song
-tempered (u.m.)
ever
-abiding (u.m.)
bearing
blooming
-constant (u.m.)
-fertile (u.m.)
glade
going
green
lasting
more
-normal (u.m.)
-present (u.m.)
-ready (u.m.)
sporting (biol.)
which
every
day (n., u.m.)
#day (each day)
one (all)
#one (distributive)
#time
evil
doer
#eye
-eyed (u.m.)
-faced (u.m.)
-looking (u.m.)
minded (u.m.)
sayer
speaker
wishing
ex
#cathedra
cathedral
communicate
-Governor
#libris
#officio
#post#facto
#rights
-serviceman
-trader
-vice-president
extra
-alimentary
-American
bold
-Britannic
-condensed (u.m.)
curricular
-fine (u.m.)
hazardous
judicial
-large (u.m.)
-long (u.m.)
marginal
mural
ordinary
polar
-strong (u.m.)
territorial
vascular
eye
#appeal
ball
bank
bar
blink
-blurred (u.m.)
bolt
brow
-conscious (u.m.)
cup
flap
glance
glass
hole
lash
lens
lid
mark
-minded (u.m.)
#opener
peep
pit
point
service
shade
shield
shot
sick
sight
sore
spot
-spotted (u.m.)
stalk
strain
string
tooth
wash
#weariness
wink
witness

F

F
-flat
-horn
-sharp
fable
#book
teller
face
-arbor (v.)
cloth
-harden (v.)
-hardened (u.m.)
lifting
mark
-off (n.)
-on (n., u.m.)
plate
up (n., u.m.)
fact
book

finding
sheet
fade
away (n., u.m.)
-in (n., u.m.)
out (n., u.m.)
fail-safe
faint
hearted
-voiced (u.m.)
fair
ground
-lead (n., u.m.)
minded
play
-skinned (u.m.)
#trade
fairy
folk
hood
tale
faithbreaker
fall
away (n., u.m.)
back (n., u.m.)
#guy
-in (n., u.m.)
out (n., u.m.)
-plow (v.)
-sow (v.)
trap
fallow#land
false
-bottomed (u.m.)
#face
-faced (u.m.)
hood
-tongued (u.m.)
fame
-crowned (u.m.)
-thirsty (u.m.)
fan
back
bearer
#belt
fare
fold
foot
-jet
-leaved (u.m.)
marker
-shaped (u.m.)
-tailed (u.m.)
fancy
-free (u.m.)
-loose (u.m.)
-woven (u.m.)
-wrought (u.m.)
far
-aloft (u.m.)
away (n., u.m.)
-borne (u.m.)
-distant (u.m.)
-eastern (u.m.)
-famed (u.m.)
fetched
flung (u.m.)
gone
-off (u.m.)
#out
-reaching (u.m.)
seeing
-seen (u.m.)
-set (u.m.)
sight
farm
-bred (u.m.)
hand
hold
owner
people
place
stead
worker
fashion
-led (u.m.)
#piece (naut.)
#plate
-setting (u.m.)
fast
-anchored (u.m.)
back
-dyed (u.m.)
going
hold
-moving (u.m.)
-read (v.)
-reading (u.m.)
fat
back
-bellied (u.m.)
-free (u.m.)
-soluble (u.m.)
father
-confessor
-in-law
land
fault
finder
line
slip
faux#pas
fax
-and-voice#
mailbox
#modem
-on-demand
fear
-free (u.m.)
nought
-pursued (u.m.)
-shaken (u.m.)
feather
bed (v.)
bedding
bone
brain
edge
-footed (u.m.)
head
-leaved (u.m.)
stitch
-stitched (u.m.)
-stitching
-tongue (v.)
weight
wing (moth)
fed-up (u.m.)
feeble
-bodied (u.m.)
minded
feed
back (n., u.m.)
bag
bin
box
crusher
cutter
head
lot
mixer
pipe
rack
store
stuff
feeder
-in
-up
fellow
craft
ship
rest two words
felt
cutter
-lined (u.m.)
packer
fence
post
#row
fern
-clad (u.m.)
leaf

-leaved (u.m.)
ferro (c.f.)
-carbon-titanium
-uranium
rest one word
ferry
boat
#car
#slip
fever
less
-stricken (u.m.)
trap
-warm (u.m.)
fiber
-faced (u.m.)
glass
#optics
stitch
Fiberglas
(copyright)
fibro (c.f.)
-osteoma
rest one word
fickleminded
fiddle
back
-faddle
head
-shaped (u.m.)
stick
string
field
ball
glass
goal
-strip
fierce
-eyed (u.m.)
-looking (u.m.)
fiery
-flaming (u.m.)
-hot (u.m.)
-red (u.m.)
-tempered (u.m.)
fig
bar
eater
leaf
shell
figure
head
-of-eight (u.m.)
#work (printing)
file
card
-hard (u.m.)
name
setter
-soft (u.m.)
fill
-in (n., u.m.)
out (n., u.m.)
-up (n., u.m.)
filler
cap
-in
-out
-up
film
cutter
goer
going
#paper
slide
strip
-struck (u.m.)
fin
back
-shaped (u.m.)
fine
-cut (u.m., v.)
-draw (v.)
-drawn (u.m.)
-featured (u.m.)
-looking (u.m.)
-set (u.m.)
finger
breadth
-cut (u.m.)
hold
hole
hook
mark
nail
parted
post
print
shell
space
spin
stall
tip
fire
arm
back (n.)
ball
bell
bolt
bomb
brand
brat
break
brick
-burnt (u.m.)
-clad (u.m.)
coat
cracker
crest
-cure (v.)
damp
#drill
-eater
fall
fang
fighter
guard
-hardened (u.m.)
horse
hose
lit
pit
place
plow
plug
-polish (v.)
power
proof
-red (u.m.)
-resistant (u.m.)
safe
side
spout
trap
truck
wall
warden
firm
-footed (u.m.)
-set (u.m.)
-up (n., u.m.)
first
#aid
-aider
-born (u.m.)
-class (u.m.)
comer
hand (u.m.)
-made (u.m.)
-named (u.m.)
-nighter
-rate (u.m.)
fish
back
bed
-bellied (u.m.)
bolt
bone
bowl
cake
eater
eye

-eyed (u.m.)
fall
#farm
-fed (u.m.)
food
garth
hook
-joint (v.)
kill
#ladder
meal
mouth
plate
pond
pool
pot
pound
trap
weir
works

fisher
folk
man
people

fishyback (n., u.m.)

fit
out (n.)
strip

five
bar
fold
-ply (u.m.)
-pointed (u.m.)
-reeler
score

flag
bearer
pole
post
-raising (u.m.)
ship
-signal (v.)
staff
stick

flame
-colored (u.m.)
-cut (v.)
out (n.)
proof
-retardant
thrower

flannelmouth

flap
cake
doodle
-eared (u.m.)
jack

flare
back (n., u.m.)
out (n., u.m.)
path
up (n., u.m.)

flash
back (n., u.m.)
bulb
card
gun
lamp
pan
point

flat
back (bookbinding)
bed (printing)
-bottomed (u.m.)
car
-compound (v.)
fold
foot (n.)
hat
head
iron
nose
out (n., u.m.)
-rolled (u.m.)
sawn
top
-topped (u.m.)
woods

flax
drop
-leaved (u.m.)
-polled (u.m.)
seed

flea
bite
-bitten (u.m.)
trap

fleet
foot
-footed (u.m.)
wing

flesh
brush
hook
-pink (u.m.)
pot
#wound

fleur-de-lis
flextime

flight
crew
-hour
path
-test (v.)

flimflam

flip
-flap
-flop
-up (n., u.m.)

flood
cock
flow
gate
lamp
lighting
mark
#plain
tide
wall
water

floor
beam
cloth
head
lamp
mat
mop
#show
space
stain
walker
#wax
-waxing (u.m.)

flophouse
floppy#disc

flour
bag
bin
#mill
sack
#sifter

flow
chart
meter
off (n., u.m.)
sheet
through (n., u.m.)

flower
bed
bud
-crowned (u.m.)
#grower
-hung (u.m.)
#piece
pot
-scented (u.m.)
#shop

flue-cure (v.)

fluid
-compressed (u.m.)

extract (pharm.) (n.)
glycerate
fluo (c.f.)
all one word
fluoro (c.f.)
all one word
flush
-cut (u.m.)
-decked (u.m.)
-decker
gate
fluvio (c.f.)
all one word
fly
away
back
ball
-bitten (u.m.)
blow
blown
-by-night (n., u.m.)
catcher
eater
-fish (v.)
-fisher
-fisherman
#fishing
flap
-free (u.m.)
leaf
paper
sheet
speck
-specked (u.m.)
tier
trap
weight
wheel
winch
flying
#boat
#fish
foam
bow
-crested (u.m.)
-white (u.m.)
fog
bound
bow
dog
eater
-hidden (u.m.)
horn
#light
-ridden (u.m.)
fold
-in
up (n., u.m.)
folk
#dance
lore
song
follow
-on
through (n., u.m.)
up (n., u.m.)
follower-up
food
-fasted (u.m.)
-fasting (v.)
packer
store
stuff
foolhardy
foolscap
foot
-and-mouth (u.m.)
ball
band
bath
blower
board
brake
breadth
bridge
candle
fall
-free (u.m.)
gear
-grain
hill
hold
lambert
licker
light(s)
lining
locker
loose
mark
note
pad
path
pick
plate
-pound
-pound-second
print
race
rail
rest
rope
scald
-second
slogger
sore
stalk
stall
step
stick
stock
stool
-ton
walk
wall
-weary (u.m.)
worn
for (pref.)
all one word
fore
-age
-and-aft (n., u.m.)
-and-after (n.)
-edge
-end
-exercise
word
rest one word
forest
-clad (u.m.)
-covered (u.m.)
#land
side
fork
head
lift
-pronged (u.m.)
tail
-tailed (u.m.)
form
fitting
#work (printing)
forth
coming
right
with
fortune
#hunter
teller
forty-niner
foul
#line
-looking (u.m.)
mouthed
-spoken (u.m.)
-tongued (u.m.)
up (n., u.m.)
fountainhead

four
-bagger
-eyed (u.m.)
flusher
fold
-footed (u.m.)
-in-hand (n., u.m.)
-masted (u.m.)
-master
penny (nail)
-ply (u.m.)
score
some
square
-wheeler
fox
-faced (u.m.)
hole
hound
#hunting
skinned
tailed
trot
fracto (c.f.)
all one word
frame-up
free
booter
born
drop
-for-all (n., u.m.)
-grown (u.m.)
hand (drawing)
handed
hold
lance
loader
-minded
masonry
#post
-spoken (u.m.)
standing (u.m.)
thinker
trader
wheel (u.m., v.)
wheeler (n.)
#will (n.)
will (u.m.)
freedom#fighter
freeze
down (n., u.m.)
out (n., u.m.)
up (n., u.m.)
freight
#house
-mile
#room
#train
fresh
-looking (u.m.)
-painted (u.m.)
water
frog
belly
-eyed (u.m.)
face
man
mouth
nose
pond
tongue (medicine)
front
-end (u.m.)
-focused (u.m.)
runner
stall
-wheel (u.m.)
fronto (c.f.)
-occipital
-orbital
rest one word
frost
bite
bow
-free (u.m.)
-hardy (u.m.)
-heaving (u.m.)
-killed (u.m.)
lamp
line
fruit
cake
#fly
growing
#shop
stalk
frying#pan
fuel
#line
#oil
full
back
-bellied (u.m.)
blood
-bound (u.m.)
-duplex
face
-fashioned (u.m.)
-flowering (u.m.)
-grown (u.m.)
-handed (u.m.)
-headed (u.m.)
-lined (u.m.)
#load
mouth
-strength (u.m.)
-text
-time (u.m.)
fundraising
funlover
funnel
form
-shaped (u.m.)
fur
-clad (u.m.)
coat
-lined (u.m.)
skin
-trimmed (u.m.)
fuse
box
#gauge
plug

G

G
-major
-man
-minor
-sharp
gabfest
gad
about (n., u.m.)
fly
gaff-topsail
gag
-check (v.)
#order
root
#rule
gain
say
-sharing (u.m.)
galact(o) (c.f.)
all one word
gallbladder
galley#proof (printing)
galvano (c.f.)
all one word
game
bag
cock
gang
boss
plank
saw
garnet-brown (u.m.)

gas
bag
bomb
-driven (u.m.)
field
-fired (u.m.)
firing
fitter
-heated (u.m.)
-laden (u.m.)
lamp
lighted
line (auto)
#line (queue)
lock
#main
#mask
meter
works
gastro (c.f.)
-omental
rest one word
gate
house
keeper
leg (u.m.)
pin
post
tender
works
gauge pin
gear
box
case
-driven (u.m.)
fitter
-operated (u.m.)
set
shift
wheel
gelatin
-coated (u.m.)
-making (u.m.)
gelatino (c.f.)
bromide
chloride
gem
cutter
-set (u.m.)
#stone
genito (c.f.)
all one word
gentle
folk
-looking (u.m.)
man
-mannered (u.m.)
mouthed
-spoken (u.m.)
woman
geo (c.f.)
all one word
germ-free (u.m.)
gerrymander
get
away (n., u.m.)
#off
-together (n., u.m.)
up (n., u.m.)
ghost
-haunted (u.m.)
write (v.)
gilt-edge (u.m.)
ginger
#ale
bread
-colored (u.m.)
snap
spice
give
-and-take (n., u.m.)
away (n., u.m.)
glacio (c.f.)
all one word
glass
blower
#ceiling
cutter
-eater
-eyed (u.m.)
-hard (u.m.)
house
works
glauco (c.f.)
all one word
glidepath
globetrotter
glosso (c.f.)
all one word
glow
lamp
meter
gluc(o) (c.f.)
all one word
glue
pot
stock
glycero (c.f.)
all one word
glyco (c.f.)
all one word
go
-ahead (n., u.m.)
-around (n., u.m.)
-as-you-please (u.m.)
-back (n., u.m.)
-between (n.)
by (n.)
cart
-devil (n.)
-getter
-getting (n., u.m.)
-off (n., u.m.)
goal
post
#setter
goat
-bearded (u.m.)
-eyed (u.m.)
herd
goat's
-hair
-horn
God
-conscious (u.m.)
-fearing (u.m.)
-forsaken (u.m.)
-given (u.m.)
head
-man
-ordained (u.m.)
-sent (u.m.)
-sped (u.m.)
speed
-taught (u.m.)
god
child
daughter
father
head
hood
less
mother
parent
send
ship
son
sonship
goggle-eyed (u.m.)
goings-on
gold
beater
brick (shirker)
#brick (of real gold)
-bright (u.m.)
-brown (u.m.)
digger
#dust
-filled (u.m.)

foil
-inlaid (u.m.)
leaf
plate (v.)
-plated (u.m.)
-plating (u.m.)
smithing
-wrought (u.m.)
golden
-fingered (u.m.)
-headed (u.m.)
good
-bye
-for-nothing (n., u.m.)
-looker
-looking (u.m.)
-natured (u.m.)
#will (kindness)
will (salable asset)
goose
bone
bumps
-cackle
#egg
-eyed (u.m.)
flesh
-footed (u.m.)
herd
mouth
neck
pimples
rump
step
wing
gospel
like
-true (u.m.)
Government (U.S. or foreign)
-in-exile
-owned (u.m.)
wide
governmentwide (State, city, etc.)
grab
-all (n., u.m.)
#bag
hook
rope
grade
finder
mark
grain
-cut (u.m.)
field
-laden (u.m.)
mark
sick
gram
-fast (u.m.)
-meter
-molecular
-negative (u.m.)
-positive (u.m.)
grand
aunt
child, etc.
stand
grant-in-aid
grape
fruit
#juice
-leaved (u.m.)
seed
stalk
vine
graph
alloy
#paper
grapho (c.f.)
all one word
grass
-clad (u.m.)
-covered (u.m.)
cutter
flat
-green (u.m.)
hop
nut
plot
roots (nonliteral)
#roots (literal)
widow
grave
clothes
digger
side
stead
gravel
-blind (u.m.)
stone
gray
back (n., u.m.)
beard (n.)
-clad (u.m.)
coat (n.)
-eyed (u.m.)
-haired (u.m.)
head
-headed (u.m.)
out (n., u.m.)
grease
#gun
#pit
proof
great
-aunt
coat
-eared (u.m.)
-grandchild, etc.
-headed (u.m.)
heart
mouthed
green
back (n., u.m.)
belt
(community)
-clad (u.m.)
-eyed (u.m.)
gage (plum)
gill
grocer
horn
keeper
-leaved (u.m.)
sand (geology)
sick
stuff
sward
town (community)
#wood (literal)
wood (forest)
greyhound
grid
iron
lock
griddlecake
grillroom
grip
sack
wheel
gross
-minded (u.m.)
#weight
ground
breaking
hog
mass
nut
path
plot
speed
#water
wave
work
group-connect (v.)
grownup (n., u.m.)
grubstake

guard
house
plate
rail
guest
chamber
house
room
guided-missile (u.m.)
guidepost
guider-in
gum
boil
chewer
digger
drop
-gum
lac
-saline (n.)
shoe
gun
#barrel
bearer
blast
builder
cotton
crew
deck
fight
fire
flint
lock
paper
pit
play
point
powder
rack
-rivet (v.)
runner
shop
shot
-shy (u.m.)
sight
stock
wale
gut
less
string
gutter
blood
-bred (u.m.)
snipe
spout
gymno (c.f.)
all one word
gyneco (c.f.)
all one word
gyro
#horizon
#mechanism
#pelorus
plane, compass, etc.

H

H
-bar
-beam
-bomb
-hour
hack
barrow
hammer
log
saw
hailstorm
hair
band
breadth
brush
-check (n.)
cloth
cut (n.)
do
dresser
-fibered (u.m.)
lock
pin
#ribbon
space (printing)
splitting
spring
streak
stroke (printing)
#trigger
half
-and-half (n., u.m.)
-afraid
-alive
-angry
back (football)
-backed (u.m.)
-baked (u.m.)
-bound (u.m.)
caste
-clear
cock (v.)
cocked (nonliteral)
-dark
#day
deck
-decked (u.m.)
-decker
-feed (v.)
hearted
-hourly (u.m.)
-life
#load
-loaded (u.m.)
-mast
-miler
-monthly (u.m.)
-on (n., u.m.)
pace
penny
-ripe
-shy
-sole (v.)
staff
stitch
-strength (u.m.)
title
tone (printing)
track
-true
-truth
-weekly (u.m.)
-yearly (u.m.)
hallmark
ham
shackle
string
hammer
cloth
dress (v.)
-hard (u.m.)
-harden (v.)
-hardened (u.m.)
head
lock
#thrower
toe
-weld (v.)
-wrought (u.m.)
hand
bag
ball
bank (v.)
barrow
bill
book
-bound (u.m.)
bow
brake
breadth
brush
-built (u.m.)
car

-carry (v.)
cart
-carve (v.)
clap
clasp
-clean (v.)
crank
cuff
-cut (v.)
-embroidered (u.m.)
-fed (v.)
fold
grasp
grenade
grip
guard
gun
-held (u.m.)
-high (u.m.)
hold
hole
-in-hand (u.m.)
kerchief
-knit (v.)
-knitter
laid
-letter (v.)
lift (truck)
liner
made
-me-down (n., u.m.)
mix (v.)
mold (v.)
mower
off (n., u.m.)
out (n., u.m.)
pick (v.)
post
press
print
rail
reading
saw
scrape (v.)
set
shake
spade
spike
splice
split
spring
spun
-stamp (v.)
stand
stitch
stroke
stuff
-tailored (u.m.)
tap
tool
-tooled (u.m.)
-tooling (u.m.)
truck
weave
wheel
worked
woven
write (v.)
written
wrought
hands#free
handlebar
hang
dog
nail
net
out (n., u.m.)
up (n.)
hanger
-back
-on
-up
happy-go-lucky
hara-kiri
harbor
master
side
hard
-and-fast (u.m.)
back (beetle)
-baked (u.m.)
-bitten (u.m)
-boiled (u.m.)
case
copy (n.)
core
#disc
#drive
fist (n.)
handed
hat (n.)
-hit (u.m.)
-looking (u.m.)
mouthed
nose
pan
-pressed (u.m.)
-set (u.m.)
#shell (n.)
ship
spun
stand
tack
top (auto)
ware
-won (u.m.)
#work
-working (u.m.)
wrought
hare
brain
foot
hound
-mad (u.m.)
harness-making (u.m.)
harum-scarum
harvesttime
has-been (n.)
hashmark
hat
band
box
brim
brush
cleaner
pin
rack
rail
stand
#tree
hatchback
hatchet-faced (u.m.)
haul
about (n., u.m.)
away (n., u.m.)
back (n.)
have-not (n., u.m.)
haversack
hawk
bill
-billed (u.m.)
head
-nosed (u.m.)
hawse
hole
pipe
hay
band
cap
cart
cock
#fever
field
fork
lift
loft
market
mow
rack

rake
rick
-scented (u.m.)
seed
stack
wire
hazardous
#waste#site
hazel
-eyed (u.m.)
nut
he-man
head
ache
achy
band
bander
block
cap
chair
cheese
chute
cloth
count
dress
-ender
first
frame
gate
gear
hunter
lamp
ledge
lighting
liner
lock
long
master
mistress
mold
most
note
-on (u.m.)
phone
plate
post
quarters
rail
reach
rest
ring
rope
set
shake
sill
space
spin
spring
stall
stand
start
stick
stock
stream
strong
waiter
wall
wind
header-up
heal-all (n., u.m.)
healthcare
heart
ache
aching
beat
block
blood
break
burn
deep
felt
free (u.m.)
grief
heavy
leaf
-leaved (u.m.)
nut
quake
seed
sick
sore
string
struck
throb
-throbbing (u.m.)
-weary (u.m.)
hearth
rug
warming
heat
drops
#pump
#rash
-resistant (u.m.)
stroke
treat (v.)
-treating (u.m.)
#wave
heaven
bound
-inspired (u.m.)
-sent (u.m.)
heaver
-off
-out
-over
heavy
back
-duty (u.m.)
-eyed (u.m.)
-footed (u.m.)
handed
-looking (u.m.)
-set (u.m.)
#water
weight (n., u.m.)
hecto (c.f.)
all one word
hedge
born
breaker
#fund
hog
hop
pig
row
#trimmer
heel
ball
band
block
cap
fast
grip
pad
path
plate
post
print
ring
stay
strap
tap
helio (c.f.)
all one word
helpmeet
helter-skelter
hema (c.f.)
all one word
hemato (c.f.)
all one word
hemi (pref.)
all one word
hemo (c.f.)
all one word
hemp
seed
string
hemstitch
hen
bill

coop
-feathered (u.m.)
house
pecked
roost
hence
forth
forward
hepato (c.f.)
all one word
hepta (c.f.)
all one word
here
about
after
at
by
from
in
inabove
inafter
inbefore
into
of
on
to
tofore
under
unto
upon
with
herringbone
hetero (c.f.)
-ousia, etc.
rest one word
hexa (c.f.)
all one word
hi-fi
hide
-and-seek (n., u.m.)
away (n., u.m.)
out (n., u.m.)
high
ball
binder
born
bred
brow (nonliteral)
-caliber (u.m.)
-class (u.m.)
-density
flier (n.)
flying (u.m.)
-foreheaded (u.m.)
#frequency
handed
-hat (v.)
jinks
lander
#light (literal)
light (nonlit.)
-minded (u.m.)
-power (u.m.)
-pressure (u.m., v.)
-priced (u.m.)
#proof
-reaching (u.m.)
-rigger (n.)
rise (building)
road
#seas
-speed (u.m.)
stepper
-tension (u.m.)
#tide
-up (u.m.)
#water
higher-up (n.)
hill
culture (farming)
side
top
hind
brain
cast
gut (n.)
head
leg
most
quarter
saddle
sight
wing
hip
bone
mold
shot
hippo (c.f.)
all one word
histo (c.f.)
all one word
hit
-and-miss (u.m.)
-and-run (u.m.)
-or-miss (u.m.)
hitchhiker
hoarfrost
hoary-haired (u.m.)
hob
goblin
nail
nob
hobbyhorse
hockshop
hocus-pocus
hod#carrier
hodgepodge
hog
back
-backed (u.m.)
-faced (u.m.)
fat
frame
hide
nose (machine)
-nosed (u.m.)
pen
sty
-tie (v.)
wash
-wild (u.m.)
hog's-back (geol.)
hogshead
hoistaway (n.)
hold
all (n., u.m.)
back (n., u.m.)
-clear (n., u.m.)
down (n., u.m.)
fast (n., u.m.)
off (n., u.m.)
out (n., u.m.)
up (n., u.m.)
holder
-forth
-on
-up
hole
#in#one
-high (u.m.)
-in-the-wall (n.)
through
hollow
back (bookbinding)
-backed (u.m.)
-eyed (u.m.)
faced
-ground (u.m.)
holo (c.f.)
all one word
holy
#day
stone
home
-baked (u.m.)
body
born

bred
brew
builder
#buyer
comer
coming
-fed (u.m.)
felt
folk
freeze (u.m., v.)
front
furnishings (n.)
going
grown
lander
life
made
maker
owner
#ownership
#page
plate
#rule
seeker
sick
spun
stead
stretch
town
woven

homeo (c.f.)
all one word

homo
#legalis
#sapiens

homo (c.f.)
-ousia, etc.
rest one word

honey
-colored (u.m.)
comb
-cured (u.m.)
dew
drop
eater
-laden (u.m.)
lipped
moon
mouthed
pot
sucker
sweet

honor
bound
#guard
#man

hood
cap
mold
wink

hoof
beat
mark
print
-printed (u.m.)

hook
ladder
nose
-nosed (u.m.)
pin
up (n., u.m.)

hooker
-off
-on
-out
-over
-up

hoopstick

hop
about (n., u.m.)
off (n., u.m.)
scotch
toad

hope#chest

hopper
burn
dozer

horehound

hormono (c.f.)
all one word

horn
bill
blende
blower
-eyed (u.m.)
pipe
stay
tip

hornyhanded

horse
back
breaker
car
cloth
dealer
fair
fight
flesh
hair
head
herd
hide
hoof
-hour
jockey
laugh
meat
mint
play
pond
power-hour
power-year
pox
race
#sense (n.)
shoe
thief
#trade
whip

hot
bed
blood
-blooded (u.m.)
brain
cake
-cold
dog
foot
head (n.)
-mix (u.m.)
pack
patch
plate
-press (v.)
rod (nonliteral)
-roll (v.)
-rolled (u.m.)
spot
-work (v).

hotelkeeper
houndshark
hourglass

house
breaking
broken
builder
#call
cleaner
-cleaning (u.m.)
coat
dress
father
furnishing(s) (n.)
guest
hold
husband
mother
owner
parent
pest
plant
-raising (u.m.)

ridden
top
trailer
wares
warming
wife

how
-do-you-do (n.)
ever
soever

hub
cap
-deep (u.m.)

humankind

humble
bee
-looking (u.m.)
mouthed
-spirited (u.m.)

humdrum

hump
back
-shouldered (u.m.)

humpty-dumpty

hunchback

hundred
fold
-legged (u.m.)
-percenter
-pounder
weight

hung-up (u.m.)

hunger
-mad (u.m.)
-worn (u.m.)

hurly-burly

hush
-hush
#money
up (n., u.m.)

hydro (c.f.)
all one word

hydro#station

hygro (c.f.)
all one word

hyper (pref.)
-Dorian, etc.
linked
text
rest one word

hypo (c.f.)
all one word

hystero (c.f.)
-oophorectomy
-salpingo-oophorectomy
rest one word

I

I
-bar
-beam
-iron
-rail

ice
berg
blind
#blindness
blink
block
bone
breaker
cap
-clad (u.m.)
-cold (u.m.)
-cooled (u.m.)
-covered (u.m.)
#cream
fall
#fishing
floe (island)
flow (current)
-free (u.m.)
maker
melt
pack
plant
plow
quake
#storm
#water

ideo (c.f.)
-unit
rest one word

idle
headed
-looking (u.m.)
-minded (u.m.)

ileo (c.f.)
all one word

ilio (c.f.)
all one word

ill
-advised (u.m.)
-being (n.)
-born (u.m.)
-bred (u.m.)
#breeding (n.)
-doing (n., u.m.)
-fated (u.m.)
-humored (u.m.)
-looking (u.m.)
-treat (v.)
-use (v.)
#will
-wisher
-wishing (u.m.)

in
-and-in (u.m.)
-and-out (u.m.)
-and-outer
-being (u.m.)
-flight (u.m.)
-house
-law (n.)
asmuch, sofar
#re, #rem, #situ, etc.

in (pref.)
active (u.m.)
breeding
depth (u.m.)
hospital (u.m.)
migration (u.m.)
service (u.m.), etc.

inch
-deep (u.m.)
-long (u.m.)
meal
-pound
-ton
worm

index-digest

indigo
-blue (u.m.)
-carmine (u.m.)

Indo (c.f.)
china
chinese
-European, etc.

infra (pref.)
-anal
-auricular
-axillary
-esophageal
-umbilical
rest one word

ink
-black (u.m.)
mixer
pot
slinger
spot
-spotted (u.m)
stain
stand
well

inner
-city (u.m.)
#man

spring
ino (c.f.)
all one word
insect-borne (u.m.)
inter (pref.)
-American, etc.
rest one word
intra (pref.)
-atomic, etc.
rest one word
intro (pref.)
all one word
Irish
-American (u.m.)
-born (u.m.)
iron
#age
back
-braced (u.m.)
clad
fisted
-free (u.m.)
handed
hard
-lined (u.m.)
mold
-red (u.m.)
shod
shot (mineral) (u.m.)
#shot (golf)
side
-willed (u.m.)
works
ironer-up
island
-born (u.m.)
-dotted (u.m.)
iso (c.f.)
-octane
-oleic
-osmosis
rest one word
ivory
-tinted (u.m.)
type (photog.)
-white (u.m.)
ivy
-clad (u.m.)
-covered (u.m.)

J

J-bolt
jack
ass
hammer
head
-in-the-box
knife
-of-all-trades
-o'-lantern
-plane (v.)
pot
rabbit
screw
jail
bird
house
jam
nut
packed
Java
#applets
Beans
Script
jaw
bone
breaker
-locked (u.m.)
twister
jay
hawk
walk
jelly
bean
roll
jerry
-build (v.)
builder
-built (u.m.)
jet
#airliner
#airplane
-black (u.m.)
lag
liner
port
-powered (u.m.)
prop
-propelled (u.m.)
#propulsion
stream
wash
jewel
-bright (u.m.)
-studded (u.m.)
jib
head
-o-jib
stay
jig
-a-jig
back
-drill (v.)
saw
job
#lot
seeker
#shop
site
joggle#piece
joint#owner
joulemeter
joy
hop
ride
stick
jump
master
off (n., u.m.)
rock
jungle
-clad (u.m.)
-covered (u.m.)
#gym
side
junkpile
jury
#box
-fixing (u.m.)
-rigged (u.m.)
just#in#time
juxta (c.f.)
-ampullar
-articular
rest one word

K

K
-ration
-term
keel
block
fat
haul
-laying (u.m.)
#line
keepsake
kerato (c.f.)
all one word
kettle
drum
stitch
key
board
bolt
hole
lock
note
punch
ring
seat

stone
stop
word
worker
kick
about (n., u.m.)
back (n., u.m.)
-in (n., u.m.)
off (n., u.m.)
out (n., u.m.)
up (n., u.m.)
killjoy
kiln
-dry (u.m., v.)
eye
hole
rib
stick
tree
kilo (pref.)
gram-meter
voltampere
watthour
rest one word
kindheart
king
bolt
#crab
head
hood
hunter
maker
piece
pin
kins
folk
people
kiss-off (n., u.m.)
kite
flier
flying
knapsack
knee
-braced (u.m.)
brush
cap
-deep (u.m.)
-high (u.m.)
hole
-jerk (u.m.)
pad
pan
strap
knick
knack
point
knight
-errant
head
hood
knitback
knock
about (n., u.m.)
away (n., u.m.)
down (n., u.m.)
-knee (n.)
-kneed (u.m.)
off (n., u.m.)
-on (n., u.m.)
out (n., u.m.)
up (n., u.m.)
knocker
-off
-up
knot
hole
horn
know
-all (n., u.m.)
-how (n., u.m.)
-it-all (n., u.m.)
-little (n., u.m.)
-nothing (n., u.m.)
knuckle
bone
buster
-deep (u.m.)
-kneed (u.m.)

L

L
-bar
-beam
-block
-shaped
-square
labio (c.f.)
all one word
laborsaving
lace
-edged (u.m.)
#edging
wing (insect)
-winged (u.m.)
worked
lackluster
ladder-backed (u.m.)
lady
beetle
finger
killer
ship
lake
bed
front
lander
shore
side
lameduck (nonliteral) (n., u.m.)
lamp
black
-blown (u.m.)
-foot
hole
-hour
house
lighter
lit
post
shade
stand
wick
land
#base
-based (u.m.)
#bird
borne
fall
fast
fill
flood
form
grabber
-grant (u.m.)
holding
lady
locked
look
lord
lubber
mark
mass
mine
#office
owner
-poor (u.m.)
right
scape
sick
side
slide
slip
spout
storm
wash
wire

wrack
lantern-jawed (u.m.)
lap
belt
-lap
robe
streak
top
weld (v.)
-welded (u.m.)
-welding (u.m.)
large
-eyed
-handed (u.m.)
-minded (u.m.)
mouthed
-scale (u.m.)
lark
-colored (u.m.)
spur
laryngo (c.f.)
all one word
last
-born (u.m.)
-cited (u.m.)
-ditcher
-named (u.m.)
latch
bolt
key
string
late
-born (u.m.)
comer
-lamented (u.m.)
-maturing (u.m.)
latero (c.f.)
all one word
lath-backed (u.m.)
lathe-bore (v.)
latter
-day (u.m.)
most
lattice
#stitch
work
laughing
#gas
stock
launch
#pad
site
laundry#room
law
-abiding (u.m.)
book
breaker
-fettered (u.m.)
giver
#office
suit
lawnmower
lay
away (n., u.m.)
back (n., u.m.)
-by (n.)
down (n., u.m.)
-minded (u.m.)
off (n., u.m.)
on (n., u.m.)
out (n., u.m.)
up (n., u.m.)
layer
-on
-out
-over
-up
lazy
bones
boots
#guy
legs
lead
-alpha
-burn (v.)
-filled (u.m.)
-gray (u.m.)
-in (n., u.m.)
line
#line (medical, naut. only)
off (n., u.m.)
out (n., u.m.)
#pencil
time
leaden
-eyed (u.m.)
pated
-souled (u.m.)
leader#line
leaf
bud
-clad (u.m.)
-eating (u.m.)
-shaped (u.m.)
stalk
lean
-faced (u.m.)
-looking (u.m.)
-to (n., u.m.)
leap
frog
#year
lease
back (n., u.m.)
hold
leased-line
leather
back
-backed (u.m.)
-bound (u.m.)
-brown (u.m.)
-covered (u.m.)
head
neck
side
ware
leavetaking
lee-bow (v.)
leech
eater
#rope
left
-bank (v.)
#field (sports)
-hand (u.m.)
-handed (u.m.)
-hander
most
-sided (u.m.)
wing (political)
leg
band
puller
rope (v.)
work
lend-lease (n., u.m.)
length
ways
wise
lepto (c.f.)
all one word
let
down (n., u.m.)
off (n., u.m.)
up (n., u.m.)
letter
bomb
#carrier
drop
gram
head
-perfect (u.m.)
press
space
writer
leuc(o) (c.f.)
all one word
liberal-minded (u.m.)

lieutenant
#colonel
-colonelcy
#governor
-governorship
life
belt
blood
boat
#buoy
#cycle
-cycle (u.m.)
drop
float
giver
giving
guard
hold
jacket
long
#net
raft
ring
saver
-size (u.m.)
-sized (u.m.)
span
spring
stream
style
tide
time
vest
weary (u.m.)
lift-off (n., u.m.)
light
-armed (u.m.)
-clad (u.m.)
-colored (u.m.)
-drab (u.m.)
-draft (u.m.)
face (printing)
-footed (u.m.)
handed
house#keeping (nautical)
#housekeeping (domestic)
mouthed
-producing (u.m.)
ship
-struck (u.m.)
weight (n., u.m.)
-year
lighter-than-air (u.m.)
like
-looking (u.m.)
-minded (u.m.)
lily
handed
-shaped (u.m.)
-white (u.m.)
lime
#juice
kiln
lighter
pit
quat
stone
wash
water
linch
bolt
pin
line
-bred (u.m.)
-breed (v.)
casting
crew
cut (printing)
finder
-item (u.m.)
up (n., u.m.)
walker
link
up (n., u.m.)
#up (v.)
lion
-bold (u.m.)
-headed (u.m.)
hearted
-maned (u.m.)
lip
read
service
stick
listener-in
litho (c.f.)
-offset
rest one word
little
-known (u.m.)
neck (clam)
-used (u.m.)
live
#load
long
stock
#stream
#wire
wire (nonliteral)
liver
-brown (u.m.)
-colored (u.m.)
wurst
living#room
loadmeter
loanword
lob
fig
lolly
lobster-tailed (u.m.)
lock
box
fast
hole
jaw
nut
out (n., u.m.)
pin
ring
step
stitch
up (n., u.m.)
washer
locker#room
lode
star
stone
log
book
in
jam
on
off
roll
sheet
loggerhead
logo (c.f.)
all one word
long
-awaited (u.m.)
beard (n.)
-bearded (u.m.)
-billed (u.m.)
bow
cloth
-distance (u.m.)
-drawn (u.m.)
felt
hair (n.)
-haired (u.m.)
hand (nonliteral)
-handed (u.m.)
-handled (u.m.)
head (n.)
horn (cattle)
-horned (u.m.)
johns
#jump

leaf
-leaved (u.m.)
-legged (u.m.)
legs (n.)
-lived (u.m.)
mouthed
-necked (u.m.)
nose (n.)
-nosed (u.m.)
-past (u.m.)
play (records)
playing (u.m.)
run (u.m.)
shoreman
spun
standing (u.m.)
stitch
#term (n.)
-term (u.m.)
wave (radio)
ways
wool (sheep)

look
down (n., u.m.)
-in (n., u.m.)
out (n., u.m.)
over (n., u.m.)
#over (v.)
through (n., u.m.)

looker-on

loop
hole
#knot
stitch

loose
leaf (u.m.)
mouthed
-tongued (u.m.)

lop
-eared (u.m.)
sided

loud
mouthed
#speaker (orator)
speaker (radio)
-voiced (u.m.)

love
bird
born
-inspired (u.m.)
#knot
lorn
seat
sick

low
born
boy
bred
brow (nonliteral)
browed (nonliteral)
-built (u.m.)
down (n., u.m.)
-downer
-lander
-lived (u.m.)
-lying (u.m.)
-power (u.m.)
-pressure (u.m.)
rise
#water

lower
case (printing)
#deck
most

lug
bolt
mark
sail

lukewarm

lumber
jack
#room

lumbo (c.f.)
-ovarian
rest one word

lumen-hour

lunch
box
#hour
room
time

lying-in (n., u.m.)

M

M-day

macebearer

machine
-finished (u.m.)
gun
-hour
-made (u.m.)
#shop
#work

macro (c.f.)
all one word

mad
brain
cap
man (n.)
#money

made
-over (u.m.)
-up (u.m.)

magnetite
-basalt
-olivinite
-spinellite

magneto (c.f.)
-optics
rest one word

mahjong

maid
#of#honor
servant

maiden
hair
head
hood
#name

mail
bag
clad
clerk
guard
-order (u.m.)
pouch
room
slot
truck

main
frame
mast
pin
sail
sheet
spring
stay
stream (nonliteral)
top
topmast
#yard

major
-domo
#league
-leaguer
-minor

make
-believe (n., u.m.)
fast (n.)
over
ready (printing)
shift
up (n., u.m.)
weight

maker
-off

-up
space
making#up
mal (c.f.)
all one word
man
back
-child
-created (u.m.)
-day
eater
-fashion (u.m.)
-grown (u.m.)
handle
hater
-high (u.m.)
hole
-hour
killer
kind
-made (u.m.)
-minute
-of-war (ship)
power
servant
-size (u.m.)
slaughter
slayer
stealer
stopper
trap
-woman
-year
manic-depressive
manifold
mantel
piece
shelf
tree
many
-colored (u.m.)
-folded (u.m.)
-layered (u.m.)
plies
-sided (u.m.)
mapreader
marble
head
-looking (u.m.)
-topped (u.m.)
-white (u.m.)
mare's
-nest
-tail
mark
down (n., u.m.)
off (n., u.m.)
shot
up (n., u.m.)
marker
-down
-off
-up
marketplace
marrowbone
marsh
buck
mallow
(confection)
#mallow (plant)
mass
-minded (u.m.)
-produce (v.)
mast
-brown (u.m.)
head
master
#at#arms
mind
#of#ceremonies
piece
ship
#stroke
#workman
mat-covered (u.m.)
match
book
head
-lined (u.m.)
mark
safe
stick
maxi (n.)
maxi (pref.)
all one word
May
#Day
-day (u.m.)
pole
tide
may
be (adv.)
beetle
day (distress call)
hap
mealymouth
mean
-acting (u.m.)
-spirited (u.m.)
time
(meanwhile)
#time
(astronomical)
tone (u.m.)
while
meat
ball
cutter
-eater
-fed (u.m.)
hook
-hungry (u.m.)
packer
works
wrapper
mechanico (c.f.)
all one word
medico (c.f.)
all one word
medio (c.f.)
all one word
medium
-brown (u.m.)
-size(d) (u.m.)
weight (n., u.m.)
meek
-eyed (u.m.)
hearted
-spirited (u.m.)
meetingplace
megalo (c.f.)
all one word
melon
grower
-laden (u.m.)
-shaped (u.m.)
melt
down (n., u.m.)
water
men
folk
kind
meningo (c.f.)
all one word
menu-driven
merry
-go-round
-meeting
-minded (u.m.)
meshbag
meso (c.f.)
all one word
mess
hall
kit
room
tin
-up (n., u.m.)
meta (pref.)
all one word

metal
ammonium
-clad (u.m.)
-coated (u.m.)
-lined (u.m.)
works
meter
-amperes
-kilogram
-kilogram-second
metro (c.f.)
all one word
mezzo
graph
relievo
soprano
tint
micro (c.f.)
-organism
rest one word
mid (c.f.)
-American, etc.
-April
day
-decade
-dish
-ice
-level
-1958
-Pacific, etc.
-Victorian, etc.
rest one word
middle
-aged (u.m.)
breaker
brow (nonliteral)
-burst (v.)
buster
#ear
#ground
man (nonliteral)
most
-of-the-roader
-sized (u.m.)
splitter
weight
midi (n.)
midi (pref.)
all one word
mighty-handed (u.m.)
mil-foot
mild
-cured (u.m.)
-mannered (u.m.)
-spoken (u.m.)
mile
-long (u.m.)
-ohm
post
-pound
-ton
-wide (u.m.)
milk
-fed (u.m.)
head
#run
shake
shed
sick
sop
-white (u.m.)
mill
cake
course
dam
feed
hand
-headed (u.m.)
pond
post
race
ring
stock
stream
wright
milli (c.f.)
gram-hour
rest one word
mincemeat
mind
#healer
-healing (u.m.)
reader
set (n.)
sight
mine
field
layer
ship
sweeper
thrower
works
mini (n.)
mini (pref.)
all one word
minor
#league
-leaguer
minute#book
mirror
-faced (u.m.)
scope
mis (pref.)
all one word
mischiefmaking
mist
bow
-clad (u.m.)
-covered (u.m.)
fall
miter
#box
-lock (v.)
mix
blood
up (n.)
mixing#room
mizzenmast
mock
-heroic (u.m.)
#turtle
up (n., u.m.)
mocker-up
mocking
stock
-up (u.m.)
mold
made (u.m.)
#shop
mole
catcher
-eyed (u.m.)
head
hill
money
bag
changer
getter
grubber
lender
-mad (u.m.)
maker
saver
monkey
-faced (u.m.)
nut
pod
pot
shine
#wrench
mono (c.f.)
-ideistic
-iodo
-iodohydrin
-ion
-ousian
rest one word
month
end
long (u.m.)

moon
beam
blind
#blindness
blink
born
-bright (u.m.)
eye
face
gazing
glow
head
lighter
lit
-mad (u.m.)
path
rise
sail
set
shade
shine
shot
sick
struck
tide
walker
-white (u.m.)
moosecall
mop
head
stick
up (n., u.m.)
mopper-up
mopping-up (u.m.)
morning
#sickness
#star
tide
mosquito
-free (u.m.)
#net
moss
back
-clad (u.m.)
-green (u.m.)
-grown (u.m.)
head
-lined (u.m.)
most-favored-nation (u.m.)
moth
ball
-eaten (u.m.)
hole
proof
mother
board
hood
-in-law
-of-pearl
moto (c.f.)
all one word
motor
bike
bus
cab
cade
car
coach
cycle
-driven (u.m.)
jet
-minded (u.m.)
#scooter
ship
truck
van
moundbuilder
mountain
-high (u.m.)
side
top
-walled (u.m.)
mouse
-brown (u.m.)
-eared (u.m.)
-eaten (u.m.)
hole
trap
mouth
-filling (u.m.)
-made (u.m.)
piece
wash
muck
rake (v.)
raker
sweat
muco (c.f.)
all one word
mud
bank
bath
-colored (u.m.)
flat
flow
guard
head
hole
lark
sill
slinger
-splashed (u.m.)
stain
sucker
track
#turtle
mule
back
#deer
skinner
multi (c.f.)
all one word
multiple-purpose (u.m.)
muscle
bound
power
music
lover
-mad (u.m.)
maker
room
musico (c.f.)
all one word
musk
#deer
melon
#ox
rat
mutton
#chop (meat)
chop (shape)
fist
head
myria (c.f.)
all one word
mytho (c.f.)
all one word
myxo (c.f.)
all one word

N

nail
bin
brush
head
-headed (u.m.)
#hole
print
puller
rod
-shaped (u.m.)
-studded (u.m.)
name
-calling (u.m.)
-dropping (u.m.)
plate
sake
nano (c.f.)
all one word

naptime
narco (c.f.)
all one word
narrow
-mouthed (u.m.)
minded
naso (c.f.)
-occipital
-orbital
rest one word
nationwide
native-born (u.m.)
navy-blue (u.m.)
naysayer
near
by
-miss
sighted
neat's-foot (u.m.)
neck
band
bone
-breaking (u.m.)
cloth
-deep (u.m.)
fast
guard
-high (u.m.)
hole
lace
line
mold
tie
necro (c.f.)
all one word
needle
bill
case
-made (u.m.)
nose (pliers)
point
-shaped (u.m.)
-sharp (u.m.)
worked
ne'er-do-well
neo (c.f.)
-Greek, etc.
rest one word
nephro (c.f.)
all one word
nerve
ache
-celled (u.m.)
-racked (u.m.)
net
ball
braider
-veined (u.m.)
work
#worth
nettle
fire
foot
some
neuro (c.f.)
all one word
never
-ending (u.m.)
more
theless
new
born
-car (u.m.)
comer
-created (u.m.)
fangled
-fashioned (u.m.)
-front (v.)
-made (u.m.)
-mown (u.m.)
-rich (u.m.)
newlywed
news
boy
case
cast
clip
dealer
#editor
letter
#media
paper
paper#work
photo
print
reader
reel
sheet
stand
story
teller
nick
-eared (u.m.)
name
nickel
plate (v.)
-plated (u.m.)
-plating (u.m.)
type
night
-black (u.m.)
#blindness
cap
-clad (u.m.)
clothes
club
dress
fall
-fly (aviation) (v.)
-flying (u.m.)
gown
-grown (u.m.)
hawk
long (u.m.)
mare
#school
shade
#shift
shirt
side
tide
walker
nimble
-fingered (u.m.)
footed
nimbostratus
(clouds)
nine
fold
#holes
-lived (u.m.)
pin
score
nitpicker
nitro (c.f.)
-hydro-carbon
rest one word
no
-account (n., u.m.)
-fault
-fee
-good (n., u.m.)
-hitter (n.)
how
#man's land
#one
-par (u.m.)
-par-value (u.m.)
-show (n., u.m.)
-thoroughfare (n.)
whit
-year (funds)
noble
-born (u.m.)
-featured (u.m.)
heartedness
-looking (u.m.)
-minded (u.m.)
nol-pros (v.)
non
-civil-service (u.m.)

-European, etc.
interactive
-pros (v.)
#sequitur, etc.
-tumor-bearing (u.m.)
as prefix, one word

none
such
theless

noon
day
tide
time

north
-central (u.m.)
east
going
most
-northeast
-sider

nose
bag
bleed
bone
dive
down (n., u.m.)
gay
guard
-high (u.m.)
hole
-led (u.m.)
over (n., u.m.)
pipe
ring
-thumbing (u.m.)
up (n., u.m.)
wheel

note
book
#paper
worthy

notwithstanding

novel
-reading (u.m.)
#writer
-writing (u.m.)

nucleo (c.f.)
all one word

nut
breaker
-brown (u.m.)
cake
cracker
hatch
hook
pecker
pick
-shaped (u.m.)
shell
sweet

O

oak
-beamed (u.m.)
-clad (u.m.)
-green (u.m.)
#leaf
-leaved (u.m.)

oar
-footed (u.m.)
lock

oarsman

oat
bin
cake
-fed (u.m.)
meal
seed

oathbreaker
object-oriented

oblong
-elliptic (u.m.)
-leaved (u.m.)
-linear (u.m.)
-ovate (u.m.)
-shaped (u.m.)
-triangular (u.m.)

occipito (c.f.)
-otic
rest one word

ocean
-born (u.m.)
borne
-girdled (u.m.)
going
side
-spanning (u.m.)

octo (c.f.)
all one word

odd
-jobber
-job man
-looking (u.m.)
man (arbiter)
-numbered (u.m.)

off
-and-on (u.m.)
beat
cast
center (u.m.)
color (u.m.)
-colored (u.m.)
cut (printing)
day
-fall (v.)
-flavor (n., u.m.)
-flow
-go (n.)
going
grade
hand
-hours
line
loading
look
-lying (u.m.)
peak
print
put
-reckoning (n.)
saddle
scape
scour
scum
-season
set
shoot
shore
side
site
-sorts (n.)
spring
stage
street
take
-the-record (u.m.)
type
-wheel (n.)
-wheeler (n.)
-white (u.m.)
#year

office
#boy
holder
seeker
-seeking (u.m.)

oftentimes
ofttimes

ohm
-ammeter
meter
-mile

oil
#burner
cake
can
cloth
coat
cup
-driven (u.m.)

-fed (u.m.)
field
-forming (u.m.)
-harden (v.)
hole
meal
paper
proofing
seed
#shale
skinned
-soaked (u.m.)
spill (n.)
stove
-temper (v.)
tightness
#well

old
-fashioned (u.m.)
-fogy (u.m.)
-growing (u.m.)
-looking (u.m.)
#maid
-maidish (u.m.)
#man
-new
style (printing)
timer
#woman
-young

oleo
#gear
margarine
#oil
#strut
as combining form, one word

olive
-brown (u.m.)
-clad (u.m.)
-drab (u.m.)
-growing (u.m.)
#oil
-skinned (u.m.)
wood
#wood (color)

omni (c.f.)
all one word

on
-and-off (n., u.m.)
board (u.m.)
-go (n.)
going
line#service
site
noun, adjective, one word

once
-over (n.)
-run (u.m.)

one
-armed (u.m.)
-decker
-eyed (u.m.)
fold
-half
-handed (u.m.)
ness
-piece (u.m.)
self
-sided (u.m.)
-sidedness
signed (u.m.)
-step (dance)
-striper
time (formerly) (u.m.)
-time (one action) (u.m.)
-two-three
-way (u.m.)

onion
peel
skin

op-ed (newspaper)

open
-air (u.m.)
-armed (u.m.)
-back (u.m.)
-backed (u.m.)
band (yarn)
cast
cut (mining)
-end (u.m.)
-ended
-faced (u.m.)
handed
#house
minded
mouthed
#shop
side (u.m.)
-sided (u.m.)
worked

opera
goer
going
#house

operating#system

ophthalmo (c.f.)
all one word

orange
ade
colored (u.m.)
peel
-red (u.m.)
stick

orchard#house

orderly#room

organo (c.f.)
all one word

ornitho (c.f.)
all one word

orrisroot

ortho (c.f.)
all one word

osteo (c.f.)
all one word

other
wise
#world
worldly

oto (c.f.)
all one word

out
-and-out (u.m.)
-and-outer (n.)
-loud (u.m.)
-Machiavelli, etc.
migration
-of-date (u.m.)
-of-door(s) (u.m.)
-of-State (u.m.)
-of-the-way (u.m.)
placement
-to-out (u.m.)
as prefix, one word

outer
-city (u.m.)
#man
most
wear

outward
-bound (u.m.)
-bounder

ovate
-acuminate (u.m.)
-oblong (u.m.)

ovato (c.f.)
-oblong
-orbicular
rest one word

oven
baked
dried
peel
ware

over
age (surplus)

age (older) (n., u.m.)
all (n., u.m.)
-the-counter (u.m.)
as combining form, one word
owl-eyed (u.m.)
ox
biter
blood (color)
bow
brake
cart
cheek
eye
-eyed (u.m.)
gall
harrow
hide
horn
shoe
tail
#team
oxy (c.f.)
all one word
oyster
bed
#crab
house
root
seed
shell
-white (u.m.)

P

pace
maker
#setter
-setting (u.m.)
pachy (c.f.)
all one word
pack
builder
cloth
horse
-laden (u.m.)
sack
saddle
staff
thread
up (n., u.m.)
packing#box
padlock
paddlefoot
page
-for-page (u.m.)
#proof (printing)
painkiller
painstaking
paint
box
brush
mixer
pot
spray
stained (u.m.)
pale
belly
-blue (u.m.)
buck
-cheeked (u.m.)
-faced (u.m.)
-looking (u.m.)
-reddish (u.m.)
paleo (c.f.)
-Christian, etc.
rest one word
pallbearer
palm
-green (u.m.)
#leaf
#oil
-shaded (u.m.)
palmi (c.f.)
all one word
pan
-American, etc.
-broil (v.)
#ice
rest one word
Pan
#American Union
hellenic
panel-lined (u.m.)
panic-stricken (u.m.)
panto (c.f.)
all one word
panty hose
paper
back (n.)
#box
#carrier
cutter
hanger
shell (n., u.m.)
-shelled (u.m.)
-thin (u.m.)
weight
-white (u.m.)
papier#mache
para (c.f. or pref.)
-analgesia
-anesthesia
legal
medic
rest one word
parcel
#carrier
-plate (v.)
#post
parchment
-covered (u.m.)
#maker
-making (u.m.)
parieto (c.f.)
-occipital
rest one word
parimutuel
park
#forest
land
way
part
-finished (u.m.)
#owner
-time (u.m.)
-timer (n.)
#way
parti (c.f.)
all one word
party#line
parvi (c.f.)
all one word
pass
back (n.)
book
key
out (n., u.m.)
port
through (n., u.m.)
way
word
passenger-mile
passer(s)-by
passion
-driven (u.m.)
-feeding (u.m.)
-filled (u.m.)
#play
paste
down (n., u.m.)
pot
up (n., u.m.)
pastureland
patent-in-fee
path
breaker
finder
way

patho (c.f.)
all one word
patri (c.f.)
all one word
patrol
man
#wagon
pattycake
pawn
broker
shop
pay
back (n., u.m.)
check
#cut
day
dirt
load
off (n., u.m.)
out (n., u.m.)
#raise
roll
sheet
-TV
pea
#coal
coat
cod
-green (u.m.)
hen
jacket
nut
pod
shooter
-sized (u.m.)
stick
peace
-blessed (u.m.)
breaker
-loving (u.m.)
maker
#pipe
time
peach
bloom
blow (color)
-colored (u.m.)
pear-shaped (u.m.)
pearl
-eyed (u.m.)
fishing
-pure (u.m.)
-set (u.m.)
-studded (u.m.)
-white (u.m.)
peat
-roofed (u.m.)
moss
stack
pebble
-paved (u.m.)
-strewn (u.m.)
peeloff (n., u.m.)
peep
eye
hole
show
sight
peer-to-peer
pegleg
pellmell
pen
-cancel (v.)
head
knife
manship
#name
point
pusher
rack
script
-shaped (u.m.)
stock
trough
pencil
#box
holder
-mark (v.)
penny
-a-liner
pincher
weight
winkle
worth
pent-up (u.m.)
penta (c.f.)
-acetate
rest one word
pepper
corn
#jelly
mint
pot
-red (u.m.)
peptalk
per
#annum
cent
#centum
compound (chemical)
current (botanical)
#diem
salt (chemical)
#se
sulfide
peri (pref.)
-insular
rest one word
permafrost
pest
hole
-ridden (u.m.)
petcock
petit
grain
#jury
#larceny
#point
petro (c.f.)
-occipital
rest one word
pharmaco (c.f.)
-oryctology
rest one word
pharyngo (c.f.)
-esophageal
-oral
rest one word
phase
-in (n., u.m.)
meter
out (n., u.m.)
-wound (u.m.)
pheno (c.f.)
all one word
philo (c.f.)
-French, etc.
rest one word
phlebo (c.f.)
all one word
phonebook
phono (c.f.)
all one word
phospho (c.f.)
all one word
photo (c.f.)
-offset
-oxidation
-oxidative
rest one word
phrasemark (music)
phreno (c.f.)
all one word
phyllo (c.f.)
all one word
phylo (c.f.)
all one word
physico (c.f.)
all one word

physio (c.f.)
all one word
phyto (c.f.)
all one word
piano
forte
graph
#player
pick
aback
ax
lock
-me-up (n., u.m.)
off (n., u.m.)
over (n., u.m.)
#over (v.)
pocket
pole
shaft
up (n., u.m.)
picker-up
picket#line
pickle-cured (u.m.)
picture
#book
#writing
pie
bald
crust
-eater
-eyed
marker
pan
plant
#plate
-stuffed (u.m.)
#tin
piece
-dye (v.)
#goods
meal
mold
piezo (c.f.)
-oscillator
rest one word
pig
-back (v.)
-backed (u.m.)
-bellied (u.m.)
belly
-eyed (u.m.)
face
-faced (u.m.)
foot
-footed (u.m.)
headed
herd
#iron
out
pen
root
stick
sty
tailed
wash
pigeon
gram
hole
-toed (u.m.)
wing
piggyback
pike
-eyed (u.m.)
staff
pile
driver
-driving (u.m.)
hammer
up (n., u.m.)
#weave
woven
pill
pusher
rolling
taker
pillow
case
made
slip
top
pilot
#boat
house
#light
pin
ball
block
bone
case
cushion
-eyed (u.m.)
fall
feather
fire
fold
head
hold
hole
hook
lock
paper
point
prick
rail
setter
spot
stripe
-tailed (u.m.)
up (n., u.m.)
wheel
pinch
back
bar
beck
cock
fist
-hit (v.)
-hitter
penny
pine
apple
-bearing (u.m.)
-clad (u.m.)
#cone
-fringed (u.m.)
#needle
#oil
-shaded (u.m.)
#tar
pink
-blossomed (u.m.)
eye (n.)
-eyed (u.m.)
pipe
-drawn (u.m.)
dream
fitter
layer
line
-shaped (u.m.)
stem
walker
welder
pisci (c.f.)
all one word
pistol-whipped (v.)
piston
head
#pin
#rod
#valve
pit
#boss
#bull
-eyed (u.m.)
fall
head
-headed (u.m.)
hole
mark
-marked (u.m.)

-rotted (u.m.)
saw
side
pitch
-black (u.m.)
blende
#box
-colored (u.m.)
-dark (u.m.)
#darkness
fork
hole
-lined (u.m.)
man
-marked (u.m.)
out (n., u.m.)
#pipe
up (n., u.m.)
place
card
kick
plague-infested (u.m.)
plain
back (fabric)
-bodied (u.m.)
clothes (u.m.)
clothesman
-headed (u.m.)
-looking (u.m.)
-spoken (u.m.)
woven (u.m.)
plane
#curve
load
-mile
-parallel (u.m.)
table (surveying)
plani (c.f.)
all one word
plano (c.f.)
all one word
plant
#food
life
site
plasterboard
plate
cutter
#glass
-incased (u.m.)
layer
mark
#proof (printing)
-roll (v.)
-rolled (u.m.)
platy (c.f.)
all one word
play
-act (v.)
back (n., u.m.)
bill
book
boy
broker
day
down (n., u.m.)
fellow
goer
going
ground
mate
off (n., u.m.)
pen
reader
room
script
suit
thing
time
wright
#yard
pleasure
-bent (u.m.)
#boat
-seeking (u.m.)
-tired (u.m.)
-weary (u.m.)
pleo (c.f.)
all one word
pleuro (c.f.)
all one word
plow
back (n., u.m.)
-bred (u.m.)
hand
horse
pan
point
-shaped (u.m.)
share
shoe
sole
staff
#tail
wright
plug
-and-play
hole
-in (n., u.m.)
tray
plumbline
plume-crowned (u.m.)
pluri (c.f.)
all one word
pluto (c.f.)
all one word
pneumato (c.f.)
-hydato-genetic (u.m.)
rest one word
pneumo (c.f.)
all one word
pock
mark
-marked (u.m.)
-pit (v.)
pocket
book (purse)
#book (book)
-eyed (u.m.)
knife
-sized (u.m.)
-veto (v.)
poet
-artist
#laureate
-painter
pointblank
Point-to-Point
poison-dipped (u.m.)
pole
arm
-armed (u.m.)
ax
burn
cat
-dried (u.m.)
horse
-pile (v.)
setter
-shaped (u.m.)
sitter
-stack (v.)
star
timber
trap
-vault (v.)
#vaulter
policy
maker
making
politico (c.f.)
-orthodox
rest one word
poll
book
#parrot
#tax

poly (c.f.)
all one word
poor
-blooded (u.m.)
farm
-spirited (u.m.)
pop
corn
eye
gun
up (n., u.m.)
poppy
-bordered (u.m.)
cock
-red (u.m.)
seed
pork
barrel (n., u.m.)
#chop
fish
#pie
port
cullis
fire
folio
hole
hook
manteau
-mouthed (u.m.)
side
#wine
post
#bellum
#boat
card
-Christian, etc.
-cold-war (u.m.)
#diem
-free (u.m.)
haste
#hospital (military)
#meridiem
#mortem (literal)
mortem (nonliteral)
#partum
#school (military)
traumatic
-traumatic (PTSD)
audit, graduate, etc.
as prefix, one word
postal#card
pot
ash
bellied
boil
eye
hanger
herb
hole
hook
hunter
latch
lid
luck
pie
pourri
rack
#roast
shot
potato#field
poultry
#keeper
-keeping (u.m.)
#raiser
-raising (u.m.)
#yard
pound
cake
-foolish (u.m.)
-foot
worth
powder
-blue (u.m.)
box
#house
#keg
#mill
#room
-scorched (u.m.)
power
boat
#mower
-operated (u.m.)
pack
plant
praise
-deserving (u.m.)
-spoiled (u.m.)
worthiness
pre (pref.)
-Incan, etc.
audit, existing, etc.
rest one word
president
-elect
#pro#tempore
press
#agent
-agentry
board
feeder
-forge (v.)
-made (u.m.)
mark
pack (v.)
plate
#proof (printing)
preter (pref.)
all one word
price
#cutter
-cutting (u.m.)
#fixer
-fixing (u.m.)
#index
list
-support (u.m.)
tag
prick
-eared (u.m.)
mark
seam
priesthood
prime
#minister
-ministerial (u.m.)
-ministership
-ministry
prince
hood
-priest
print
cloth
out
script
printing
-in (n., u.m.)
#ink
#office
-out (n., u.m.)
prison
bound
-free (u.m.)
-made (u.m.)
prisoner-of-war (u.m.)
prize
fighter
#ring
taker
winner
-winning (u.m.)
pro
-Ally, etc.
-choice

#football, etc.
#forma
-life
#rata
#tem
#tempore
as prefix, one word
problem-solver
procto (c.f.)
all one word
profit
-and-loss (u.m.)
-sharing (u.m.)
prong
buck
-hoe (v.)
horn
-horned (u.m.)
proof
#press
read
reader
room
sheet
prop
jet
wash
proso (c.f.)
all one word
proto (c.f.)
-Egyptian, etc.
rest one word
proud
hearted
-looking (u.m.)
-minded (u.m.)
psalmbook
pseudo (c.f.)
-Messiah, etc.
-occidental
-official
-orthorhombic
-osteomalacia
-owner
rest one word
psycho (c.f.)
-organic
rest one word
ptero (c.f.)
all one word
public
hearted
-minded (u.m.)
-spirited (u.m.)
#works
pug
nose
-pile (v.)
pull
back (n., u.m.)
#box
down (n., u.m.)
-in (n., u.m.)
off (n., u.m.)
-on (n., u.m.)
out (n., u.m.)
-push (u.m.)
through (n., u.m.)
up (n., u.m.)
puller
-in
-out
pulp
board
wood
punch
board
bowl
card
-drunk (u.m.)
mark
-marked (u.m.)
out (n.)
punctureproof
pup#tent
pure
blood
bred
#line (biological)
purple
-blue (u.m.)
-clad (u.m.)
-colored (u.m.)
heart (wood)
purse
making
-proud (u.m.)
#strings
push
button
card
cart
off (n., u.m.)
-pull (u.m.)
up (n., u.m.)
pussy
cat
foot
#willow
put
back (n., u.m.)
off (n., u.m.)
-on (n., u.m.)
out (n., u.m.)
-put (n.)
-up (n., u.m.)
putter
-forth
-in
-off
-on
-out
-through
-up
pyo (c.f.)
all one word
pyro (c.f.)
all one word

Q

Q
-boat
-fever
quadri (c.f.)
-invariant
rest one word
quarrystone
quarter
-angled (u.m.)
back
-bloom (u.m.)
#boards
-bound (u.m.)
-breed (u.m.)
-cast (u.m.)
-cut (u.m.)
deck
-miler
#note
pace
-phase (u.m.)
saw (v.)
staff
stretch
-yearly (u.m.)
quartermaster
#general
-generalship
quasi
all hyphened
queen#bee
quick
-change (u.m., v.)
-drawn (u.m., v.)
freeze (u.m., v.)
lime
sand

set
silver
step
#time
-witted (u.m.)
quin (c.f.)
all one word
quit
claim
rent

R

rabbit
-backed (u.m.)
-eared (u.m.)
#fever
#foot
skin
race
about (n., u.m.)
course
goer
horse
track
way
radarscope
radio
generally two words except the following forms
frequency
isotope
telegraph
telephone
rag
bolt
#doll
-made (u.m.)
sorter
tag
time
rail
bird
car
guard
head
-ridden (u.m.)
road
setter
splitter
#train
way#maker
wayman
rain
band
-beaten (u.m.)
bow
check
coat
drop
fall
#forest
-soft (u.m.)
spout
storm
wash
water
rakeoff (n., u.m.)
ram
jet
rod
shackle
ranch
#hand
house
random-access (u.m.)
range
finder
#light
rider
rapid
#fire
#transit
rat
bite
catcher
hole
-infested (u.m.)
#race
-tailed (u.m.)
-tight (u.m.)
trap
rate
#cutter
-cutting (u.m.)
-fixing (u.m.)
payer
-raising (u.m.)
setting
rattle
brain
snake
trap
raw
boned
-edged (u.m.)
hide
-looking (u.m.)
razor
back
-billed (u.m.)
#blade
edge
-keen (u.m.)
-sharp (u.m.)
strop
razzle-dazzle
re (pref.)
-cover (cover again)
-create (create again), etc.
-cross-examination
-ice
-ink
-redirect
evaluate, process, etc.
rest one word
reading#room
read
out (n.)
through (n., u.m.)
real
time (n.)
-time (u.m.)
ready
-built (u.m.)
-handed (u.m.)
made (u.m.)
-mix (u.m.)
#reference
room
-witted (u.m.)
rear
#end
guard
most
view (u.m.)
ward
reception#room
recordbreaker
recti (c.f.)
all one word
recto (c.f.)
all one word
red
bait (v.)
-billed (u.m.)
-blooded (u.m.)
buck
cap (porter)
coat (n.)
eye (n.)
-eyed (u.m.)
-faced (u.m.)
-haired (u.m.)
handed

head (n.)
-hot (u.m.)
-legged (u.m.)
#line (literal)
out (n., u.m.)
-skinned (u.m.)
tape (nonliteral)
#tape (literal)
-throated (u.m.)
-yellow (u.m.)
reformat
regionwide
religio (c.f.)
all one word
remote-access
repair#shop
representative
#at#large
-elect
research#worker
resino (c.f.)
all one word
retro (c.f.)
-ocular
-omental
-operative
-oral
rest one word
rheo (c.f.)
all one word
rhino (c.f.)
all one word
rhizo (c.f.)
all one word
rhod(o) (c.f.)
all one word
rhomb(o) (c.f.)
all one word
rice
growing
#water
rich
-bound (u.m.)
-clad (u.m.)
-looking (u.m.)
rickrack
ridge
band
pole
top
riffraff
rifleshot
rig
out (n., u.m.)
-up (n., u.m.)
right
about
about-face
-angle (u.m., v.)
-angled (u.m.)
#away
#field (sports)
-handed (u.m.)
-hander
-headed (u.m.)
most
-of-way
wing (political)
rim
-deep (u.m.)
fire
lock
rock
ring
-adorned (u.m.)
-banded (u.m.)
-billed (u.m.)
bolt
giver
head
-in (n., u.m.)
lead (v.)
leader
-necked (u.m.)
-off (n., u.m.)
pin
-porous (u.m.)
-shaped (u.m.)
side
sight
stand
stick
-tailed (u.m.)
-up (n., u.m.)
worm
rip
cord
-off (n., u.m.)
rap
roaring
sack
saw
snorter
tide
-up (n., u.m.)
river
bank
bed
#bottom
flow
-formed (u.m.)
front
head
scape
side
wash
-worn (u.m.)
road
bank
bed
block
builder
head
hog
kill
map
#runner (bird)
#show
side
-test (v.)
way
-weary (u.m.)
rock
abye
bottom
(nonliteral)
#climber
-climbing (u.m.)
fall (n.)
-fallen (u.m.)
fill
firm
pile
-ribbed (u.m.)
#salt
shaft
slide
rod-shaped (u.m.)
roe
buck
#deer
roentgeno (c.f.)
all one word
roll
about (n., u.m.)
back (n., u.m.)
call
-fed (v.)
film
off (n., u.m.)
-on (n., u.m.)
out (n., u.m.)
over (n., u.m.)
top
up (n., u.m.)
roller
#blade
#coaster
-made (u.m.)
-milled (u.m.)
#skate

Romano (c.f.)
-canonical, etc.
-Gallic, etc.
roof
garden
line
top
tree
room
#clerk
keeper
mate
roominghouse
root
bound
cap
-cutting (u.m.)
fast
hold
#mean#square
#rot
stalk
stock
rope
dance
layer
stitch
walk
rose
-bright (u.m.)
bud
bush
head
-headed (u.m.)
-scented (u.m.)
-sweet (u.m.)
tan
#water
rotor
craft
ship
rotten
-dry (u.m.)
-minded (u.m.)
rough
-and-ready (u.m.)
-and-tumble (n., u.m.)
cast (u.m., v.)
-coat (v.)
-cut (u.m.)
draw (v.)
dress (v.)
dry (u.m., v.)
-face (v.)
-faced (u.m.)
hew
house
-legged (u.m.)
-looking (u.m.)
neck
rider
setter
shod
-sketch (v.)
stuff
tailed
#work (n.)
work (v.)
wrought
rougher
-down
-out
-up
roughing-in (u.m.)
round
about (n., u.m.)
about-face
-faced (u.m.)
head
-made (u.m.)
mouthed
nose (tool)
out (n., u.m.)
robin (petition)
seam
table (panel)
-tailed (u.m.)
-topped (u.m.)
#trip
-tripper
up (n., u.m.)
rub
-a-dub
down (n., u.m.)
rubber
band
-down
-lined (u.m.)
neck
-off
-set (u.m.)
stamp (nonliteral) (n., u.m., v.)
#stamp (n.)
-stamped (u.m.)
ruby
-hued (u.m.)
-red (u.m.)
-set (u.m.)
-throated (u.m.)
rudder
head
hole
post
stock
rule#of#thumb
rum
-crazed (u.m.)
runner
seller
rumpus#room
run
about (n., u.m.)
around (n., u.m.)
away (n., u.m.)
back (n., u.m.)
by (n.)
down (n., u.m.)
-in (n., u.m.)
off (n., u.m.)
-on (n., u.m.)
out (n., u.m.)
over (n., u.m.)
through (n., u.m.)
up (n., u.m.)
runner-up
Russo (c.f.)
-Chinese, etc.
rest one word
rust
-brown (u.m.)
-eaten (u.m.)
proofing
-resistant (u.m.)
-stained (u.m.)
rye#field

S

S
-bend
-brake
-iron
-ray
-shaped
-trap
-wrench
saber
-legged (u.m.)
tooth
-toothed (u.m.)
sable-cloaked (u.m.)
Sabrejet
saccharo (c.f.)
all one word
sack
bearer
cloth
#coat
-coated (u.m.)
-making (u.m.)

-shaped (u.m.)
sacro (c.f.)
all one word
sad
-eyed (u.m.)
iron
#sack
-voiced (u.m.)
saddle
back
-backed (u.m.)
bag
bow
cloth
-graft (v.)
#horse
-making (u.m.)
nose
-nosed (u.m.)
sore
-stitched (u.m.)
tree
-wire (u.m.)
safe
blower
cracker
-deposit (u.m.)
guard
hold
#house
#site
sage
brush
leaf
-leaved (u.m.)
sail
cloth
-dotted (u.m.)
flying
saintlike
sales
book
clerk
manship
people
person
salmon
-colored (u.m.)
-red (u.m.)
salpingo (c.f.)
-oophorectomy
-oophoritis
-ovariotomy
-ovaritis
rest one word
salt
box
cellar
-cured (u.m.)
#lick
mouth
pack
pan
peter
pit
pond
shaker
spoon
sprinkler
water
works
salver
form
-shaped (u.m.)
same-sex (u.m.)
sample
#book
#box
maker
-making (u.m.)
sand
bag
bank
bar
bath
bin
blast
blown
box
-built (u.m.)
-buried (u.m.)
-cast (u.m., v.)
culture
#dune
fill
flea
glass
heat
hill
-hiller
hog
hole
lapper
lot
paper
pile
pipe
pit
-pump (u.m., v.)
shoe
spit
storm
table
weld (v.)
-welded (u.m.)
-welding (u.m.)
sandy-bottomed (u.m.)
sangfroid
sans
#serif
#souci
sapphire
-blue (u.m.)
-colored (u.m.)
sarco (c.f.)
all one word
sashcord
satin
#cloth
-lined (u.m.)
-smooth (u.m.)
sauce
dish
pan
sauer
braten
kraut
save-all (n., u.m.)
saw
back
belly
bill (bird)
-billed (u.m.)
bones (n.)
buck
dust
-edged (u.m.)
horse
setter
timber
tooth
-toothed (u.m.)
sax
cornet
horn
tuba
say
-nothing (n., u.m.)
-so (n.)
scale
bark
down (n., u.m.)
pan
-reading (u.m.)
scapegoat
scapulo (c.f.)
all one word
scar
-clad (u.m.)
face

-faced (u.m.)
#tissue
scare
crow
head
scarfpin
scarlet
-breasted (u.m.)
#fever
-red (u.m.)
scatter
brain
good
#rug
scene
shifter
wright
schisto (c.f.)
all one word
schizo (c.f.)
all one word
school
bag
#board
book
bus
children
day
-made (u.m.)
mate
ship
teacher
-trained (u.m.)
#year
scientifico (c.f.)
all one word
scissor
bill
-tailed (u.m.)
-winged (u.m.)
scissors
hold
-shaped (u.m.)
#smith
sclero (c.f.)
-oophoritis
-optic
rest one word
score
board
book
card
sheet
scot-free
Scoto (c.f.)
-Britannic, etc.
Scotsman
scout
#badge
#car
hood
master
scrap
basket
book
#paper
works
scratch
brush
-brusher
-coated (u.m.)
#pad
#test
screen
out (n., u.m.)
play
screw
ball
bolt
cap
down (u.m.)
drive (v.)
-driven (u.m.)
driver
head
hook
jack
-lifted (u.m.)
nut
ship
#thread
-threaded (u.m.)
-turned (u.m.)
scroll
-back
head
work
scuttlebutt
scythe-shaped (u.m.)
sea
#base
-based (u.m.)
-bathed (u.m.)
beach
-beaten (u.m.)
bed
#bird
-blue (u.m.)
board
#boat
-born (u.m.)
borne
bound
-bred (u.m.)
coast
-deep (u.m.)
dog
-driven (u.m.)
drome
-encircled (u.m.)
fare (food)
fighter
#floor
folk
food
front
girt
goer
going
hound
lane
#level
lift
#lion
mark
port
quake
#room
scape
#scout
scouting
shell
shine
shore
sick
side
stroke
#time (clock)
wall
weed
wing
worn
worthiness
-wrecked (u.m.)
seam
blasting
rend (v.)
stitch
weld (v.)
-welded (u.m.)
search
#engine
light
plane
seat
belt
#cover
-mile
second
-class (u.m.)
-degree (u.m.)

-foot
-guess (v.)
hand (adv., u.m.)
#hand (n.)
#in#command
-rate (u.m.)
#sight
-sighted (u.m.)
Secret Service
secretary
#general
-generalcy
-generalship
section#man
seed
bed
cake
case
coat
kin
stalk
seer
band
hand
sucker
seesaw
seismo (c.f.)
all one word
self
dom
-extracting
hood
less
ness
same
reflexive prefix, use hyphen
sell
off (n., u.m.)
out (n., u.m.)
semi (pref.)
-armor-piercing (u.m.)
-Christian, etc.
-idleness
-indirect, etc.
annual, arid, etc.
rest one word
send
off (n., u.m.)
out (n., u.m.)
senso (c.f.)
all one word
septi (c.f.)
all one word
septo (c.f.)
all one word
sergeant#at#arms
serio (c.f.)
all one word
sero (c.f.)
all one word
serrate
-ciliate (u.m.)
-dentate (u.m.)
server-based
service
-connected (u.m.)
man
#man#and #woman
member
person
wide
woman
servo
accelerometer
amplifier
control
mechanism
motor
system
sesqui (c.f.)
all one word
set
-aside (n., u.m.)
back (n., u.m.)
bolt
down (n., u.m.)
-fair (n.)
head
-in (n., u.m.)
off (n., u.m.)
-on (n., u.m.)
out (n., u.m.)
over (n., u.m.)
pin
screw
-stitched (u.m.)
-to (n., u.m.)
up (n., u.m.)
setter
-forth
-in
-on
-out
-to
-up
seven
-branched (u.m.)
fold
penny (nail)
score
-shooter
-up (n.)
severalfold
shade
-giving (u.m.)
-grown (u.m.)
shadow
boxing
gram
graph
#line
shag
bark
-haired (u.m.)
#rug
shake
down (n., u.m.)
out (n., u.m.)
up (n., u.m.)
shallow
-draft (u.m.)
-headed (u.m.)
shame
-crushed (u.m.)
faced
shank
bone
#mill
shapeup (n., u.m.)
share
bone
broker
cropper
holder
out (n., u.m.)
ware
sharp
-angled (u.m.)
-cut (u.m.)
-edged (u.m.)
-freeze (u.m., v.)
-freezer
-looking (u.m.)
naysayer
-set (u.m.)
shod
shooter
-tailed (u.m.)
-witted (u.m.)
shavetail
shear
pin
waters
shedhand
sheep
biter
crook
dip

#dog
faced
#farm
fold
gate
herder
hook
kill
-kneed (u.m.)
nose (apple)
pen
shank
shear (v.)
shearer (n.)
shed
stealer
walk
-white (u.m.)
sheer
off (n., u.m.)
up (n., u.m.)
sheet
block
flood
#glass
rock
ways
shell
back
burst
fire
fishery
#game
hole
-like
shocked
shelterbelt
shield-shaped (u.m.)
shilly-shally
shin
bone
guard
plaster
shiner-up
ship
breaker
broken
broker
builder
lap
mast
owning
-rigged (u.m.)
shape
side
wreck
shipping
#master
#room
shirt
band
#sleeve
tail
waist
shock
#therapy
#troops
#wave
shoe
black
brush
horn
lace
pack
scraper
shine
store
string
tree
shootoff (n., u.m.)
shop
folk
lifter
-made (u.m.)
mark
owner
-soiled (u.m.)
talk
walker
window
shore
#bird
#boat
fast
going
#leave
side
short
-armed (u.m.)
bread
cake
change (v.)
changer
#circuit
-circuited (u.m.)
coming
cut (n., u.m., v.)
fall (n.)
-fed (u.m.)
hand (writing)
-handed (u.m.)
head (whale)
horn (n., u.m.)
-horned (u.m.)
-lasting (u.m.)
leaf (u.m.)
-lived (u.m.)
rib
run (u.m.)
sighted
staff
stop
#term
-term (u.m.)
wave (radio)
shot
gun
hole
put
star
shoulder
#belt
#blade
-high (u.m.)
#strap
show
boat
card
case
down (n., u.m.)
off (n., u.m.)
piece
place
room
through (printing) (n., u.m.)
up (n., u.m.)
shredout (n., u.m.)
shroud
-laid (u.m.)
plate
shut
away (n., u.m.)
down (n., u.m.)
eye (n., u.m.)
-in (n., u.m.)
-mouthed (u.m.)
off (n., u.m.)
out (n., u.m.)
up (u.m.)
shuttlecock
sick
bay
bed
#call
#leave
list
room
sickle cell (n.)
sickle-cell (u.m.)

side
arms
band
board
bone
burns
car
check
-cut (u.m.)
dress (v.)
flash
head (printing)
hill
hook
kick
lap
#light (literal)
light (nonliteral)
#line (literal)
line (nonliteral)
long
note
plate
play
saddle
show
slip
splitting
step
stitch
-stitched (u.m.)
sway
swipe
track
walk
wall
-wheeler
winder
sight
hole
read
saver
seeing
setter
sign
off (n., u.m.)
-on (n., u.m.)
post
up (n., u.m.)
silico (c.f.)
all one word
silk
#screen
-stockinged (u.m.)
works
siltpan
silver
-backed (u.m.)
beater
-bright (u.m.)
fish
-gray (u.m.)
-haired (u.m.)
-lead (u.m.)
-leaved (u.m.)
plate (v.)
-plated (u.m.)
point (drawing)
print
tip
-tongued (u.m.)
top
simon-pure (u.m.)
simple
-headed (u.m.)
-minded (u.m.)
-rooted (u.m.)
-witted (u.m.)
simulcast
sin
-born (u.m.)
-bred (u.m.)
sine#die
single
bar
-breasted (u.m.)
-decker
-edged (u.m.)
handed
hood
-loader
-minded (u.m.)
-phase (u.m.)
-seater
stick
#stitch
tree
singsong
sink
head
hole
Sino (c.f.)
-Japanese, etc.
sister
hood
-in-law
sit
down (n., u.m.)
-downer
fast (n., u.m.)
-in
up (n., u.m.)
sitter
-by
-in
-out
sitting#room
sitz
#bath
mark
six
-cylinder (u.m.)
fold
penny (nail)
-ply (u.m.)
-shooter
-wheeler
sizeup (n., u.m.)
ski
#jump
#lift
plane
#suit
skid
lift (truck)
road
#row
skin
-clad (u.m.)
deep
diver
flint
-graft (v.)
skipjack
skirtmarker
skullcap
sky
-blue (u.m.)
gazer
-high (u.m.)
jacker
lift
look (v.)
rocket
sail
scape
scraper
shine
writer
slab-sided (u.m.)
slack
-bake (v.)
-filled (u.m.)
#water
slambang
slap
bang
dab
dash
down (n., u.m.)
happy

jack
stick
-up (n., u.m.)
slate
-blue (u.m.)
-colored (u.m.)
works
slaughter
house
pen
slave
holding
#market
owner
pen
Slavo (c.f.)
-Hungarian, etc.
sledge
#hammer
-hammered (u.m.)
meter
sleep
-filled (u.m.)
talker
walker
sleepy
-eyed (u.m.)
head
-looking (u.m.)
sleetstorm
sleeveband
sleuthhound
slide
film
knot
#rule
sling
ball
shot
slip
along (u.m.)
band
case
cover
knot
#law
-on (n., u.m.)
#proof (printing)
proof
ring
sheet
shod
sole
step
stitch
stream
-up (n., u.m.)
washer
slit
shell
#skirt
slop
-molded (u.m.)
seller
slopeways
slow
belly
down (n., u.m.)
-footed (u.m.)
going
-motion (u.m.)
mouthed
poke
#time
up (n., u.m.)
-witted (u.m.)
sluice
box
#gate
slum
dweller
gullion
gum
lord
slumber-bound (u.m.)
small
#arms
#businessman
pox
-scale (u.m.)
sword
talk
-time (u.m.)
town (u.m.)
smart
#aleck
-alecky (u.m.)
-looking (u.m.)
#set
-tongued (u.m.)
smashup (n., u.m.)
smearcase
smoke
-blinded (u.m.)
bomb
chaser
-dried (u.m.)
-dry (v.)
-dyed (u.m.)
-filled (u.m.)
house
jack
jumper
-laden (u.m.)
pot
screen
stack
smoking#room
smooth
bore
-browed (u.m.)
-cast (u.m.)
-mouthed (u.m.)
-tongued (u.m.)
-working (u.m.)
snackbar
snail
-paced (u.m.)
-slow (u.m.)
snail's#pace
snake
bite
-bitten (u.m.)
-eater
-eyed (u.m.)
head
hole
pit
snap
dragon
head
hook
-on (n., u.m.)
out (n.)
ring
roll
shooter
shot
-up (u.m.)
snapper
-back
-up
snipe
bill
#eel
-nosed (u.m.)
sniperscope
snooperscope
snow
ball
bank
berg
blind
#blindness
blink
block
-blocked (u.m.)
blower
break
capped
-choked (u.m.)

clad (u.m.)
#cover
-covered (u.m.)
drift
fall
field
flake
line
melt
-melting (u.m.)
mobile
pack
pit
plow
scape
shade
shed
shine
shoe
sled
slide
slip
storm
suit
-topped (u.m.)
#water
-white (u.m.)
snuffbox
so
-and-so
beit (n., conj.)
-called (u.m.)
-seeming (u.m.)
-so
soap
box
bubble
dish
flakes
#opera
rock
stock
suds
sob
#sister
#story
sober
-minded (u.m.)
sides
social
#work
#worker
socio (c.f.)
-official
economic, etc.
sod
buster
culture
#house
soda
jerk
#pop
#water
sofa
#bed
#maker
-making (u.m.)
-ridden (u.m.)
soft
ball
-boiled (u.m.)
#coal
#copy
#drink
#goods
head
-pedal (v.)
-shelled (u.m.)
-soap (nonliteral) (v.)
-soaper (nonliteral) (n.)
-spoken (u.m.)
tack
ware
wood
sole
cutter
plate
somato (c.f.)
all one word
some
day
how
one (anyone)
#one (distributive)
place (adv.)
time (adv., u.m.)
#time (some time ago)
what
son-in-law
song
bird
fest
writer
sonobuoy
sooth
fast
sayer
sore
-eyed (u.m.)
foot (n.)
footed (u.m.)
head (n., u.m.)
sorry-looking (u.m.)
soul
-deep (u.m.)
mate
-searching (u.m.)
sick
sound
-absorbing (u.m.)
#field
film
-minded (u.m.)
off (n., u.m.)
track
#wave
soup
bone
#bowl
#kitchen
#plate
spoon
sour
belly
bread
dough (n.)
faced
-natured (u.m.)
-sweet
source
book
#code
#file
south
-born (u.m.)
bound
-central (u.m.)
east
going
lander
paw
#side
-sider
-southeast
west
soybean
sow
back
belly
space
bar
craft
-cramped (u.m.)
#key
mark
ship
#time
spade
-dug (u.m.)

foot
-footed (u.m.)
-shaped (u.m.)
Spanish
-American (u.m.)
-born (u.m.)
-speaking (u.m.)
spare
-bodied (u.m.)
rib
#room
spark
#plug (literal)
plug (nonliteral)
speakeasy (n.)
spear
cast
head
-high (u.m.)
-shaped (u.m.)
spectro (c.f.)
all one word
speech
-bereft (u.m.)
-read (v.)
speed
boating
trap
up (n., u.m.)
spell
binding
check
down (n., u.m.)
-free (u.m.)
spend
-all (n.)
thrift
spermato (c.f.)
all one word
spermo (c.f.)
all one word
spheno (c.f.)
-occipital
rest one word
sphygmo (c.f.)
all one word
spice
-burnt (u.m.)
cake
-laden (u.m.)
spider
#crab
-legged
-spun (u.m.)
#web (n.)
web (u.m., v.)
spike
horn
-kill (v.)
-pitch (v.)
spill
over (n., u.m.)
way
spin
back
#doctor (slang)
off
spindle
-formed (u.m.)
head
-legged (u.m.)
legs
shanks
spine
bone
-broken (u.m.)
-pointed (u.m.)
spino (c.f.)
-olivary
rest one word
spirit
-born (u.m.)
-broken (u.m.)
#writing
spit
ball
fire
splanchno (c.f.)
all one word
splay
footed
mouthed
spleen
-born (u.m.)
sick
-swollen (u.m.)
spleno (c.f.)
all one word
split
finger
(crustacean)
fruit
mouth
saw
#second
-tongued (u.m.)
up (n., u.m.)
spoilsport
spondylo (c.f.)
all one word
sponge
#bath
cake
diver
-diving (u.m.)
-shaped (u.m.)
spongio (c.f.)
all one word
spool#winder
spoon
-beaked (u.m.)
-billed (u.m.)
bread
-fed (u.m.)
-shaped (u.m.)
ways
sporeformer
sporo (c.f.)
all one word
sports
#editor
person
wear
writer
spot
#check
-checked (u.m.)
-face (v.)
light
weld (v.)
welded (u.m.)
-welding (u.m.)
spray-washed (u.m.)
spread
-eagle (u.m., v.)
head
out (n., u.m.)
over (n., u.m.)
-set (v.)
spring
back
(bookbinding)
bok
-born (u.m.)
buck
-clean (v.)
#fever
finger
-grown (u.m.)
halt
head
-plow (v.)
-plowed (u.m.)
tide (season)
time
trap
spritsail
spur
-clad (u.m.)
-driven (u.m.)
gall
-galled (u.m.)

-heeled (u.m.)
spy
glass
hole
tower
square
-bottomed (u.m.)
-built (u.m.)
-faced (u.m.)
flipper
head
-headed
#mile
-rigged (u.m.)
#root
-set (u.m.)
shooter
squeeze
-in (n., u.m.)
out (n., u.m.)
up (n., u.m.)
squirrel-headed (u.m.)
stackup (n., u.m.)
staff
-herd (v.)
-hour
time
stag
-handled (u.m.)
head
-headed (u.m.)
horn
-horned (u.m.)
hound
hunter
stage
coach
hand
#set
-struck (u.m.)
stair
case
head
step
well
stake
head
holder
out (n.)
stale-worn (u.m.)
stall
-fed (u.m.)
-feed (v.)
stand
by (n., u.m.)
down (n., u.m.)
fast (n., u.m.)
-in (n., u.m.)
off (n., u.m.)
offish
out (n., u.m.)
pat
pipe
point
post
still (n., u.m.)
up (n., u.m.)
standard
#bearer
bred
#gauge
#time
staphylo (c.f.)
all one word
star
blind
bright
dust
gazer
-led (u.m.)
light
lit
lite (gem)
nose (mole)
shake
shine
shoot
-spangled (u.m.)
stroke
-studded (u.m.)
#time
stark
-blind (u.m.)
-mad (u.m.)
-naked (u.m.)
-raving (u.m.)
starter-off
start-stop
startup (n., u.m.)
stat (pref.)
all one word
State
-aided (u.m.)
#line
-owned (u.m.)
state
hood
-of-the-art (u.m.)
quake
room
side
station#house
stato (c.f.)
all one word
statute
-barred (u.m.)
#book
stay
-at-home (n., u.m.)
#bar
bolt
boom
lace
log
pin
plow
sail
wire
steam
boating
car
-cooked (u.m.)
-driven (u.m.)
fitter
pipe
plant
-pocket (v.)
power (n.)
#powerplant
-propelled (u.m.)
roll (v.)
roller (u.m., v.)
ship
table
tightness
steamer#line
steel
-blue (u.m.)
-bright (u.m.)
-cased (u.m.)
clad
-framed (u.m.)
-hard (u.m.)
head
plate
works
steep
-rising (u.m.)
-to (u.m.)
-up (u.m.)
-walled (u.m.)
steeple
chase
-high (u.m.)
jack
top
stem
head
post
winder
stencil-cutting (u.m.)

steno (c.f.)
all one word
step
aunt
child, etc.
dance
down (n., u.m.)
-in (n., u.m.)
ladder
off (n., u.m.)
-on (n., u.m.)
over (n., u.m.)
-up (n., u.m.)
stepping
-off (u.m.)
-out (u.m.)
stone
stereo (c.f.)
all one word
stern
castle
-faced (u.m.)
-heavy (u.m.)
-looking (u.m.)
most
post
#wheel
-wheeler
sterno (c.f.)
all one word
stetho (c.f.)
all one word
stew
pan
pot
stick
-at-it (n., u.m.)
fast (n.)
-in-the-mud (n., u.m.)
out (n., u.m.)
pin
-to-it-iveness (n.)
up (n., u.m.)
sticker
-in
-on
-up
stiff
-backed (u.m.)
neck
-necked (u.m.)
still
-admired (u.m.)
birth
born
-burn (v.)
-fish (v.)
-hunt (v.)
#life
-recurring (u.m.)
stand
stink
ball
bomb
bug
damp
pot
stir
about (n., u.m.)
fry
-up (n., u.m.)
stitch
down (n., u.m.)
up (n., u.m.)
stock
breeder
broker
#car
feeder
holding
jobber
judging
list
pile
pot
rack
raiser
-still (u.m.)
taker
truck
stoke
hold
hole
stomach
#ache
-filling (u.m.)
#pump
-shaped (u.m.)
-sick (u.m.)
-weary (u.m.)
stomato (c.f.)
all one word
stone
biter
blind
brash
breaker
broke
brood
cast
-cold (u.m.)
#crab
crusher
cutter
-dead (u.m.)
-deaf (u.m.)
-eyed (u.m.)
head
layer
lifter
mason
shot
#wall (n.)
wall (u.m., v.)
#writing
stony
-eyed (u.m.)
#land
stop
back (n.)
block
clock
cock
gap
hound
list
log
-loss (u.m.)
off (n., u.m.)
watch
storage#room
store
front
house
storm
-beaten (u.m.)
cock
flow
-laden (u.m.)
-swept (u.m.)
-tossed (u.m.)
#trooper
wind
#window
storyteller
stout
-armed (u.m.)
heartedness
-minded (u.m.)
stove
brush
-heated (u.m.)
pipe
stow
away (n., u.m.)
down (n., u.m.)
straddle
back
-face (v.)
-legged (u.m.)

straight
away
-backed (u.m.)
-cut (u.m.)
edge
-edged (u.m.)
#face
-faced (u.m.)
forward
head
-legged (u.m.)
#line
-lined (u.m.)
-out (n., u.m.)
-spoken (u.m.)
#time
-up (u.m.)
-up-and-down (u.m.)
strainslip
strait
-chested (u.m.)
jacket
laced
stranglehold
strap
-bolt (v.)
hanger
head
-shaped (u.m.)
watch
strato (c.f.)
all one word
straw
berry#field
boss
-built (u.m.)
hat
#poll
-roofed (u.m.)
splitting
stack
-stuffed (u.m.)
#vote
walker
-yellow (u.m.)
stray
away (n., u.m.)
#line
mark
stream
bank
bed
flow
head
lined
side
street
-bred (u.m.)
car
cleaner
-cleaning (u.m.)
sweeper
walker
strepto (c.f.)
all one word
stretchout (n., u.m.)
strike
breaker
-in (n., u.m.)
out (n., u.m.)
-over (n., u.m.)
striker
-in
-out
-over
string
course
halt
#proof (density)
ways
strip
cropping
#mine
tease
strong
-arm (u.m., v.)
back (nautical)
-backed (u.m.)
box
hold
#man (literal)
man (nonliteral)
-minded (u.m.)
point (n.)
stub
runner
-toed (u.m.)
wing
stubble
#field
-mulch (u.m.)
stubbornminded
stucco-fronted (u.m.)
stuck
up (n., u.m.)
-uppish (u.m.)
stud
bolt
horse
mare
stuntman
sturdy-limbed (u.m.)
stylebook
stylo (c.f.)
all one word
sub (pref.)
-Himalayan, etc.
machinegun
#rosa, #specie, etc.
-subcommittee
polar, standard, etc.
rest one word
subject
-object
-objectivity
subter (pref.)
all one word
such-and-such
suck
-egg (n., u.m.)
hole
-in (n., u.m.)
sugar
#beet
#bowl
cake
cane
-coat (v.)
-coated (u.m.)
-cured (u.m.)
loaf
plum
spoon
sweet
#water
works
sulfa (c.f.)
all one word
sulfo (c.f.)
all one word
sulfon (c.f.)
all one word
sullen
hearted
-natured (u.m.)
summer
-clad (u.m.)
-dried (u.m.)
-fallow (v.)
-made (u.m.)
tide
time (season)
#time (daylight saving)
sun
-baked (u.m.)
bath
-bathed (u.m.)

beam
blind
#blindness
bonnet
bow
break
burn
burst
-cured (u.m.)
dial
dog
down
dress
-dried (u.m.)
-dry (v.)
fall
fast
glade
glare
glow
#hat
lamp
lit
quake
ray
rise
scald
set
shade
shine
-shot (u.m.)
shower
spot
stricken
stroke
struck
tan
#time (measure)
time (dawn)
up

sunny
-looking (u.m.)
-natured (u.m.)

super (pref.)
-Christian, etc.
#high frequency
-superlative
highway, market, etc.
rest one word

Super Bowl

supra (pref.)
-abdominal
-acromial
-aerial
anal
-angular
-arytenoid
-auditory
-auricular
-axillary
-Christian, etc.
rest one word

sur (pref.)
all one word

sure
-fire (u.m.)
-footed (u.m.)
-slow

surf
-battered (u.m.)
board
#fish
-swept (u.m.)

swallow
pipe
-tailed (u.m.)

swampside

swan
-bosomed (u.m.)
dive
herd
mark
neck
song

swansdown

swash
buckler
plate

sway
back (n., u.m.)
-backed (u.m.)
bar
-brace (v.)

swearer-in

sweat
band
#gland
shirt
shop

sweep
back (aviation) (n., u.m.)
forward (aviation) (n., u.m.)
stake
through (n., u.m.)
washer

sweet
bread
-breathed (u.m.)
brier
faced
heart
meat
mouthed
-pickle (v.)
-sour

swell
-butted (u.m.)
head
toad

swelled-headed (u.m.)

swept
back (n., u.m.)
forward (n., u.m.)
wing (n., u.m.)

swift
foot
-footed (u.m.)
-handed (u.m.)
-running (u.m.)

swill
bowl
tub

swimsuit

swine
-backed (u.m.)
bread
head
herd
pox
sty

swing
back (n., u.m.)
bar
dingle
#gate
#shift
stock
tree

swingle
bar
tree

switch
back
blade
box
gear
plate
plug
rail
tender

swivel
#chair
eye
-eyed (u.m.)
-hooked (u.m.)

sword
-armed (u.m.)

bearer
#belt
bill
fishing
play
-shaped (u.m.)
stick

syn (pref.)
all one word

synchro
cyclotron
flash
mesh
tron

Syro (c.f.)
-Arabian, etc.
phenician

T

T
-ball
-bandage
-beam
-boat
-bone
-cloth
-iron
-man
-rail
-scale (score)
-shape
-shaped
-shirt
-square

table
cloth
-cut (u.m.)
cutter
-cutting (u.m.)
-formed (u.m.)
#linen
-shaped (u.m.)
spoon
talk
top
ware

tachy (c.f.)
all one word

tag
-affixing (u.m.)
lock
rag
sore

tail
band
#coat
-cropped (u.m.)
#end
-ender
first
foremost
gate
head
-heavy (u.m.)
hook
lamp
pin
pipe
race
spin
stock
-tied (u.m.)
twister
-up (n., u.m.)
wheel
wind

tailor
-cut (u.m.)
made (u.m.)
-suited (u.m.)

take
-all (n.)
down (n., u.m.)
-home (n., u.m.)
-in (n., u.m.)
off (n., u.m.)
out (n., u.m.)
over (n., u.m.)
up (n., u.m.)

taker
-down
-in
-off
-over
-up

tale
bearer
carrier
teller

talkfest
talking-to (n.)

tall
boy (n.)
-built (u.m.)
-looking (u.m.)

tallow
-faced (u.m.)
-pale (u.m.)

tally
#board
#clerk
ho
#room
#sheet

tame
-grown (u.m.)
-looking (u.m.)

tan
bark
works

tangent
-cut (v.)
-saw (v.)

tangle
foot
-haired (u.m.)

tank
#car
farm
ship
town

tap
bolt
dance
hole
net
off (n., u.m.)
-riveted (u.m.)
room
root
-tap
water

tape
#deck
#drive
#measure
string
-tied (u.m.)

taper
bearer
-fashion (u.m.)
-headed (u.m.)

tapestry
-covered (u.m.)
#maker
-making (u.m.)
#work

tar
-brand (v.)
brush
-coal (u.m.)
-dipped (u.m.)
#paper
-paved (u.m.)
pot
-roofed (u.m.)
works

tariff-protected (u.m.)

tarpaulin
-covered (u.m.)
#maker

-making (u.m.)
tarso (c.f.)
all one word
task
#force
setter
tattletale
tauro (c.f.)
all one word
tax
-burdened (u.m.)
#collector
eater
-exempt (u.m.)
-free (u.m.)
gatherer
-laden (u.m.)
paid
payer
#roll
-supported (u.m.)
taxi
auto
bus
cab
meter
stand
tea
ball
cake
cart
-colored (u.m.)
cup
dish
kettle
#party
pot
room
-scented (u.m.)
spoon
taster
teamplay
tear
bomb
-dimmed (u.m.)
down (n., u.m.)
drop
#gas
-off (n., u.m.)
-out (n., u.m.)
pit
sheet
stain
-stained (u.m.)
teen
age (u.m.)
ager
teeter-totter
tele (c.f.)
all one word
teleo (c.f.)
all one word
tell
tale
truth
telo (c.f.)
all one word
tempest-rocked (u.m.)
temporo (c.f.)
-occipital
rest one word
ten
fold
penny (nail)
pins
tender
#boat
-faced (u.m.)
foot
-footed (u.m.)
footish
-handed (u.m.)
heart
loin
-looking (u.m.)
tenement#house
tent
-dotted (u.m.)
pole
-sheltered (u.m.)
#show
terra
#cotta
#firma
mara
terrace-fashion (u.m.)
test-fly (v.)
tetra (c.f.)
all one word
thanksgiving
thatch-roofed (u.m.)
text
-based
#file
#mode
theater
goer
going
thenceforth
theo (c.f.)
all one word
theologico (c.f.)
all one word
there
about(s)
above
across
after
against
among
around
at
away
before
between
by
for
fore
from
in
inafter
inbefore
into
on
over
through
tofore
under
until
unto
upon
with
thermo (c.f.)
all one word
thick
-blooded (u.m.)
head
-looking (u.m.)
pated
set (n., u.m.)
skinned
skull (n.)
skulled
-tongued (u.m.)
wit
-witted (u.m.)
-wooded (u.m.)
-woven (u.m.)
thin
-clad (u.m.)
down (n., u.m.)
set (u.m.)
-voiced (u.m.)
thio (c.f.)
all one word
third
-class (u.m.)
-degree (u.m.)

hand (adv., u.m.)
#house
-rate (u.m.)
-rater
thistledown
thoraco (c.f.)
all one word
thorn
back
bill
-covered (u.m.)
-set (u.m.)
-strewn (u.m.)
tail
thorough
-bind (v.)
bred
-dried (u.m.)
fare
going
-made (u.m.)
paced
pin
thought
-free (u.m.)
-out (u.m.)
-provoking (u.m.)
thousand
fold
-headed (u.m.)
-legged (u.m.)
legs (worm)
thrall
born
dom
-less
thread
bare
-leaved (u.m.)
worn
three
-bagger
-cornered (u.m.)
-dimensional (u.m.)
fold
-in-hand
-master
penny (nail)
-piece (u.m.)
-ply (u.m.)
score
some
-spot
-square
-striper
throat
band
cutter
latch
strap
thrombo (c.f.)
all one word
through
out
put
#road
way
throw
away (n., u.m.)
back (n., u.m.)
-in (n., u.m.)
#line
off (n., u.m.)
-on (n., u.m.)
out (n., u.m.)
over (n., u.m.)
-weight
thrust-pound
thumb
#hole
-made (u.m.)
mark
-marked (u.m.)
nail
print
screw
stall
string
sucker
tack
worn
thunder
bearer
blast
bolt
clap
cloud
head
peal
shower
storm
struck
thymo (c.f.)
all one word
thyro (c.f.)
all one word
tibio (c.f.)
all one word
tick
#feed
seed
tacktoe
tick
tock
ticket
#seller
-selling (u.m.)
#writer
tidal#wave
tiddlywink
tide
flat
head
mark
-marked (u.m.)
race
table
-tossed (u.m.)
waiter
-worn (u.m.)
tie
back (n.)
#bar
#beam
down (n., u.m.)
-in (n., u.m.)
-on (n., u.m.)
-out (n., u.m.)
pin
-plater
#rod
#tack
up (n., u.m.)
tierlift (truck)
tiger
eye
#lily
#shark
-striped (u.m.)
tight
-belted (u.m.)
fisted
-fitting (u.m.)
lipped
rope
-set (u.m.)
-tie (v.)
wad
wire
tile
-clad (u.m.)
#drain
-red (u.m.)
setter
works
wright
tilt
hammer
rotor
up (n.)

timber
-built (u.m.)
head
-headed (u.m.)
jack
line
-propped (u.m.)
#wolf
wright
time
bomb
born
card
clerk
clock
-consuming (u.m.)
frame
-honored (u.m.)
keeper
killer
lag
lock
outs (n., u.m.)
piece
pleaser
saver
server
sheet
slip
slot
span
-stamp (v.)
study
table
taker
waster
worn
tin
-bearing (u.m.)
#can
-capped (u.m.)
-clad (u.m.)
#cup
#fish (torpedo)
foil
horn
kettle
-lined (u.m.)
man
pan
plate
-plated (u.m.)
pot
-roofed (u.m.)
type
-white (u.m.)
tinsel
-bright (u.m.)
-clad (u.m.)
-covered (u.m.)
#town
tintblock (printing)
tip
burn
cart
-curled (u.m.)
head
-in (n., u.m.)
most
off (n., u.m.)
over (n., u.m.)
staff
stock
tank
-tap
toe
top
-up (u.m.)
tire
changer
dresser
fitter
#gauge
#iron
-mile
#rack
shaper
some
tit
bit
#for#tat
mouse
titano (c.f.)
all one word
tithe
book
-free (u.m.)
payer
right
title
holder
-holding (u.m.)
#page
winner
-winning (u.m.)
to
-and-fro
-do (n.)
#wit
toad
back
-bellied (u.m.)
blind
fish
-green (u.m.)
stool
tobacco
#grower
-growing (u.m.)
#shop
toe
cap
#dance
hold
-in (n., u.m.)
-mark (v.)
nail
plate
print
toil
-beaten (u.m.)
some
-stained (u.m.)
-weary (u.m.)
worn
toilet#room
toll
bar
#bridge
#call
gate
gatherer
house
#line
payer
road
taker
tom
boy
cat
foolery
-tom
tommy
gun
rot
ton
-hour
-kilometer
-mile
-mileage
-mile-day
tone
-deaf (u.m.)
down (n., u.m.)
-producing (u.m.)
up (n., u.m.)
tongue
-baited (u.m.)
-bound (u.m.)
-free (u.m.)
-lash (v.)
#lashing

play
-shaped (u.m.)
shot
sore
tack
-tied
tip
#twister
-twisting (u.m.)
tool
bag
#belt
box
builder
#chest
crib
dresser
fitter
#grinder
-grinding (u.m.)
head
holding
kit
mark
plate
post
rack
setter
shed
slide
stock
tooth
ache
#and#nail
-billed (u.m.)
brush
drawer
mark
-marked (u.m.)
paste
pick
plate
powder
puller
-pulling (u.m.)
-set (u.m.)
-shaped (u.m.)
some
wash
top
#brass
cap (n.)
coat
cutter
#dog
-drain (v.)
#drawer
dress (v.)
flight (u.m.)
full
gallant (n., u.m.)
-graft (v.)
hat
-hatted (u.m.)
heavy
kick
knot
liner
mark
mast
milk
most
notch (nonliteral)
rail
rope
sail
-secret (u.m.)
-shaped (u.m.)
side (naut.)
soil
topo (c.f.)
all one word
topsy-turvy
torch
bearer
#holder
lighted
lit
torpedo
#boat
#room
torquemeter
toss
pot
up (n., u.m.)
touch
#and#go
back (n., u.m.)
down (n., u.m.)
hole
-me-not (n., u.m.)
pan
reader
stone
up (n., u.m.)
tough
-headed (u.m.)
-looking (u.m.)
-skinned (u.m.)
tow
away
boat
head
line
mast
#net
-netter
path
rope
#truck
tower
-high (u.m.)
-shaped (u.m.)
town
-bred (u.m.)
#clerk
#crier
-dotted (u.m.)
folk
gate
going
hall
lot
ship
side
site
talk
-weary (u.m.)
towns
fellow
people
toy
#dog
-sized (u.m.)
town
tracheo (c.f.)
all one word
trachy (c.f.)
all one word
track
barrow
hound
layer
mark
-mile
side
walker
tractor-trailer
trade
#board
-in (n., u.m.)
-laden (u.m.)
-made (u.m.)
mark
#name
off
#union
#wind
tradespeople
traffic-mile
tragico (c.f.)
all one word

trail
blazer
breaker
-marked (u.m.)
side
sight
-weary (u.m.)
train
bearer
bolt
crew
line
-mile
shed
sick
stop
tram
-borne (u.m.)
car
rail
road
way
trans (pref.)
alpine
atlantic
-Canadian, etc.
gender
pacific
uranic
rest one word
transit#time
trap
door
fall
shoot
trashrack
travel
-bent (u.m.)
time
-tired (u.m.)
-worn (u.m.)
trawlnet
tread
mill
wheel
treasure
-filled (u.m.)
#house
-laden (u.m.)
treaty
breaker
-sealed (u.m.)
tree
#belt
-clad (u.m.)
#line
-lined (u.m.)
nail
-ripe (u.m.)
scape
top
#trunk
trellis-covered (u.m.)
trench
back
coat
foot
#knife
mouth
#plow
-plowed (u.m.)
tri (c.f.)
-iodide
-ply (u.m.)
state, etc.
rest one word
tribespeople
tribo (c.f.)
all one word
tricho (c.f.)
all one word
trim
-cut (u.m.)
-dressed (u.m.)
-looking (u.m.)
trinitro (c.f.)
all one word
trip
-free (u.m.)
hammer
wire
triple
-acting (u.m.)
back (sofa)
branched (u.m.)
-edged (u.m.)
fold
#play
-tailed (u.m.)
tree (n.)
trolley#line
troop
ship
#train
tropho (c.f.)
all one word
tropo (c.f.)
all one word
trouble
-free (u.m.)
-haunted (u.m.)
maker
shooter
some
truce
breaker
-seeking (u.m.)
truck
driver
#farm
-mile
stop
true
-aimed (u.m.)
-blue (u.m.)
born
bred
-eyed (u.m.)
-false
love (n., u.m.)
penny (n.)
#time
trunk
back
nose
trust
breaking
buster
-controlled (u.m.)
-ridden (u.m.)
worthy
truth
-filled (u.m.)
lover
seeker
-seeking (u.m.)
teller
try
-on (n., u.m.)
out (n., u.m.)
square
works
tube
-eyed (u.m.)
-fed (u.m.)
head
-nosed (u.m.)
works
tuberculo (c.f.)
all one word
tubo (c.f.)
-ovarian
rest one word
tug
boat
#of#war
tumbledown (n., u.m.)
tune
out (n., u.m.)

up (n., u.m.)
tunnel
-boring (u.m.)
-shaped (u.m.)
#vision
turbo (c.f.)
-ramjet (u.m.)
rest one word
turf
-built (u.m.)
-clad (u.m.)
-covered (u.m.)
#war
turkey
back
#buzzard
#gobbler
#trot
Turko (c.f.)
-Greek, etc.
rest one word
turn
about (n., u.m.)
about-face
again (n., u.m.)
around (n., u.m.)
back (n., u.m.)
buckle
cap
coat
cock
down (n., u.m.)
gate
-in (n., u.m.)
key
off (n., u.m.)
out (n., u.m.)
over (n., u.m.)
pike
pin
plate
round (n., u.m.)
screw
sheet
sole
stile
stitch
table
tail
-to (n.)
under (n., u.m.)
up (n., u.m.)
turned
-back (u.m.)
-down (u.m.)
-in (u.m.)
-on (u.m.)
-out (u.m.)
-over (u.m.)
turner-off
turtle
back
dove
-footed (u.m.)
neck (u.m.)
#shell
twelve
fold
penny (nail)
score
twenty
-first
fold
-one
twice
-born (u.m.)
-reviewed (u.m.)
-told (u.m.)
twin
#boat
born
-engined (u.m.)
fold
-jet (u.m.)
-motor (u.m.)
-screw (u.m.)
two
-a-day (u.m.)
-along (n.)
(bookbinding)
-decker
-faced (u.m.)
fold
-handed (u.m.)
penny (nail)
-piece (u.m.)
-ply (u.m.)
score
-seater
some
-spot
-step (dance)
-striper
-suiter
-up (n., u.m.)
-way (u.m.)
-wheeler
tympano (c.f.)
all one word
type
case
cast
cutter
face
foundry
script
set
write (v.)
typho (c.f.)
all one word
typo (c.f.)
all one word
tyro (c.f.)
all one word

U

U
-boat
-cut
-magnet
-rail
-shaped
-tube
ultra (pref.)
-ambitious,
-atomic, etc.
-English, etc.
high#frequency
-high-speed (u.m.)
#valorem, etc.
rest one word
un (pref.)
-American, etc.
called-for (u.m.)
heard-of (u.m.)
-ionized (u.m.)
self-conscious
sent-for (u.m.)
thought-of (u.m.)
rest one word
under
age (deficit)
age (younger)
(n., u.m.)
#cultivation
(tillage)
cultivation
(insufficient)
#secretary
-secretaryship
way
as prefix, one word
uni (c.f.)
-univalent
rest one word
union
-made (u.m.)
#shop
unit-set (u.m.)
up
-anchor (u.m., v.)

-and-coming (u.m.)
#and#up
beat
coast
country
dip
end (v.)
front (n., u.m.)
grade
gradient
keep
lift
load
-over (u.m.)
rate
river
stairs
state
stream
swing
take
tight (n., u.m.)
#tight (v.)
-to-date (u.m.)
#to#date
town
trend
turn
wind
upper
case (printing)
#class
classman
crust (n., u.m.)
cut
#deck
most
urano (c.f.)
all one word
uretero (c.f.)
all one word
urethro (c.f.)
all one word
uro (c.f.)
all one word
used-car (u.m.)
user
#default
-defined
-friendly
#group
#interface
utero (c.f.)
all one word

V

V
-connection
-curve
-engine
-neck
-shaped
-type
vacant
-eyed (u.m.)
-looking (u.m.)
-minded (u.m.)
vagino (c.f.)
all one word
vainglorious
valve
-grinding (u.m.)
-in-head (u.m.)
van
driver
guard
pool
vapor
-filled (u.m.)
-heating (u.m.)
#lock
vase-shaped (u.m.)
vaso (c.f.)
all one word
vegeto (c.f.)
all one word
vein
-mining (u.m.)
-streaked (u.m.)
vellum
-bound (u.m.)
-covered (u.m.)
velvet
-crimson (u.m.)
-draped (u.m.)
-green (u.m.)
-pile (u.m.)
venthole
ventri (c.f.)
all one word
ventro (c.f.)
all one word
vertebro (c.f.)
all one word
vesico (c.f.)
all one word
vibro (c.f.)
all one word
vice
#admiral
-admiralty
#consul
-consulate
#governor
-governorship
#minister
-ministry
-presidency
#president
-president-elect
-presidential
#rector
-rectorship
regal
-regency
#regent
royal
#squad
#versa
#warden
videotape
Vietcong
view
finder
point
vile-natured (u.m.)
vine
-clad (u.m.)
-covered (u.m.)
dresser
growing
stalk
vinegar
-flavored (u.m.)
-hearted (u.m.)
-making (u.m.)
-tart (u.m.)
violet
-blue (u.m.)`
-colored (u.m.)
-eared (u.m.)
#ray
-rayed (u.m.)
#water
violin-shaped (u.m.)
vis-a-vis
viscero (c.f.)
all one word
vitreo (c.f.)
all one word
vitro (c.f.)
-clarain
-di-trina
rest one word
vivi (c.f.)
all one word
voice
-capable
#mail
over (n.)

volleyball
volt
ammeter
-ampere
-coulomb
meter
ohmmeter
-second
volta (c.f.)
all one word
vote
-casting (u.m.)
getter
-getting (u.m.)
vow
-bound (u.m.)
breaker
-pledged (u.m.)
vulvo (c.f.)
all one word

W

W
-engine
-shaped
-surface
-type
wage
#earner
-earning (u.m.)
#scale
worker
waist
band
belt
cloth
coat
-deep (u.m.)
-high (u.m.)
line
waiting
#list
#man
#room
#woman
walk
around (n., u.m.)
away (n., u.m.)
-on (n., u.m.)
out (n., u.m.)
over (n., u.m.)
up (n., u.m.)
way
walkie-talkie
wall
board
eyed
flower
-like
-painting (u.m.)
paper
plate
-sided (u.m.)
walled
-in (u.m.)
-up (u.m.)
war
#dance
-disabled (u.m.)
-famed (u.m.)
fare
head
horse (nonliteral)
like
monger
-made (u.m.)
path
plane
ship
-swept (u.m.)
#time (clock)
time (duration)
ward
#heeler
robe
ship
warm
blooded
-clad (u.m.)
up (n., u.m.)
warmed-over (u.m.)
warpsetter
wash
basin
basket
board
bowl
cloth
-colored (u.m.)
day
down (n., u.m.)
-in (n., u.m.)
off (n., u.m.)
out (n., u.m.)
pot
rag
#sale
stand
tray
trough
tub
up (n., u.m.)
washed
-out (u.m.)
-up (u.m.)
waste
basket
land
leaf
(bookbinding)
paper
site
word
watch
band
case
#chain
cry
dog
-free (u.m.)
glass
tower
water
bag
bank
bearer
-bearing (u.m.)
-beaten (u.m.)
-bind (v.)
#blister
bloom
buck
color
-colored (u.m.)
-cool (v.)
-cooled (u.m.)
#cooler
course
craft
dog
-drinking (u.m.)
drop
fall
-filled (u.m.)
finder
flood
flow
fog
-free (u.m.)
front
gate
head
hole
horse
-inch
-laden (u.m.)
lane
leaf
#line
-lined (u.m.)
locked
log

#main
mark
melon
meter
plant
pot
power
proofing
quake
-rot (v.)
scape
shed
shoot
side
-soak (v.)
-soaked (u.m.)
-soluble (u.m.)
spout
stain
#table
tight
wall
works
worn
watt
-hour
meter
-second
wave
-cut (u.m.)
form
guide
-lashed (u.m.)
length
mark
meter
-moist (u.m.)
-on (n., u.m.)
off (n., u.m.)
-swept (u.m.)
-worn (u.m.)
wax
bill
-billed (u.m.)
chandler
cloth
-coated (u.m.)
-headed (u.m.)
#paper
#stone
-yellow (u.m.)
way
back (n., u.m.)
beam
bill
down (n., u.m.)
farer
fellow
going
laid
lay
mark
post
side
-sore (u.m.)
-up (n., u.m.)
worn
weak
-backed (u.m.)
-eyed (u.m.)
handed
-kneed (u.m.)
minded
mouthed
weather
beaten
blown
-borne (u.m.)
break
cock
glass
going
-hardened (u.m.)
#house
-marked (u.m.)
most
proofing
-stain (v.)
strip
-stripped (u.m.)
worn
web
-fingered (u.m.)
foot
-footed (u.m.)
master
#page
#press
site
wedge
-billed (u.m.)
-shaped (u.m.)
weed
-choked (u.m.)
-hidden (u.m.)
hook
killer
week
day
end
-ender
-ending (u.m.)
long (u.m.)
-old (u.m.)
weigh
bridge
-in (n., u.m.)
lock
out (n., u.m.)
shaft
well
-being (n.)
-beloved (u.m.)
-born (u.m.)
-bound (u.m.)
-bred (u.m.)
-clad (u.m.)
-deserving (u.m.)
-doer
-doing (n., u.m.)
-drained (u.m.)
-drilling (u.m.)
#field
-grown (u.m.)
head
-headed (u.m.)
hole
-informed (u.m.)
-known (u.m.)
-looking (u.m.)
-meaner
-nigh (u.m.)
-off (u.m.)
-read (u.m.)
-set-up (u.m.)
-settled (u.m.)
side
-spoken (u.m.)
spring
stead
-thought-of (u.m.)
-thought-out (u.m.)
-to-do (u.m.)
-wisher
-wishing (u.m.)
-worn (u.m.)
welterweight
werewolf
west
bound
-central (u.m.)
#end
-faced (u.m.)
going
most
-northwest
#side
-sider
wet
#bar
-cheeked (u.m.)

-clean (v.)
land
-nurse (v.)
pack
wash
whale
back
-backed (u.m.)
bone
-built (u.m.)
-headed (u.m.)
-mouthed (u.m.)
ship
wharf
#boat
hand
head
side
what
abouts (n.)
ever
-is-it (n.)
not (n.)
soever
-you-may-call-it (n.)
wheat
cake
-colored (u.m.)
ear
-fed (u.m.)
field
grower
-rich (u.m.)
stalk
wheel
band
barrow
base
chair
-cut (u.m.)
going
horse (nonliteral)
#load
-made (u.m.)
plate
race
spin
stitch
-worn (u.m.)
wright
when
ever
-issued (u.m.)
soever
where
abouts
after
as
at
by
for
fore
from
in
insoever
into
of
on
over
soever
through
to
under
upon
with
withal
wherever
which
ever
soever
whiffletree
whip
cord
crack
-graft (v.)
#hand
lash
-marked (u.m.)
post
saw
-shaped (u.m.)
socket
staff
stalk
stall
stick
stitch
stock
-tailed (u.m.)
whipper
-in
snapper
whirl
about (n., u.m.)
blast
pool
-shaped (u.m.)
wind
whirlybird
whisk
broom
#tail
whistle
blower (nonliteral)
#blower (literal)
stop
white
back
beard (n.)
#book (diplomatic)
cap (n.)
coat (n.)
-collar (u.m.)
comb (n.)
corn
-eared (u.m.)
-eyed (u.m.)
face
-faced (u.m.)
foot (n.)
-footed (u.m.)
handed
-hard (u.m.)
head
-headed (u.m.)
-hot (u.m.)
#line
out (u.m., v.)
pot
tail
-tailed (u.m.)
-throated (u.m.)
top (n.)
vein
wash
who
ever
soever
whole
-headed (u.m.)
#hog
-hogger
sale
some
whomsoever
whooping#cough
wicker-woven (u.m.)
wicket
keeper
keeping
wide
-angle (u.m.)
-awake (u.m.)
-handed (u.m.)
mouthed
-open (u.m.)
spread
-spreading (u.m.)

widow
#bird
hood
wigwag
wild
cat (n.)
-eyed (u.m.)
fire
#land
life
#man
wind
will
-less
-o'-the-wisp
power
wilt-resistant (u.m.)
wind (v.)
down (n., u.m.)
up (n., u.m.)
bag
ball
blown
brace
breaker
burn
catcher
-chapped (u.m.)
chill
fall
#farm
fast
-fertilized (u.m.)
firm
flow
#force
gall
-galled (u.m.)
#gauge
hole
-hungry (u.m.)
jammer
lass
mill
pipe
-pollinated (u.m.)
#power
-rode (u.m.)
row
screen
-shaken (u.m.)
-shear (u.m.)
shield
shock
side
sleeve
sock
speed
stop
storm
stream
swept
#tunnel
worn
window
breaker
-breaking (u.m.)
#cleaner
-cleaning (u.m.)
#dresser
-dressing (u.m.)
pane
#shade
-shop (v.)
-shopping (u.m.)
sill
#work
wine
bag
-black (u.m.)
-drinking (u.m.)
glass
growing
-hardy (u.m.)
pot
#press
-red (u.m.)
seller
taster
tester
vat
wing
band
bar
beat
bolt
bone
borne
bow
cut
#flap
-footed (u.m.)
handed
-heavy (u.m.)
-loading (u.m.)
-loose (u.m.)
nut
over (n., u.m.)
-shaped (u.m.)
-shot (u.m.)
span
-swift (u.m.)
tip
top
wall
-weary (u.m.)
winter
-beaten (u.m.)
-clad (u.m.)
-fallow (v.)
-fed (u.m.)
feed
#green (color)
green (plant, etc.)
-hardy (u.m.)
kill
-made (u.m.)
-sown (u.m.)
tide
time
-worn (u.m.)
wire
bar
-caged (u.m.)
-cut (u.m.)
cutter
dancer
draw (v.)
-edged (u.m.)
#gauge
hair (dog)
-haired (u.m.)
less
#line
photo
puller
#rope
spun
stitch
-stitched (u.m.)
-tailed (u.m.)
tap
walker
works
-wound (u.m.)
wise
acre
crack
guy
head (n.)
-headed (u.m.)
-spoken (u.m.)
wishbone
witch
craft
#hazel
#hunt
-hunting (u.m.)
with
draw
hold
in

out
stand
within
-bound (u.m.)
-named (u.m.)
woe
begone
worn
wolf
-eyed (u.m.)
#fish
hound
pack
woman
folk
hood
kind
womenfolk
wonder
land
strong
-struck (u.m.)
wood
bark (color)
bin
bined
block
-built (u.m.)
-cased (u.m.)
chipper
chopper
chuck
craft
cut
grub
hole
horse
hung (u.m.)
land
-lined (u.m.)
lot
-paneled (u.m.)
pecker
pile
-planing (u.m.)
print
pulp
ranger
rock
#rot
shed
side
stock
turner
-turning (u.m.)
-walled (u.m.)
wind (music)
working (u.m.)
wooden
head (n.)
-hulled (u.m.)
wool
fell
gatherer
grader
growing
head
-laden (u.m.)
-lined (u.m.)
pack
press
shearer
shed
sorter
stock
washer
wheel
-white (u.m.)
winder
woolly
-coated (u.m.)
-headed (u.m.)
-looking (u.m.)
-white (u.m.)
word
-blind (u.m.)
book
builder
catcher
-clad (u.m.)
-deaf (u.m.)
flow
list
-perfect (u.m.)
play
seller
smith
work
aday (n., u.m.)
-and-turn (u.m.)
away (n., u.m.)
bag
basket
bench
book
card
day
-driven (u.m.)
fare
flow
folk
force
group
hand
-hardened (u.m.)
horse
-hour (u.m.)
housed
life
load
manship
out (n., u.m.)
pace
pan
paper
people
place
room
saving
sheet
shoe
shop
-shy (n., u.m.)
-shyness
site
slip
space
-stained (u.m.)
stand
station
stream
study
table
time
up (n., u.m.)
ways
-weary (u.m.)
week
worn
working
#capital
#load
#room
world
beater
-conscious (u.m.)
#consciousness
#line
#power
-shaking (u.m.)
-weary (u.m.)
worm
-eaten (u.m.)
-eating (u.m.)
hole
-riddled (u.m.)
-ripe (u.m.)
seed
shaft
wood
worn
#away

down (u.m.)
out (u.m.)
outness
worrywart
worth
less
while (n., u.m.)
whileness (n.)
wrap
around (n., u.m.)
-up (n., u.m.)
wreath-crowned (u.m.)
wreck-free (u.m.)
wring
bolt
staff
wrist
band
bone
drop
fall
lock
#pin
plate
watch
write
back (n., u.m.)
-in (n., u.m.)
off (n., u.m.)
-protect
up (n., u.m.)
writing#room
wrong
doer
-ended (u.m.)
-minded (u.m.)
-thinking (u.m.)
wrought
#iron
-up (u.m.)
wry
bill
-billed (u.m.)
-faced (u.m.)
-looking (u.m.)
-mouthed (u.m.)
neck
-set (u.m.)

X

X
-body
-chromosome
-disease
#rated
-shaped
-virus
x
-axis
#ray (n.)
-ray (u.m.)
xantho (c.f.)
all one word
xeno (c.f.)
all one word
xero (c.f.)
all one word
xylo (c.f.)
all one word

Y

Y
-chromosome
-joint
-level
-potential
-shaped
-track
-tube
Yankee-Doodle
yard
arm
-deep (u.m.)
-long (u.m.)
stick
-wide (u.m.)
yaw
meter
-sighted (u.m.)
year
book
day
end
-hour (u.m.)
long (u.m.)
-old (u.m.)
-round (u.m.)
yellow
back
-backed (u.m.)
-bellied (u.m.)
belly
-billed (u.m.)
brush
#fever
-headed (u.m.)
-tailed (u.m.)
-throated (u.m.)
top
yes
-man
-no
yester
day
year
yoke
fellow
mating
-toed (u.m.)
young
eyed (u.m.)
-headed (u.m.)
-ladylike
-looking (u.m.)
-manlike
-old
-womanhood
youthtide
yuletide

Z

Z
-bar
zero
axial
-dimensional (u.m.)
#gravity
#hour
zigzag
zinc
-coated (u.m.)
-white (u.m.)
zip
#gun
line
-lipped (u.m.)
lock
zoo (c.f.)
all one word
zoologico (c.f.)
all one word
zygo (c.f.)
all one word
zygomatico (c.f.)
-orbital
rest one word
zymo (c.f.)
all one word

8. Punctuation

8.1. Punctuation is used to clarify the meaning of written or printed language. Well-planned word order requires a minimum of punctuation. The trend toward less punctuation calls for skillful phrasing to avoid ambiguity and to ensure exact interpretation. The GPO STYLE MANUAL can offer only general rules of text treatment. A rigid design or pattern of punctuation cannot be laid down, except in broad terms. The adopted style, however, must be consistent and based on sentence structure.

8.2. The general principles governing the use of punctuation are: If it does not clarify the text it should be omitted; and, in the choice and placing of punctuation marks, the sole aim should be to bring out more clearly the author's thought. Punctuation should aid reading and prevent misreading.

Apostrophes and possessives

8.3. The possessive case of a singular or plural noun not ending in *s* is formed by adding an apostrophe and *s*. The possessive case of a singular or plural noun ending in *s* or with an *s* sound is formed by adding an apostrophe only. Some irregular plurals require both an apostrophe and an *s*. (For possessives of italicized nouns, see rule 11.6.)

boss', bosses'
child's, children's
citizen's, citizens'
Congress', Congresses'
criterion's, criteria's
Co.'s, Cos.'
erratum's, errata's
hostess', hostesses'
lady's, ladies'
man's, men's
medium's, media's
people's, peoples'
Essex's, Essexes'
Jones', Joneses'
Jesus'
Mars'
Dumas'
Schmitz'

8.4. In compound nouns, the *'s* is added to the element nearest the object possessed.

comptroller general's decision
attorneys general's appointments
Mr. Brown of New York's motion
attorney at law's fee
John White, Jr.'s (no comma) account

8.5. Joint possession is indicated by placing an apostrophe on the last element of a series, while individual or alternative possession requires the use of an apostrophe on each element of a series.

soldiers and sailors' home	editor's or proofreader's opinion
Brown & Nelson's store	Bush's or Obama's administration
men's, women's, and children's clothing	Mrs. Smith's and Mrs. Allen's children
	the Army's and the Navy's work
St. Michael's Men's Club	master's and doctor's degrees

8.6. In the use of an apostrophe in firm names, the names of organizations and institutions, the titles of books, and geographic names, the authentic form is to be followed. (Note use of "St.")

Masters, Mates & Pilots' Association	Johns Hopkins University
Dentists' Supply Co. of New York	Hinds' Precedents
International Ladies' Garment Workers' Union	Hells Canyon
	Reader's Digest
Court of St. James's	Actor's Equity Association
St. Peter's Church	Harpers Ferry
St. Elizabeths Hospital	*but* Martha's Vineyard

8.7. Generally, the apostrophe should not be used after names of countries and other organized bodies ending in *s*, or after words more descriptive than possessive (not indicating personal possession), except when plural does not end in *s*.

United States control	teachers college
United Nations meeting	merchants exchange
Southern States industries	children's hospital
Massachusetts laws	Young Men's Christian Association
Bureau of Ships report	
House of Representatives session	*but*
Teamsters Union	Veterans' Administration
editors handbook	(now Department of Veterans Affairs)
syrup producers manual	
technicians guide	Congress' attitude

8.8. Possessive pronouns do not take an apostrophe.

its	yours
ours	hers
theirs	whose

8.9. Possessive indefinite or impersonal pronouns require an apostrophe.

each other's books
some others' plans
one's home is his castle
another's idea
someone's guesstimate

8.10. The singular possessive case is used in such general terms as the following:

arm's length
attorney's fees
author's alterations
confectioner's sugar
cow's milk
distiller's grain
fuller's earth
miner's inch
printer's ink
traveler's checks
writer's cramp

8.11. While an apostrophe is used to indicate possession and contractions, it is not generally necessary to use an apostrophe simply to show the plural form of most acronyms, initialisms, or abbreviations, except where clarity and sense demand such inclusion.

49ers
TVers
OKs
MCing
RIFing
RIFs
RIFed
YWCAs
ABCs
1920s
IOUs
10s (thread)
4½s (bonds)
3s (golf)
2 by 4s
IQs
don't (do not)
I've (I have)
it's (it is/it has)
ne'er (never)

e'er (ever)
class of '08 (2008)
spirit of '76 (1776)

not in her '70s (age)
better: in her seventies

not during the '90s
better: during the 1990s or during the nineties

but
he never crosses his t's
she fails to dot her i's
a's, &'s, 7's
watch your p's and q's
are they l's or 1's
the Oakland A's
a number of s's
his résumé had too many I's

When the plural form of an acronym appears in parentheses, a lowercase *s* is included within the parentheses.

(MPDs)
(MP3s)
(JPEGs)
(IPOs)
(SUVs)
(EVs)

8.12. The apostrophe is omitted in abbreviations, and also in shortened forms of certain other words.

Danl., *not* Dan'l
phone, *not* 'phone
coon, *not* 'coon
possum, *not* 'possum
Halloween, *not* Hallowe'en
copter, *not* 'copter
but ma'am

8.13. The plural of spelled-out numbers, of words referred to as words, and of words containing an apostrophe is formed by adding *s* or *es*; but *'s* is added to indicate the plural of words used as words if omission of the apostrophe would cause difficulty in reading.

twos, threes, sevens
ands, ifs, and buts
ins and outs
the haves and have-nots
ups and downs
whereases and wherefores
pros and cons
yeses and noes
yeas and nays
but
do's and don'ts
which's and that's

8.14. The possessive case is often used in lieu of an objective phrase even though ownership is not involved.

1 day's labor (labor for 1 day)
12 days' labor
2 hours' traveltime
a stone's throw
2 weeks' pay
for charity's sake
for pity's sake
several billion dollars' worth
but $10 billion worth

8.15. The possessive case is not used in such expressions as the following, in which one noun modifies another.

day labor (labor by the day)
quartermaster stores
State prison
States rights

8.16. For euphony, nouns ending in *s* or *ce* and followed by a word beginning with *s* form the possessive by adding an apostrophe only.

for goodness' sake
Mr. Hughes' service
for old times' sake
for acquaintance' sake
for conscience' sake

8.17. A possessive noun used in an adjective sense requires the addition of *'s*.

He is a friend of John's.
Stern's is running a sale.

8.18. A noun preceding a gerund should be in the possessive case.

in the event of Mary's leaving
the ship's hovering nearby

Brackets

Brackets, in pairs, are used—

8.19. In transcripts, congressional hearings, the Congressional Record, testimony in courtwork, etc., to enclose interpolations that are not specifically a part of the original quotation, such as a correction, explanation, omission, editorial comment, or a caution that an error is reproduced literally.

We found this to be true at the Government Publishing Office [GPO].
He came on the 3d [2d] of July.
Our conference [lasted] 2 hours.
The general [Washington] ordered him to leave.
The paper was as follows [reads]:
I do not know. [Continues reading:]
[Chorus of "Mr. Chairman."]
They fooled only themselves. [Laughter.]
Our party will always serve the people [applause] in spite of the opposition [loud applause]. (If more than one bracketed interpolation, both are included within the sentence.)
The WITNESS. He did it that way [indicating].
Q. Do you know these men [handing witness a list]?
The bill had *not* been paid. [Italic added.] *or* [Emphasis added.]
The statue [sic] was on the statute books.
The WITNESS. This matter is classified. [Deleted.]
[Deleted.]
Mr. JONES. Hold up your hands. [Show of hands.]
Answer [after examining list]. Yes; I do.
Q. [Continuing.]
A. [Reads:]

A. [Interrupting.]
[Discussion off the record.]
[Pause.]
The WITNESS [interrupting]. It is known——
Mr. JONES [continuing]. Now let us take the next item.
Mr. SMITH [presiding]. Do you mean that literally?
Mr. JONES [interposing]. Absolutely.
[The matter referred to is as follows:]
The CHAIRMAN [to Mr. Smith].
The CHAIRMAN [reading]:
Mr. KELLEY [to the chairman]. From 15 to 25 percent.
[Objected to.]
[Mr. Smith nods.]
[Mr. Smith aside.]
[Mr. Smith makes further statement off the record.]
Mr. JONES [for Mr. Smith].
A VOICE FROM AUDIENCE. Speak up.
SEVERAL VOICES. Quiet!

8.20. In bills, contracts, laws, etc., to indicate matter that is to be omitted.

8.21. In mathematics, to denote that enclosed matter is to be treated as a unit.

8.22. When matter in brackets makes more than one paragraph, start each paragraph with a bracket and place the closing bracket at end of last paragraph.

Colon

The colon is used—

8.23. To introduce any matter that forms a question or a quotation.

The following question came up for discussion: What policy should be adopted?
She said: "We believe the time is now or never."

8.24. After an introductory independent clause that describes or defines what follows. If a complete sentence follows the colon, capitalize its first word.

And then came the surprise: cake all around!
His only rule was this: Chickens are not allowed past the front parlor.

8.25. Before a final clause that extends or amplifies the preceding independent clause. Even if a complete sentence follows the colon, lowercase its first word.

> Give up conveniences; do not demand special privileges; do not stop work: these are necessary while we are at war.
>
> Railroading is not a variety of outdoor sport: it is service.

8.26. Following a sentence introducing an extract.

> The Clerk will read as follows:
>
> > Amendment by Mr. STEARNS: In line 4, after the word "pay", add a comma and the following words: "out of any money in the Treasury not otherwise appropriated".

8.27. To introduce a run-in list.

> There are three primary pigment colors: magenta, yellow, and cyan.
>
> The vote was as follows: in the affirmative, 23; in the negative, 11; not voting, 3.
>
> These are what he missed most: walking along the river at dawn, napping under the old maple tree, chasing birds in the park.
>
> His goals were these: (1) learn Spanish, (2) see the Grand Canyon, and (3) climb Mt. Everest.

8.28. To introduce a bulleted or enumerated list that is not run in. There are many ways to construct such a list—far too many to detail here—depending on the contents of the list and the intent of the author; however, a few guidelines concerning consistency should be kept in mind.

Punctuation at the end of each list item may be commas, semicolons, periods, or even none at all, as long as its use is consistent within a list. The exception to this is that if commas or semicolons are used, the last item should end with a period, unless the list is part of a sentence that continues on after the list.

List items should be lowercased in a list using commas or semicolons after each list item. For lists using periods or no punctuation, capitalization should be determined by context—lists of single words are usually lowercased, whereas lists of independent clauses are more appropriately capitalized. Whatever choice is made concerning capitalization, it should be applied to all the list items; the first item is not handled differently.

A conjunction (and, or, nor) should follow the penultimate item in a list using commas or semicolons after each list item, but not otherwise.

His goals were these:

- Learn Spanish.
- See the Grand Canyon.
- Climb Mt. Everest.

His goals were these:

(1) learn Spanish,
(2) see the Grand Canyon, and
(3) climb Mt. Everest.

His goals were these:

(a) learn Spanish,
(b) see the Grand Canyon, and
(c) climb Mt. Everest;

but he knew it was unlikely he would meet them.

8.29. To introduce subentries in tables and leaderwork. Single subentries are run in following the colon and are initial cap.

Seward Peninsula: Council district: (single subentry runs in).
Mining and manufacturing.
Shipping and trade.

Seward Peninsula:
Council district:
Mining and manufacturing.
Shipping and trade.
Fairhaven district: Tourism (single subentry runs in).

8.30. After a salutation.

MY DEAR SIR:
Ladies and Gentlemen:
To Whom It May Concern:

8.31. In expressing clock time.

2:40 p.m.

8.32. In Biblical and other citations.

Luke 4:3.
I Corinthians 13:13.
Journal of Education 3:342–358.

8.33. In bibliographic references, between place of publication and name of publisher.

Congressional Directory. Washington: U.S. Government Publishing Office.

8.34. To separate book titles and subtitles.

Financial Aid for College Students: Graduate
Germany Revisited: Education in the Federal Republic

8.35. In imprints before the year (en space each side of colon).

U.S. Government Publishing Office
Washington : 2016

8.36. In proportions.

Concrete mixed 5:3:1
but 5–2–1 *or* 5-2-1 (when so in copy)

8.37. In double colon as ratio sign.

1:2::3:6

Comma

The comma is used—

8.38. To separate two words or figures that might otherwise be misunderstood.

Instead of hundreds, thousands came.
Instead of 20, 50 came.
December 7, 1941.
In 2003, 400 men were dismissed.
To John, Smith was very kind.
What the difficulty is, is not known.
but He suggested that that committee be appointed.

8.39. Before a direct quotation of only a few words following an introductory phrase.

He said, "Now or never."

8.40. To indicate the omission of a word or words.

Then we had much; now, nothing.

8.41. After each of a series of coordinate qualifying words.

short, swift streams; *but* short tributary streams

8.42. Between an introductory modifying phrase and the subject modified.

Beset by the enemy, they retreated.

8.43. Before and after *Jr., Sr., Esq., Ph.D., F.R.S., Inc.*, etc., within a sentence except where possession is indicated.

Henry Smith, Jr., chairman
Peter Johns, F.R.S., London
Washington, DC, schools
Google, Inc., technology
Brown, A.H., Jr. (*not* Brown, Jr., A.H.)
Milan, Italy, vacation
University of California, Santa Cruz, mascot

but
John Smith 2d (*or* II); Smith, John, II
Mr. Smith, Junior, also spoke
(where only last name is used)
Alexandria, VA's waterfront

8.44. To set off parenthetic words, phrases, or clauses.

Mr. Jefferson, who was then Secretary of State, favored the location of the National Capital at Washington.
It must be remembered, however, that the Government had no guarantee.
It is obvious, therefore, that this office cannot function.
The atom bomb, which was developed at the Manhattan project, was first used in World War II.
Their high morale might, he suggested, have caused them to put success of the team above the reputation of the college.
The restriction is laid down in title IX, chapter 8, section 15, of the code.
but The man who fell [restrictive clause] broke his back.
The dam that gave way [restrictive clause] was poorly constructed.
He therefore gave up the search.

8.45. To set off words or phrases in apposition or in contrast.

Mr. Green, the lawyer, spoke for the defense.
Mr. Jones, attorney for the plaintiff, signed the petition.
Mr. Smith, not Mr. Black, was elected.
James Roosevelt, Democrat, of California.
Jean's sister, Joyce, was the eldest. (Jean had one sister.)
but Jonathan's brother Moses Taylor was appointed. (Jonathan had more than one brother.)

8.46. After each member within a series of three or more words, phrases, letters, or figures used with *and, or,* or *nor.*

red, white, and blue
horses, mules, and cattle; *but* horses and mules and cattle
by the bolt, by the yard, or in remnants

a, b, and c
neither snow, rain, nor heat
2 days, 3 hours, and 4 minutes (series); *but* 70 years 11 months 6 days (age)

8.47. Before the conjunction in a compound sentence containing two or more independent clauses, each of which could have been written as a simple sentence.

Fish, mollusks, and crustaceans were plentiful in the lakes, and turtles frequented the shores.
The boy went home alone, and his sister remained with the crowd.

8.48. After a noun or phrase in direct address.

Senator, will the measure be defeated?
Mr. Chairman, I will reply to the gentleman later.
but Yes, sir; he did see it.
No, ma'am; I do not recall.

8.49. After an interrogative clause, followed by a direct question.

You are sure, are you not?
You will go, will you not?

8.50. Between the title of a person and the name of an organization in the absence of the words *of* or *of the*.

Chief, Division of Finance
chairman, Committee on Appropriations
colonel, 12th Cavalry Regiment
president, University of Virginia

8.51. Inside closing quotation mark.

He said "four," not "five."
"Freedom is an inherent right," he insisted.
Items marked "A," "B," and "C," inclusive, were listed.

8.52. To separate thousands and millions in numerical figures.

4,230
50,491
1,250,000
but 1,000,000,000 is more clearly illustrated as 1 billion

8.53. After the year in complete dates (month, day, year) within a sentence.

The dates of September 11, 1993, to June 12, 1994, were erroneous.
This was reflected in the June 13, 2007, report.
but Production for June 2008 was normal.
The 10 February 2008 deadline passed.

The comma is omitted—

8.54. Between superior figures or letters in footnote references.

Numerous instances may be cited.[1] [2]
Data are based on October production.[a] [b]

8.55. Before ZIP (Zone Improvement Plan) Code postal-delivery number.

Washington, DC 20401–0003, for the GPO
East Rochester, OH 44625–9701 USA, was his hometown

8.56. Between month, holiday, or season and year in dates.

June 2016
22d of May 2016
February and March 2016
January, February, and March 2016
January 24 A.D. 2016; 15th of June A.D. 2016

150 B.C.
Labor Day 2016
Easter Sunday 2016
5 January 2016 (military usage)
spring 2016
autumn 2016

8.57. Between the name and number of an organization.

Columbia Typographical Union No. 101–12
American Legion Post No. 33

8.58. In fractions, in decimals, and in serial numbers, except patent numbers.

$\frac{1}{2500}$
1.0947
page 2632
202–512–1800 (telephone number)
1721–1727 St. Clair Avenue
Executive Order 11242
motor No. 189463
1450 kilocycles; 1100 meters

8.59. Between two nouns one of which identifies the other.

The Children's Bureau's booklet "Infant Care" continues to be a bestseller.

8.60. Before an ampersand (&).

Brown, Wilson & Co.
Mine, Mill & Smelter Workers

8.61. Before abbreviations of compass directions.

6430 Princeton Dr. SW

8.62. In bibliographies, between name of the publication and volume or similar number.

American Library Association Bulletin 34:238, April 1940.

8.63. Wherever possible without danger of ambiguity.

$2 gold
Executive Order No. 21
General Order No. 12; *but* General Orders, No. 12
Public Law 85–1
He graduates in the year 2010 (not the year 2,010)
My age is 30 years 6 months 12 days.
John Lewis 2d (*or* II)
Murphy of Illinois; Murphy of New York (where only last name is used)
Carroll of Carrollton; Henry of Navarre (person closely identified with place); *but* Clyde Leo Downs, of Maryland; President Levin, of Yale University
James Bros. et al.; but James Bros., Nelson Co., et al. (last element of series)

Dash

A 1-em dash is used—

8.64. To mark a sudden break or abrupt change in thought.

He said—and no one contradicted him—"The battle is lost."
If the bill should pass—which God forbid!—the service will be wrecked.
The auditor—shall we call him a knave or a fool?—approved an inaccurate statement.

8.65. To indicate an interruption or an unfinished word or sentence. A 2-em dash is used when the interruption is by a person other than the speaker, and a 1-em dash will show self-interruption. Note that extracts must begin with a true paragraph. Following extracts, colloquy must start as a paragraph.

"Such an idea can scarcely be——"
"The word 'donation'——"
"The word 'dona'——"
He said: "Give me lib——"
The bill reads "repeal," not "am——"
Q. Did you see——
A. No, sir.

Mr. Brown [reading]: "The report goes on to say that"—Observe this closely—"during the fiscal year . . . ."

8.66. Instead of commas or parentheses if the meaning may thus be clarified.

> These are shore deposits—gravel, sand, and clay—but marine sediments underlie them.

8.67. Before a final clause that summarizes a series of ideas.

> Freedom of speech, freedom of worship, freedom from want, freedom from fear—these are the fundamentals of moral world order.

8.68. After an introductory phrase reading into the following lines and indicating repetition of such phrase.

> I recommend—
> that we submit them for review and corrections;
> that we then accept them as corrected; and
> that we also publish them.

8.69. With a preceding question mark, in lieu of a colon.

> How can you explain this?—"Fee paid, $5."

8.70. To precede a credit line or a run-in credit or signature.

> Lay the proud usurpers low!
> Tyrants fall in every foe!
> Liberty's in every blow!
> Let us do or die!
> —Robert Burns.

> Every man's work shall be made manifest.—I Corinthians 3:13.
> This statement is open to question.—GERALD H. FORSYTHE.

8.71. After a run-in sidehead.

8.72. To separate run-in questions and answers in testimony.

> Q. Did he go?—A. No.

A 1-em dash is not used—

8.73. At the beginning of any line of type, except as shown in rule 8.70.

8.74. Immediately after a comma, colon, or semicolon.

A 3-em dash is used—

8.75. In bibliographies to indicate repetition.

> Powell, James W., Jr., Hunting in Virginia's lowlands. 1972. 200 pp.
> ———Fishing off Delmarva. 1972. 28 pp.

An en dash is used—

8.76. In a combination of figures and/or letters, including acronyms (even if the acronym spells out a word (e.g. PATRIOT)). But use a hyphen to combine such letters and/or figures with a word or abbreviation, or in chemical nomenclature.

figures:

5–20 (bonds)

85–1—85–20 (Public laws; use em dash between two elements with en dashes)

1–703–555–6593 (telephone number)

123–45–6789 (Social Security number)

$15–$20 (range)

letters:

WTOP–AM–FM–TV (radio and television stations)

CBS–TV

AFL–CIO

C–SPAN

s–NOM (scientific term)

figures and letters:

6–A (exhibit identification)

DC–14 (airplane)

MiG–25 (airplane, mixed letters with figure)

I–95 (interstate roadway)

4–H (Club)

LK–66–A(2)–74, 15A–x–3 (serial numbers)

SE–BatsCZX–2015–65 (SEC file number)

rule 13e–4

Section 12(a)–(d) (range)

but a hyphen is used with:

ACF-Brill Motors Co. (hyphen with capital letters and a word)

loran-C (coined word plus letter)

ALL-AMERICAN ESSAY CONTEST (hyphen in capitalized heading)

Four Corners Monument, AZ-NM-UT-CO (hyphen with two-letter state abbreviations)

U-235, Cr-Ni-Mo (chemical symbols)

δ-HCH (chemical nomenclature)

8.77. In the absence of the word *to* when denoting a span of time.

2005–2008 January–June Monday–Friday

An en dash is not used—

8.78. For *to* when the word *from* precedes the first of two related figures or expressions.

From June 1 to July 30, 2016; *not* from June 1–July 30, 2016

8.79. For *and* when the word *between* precedes the first of two related figures or expressions.

Between 2000 and 2016; *not* between 2000–16

Ellipses

8.80. Three periods or three asterisks, separated by en spaces, are used to denote an ellipsis within a sentence, at the beginning or end of a sentence, or in two or more consecutive sentences. To achieve faithful reproduction of excerpt material, editors using period ellipses should indicate placement of the terminal period in relation to an ellipsis at the end of a sentence. Note, in the following examples, the additional spacing necessary to clearly define commas and the terminal period when period ellipses are employed.

> The Senate having tried Andrew Johnson, President of the United States, upon articles of impeachment exhibited against him by the House of Representatives, and two-thirds of the Senators present not having found him guilty of the charges contained in the second, third, and eleventh articles of impeachment, it is therefore
>
> *Ordered and adjudged.* That the said Andrew Johnson, President of the United States be, and he is, acquitted of the charges in said articles made and set forth.

> The Senate having tried Andrew Johnson . . . upon articles of impeachment . . . , and two-thirds of the Senators present not having found him guilty of the charges . . . , it is therefore
>
> *Ordered and adjudged.* That the said Andrew Johnson, President of the United States be . . . acquitted of the charge . . . .

> The Senate having tried Andrew Johnson * * * upon articles of impeachment * * *, and two-thirds of the Senators present not having found him guilty of the charges * * *, it is therefore
>
> *Ordered and adjudged.* That the said Andrew Johnson, President of the United States be * * * acquitted of the charges * * *.

8.81. Ellipses are not overrun alone at the end of a paragraph.

8.82. Copy will be followed for period or asterisk ellipses, even if inconsistent.

8.83. A line of asterisks indicates an omission of one or more entire paragraphs. In 26½-pica or wider measure, a line of "stars" means seven asterisks indented 2 ems at each end of the line, with the remaining space divided evenly between the asterisks. In measures less than 26½ picas, five asterisks are used. Quotation marks are not used on a line of asterisks in quoted matter. Where an ellipsis line ends a complete quotation, no closing quote is used.

* * * * * * *

8.84. Indented matter in 26½-pica or wider measure also requires a seven-asterisk line to indicate the omission of one or more entire paragraphs.

8.85. If an omission occurs in the last part of a paragraph immediately before a line of asterisks, three periods or asterisks are used, in addition to the line of asterisks, to indicate such an omission.

8.86. Equalize spacing above and below an ellipsis line.

Exclamation point

8.87. The exclamation point is used to mark surprise, incredulity, admiration, appeal, or other strong emotion which may be expressed even in a declarative or interrogative sentence.

> Who shouted, "All aboard!" [Note omission of question mark.]
> "Great!" he shouted. [Note omission of comma.]
> He acknowledged the fatal error!
> How breathtakingly beautiful!
> Timber!
> Mayday! Mayday!

8.88. In direct address, either to a person or a personified object, *O* is used without an exclamation point, or other punctuation; but if strong feeling is expressed, an exclamation point is placed at the end of the statement.

> O my friend, let us consider this subject impartially.
> O Lord, save Thy people!

8.89. In exclamations without direct address or appeal, *oh* is used instead of *O*, and the exclamation point is omitted.

Oh, but the gentleman is mistaken.
Oh dear; the time is so short.

Hyphen

The hyphen (a punctuation mark, not an element in the spelling of words) is used—

8.90. To connect the elements of certain compound words. (See Chapter 6 "Compounding Rules.")

8.91. To indicate continuation of a word divided at the end of a line.

8.92. Between the letters of a spelled word.

The Style Board changed New Jerseyite to New J-e-r-s-e-y-a-n.
A native of Halifax is a H-a-l-i-g-o-n-i-a-n.
The Chinese repressive action took place in T-i-a-n-a-n-m-e-n Square.

8.93. To separate elements of chemical formulas.

The hyphen, as an element, may be used—

8.94. To represent letters deleted or illegible words in copy.

Oakland's - - bonic plague   Richard Emory H - - - -

Parentheses

Parentheses are used—

8.95. To set off important matter not intended to be part of the main statement that is not a grammatical element of the sentence. In colloquy, brackets must be substituted.

This case (124 U.S. 329) is not relevant.
The result (see fig. 2) is most surprising.
The United States is the principal purchaser (by value) of these exports (23 percent in 1995 and 19 percent in 1996).

8.96. To enclose a parenthetic clause where the interruption is too great to be indicated by commas.

You can find it neither in French dictionaries (at any rate, not in Littré) nor in English dictionaries.

8.97. To enclose an explanatory word not part of a written or printed statement.

the Winchester (VA) Star; *but* the Star of Winchester, VA
Portland (OR) Chamber of Commerce; *but* Athens, GA, schools

8.98. To enclose letters or numbers designating items in a series, either at the beginning of paragraphs or within a paragraph.

The order of delivery will be: (a) food, (b) clothing, and (c) tents and other housing equipment.
You will observe that the sword is (1) old fashioned, (2) still sharp, and (3) unusually light for its size.
Paragraph 7(B)(1)(*a*) will be found on page 6. (Note parentheses closed up.)

8.99. To enclose a figure inserted to confirm a written or printed statement given in words if double form is specifically requested.

This contract shall be completed in sixty (60) days.

8.100. A reference in parentheses at the end of a sentence is placed before the period, unless it is a complete sentence in itself.

The specimen exhibits both phases (pl. 14, *A*, *B*).
The individual cavities show great variation. (See pl. 4.)

8.101. If a sentence contains more than one parenthetic reference, the one at the end is placed before the period.

This sandstone (see pl. 6) is in every county of the State (see pl. 1).

8.102. When a figure is followed by a letter in parentheses, no space is used between the figure and the opening parenthesis; but, if the letter is not in parentheses and the figure is repeated with each letter, the letter is closed up with the figure.

15(*a*). Classes, grades, and sizes.
15*a*. Classes, grades, and sizes.

8.103. If both a figure and a letter in parentheses are used before each paragraph, a period and an en space are used after the closing parenthesis. If the figure is not repeated before each letter in parentheses but is used only before the first letter, the period is placed after the figure. However, if the figure is not repeated before each letter in parentheses and no period is used, space is inserted after the number if at least one other lettered subsection appears.

15(*a*). When the figure is used before the letter in each paragraph—
15(*b*). The period is placed after the closing parenthesis.
15. (*a*) When the figure is used before the letter in the first paragraph but not repeated with subsequent letters—
(*b*) The period is used after the figure only.
Sec. 12 (a) When no period is used and a letter in parentheses appears after a numbered item—
(b) Space must be used after the number if at least one other lettered subsection is shown.

8.104. Note position of the period relative to closing parenthesis:

The vending stand sells a variety of items (sandwiches, beverages, cakes, etc.).
The vending stand sells a variety of items (sandwiches, beverages, cakes, etc. (sometimes ice cream)).
The vending stand sells a variety of items. (These include sandwiches, beverages, cakes, etc. (sometimes ice cream).)

8.105. To enclose bylines in congressional work.

(By Harvey Hagman, archeological correspondent)

8.106. When matter in parentheses makes more than one paragraph, start each paragraph with a parenthesis and place the closing parenthesis at the end of the last paragraph.

Period

The period is used—

8.107. After a declarative sentence that is not exclamatory or after an imperative sentence.

Stars are suns.
He was employed by Sampson & Company.
Do not be late.
On with the dance.

8.108. After an indirect question or after a question intended as a suggestion and not requiring an answer.

Tell me how he did it.
May we hear from you.
May we ask prompt payment.

8.109. In place of a closing parenthesis after a letter or number denoting a series.

a. Bread well baked	1. Punctuate freely
b. Meat cooked rare	2. Compound sparingly
c. Cubed apples stewed	3. Index thoroughly

8.110. To indicate an ellipsis. (See rules 8.80 and 8.82.)

8.111. After a run-in sidehead.

Conditional subjunctive.—The conditional subjunctive is required for all unreal and doubtful conditions.

2. Peacetime preparation.—*a.* The Chairman of the National Security Resources Board, etc.

2. Peacetime preparation.—Industrial mobilization plans.—The Chairman of the National Security Resources Board, etc.

2. Peacetime preparation.—*Industrial mobilization.*—The Chairman of the National Security Resources Board, etc.

62. *Determination of types.—a. Statement of characteristics.*—Before types of equipment, etc.

Steps in planning for procurement.—(1) *Determination of needs.*—To plan for the procurement of such arms, etc.

62. *Determination of types.—(a) Statement of characteristics.*—Before, etc.

DETERMINATION OF TYPES.—Statement of characteristics.—Before types of, etc.

but NOTE.—The source material was furnished.
Source: U.S. Department of Commerce, Bureau of the Census.

8.112. Paragraphs and subparagraphs may be arranged according to the following scheme. The sequence is not fixed, and variations, in addition to the use of center and side heads or indented paragraphs, may be adopted, depending on the number of parts.

I. Outlines can begin with a capital Roman numeral.
   A. The number of levels and the width of the column determine alignment and indention.
      1. A set space (en space) following the identifier aids alignment.
         a. Usually, typefaces and sizes are chosen to agree with the hierarchy of the head breakdowns.
            (1) Aligning runover lines with the first word which follows the number or letter aids readability.

(*a*) It is important to vary (alternate) the use of letters and numbers in any outline.

(i) The lowercase Roman numerals (i), (ii), etc. may be used as parts of the outline or to identify subparts of any previous parts.

(*aa*) When absolutely necessary, double (or triple) lowercase letters may be used.

II. Where not needed, the capital Roman numerals may be discarded and the outline can begin with the letter A. As in any composition, consistency in indentions and order is essential.

8.113. To separate integers from decimals in a single expression.

13.75 percent	1.25 meters
$3.50	0.08 mile

8.114. In continental European languages, to indicate thousands.

1.317	72.190.175

8.115. After abbreviations, unless otherwise specified. (See Chapter 9, "Abbreviations and Letter Symbols.")

Apr.	*but*
Co.	m (meter)
fig.	kc (kilocycle)
Ry.	NY (New York)
Ph.D.	RR
p.m.	SSE (south-southeast)

8.116. After legends and explanatory matter beneath illustrations. Legends without descriptive language do not receive periods.

FIGURE 1.—Schematic drawing.
FIGURE 1.—Continued.
but FIGURE 1 (without legend, no period)

8.117. After *Article 1, Section 1,* etc., at the beginning of paragraphs.

A center period is sometimes used—

8.118. To indicate multiplication. (Use of a multiplication sign is preferable.)

$a \cdot b$	$a \times b$

The period is omitted—

8.119. After—

Lines in title pages
Center, side, and running heads; *but* is not omitted after run-in sideheads
Continued lines
Boxheads of tables
Scientific, chemical, or other symbols

This rule does not apply to abbreviation periods.

8.120. After a quotation mark that is preceded by a period.

She said: "I believe the time is now or never."

8.121. After letters used as names without specific designation.

Officer B, Subject A, Brand X, etc.
A said to B that all is well.
Mr. A told Mr. B that the case was closed.
Mr. X (for unknown or censored name).
but Mr. A. [for Mr. Andrews]. I do not want to go.
Mr. K. [for Mr. King]. The meeting is adjourned.

8.122. After a middle initial which is merely a letter and not an abbreviation of a name.

Daniel D Tompkins
Ross T McIntire
but Harry S. Truman (President Truman's preference)

8.123. After a short name which is not an abbreviation of the longer form.

Alex	Mac
Ed	Sam

8.124. After Roman numerals used as ordinals.

King George V	Super Bowl XLIX, LI
Apollo XII insigne	*but* Super Bowl 50

8.125. After words and incomplete statements listed in columns. Full-measure matter is not to be regarded as a column.

8.126. After explanatory matter under leaders or rules.

....	....	....
(Name)	(Address)	(Position)

8.127. Immediately before leaders, even if an abbreviation precedes the leaders.

Question mark

The question mark is used—

8.128. To indicate a direct query, even if not in the form of a question.

Did he do it?
He did what?
Can the money be raised? is the question.
Who asked, "Why?" [Note single question mark.]
"Did you hurt yourself, my son?" she asked.

8.129. To express more than one query in the same sentence.

Can he do it? or you? or anyone?

8.130. To express doubt.

He said the boy was 8(?) feet tall. (No space before question mark.)
The statue(?) was on the statute books.
The scientific identification *Dorothia*? was noted. (Roman "?".)

Quotation marks

Quotation marks are used—

8.131. To enclose direct quotations. (Each part of an interrupted quotation begins and ends with quotation marks.)

The answer is "No."
He said, "John said, 'No.' " (Note thin space between single and double closing quotes.)
"John," asked Henry, "why do you go?"

8.132. To enclose any matter following such terms as *entitled, the word, the term, marked, designated, classified, named, endorsed, cited as, referred to as,* or *signed;* however, quotation marks are not used to enclose expressions following the terms *known as, called, so-called,* etc., unless such expressions are misnomers or slang.

Congress passed the act entitled "An act . . . ."
After the word "treaty," insert a comma.
Of what does the item "Miscellaneous debts" consist?
The column "Imports from foreign countries" was not well written.
The document will be marked "Exhibit No. 21;" *but* The document may be made exhibit No. 21.
The check was endorsed "John Adamson."

It was signed "John."
but Beryllium is known as glucinium in some European countries.
It was called profit and loss.
The so-called investigating body.

8.133. To enclose titles of addresses, albums, articles, awards, books, captions, editorials, essays, headings, headlines, hearings, motion pictures and plays (including television and radio programs), operas, papers, short poems, reports, songs, studies, subheadings, subjects, and themes. All principal words are to be capitalized.

An address on "Uranium-235 in the Atomic Age"
The article "Germany Revisited" appeared in the last issue.
He received the "Man of the Year" award.
"The Conquest of Mexico," a published work (book)
Under the caption "Long-Term Treasurys Rise"
The subject was discussed in "Punctuation." (chapter heading)
It will be found in "Part XI: Early Thought."
The editorial "Haphazard Budgeting"
"Compensation," by Emerson (essay)
"United States To Appoint Representative to U.N." (heading or headline)
In "Search for Paradise" (motion picture)
"South Pacific" (play)
A paper on "Constant-Pressure Combustion" was read.
"O Captain! My Captain!" (short poem)
The report "Atomic Energy: What It Means to the Nation"; *but* annual report of the Director of the Government Publishing Office
This was followed by the singing of "The Star-Spangled Banner."
The information is located under the subhead "Sixty Days of Turmoil."
The subject (or theme) of the conference is "Peaceful Uses of Atomic Energy."
also Account 5, "Management fees."
Under the heading "Management and Operation."
Under the appropriation "Building of ships, Navy."

8.134. At the beginning of each paragraph of a quotation, but at the end of the last paragraph only.

8.135. To enclose a letter or communication that bears both date and signature.

8.136. To enclose misnomers, slang expressions, sobriquets, coined words, or ordinary words used in an arbitrary way.

His report was "bunk."
It was a "gentlemen's agreement."

The "invisible government" is responsible.
George Herman "Babe" Ruth.
but He voted for the lameduck amendment.

8.137. To close up characters except when they precede a fraction or an apostrophe or precede or follow a superior figure or letter, in which case a thin space is used. A thin space is used to separate double and single quotation marks.

8.138. The comma and the final period will be placed inside the quotation marks. Other punctuation marks should be placed inside the quotation marks only if they are a part of the matter quoted.

Ruth said, "I think so."
"The President," he said, "will veto the bill."
The conductor shouted, "All aboard!"
Who asked, "Why?"
The President suggests that "an early occasion be sought."
Why call it a "gentlemen's agreement"?

8.139. In congressional and certain other classes of work showing amendments, and in courtwork with quoted language, punctuation marks are printed after the quotation marks when not a part of the quoted matter.

Insert the words "growth", "production", and "manufacture".
To be inserted after the words "cadets, U.S. Coast Guard;".
Change "February 1, 1983", to "June 30, 2016".
"Insert in lieu thereof 'July 1, 1983,'."

8.140. When occurring together, quotation marks should precede footnote reference numbers.

The commissioner claimed that the award was "unjustified." [1]
Kelly's exact words were: "The facts in the case prove otherwise." [2]

8.141. Quotation marks should be limited, if possible, to three sets (double, single, double).

"The question in the report is, 'Can a person who obtains his certificate of naturalization by fraud be considered a "bona fide" citizen of the United States?' "

Quotation marks are not used—

8.142. To enclose titles of works of art: paintings, statuary, etc.

8.143. To enclose names of newspapers or magazines.

8.144. To enclose complete letters having date and signature.

8.145. To enclose extracts that are indented or set in smaller type, or solid extracts in leaded matter; but indented matter in text that is already quoted carries quotation marks.

8.146. In indirect quotations.

Tell her yes. He could not say no.

8.147. Before a display initial which begins a quoted paragraph.

Semicolon

The semicolon is used—

8.148. To separate clauses containing commas.

Donald A. Peters, Jr., president of the First National Bank, was also a director of New York Central; Harvey D. Jones was a director of Oregon Steel Co. and New York Central; Thomas W. Harrison, chairman of the board of McBride & Co., was also on the board of Oregon Steel Co.

Reptiles, amphibians, and predatory mammals swallow their prey whole or in large pieces, bones included; waterfowl habitually take shellfish entire; and gallinaceous birds are provided with gizzards that grind up the hardest seeds.

Yes, sir; he did see it.

No, sir; I do not recall.

8.149. To separate statements that are too closely related in meaning to be written as separate sentences, and also statements of contrast.

Yes; that is right.

No; we received one-third.

It is true in peace; it is true in war.

War is destructive; peace, constructive.

8.150. To set off explanatory abbreviations or words that summarize or explain preceding matter.

The industry is related to groups that produce finished goods; i.e., electrical machinery and transportation equipment.

There were three metal producers involved; namely, Jones & Laughlin, Armco, and Kennecott.

The semicolon is not used—

8.151. Where a comma will suffice.

Offices are located in New York, NY, Chicago, IL, and Dallas, TX.

Single punctuation

8.152. Single punctuation should be used wherever possible without ambiguity.

124 U.S. 321 (no comma)
Sir: (no dash)
Joseph replied, "It is a worthwhile effort." (no outside period)

Type

8.153. All punctuation marks, including parentheses, brackets, and superior reference figures, are set to match the type of the words which they adjoin. A lightface dash is used after a run-in boldface sidehead followed by lightface matter. Lightface brackets, parentheses, or quotation marks shall be used when both boldface and lightface matter are enclosed.

Charts: C&GS 5101 (N.O. **18320**), page **282 (see above);** N.O. **93491 (Plan);** page **271.**

9. Abbreviations and Letter Symbols

9.1. Abbreviations and letter symbols are used to save space and to avoid distracting the reader by use of repetitious words or phrases.

9.2. The nature of the publication governs the extent to which abbreviations are used. In the text of technical and legal publications, and in parentheses, brackets, footnotes, sidenotes, tables, leaderwork, and bibliographies, many words are frequently abbreviated. Heads, legends, tables of contents, and indexes follow the style of the text.

9.3. Internal and terminal punctuation in symbols representing units of measure are to be omitted to conform with practice adopted by scientific, technical, and industrial groups. Where the omission of terminal punctuation causes confusion; e.g., the symbol *in* (inch) mistaken for the preposition *in*, the symbol should be spelled out.

9.4. Standard and easily understood forms are preferable, and they should be uniform throughout a job. Abbreviations not generally known should be followed in the text by the spelled-out forms in parentheses the first time they occur; in tables and leaderwork such explanatory matter should be supplied in a footnote. As the printer cannot rewrite the copy, the author should supply these explanatory forms.

9.5. In technical matter, symbols for units of measure should be used only with figures; similarly, many other abbreviations and symbols should not appear in isolation. For example, *energy is measured in foot-pounds,* NOT *energy is measured in ft•lbs.* See ASME Y14.38 ("Abbreviations and Acronyms for use on Drawings and Related Documents") for an extended list of technical abbreviations.

Capitals, hyphens, periods (points), and spacing

9.6. In general, an abbreviation follows the capitalization and hyphenation of the word or words abbreviated. It is followed by a period unless otherwise indicated.

c.o.d. St. *but* ft•lb

9.7. Abbreviations and initials of a personal name with points are set without spaces. Abbreviations composed of contractions and initials or numbers, will retain space.

F.D.R.	i.e., e.g. (*but* op. cit.)
J.F.K.	B.S., LL.D., Ph.D., B.Sc.
L.B.J.	H.R. 116 (*but* S. 116, S. Con. Res. 116)
B.C. Forrest, D.D.S.	C.A.D.C. (*but* App. D.C.)
U.S.	*but*
U.N.	AT&T
U.S.C. (*but* Rev. Stat.)	Texas A&M
A.F. of L.-CIO (AFL–CIO preferred)	R&D
A.D., B.C.	

9.8. Except as otherwise designated, points and spaces are omitted after initials used as shortened names of governmental agencies and of other organized bodies. "Other organized bodies" will be interpreted to mean organized bodies that have become popularly identified with a symbol, such as MIT (Massachusetts Institute of Technology), GM (General Motors), AFLAC (American Family Life Assurance Company), etc. (See also rule 9.61.) Symbols, when they appear in copy, may be used for acts of Congress. Example: ARA (Area Redevelopment Act).

VFW	TVA	ARC
NLRB	AFL–CIO	ASTM

Geographic terms

9.9. *United States* must be spelled out when appearing in a sentence containing the name of another country. The abbreviation *U.S.* will be used when preceding the word *Government* or the name of a Government organization, except in formal writing (treaties, Executive orders, proclamations, etc.); congressional bills; legal citations and courtwork; and covers and title pages.

U.S. Government
U.S. Congress
U.S. Department of Health and Human Services
U.S. district court
U.S. Supreme Court (*but* Supreme Court of the United States)
U.S. Army (*but* Army of the United States)
U.S. monitor *Nantucket*

U.S.-NATO assistance
U.S. Government efforts to control inflation must be successful if the United States is to have a stable economy.
but British, French, and United States Governments; United States-British talks

9.10. With the exceptions in the preceding rule, the abbreviation *U.S.* is used in the adjective position, but is spelled out when used as a noun.

U.S. foreign policy
U.S. farm-support program
U.S. attorney
U.S. citizen
United States Code (official title)
United States Steel Corp. (legal title)
Foreign policy of the United States
not Temperatures vary in the U.S.

9.11. The names of foreign countries are not abbreviated, with the exception of the former U.S.S.R., which is abbreviated due to its length.

9.12. In other than formal usage as defined in rule 9.9, all States of the United States, Puerto Rico, the Virgin Islands, and freely associated states are abbreviated immediately following any capitalized geographic term, including armory, arsenal, airbase, airport, barracks, depot, fort, Indian agency, military camp, national cemetery (also forest, historic site, memorial, seashore, monument, park), naval shipyard, proving ground, reservation (forest, Indian, or military), and reserve or station (military or naval).

Prince George's County, MD
Mount Rainier National Forest, WA
Stone Mountain, GA
National Naval Medical Center, Bethesda, MD
Mark Twain National Wildlife Refuge, IL-IA-MO (note use of hyphens here)
Richmond, VA
Arlington National Cemetery, VA
Aberdeen Proving Ground, MD
Washington Dulles International Airport, VA
Redstone Arsenal, AL

but
Leavenworth freight yards, Kansas
Altoona sidetrack, Wisconsin

9.13. The Postal Service style of two-letter State, Province, and freely associated State abbreviations is to be used.

United States

[Including freely associated States]

Alabama	AL	Kentucky	KY	Ohio	OH
Alaska	AK	Louisiana	LA	Oklahoma	OK
American Samoa	AS	Maine	ME	Oregon	OR
Arizona	AZ	Marshall Islands	MH	Palau	PW
Arkansas	AR	Maryland	MD	Pennsylvania	PA
California	CA	Massachusetts	MA	Puerto Rico	PR
Colorado	CO	Michigan	MI	Rhode Island	RI
Connecticut	CT	Minnesota	MN	South Carolina	SC
Delaware	DE	Mississippi	MS	South Dakota	SD
District of Columbia	DC	Missouri	MO	Tennessee	TN
Federated States of Micronesia	FM	Montana	MT	Texas	TX
Florida	FL	Nebraska	NE	Utah	UT
Georgia	GA	Nevada	NV	Vermont	VT
Guam	GU	New Hampshire	NH	Virgin Islands	VI
Hawaii	HI	New Jersey	NJ	Virginia	VA
Idaho	ID	New Mexico	NM	Washington	WA
Illinois	IL	New York	NY	West Virginia	WV
Indiana	IN	North Carolina	NC	Wisconsin	WI
Iowa	IA	North Dakota	ND	Wyoming	WY
Kansas	KS	Northern Mariana Islands	MP		

Canada

Alberta	AB	Northwest Territories	NT	Prince Edward Island	PE
British Columbia	BC	Nova Scotia	NS	Quebec	QC
Manitoba	MB	Nunavut	NU	Saskatchewan	SK
New Brunswick	NB	Ontario	ON	Yukon	YT
Newfoundland and Labrador	NL				

9.14. The names of other insular possessions, trust territories, and *Long Island, Staten Island,* etc., are not abbreviated.

9.15. The names of Canadian Provinces and other foreign political subdivisions are not abbreviated except as noted in rule 9.13.

Addresses

9.16. Words such as *Street, Avenue, Place, Road, Square, Boulevard, Terrace, Drive, Court,* and *Building,* following a name or number, are abbreviated in footnotes, sidenotes, tables, leaderwork, and lists.

9.17. In addresses, no period is used with the abbreviations *NW, SW, NE, SE* (indicating sectional divisions of cities) following name or number. *North, South, East,* and *West* are spelled out at all times.

9.18. The word *Street* or *Avenue* as part of a name is not abbreviated even in parentheses, footnotes, sidenotes, tables, lists, or leaderwork.

14th Street Bridge   Ninth Avenue Bldg.

9.19. The words *County, Fort, Mount, Point,* and *Port* are not abbreviated. *Saint* (*St.*) and *Sainte* (*Ste.*) should be abbreviated.

Descriptions of tracts of land

9.20. In the description of tracts of public land the following abbreviations are used (periods are only used after compass directional abbreviations that describe township(s) (T./Tps.) and range(s) (R./Rs.)):

SE¼NW¼ sec. 4, T. 12 S., R. 15 E., of the Boise Meridian
lot 6, NE¼ sec. 4, T. 6 N., R. 1 W.
N½ sec. 20, T. 7 N., R. 2 W., sixth principal meridian
Tps. 9, 10, 11, and 12 S., Rs. 12 and 13 W.
T. 2 S., Rs. 8, 9, and 10 E., sec. 26
T. 3 S., R. 1 E., sec. 34, W½E½, W½, and W½SE¼SE¼
sec. 32 (with or without a township number)

9.21. If fractions are spelled out in land descriptions, *half* and *quarter* are used (not *one-half* or *one-quarter*).

south half of T. 47 N., R. 64 E.

9.22. In case of an unavoidable break in a land-description symbol group at end of a line, use no hyphen and break after fraction.

Names and titles

9.23. The following forms are not always abbreviations, and copy should be followed as to periods:

Al	Ben	Fred	Walt
Alex	Ed	Sam	Will

9.24. In signatures, an effort should be made to retain the exact form used by the signer.

George Wythe   Geo. Taylor

9.25. In company and other formal names, if it is not necessary to preserve the full legal title, such forms as *Bro., Bros., Co., Corp., Inc., Ltd.,* and *&* are used. *Association* and *Manufacturing* are not abbreviated.

Radio Corp. of America
Aluminum Co. of America
Standard Oil Co. of New Jersey
H.J. Baker & Bro.
Jones Bros. & Co.
American Telephone & Telegraph Co.
Norton Enterprises, Inc.
Maryland Steamship Co., Ltd.
Chesapeake & Delaware Canal
Fairmount Building & Loan Association
Electronics Manufacturing Co.
Texas College of Arts & Industries
Robert Wilson & Associates, Inc.
U.S. News & World Report
Baltimore & Ohio Railroad
Mine, Mill & Smelter Workers

but
Little Theater Company
Senate Banking, Housing and Urban Affairs Committee

9.26. *Company* and *Corporation* are not abbreviated in names of Federal Government units.

Commodity Credit Corporation
Federal Savings and Loan Insurance Corporation
Pension Benefit Guaranty Corporation

9.27. In parentheses, footnotes, sidenotes, tables, and leaderwork, abbreviate the words *railroad* and *railway* (*RR* and *Ry.*), except in such names as "Washington Railway & Electric Co." and "Florida Railroad & Navigation Corp." *SS* for *steamship, MS* for *motorship,* etc., preceding name are used at all times.

9.28. In the names of informal companionships the word *and* is spelled out.

Lennon and McCartney   Currier and Ives

9.29. In other than formal usage, a civil, military, or naval title preceding a name is abbreviated if followed by first or given name or initial; but *Mr., Mrs., Miss, Ms., M., MM., Messrs., Mlle., Mme.,* and *Dr.* are abbreviated with or without first or given name or initial.

United States military titles and abbreviations

Officer rank

Officer ranks in the United States military consist of commissioned officers and warrant officers. The commissioned ranks are the highest in the military. These officers hold presidential commissions and are confirmed at their ranks by the Senate. Army, Air Force, and Marine Corps officers are called company grade officers in the pay grades of O-1 to O-3, field grade officers in pay grades O-4 to O-6, and general officers in pay grades O-7 and higher. The equivalent officer groupings in the Navy are called junior grade, mid-grade, and flag.

Warrant officers hold warrants from their service secretary and are specialists and experts in certain military technologies or capabilities. The lowest ranking warrant officers serve under a warrant, but they receive commissions from the President upon promotion to chief warrant officer 2. These commissioned warrant officers are direct representatives of the President of the United States. They derive their authority from the same source as commissioned officers but remain specialists, in contrast to commissioned officers, who are generalists. There are no warrant officers in the Air Force.

	Army	**Navy Coast Guard**	**Marines**	**Air Force**
	General of the Army (Reserved for wartime only)	Fleet Admiral (Reserved for wartime only)		General of the Air Force (Reserved for wartime only)
O10	General GEN Army Chief of Staff	Admiral ADM Chief of Naval Operations and Commandant of the Coast Guard	General Gen. Commandant of the Marine Corps	General Gen. Air Force Chief of Staff
O9	Lieutenant General LTG	Vice Admiral VADM	Lieutenant General Lt. Gen.	Lieutenant General Lt. Gen.
O8	Major General MG	Rear Admiral Upper Half RADM	Major General Maj. Gen.	Major General Maj. Gen.
O7	Brigadier General BG	Rear Admiral Lower Half RDML	Brigadier General Brig. Gen.	Brigadier General Brig. Gen.
O6	Colonel COL	Captain CAPT	Colonel Col.	Colonel Col.
O5	Lieutenant Colonel LTC	Commander CDR	Lieutenant Colonel Lt. Col.	Lieutenant Colonel Lt. Col.
O4	Major MAJ	Lieutenant Commander LCDR	Major Maj.	Major Maj.
O3	Captain CPT	Lieutenant LT	Captain Capt.	Captain Capt.

	Army	Navy Coast Guard	Marines	Air Force
O2	First Lieutenant 1LT	Lieutenant Junior Grade LTJG	First Lieutenant 1st Lt.	First Lieutenant 1st Lt.
O1	Second Lieutenant 2LT	Ensign ENS	Second Lieutenant 2nd Lt.	Second Lieutenant 2nd Lt.
W5	Chief Warrant Officer CW5	Chief Warrant Officer CWO5	Chief Warrant Officer 5 CWO5	NO WARRANT
W4	Chief Warrant Officer 4 CW4	Chief Warrant Officer 4 CWO4	Chief Warrant Officer 4 CWO4	NO WARRANT
W3	Chief Warrant Officer 3 CW3	Chief Warrant Officer 3 CWO3	Chief Warrant Officer 3 CWO3	NO WARRANT
W2	Chief Warrant Officer 2 CW2	Chief Warrant Officer 2 CWO2	Chief Warrant Officer 2 CWO2	NO WARRANT
W1	Warrant Officer 1 WO1	Warrant Officer 1 WO1	Warrant Officer 1 WO	NO WARRANT

Source: http://www.defense.gov/About-DoD/Insignias/Officers.

Enlisted rank

Service members in pay grades E–1 through E–3 are usually either in some kind of training status or on their initial assignment. The training includes the basic training phase where recruits are immersed in military culture and values and are taught the core skills required by their service component.

Basic training is followed by a specialized or advanced training phase that provides recruits with a specific area of expertise or concentration. In the Army and Marines, this area is called a military occupational specialty; in the Navy it is known as a rate; and in the Air Force it is simply called an Air Force specialty.

Leadership responsibility significantly increases in the mid-level enlisted ranks. This responsibility is given formal recognition by use of the terms noncommissioned officer and petty officer. An Army sergeant, an Air Force staff sergeant, and a Marine corporal are considered NCO ranks. The Navy NCO equivalent, petty officer, is achieved at the rank of petty officer third class.

At the E–8 level, the Army, Marines, and Air Force have two positions at the same pay grade. Whether one is, for example, a senior master sergeant or a first sergeant in the Air Force depends on the person's job. The same is true for the positions at the E–9 level. Marine Corps master gunnery sergeants and sergeants major receive the same pay but have different responsibilities. E–8s and E–9s have 15 to 30 years on the job, and are commanders' senior advisers for enlisted matters.

A third E–9 element is the senior enlisted person of each service. The sergeant major of the Army, the sergeant major of the Marine Corps, the master chief petty officer of the Navy, and the chief master sergeant of the Air Force are the spokespersons of the enlisted force at the highest levels of their services.

<table>
<tr><th></th><th colspan="2">Army</th><th colspan="2">Navy
Coast Guard</th><th colspan="2">Marines</th><th colspan="3">Air Force</th></tr>
<tr><td>E9</td><td colspan="2">Sergeant Major of the Army (SMA)</td><td colspan="2">Master Chief Petty Officer of the Navy (MCPON)
and
Coast Guard (MCPOCG)</td><td colspan="2">Sergeant Major of the Marine Corps (SgtMajMC)</td><td colspan="3">Chief Master Sergeant of the Air Force (CMSAF)</td></tr>
<tr><td>E9</td><td>Sergeant Major (SGM)</td><td>Command Sergeant Major (CSM)</td><td>Master Chief Petty Officer (MCPO)</td><td>Fleet/Command Master Chief Petty Officer</td><td>Sergeant Major (SgtMaj)</td><td>Master Gunnery Sergeant (MGySgt)</td><td>Chief Master Sergeant (CMSgt)</td><td>First Sergeant</td><td>Command Chief Master Sergeant (CCM)</td></tr>
<tr><td>E8</td><td>Master Sergeant (MSG)</td><td>First Sergeant (1SG)</td><td colspan="2">Senior Chief Petty Officer (SCPO)</td><td>Master Sergeant (MSgt)</td><td>First Sergeant</td><td>Senior Master Sergeant (SMSgt)</td><td colspan="2">First Sergeant</td></tr>
<tr><td>E7</td><td colspan="2">Sergeant First Class (SFC)</td><td colspan="2">Chief Petty Officer (CPO)</td><td colspan="2">Gunnery Sergeant (GySgt)</td><td>Master Sergeant (MSgt)</td><td colspan="2">First Sergeant</td></tr>
<tr><td>E6</td><td colspan="2">Staff Sergeant (SSG)</td><td colspan="2">Petty Officer First Class (PO1)</td><td colspan="2">Staff Sergeant (SSgt)</td><td colspan="3">Technical Sergeant (TSgt)</td></tr>
<tr><td>E5</td><td colspan="2">Sergeant (SGT)</td><td colspan="2">Petty Officer Second Class (PO2)</td><td colspan="2">Sergeant (Sgt)</td><td colspan="3">Staff Sergeant (SSgt)</td></tr>
<tr><td>E4</td><td>Corporal (CPL)</td><td>Specialist (SPC)</td><td colspan="2">Petty Officer Third Class (PO3)</td><td colspan="2">Corporal (Cpl)</td><td colspan="3">Senior Airman (SrA)</td></tr>
</table>

	Army	Navy Coast Guard	Marines	Air Force
E3	Private First Class (PFC)	Seaman (SN)	Lance Corporal (LCpl)	Airman First Class (A1C)
E2	Private E-2 (PV2)	Seaman Apprentice (SA)	Private First Class (PFC)	Airman (Amn)
E1	Private	Seaman Recruit (SR)	Private	Airman Basic

Source: http://www.defense.gov/About-DoD/Insignias/Enlisted.

9.30. Spell out *Senator, Representative,* and *commandant.*

9.31. Unless preceded by *the*, abbreviate *Honorable, Reverend,* and *Monsignor* when followed by the first name, initials, or title.

Hon. John Kerry; the Honorable John Kerry; the Honorable Mr. Kerry

the Honorables John Roberts, Elena Kagan, and Ruth Bader Ginsberg

Rev. Martin Luther King, Jr.; the Reverend Dr. King; Rev. Dr. King; Reverend King (*not* Rev. King, *nor* the Reverend King)

Rt. Rev. James E. Freeman; the Right Reverend James E. Freeman; Very Rev. Henry Boyd; the Very Reverend Henry Boyd

Rt. Rev. Msgr. John Bird; the Right Reverend Monsignor John Bird

9.32. The following and similar forms are used after a name:

Esq., Jr., Sr.

2d, 3d (*or* II, III) (not preceded by comma)

Degrees: LL.D., M.A., Ph.D., etc.

Fellowships, orders, etc.: FSA Scot, F.R.S., K.C.B., C.P.A., etc.

9.33. The abbreviation *Esq.* and other titles such as *Mr., Mrs.,* and *Dr.,* should not appear with any other title or with abbreviations indicating scholastic degrees.

John L. Smith, Esq., *not* Mr. John L. Smith, Esq., *nor* John L. Smith, Esq., A.M.; *but* James A. Jones, Jr., Esq.

Ford Maddox, A.B., Ph.D., *not* Mr. Ford Maddox, A.B., Ph.D.

George Gray, M.D., *not* Mr. George Gray, M.D., *nor* Dr. George Gray, M.D.

Dwight A. Bellinger, D.V.M., *but* Major John P. Pryor, M.D.

9.34. *Sr.* and *Jr.* should not be used without first or given name or initials, but may be used in combination with any title.

A.K. Jones, Jr., or Mr. Jones, Junior, *not* Jones, Jr., *nor* Jones, Junior

President J.B. Nelson, Jr.

9.35. When name is followed by abbreviations designating religious and fraternal orders and scholastic and honorary degrees, their sequence is as follows: Orders, religious first; theological degrees; academic degrees earned in course; and honorary degrees in order of bestowal.

Henry L. Brown, D.D., A.M., D.Lit.
T.E. Holt, C.S.C., S.T.Lr., LL.D., Ph.D.
Samuel J. Deckelbaum, P.M.

9.36. Academic degrees standing alone may be abbreviated.

John was graduated with a B.A. degree; *but* bachelor of arts degree (lowercase when spelled out).
She earned her Ph.D. by hard work.

9.37. In addresses, signatures, lists of names, and leaderwork but not in tables nor in centerheads, *Mr., Mrs.,* and other titles preceding a name, and *Esq., Ph.D., Jr.,* and *Sr.* following a name, are set in roman caps and lowercase if the name is in caps and small caps. If the name is in caps, they are set in caps and small caps, if small caps are available—otherwise in caps and lowercase.

Parts of publications

9.38. The following abbreviations are used for parts of publications mentioned in parentheses, brackets, footnotes, sidenotes, list of references, tables, and leaderwork, when followed by figures, letters, or Roman numerals.

app., apps. (appendix, appendixes)
art., arts. (article, articles)
bull., bulls. (bulletin, bulletins)
ch., chs. (chapter, chapters)
col., cols. (column, columns)
ed., eds. (edition, editions)
fig., figs. (figure, figures)
fn., fns. (footnote, footnotes)
No., Nos. (number, numbers)
p., pp. (page, pages)
par., pars. (paragraph, paragraphs)
pl., pls. (plate, plates)
pt., pts. (part, parts)
sec., secs. (section, sections)
subch., subchs. (subchapter, subchapters)
subpar., subpars. (subparagraph, subparagraphs)
subpt., subpts. (subpart, subparts)
subsec., subsecs. (subsection, subsections)
supp., supps. (supplement, supplements)
vol., vols. (volume, volumes)

9.39. The word *article* and the word *section* are abbreviated when appearing at the beginning of a paragraph and set in caps and small caps followed by a period and an en space, except that the first of a series is spelled out.

ART. 2; SEC. 2; etc.; *but* ARTICLE 1; SECTION 1
ART. II; SEC. II; etc.; *but* ARTICLE I; SECTION I

9.40. At the beginning of a legend, the word *figure* preceding the legend number is not abbreviated.

FIGURE 4.—Landscape.

Terms relating to Congress

9.41. The words *Congress* and *session*, when accompanied by a numerical reference, are abbreviated in parentheses, brackets, and text footnotes. In sidenotes, lists of references, tables, leaderwork, and footnotes to tables and leaderwork, the following abbreviations are used:

106th Cong., 1st sess.
1st sess., 106th Cong.
Public Law 84, 102d Cong.
Private Law 68, 102d Cong.

9.42. In references to bills, resolutions, documents and reports in parentheses, brackets, footnotes, sidenotes, tables, and leaderwork, the following abbreviations are used:

H.R. 416 (House bill)
S. 116 (Senate bill)
The examples above may be abbreviated or spelled out in text.
H. Res. 5 (House resolution)
H. Con. Res. 10 (House concurrent resolution)
H.J. Res. 21 (House joint resolution)
S. Res. 50 (Senate resolution)
S. Con. Res. 17 (Senate concurrent resolution)
S.J. Res. 45 (Senate joint resolution)
H. Conf. Rept. 10 (House conference report)
H. Doc. 35 (House document)
S. Doc. 62 (Senate document)
H. Rept. 214 (House report)
S. Rept. 410 (Senate report)
Ex. Doc. B (Executive document)
Ex. F (92d Cong., 2d sess.)
Ex. Rept. 9 (92d Cong., 1st sess.)
Misc. Doc. 16 (miscellaneous document)
Public Res. 47

9.43. References to statutes in parentheses, footnotes, sidenotes, tables, leaderwork, and congressional work are abbreviated.

Rev. Stat. (Revised Statutes); 43 Rev. Stat. 801; 18 U.S.C. 38
Supp. Rev. Stat. (Supplement to the Revised Statutes)
Stat. L. (Statutes at Large)
but Public Law 85–1; Private Law 68

Calendar divisions

9.44. Names of months followed by the day, or day and year, are abbreviated in footnotes, tables, leaderwork, sidenotes, and in bibliographies. (See examples, rule 9.45.) *May, June,* and *July* are always spelled out. In narrow columns in tables, however, the names of months may be abbreviated even if standing alone. Preferred forms follow:

Jan.	Apr.	Oct.
Feb.	Aug.	Nov.
Mar.	Sept.	Dec.

9.45. In text only, dates as part of a citation or reference within parentheses or brackets are also abbreviated.

(Op. Atty. Gen., Dec. 4, 2005)
(Congressional Record, Sept. 25, 2007)
[From the New York Times, Mar. 4, 2008]
[From the Mar. 4 issue]
On Jan. 25 (we had commenced on Dec. 26, 2005) the work was finished. (In footnotes, tables, leaderwork, and sidenotes)
On January 25, a decision was reached (Op. Atty. Gen., Dec. 4, 2006). (Text, but with citation in parentheses)

but On January 25 (we had commenced on December 26, 2008) the work was finished. (Not a citation or reference in text)

9.46. Weekdays are not abbreviated, but the following forms are used, if necessary, in lists or in narrow columns in tables:

Sun.	Wed.	Fri.
Mon.	Thurs.	Sat.
Tues.		

Time zones

9.47. The following forms are to be used when abbreviating names of time zones:

AKDT—Alaska daylight time
AKST—Alaska standard time
AKT—Alaska time (implies standard or daylight time)
AST—Atlantic standard time
AT—Atlantic time
CDT—central daylight time
CST—central standard time
CT—central time
ChST—Chamorro standard time (DST not observed)
DST—daylight saving (no "s") time
EDT—eastern daylight time
EST—eastern standard time
ET—eastern time
GCT—Greenwich civil time
GMAT—Greenwich mean astronomical time
GMT—Greenwich mean time
HDT—Hawaii-Aleutian daylight time (not observed in HI)
HST—Hawaii-Aleutian standard time
LST—local standard time
MDT—mountain daylight time
MST—mountain standard time
MT— mountain time
PDT—Pacific daylight time
PST—Pacific standard time
PT—Pacific time
SST—Samoan standard time (DST not observed)
UTC—coordinated universal time

Acronyms and coined words

9.48. To obtain uniform treatment in the formation of acronyms and coined words, apply the formulas that follow:

Use all capital letters when only the first letter of each word or selected words is used to make up the symbol:

APPR (Army package power reactor)
EPCOT (Experimental Prototype Community of Tomorrow)
MAG (Military Advisory Group)
MIRV (multiple independently targetable reentry vehicle)
SALT (strategic arms limitation talks); (*avoid* SALT talks)

Use all capital letters where first letters of prefixes and/or suffixes are utilized as part of established expressions:

CPR (*c*ardio*p*ulmonary *r*esuscitation)
ESP (*e*xtra*s*ensory *p*erception)
FLIR (*f*orward-*l*ooking *i*nfra*r*ed)

Copy must be followed where an acronym or abbreviated form is copyrighted or established by law:

ACTION (agency of Government; not an acronym)
MARAD (*Mar*itime *Ad*ministration)
NACo (*N*ational *A*ssociation of *Co*unties)
MEDLARS (*Med*ical *L*iterature *A*nalysis and *R*etrieval *S*ystem)

Use caps and lowercase when proper names are used in shortened form, any word of which uses more than the first letter of each word:

Conrail (Consolidated Rail Corporation)
Pepco (Potomac Electric Power Co.)
Inco (International Nickel Co.)
Aramco (Arabian-American Oil Co.)
Unprofor (United Nations Protection Force)
but USAJOBS

Use lowercase in common-noun combinations made up of more than the first letter of lowercased words:

loran (*lo*ng-*ra*nge *n*avigation)
sonar (*so*und *na*vigation *r*anging)
secant (*se*paration *c*ontrol of *a*ircraft by *n*onsynchronous *t*echniques)

9.49. The words *infra* and *supra* are not abbreviated.

Terms of measure

9.50. The only instance where a period is used with a compass directonal abbreviation is in a land tract description with township(s) (T./Tps.) and range(s) (R./Rs.). (See rule 9.20.) Compass directionals are abbreviated as follows:

N	S	ESE
NE	NNW	10° N 25° W
E	W	*but*
NW by N ¼ W	SW	T. 2 S., R. 1 E.

9.51. The words *latitude* and *longitude,* followed by figures, are abbreviated in parentheses, brackets, footnotes, sidenotes, tables, and leaderwork, and the figures are always closed up.

lat. 52°33'05" N   long. 13°21'10" E

9.52. Avoid breaking latitude and longitude figures at end of line; space out line instead. In case of an unavoidable break at end of line, use hyphen.

9.53. Temperature and gravity are expressed in figures. When the degree mark is used, it must appear closed up to the capital letter, not against the figures. Note the following related abbreviations and letter symbols and their usages:

abs, absolute	API, American Petroleum Institute
Bé, Baumé	Twad, Twaddell
°C,[1] degree Celsius[2]	100 °C
°F, degree Fahrenheit	212 °F[1]
°R, degree Rankine	671.67 °R
K, kelvin; *but* Kelvin scale	18 °API
273.15 K	
°API	

9.54. References to meridian in statements of time are abbreviated as follows:

10 a.m. (*not* 10:00 a.m.)	12 p.m. (12 noon)
2:30 p.m.	12 a.m. (12 midnight)

9.55. The word *o'clock* is not used with abbreviations of time.

not 10 o'clock p.m.

9.56. Metric unit letter symbols are set lowercase roman unless the unit name has been derived from a proper name, in which case the first letter of the symbol is capitalized (for example Pa for pascal and W for watt). The exception is the letter L for liter. The same form is used for singular and plural. The preferred symbol for *cubic centimeter* is *cm*³; use *cc* only when requested.

A space is used between a figure and a unit symbol except in the case of the symbols for degree, minute, and second of plane angle.

3 m   45 mm   25 °C   *but* 33°15'21"

Prefixes for multiples and submultiples				*Metric units*	
Y	yotta (10^{24})	d	deci (10^{-1})	m	meter (for length)
Z	zetta (10^{21})	c	centi (10^{-2})	g	gram (for weight or mass)
E	exa (10^{18})	m	milli (10^{-3})	L	liter (for capacity)
P	peta (10^{15})	μ	micro (10^{-6})		
T	tera (10^{12})	n	nano (10^{-9})		
G	giga (10^{9})	p	pico (10^{-12})		
M	mega (10^{6})	f	femto (10^{-15})		
k	kilo (10^{3})	a	atto (10^{-18})		
h	hecto (10^{2})	z	zepto (10^{-21})		
da	deka (10)	y	yocto (10^{-24})		

[1]Without figures preceding it, °C or °F should be used only in boxhead and over figure columns in tables.
[2]Preferred form (superseding Centigrade).

	Length		*Area*		*Volume*
km	kilometer	km^2	square kilometer	km^3	cubic kilometer
hm	hectometer	hm^2	square hectometer	hm^3	cubic hectometer
dam	decameter	dam^2	square decameter	dam^3	cubic dekameter
m	meter	m^2	square meter	m^3	cubic meter
dm	decimeter	dm^2	square decimeter	dm^3	cubic decimeter
cm	centimeter	cm^2	square centimeter	cm^3	cubic centimeter
mm	millimeter	mm^2	square millimeter	mm^3	cubic millimeter

	Weight		*Land area*		*Capacity of containers*
kg	kilogram	ha	hectare	kL	kiloliter
hg	hectogram	a	acre	hL	hectoliter
dag	dekagram			daL	dekaliter
g	gram			L	liter
dg	decigram			dL	deciliter
cg	centigram			cL	centiliter
mg	milligram			mL	milliliter
μg	microgram				

9.57. A similar form of abbreviation applies to any unit of the metric system.

A	ampere	V	volt	mF	millifarad
VA	voltampere	W	watt	mH	millihenry
F	farad	kc	kilocycle	μF	microfarad (one-millionth of a farad)
H	henry	kV	kilovolt		
Hz	hertz	kVA	kilovoltampere		
J	joule	kW	kilowatt		

9.58. The following forms are used when units of English weight and measure and units of time are abbreviated, the same form of abreviation being used for both singular and plural:

	Length		*Area and volume*
in	inch	in^2	square inch
ft	foot	in^3	cubic inch
yd	yard	mi^2	square mile
mi	mile (statute)	ft^3	cubic foot

	Time		*Weight*		*Capacity*
yr	year	gr	grain	gill	(not abbreviated)
mo	month	dr	dram	pt	pint
d	day	oz	ounce	qt	quart
h	hour	lb	pound	gal	gallon
min	minute	cwt	hundredweight	pk	peck
s	second	dwt	pennyweight	bu	bushel
		ton(s)	(not abbreviated)	bbl	barrel
		but t	metric ton (tonne)		

9.59. In astrophysical and similar scientific matter, magnitudes and units of time may be expressed as follows:

$5^h3^m9^s$ 4.5^h

Money

9.60. The following are some of the abbreviations and symbols used for indicating money:

(For the abbreviations of other terms indicating currency, see the table "Currency" in Chapter 17 "Useful Tables.")

$, dol (dollar)
c, ct, ¢ (cent, cents)
TRL175 (Turkish)
USD15,000
€ (euro)
Mex $2,650
₱ (peso)
£ (pound)
d (pence)

Use "USD" if omission would result in confusion.

Standard word abbreviations

9.61. For a more complete list of Government acronyms visit the U.S. Government Manual: https//www.govinfo.gov/content/pkg/GOVMAN-2015-07-01/pdf/GOVMAN-2015-07-01-Commonly-Used-Agency-Acronyms-105.pdf. Use these forms if abbreviations are required:

2,4D (insecticide)
2d—second
3d—third
3D—three dimensional
4°—quarto
8°—octavo
A1 (rating)
A.A.—Alcoholics Anonymous
AARP—American Association of Retired Persons
abbr.—abbreviation
abs.—abstract

acct.—account
ACTH—adrenocorticotropic hormone
A.D.—(anno Domini) in the year of our Lord (A.D. 937)
ADDH—attention deficit disorder with hyperactivity
ADHD—attention deficit hyperactivity disorder
AF—audiofrequency
AFB—Air Force Base
AFL-CIO—American Federation of Labor and Congress of Industrial Organizations
AIDS—acquired immunodeficiency syndrome
a.k.a.—also known as
A.L.R.—American Law Reports
ALS—amyotrophic lateral sclerosis
AM—amplitude modulation (no periods)
A.M.—(anno mundi) in the year of the world
A.M. or M.A.—master of arts
a.m.—(ante meridiem) before noon
Am. Repts.—American Reports
Amtrak—National Railroad Passenger Corporation
AMVETS—American Veterans; Amvet(s) (individual)
ANSI—American National Standards Institute
antilog—antilogarithm (no period)
AOA—Administration on Aging
APEC—Asia-Pacific Economic Cooperation
API—American Petroleum Institute
APO—Army post office (no periods)
App. D.C.—District of Columbia Appeal Cases
App. Div.—Appellate Division
approx.—approximately
ARC—American Red Cross
ARS—Agricultural Research Service
ASD—autism spectrum disorder
ASME—American Society of Mechanical Engineers
ASTM—American Society for Testing and Materials
ATM—automatic teller machine
Atl.—Atlantic Reporter; A.2d, Atlantic Reporter, second series
AUS—Army of the United States
Ave.—avenue
AWACS—airborne warning and control system
AWOL—absent without leave
B.A. or A.B.—bachelor of arts
BAC—billing address code
BBB—Better Business Bureau
B.C.—before Christ (1200 B.C.)
B.C.E.—Before Common Era
BCG—(bacillus Calmette-Guerin) antituberculosis vaccine
bf.—boldface
BGN—Board on (*not* of) Geographic Names
BIA—Bureau of Indian Affairs
BIS—Bank for International Settlements
Blatch. Pr. Cas.—Blatchford's Prize Cases
Bldg.—building
B.Lit(t). or Lit(t).B.—bachelor of literature
BLM—Bureau of Land Management
BLS—Bureau of Labor Statistics
Blvd.—boulevard
b.o.—buyer's option
B.S. or B.Sc.—bachelor of science
c. and s.c.—caps and small caps
ca.—(circa) about
ca—centiare

CACM—Central American Common Market
CAD—computer-aided design
CAP—Civil Air Patrol
CAT scan—computerized axial tomography
C.C.A.—Circuit Court of Appeals
CCC—Commodity Credit Corporation
C.Cls.—Court of Claims
C.Cls.R.—Court of Claims Reports
C.C.P.A.—Court of Customs and Patents Appeals
CCSDS—Consultative Committee for Space Data Systems
CDC—Centers for Disease Control and Prevention
C.E.—Common Era
CEA—Council of Economic Advisers
cf.—(confer) compare or see
CFR—Code of Federal Regulations
CFR Supp.—Code of Federal Regulations Supplement
CHAMPUS—Civilian Health and Medical Program of the Uniformed Services
CIA—Central Intelligence Agency
C.J.—(corpus juris) body of law; Chief Justice
CMYK—cyan, magenta, yellow, black
CNN—Cable News Network
CO—commanding officer
Co.—company (commercial)
c.o.d.—cash on delivery
COLA—cost-of-living adjustment
Comp. Dec.—Comptroller's Decisions (Treasury)
Comp. Gen.—Comptroller General Decisions
con.—continued
Conus—continental United States
Corp.—corporation (commercial)
cos—cosine (no period)
cosh—hyperbolic cosine (no period)
cot—cotangent (no period)
coth—hyperbolic cotangent (no period)
c.p.—chemically pure
C.P.A.—certified public accountant
CPI—Consumer Price Index
CPR—cardiopulmonary resuscitation
cr.—credit; creditor
C-SPAN—Cable Satellite Public Affairs Network
csc—cosecant (no period)
csch—hyperbolic cosecant (no period)
Ct.—court
Dall.—Dallas (U.S. Supreme Court Reports)
DAR—Daughters of the American Revolution
d.b.a.—doing business as
d.b.h.—diameter at breast height
D.D.—doctor of divinity
D.D.S.—doctor of dental surgery
DDT—dichlorodiphenyl-trichloroethane
DHS—Department of Homeland Security
Dist. Ct.—District Court
D.Lit(t). or Lit(t).D.—doctor of literature
DNC—Domestic Names Committee (BGN)
do.—(ditto) the same
DOC—Department of Commerce
DoD—Department of Defense
DOE—Department of Energy
DOI—Department of the Interior
DOJ—Department of Justice

DOL—Department of Labor
DoS—Department of State
DOT—Department of Transportation
DP—displaced person (no period)
D.P.H.—doctor of public health
D.P.Hy.—doctor of public hygiene
DPT—diphtheria, pertussis, tetanus innoculation
dr.—debit; debtor
Dr.—doctor; drive
DST—daylight saving (no "s") time
D.V.M.—doctor of veterinary medicine
E—east
e-CFR—electronic Code of Federal Regulations
EDGAR—Electronic Data Gathering, Analysis and Retrieval (SEC)
EEOC—Equal Employment Opportunity Commission
EFTA—European Free Trade Association
EFTS—electronic funds transfer system
e.g.—(exempli gratia) for example
EHF—extremely high frequency
emcee—master of ceremony
e.o.m.—end of month
EOP—Executive Office of the President
EPA—Environmental Protection Agency
ESE—east-southeast
et al.—(et alii) and others
et seq.—(et sequentia) and the following
etc.—(et cetera) and so forth
EU—European Union
Euratom—European Atomic Energy Community
Euro—currency (common)
Eurodollars—U.S. dollars used to finance foreign trade
Ex. Doc. (with letter)—executive document
EXIM Bank—Export-Import Bank of the United States
f., ff.—and following page (pages)
FAA—Federal Aviation Administration
FACS—Faculty of the American College of Surgeons
Fannie Mae—Federal National Mortgage Association
FAO—Food and Agriculture Organization
FAQ—frequently asked question
FAR—Federal Acquisition Regulation
f.a.s.—free alongside ship
FAS—Foreign Agricultural Service
FBI—Federal Bureau of Investigation
FCA—Farm Credit Administration
FCC—Federal Communications Commission
FCIC—Federal Crop Insurance Corporation
FCSC—Foreign Claims Settlement Commission
FDA—Food and Drug Administration
FDIC—Federal Deposit Insurance Corporation
FDLP—Federal Depository Library Program
Fed.—Federal Reporter; F.3d, Federal Reporter, third series
FEOF—Foreign Exchange Operations Fund
FERC—Federal Energy Regulatory Commission

FHA—Federal Housing Administration
FHFA—Federal Housing Finance Agency
FmHA—Farmers Home Administration
FHWA—Federal Highway Administration
FICA—Federal Insurance Contributions Act
FLSA—Fair Labor Standards Act
FM—frequency modulation
FMC—Federal Maritime Commission
FMCS—Federal Mediation and Conciliation Service
FNS—Food and Nutrition Service
f°—folio
FOB—free on board
FPO—fleet post office (no periods)
FR—Federal Register (publication)
FRG—Federal Republic of Germany
FRS—Federal Reserve System
FS—Forest Service
FSLIC—Federal Savings and Loan Insurance Corporation
F. Supp.—Federal Supplement
FTC—Federal Trade Commission
FWS—Fish and Wildlife Service
GAO—Government Accountability Office
GATT—General Agreement on Tariffs and Trade
GDP—Gross Domestic Product
GFE—government furnished equipment
GFI—government furnished information
GI—general issue; Government issue
GIS—geographic information system
G.M.&S.—general, medical, and surgical
GNMA—Government National Mortgage Association (Ginnie Mae)
Gov.—Governor
GPO—Government Publishing Office
GPS—Global Positioning System
gr. wt.—gross weight
GSA—General Services Administration
GSE—Government-Sponsored Enterprise
G7—Group of Seven
H.C.—House of Commons
H. Con. Res. (with number)—House concurrent resolution
H. Doc. (with number)—House document
hazmat—hazardous material
HDTV—high definition television
HE—high explosive (no periods)
HF—high frequency (no periods)
HHS—Health and Human Services (Department of)
HIV—human immunodeficiency virus
H.J. Res. (with number)—House joint resolution
HMO—health-maintenance organization
HOV—high-occupancy vehicle
How.—Howard (U.S. Supreme Court Reports)
H.R. (with number)—House bill
H. Rept. (with number)—House report
H. Res. (with number)—House resolution
HUD—Housing and Urban Development (Department of)
IADB—Inter-American Defense Board

IAEA—International Atomic Energy Agency
ibid.—(ibidem) in the same place
ICBM—intercontinental ballistic missile
id.—(idem) the same
ID—Information Dissemination
IDA—International Development Association
IDE—integrated drive electronics
i.e.—(id est) that is
IEEE—Institute of Electrical and Electronic Engineers
IF—intermediate frequency (no periods)
IFC—International Finance Corporation
IMF—International Monetary Fund
Insp. Gen. (also IG)—inspector general
Interpol—International Criminal Police Organization
IOU—I owe you
IQ—intelligence quotient
IRA—individual retirement account
IRBM—intermediate range ballistic missile
IRE—Institute of Radio Engineers
IRS—Internal Revenue Service
ISIL—Islamic State of Iraq and the Levant (Intelligence Community standard)
ISIS—Islamic State of Iraq and Syria
ISO—International Organization for Standardization
ISS—International Space Station
ISSN—International Standard Serial Number
JAG—Judge Advocate General
jato—jet-assisted takeoff
J.D.—(jurum or juris doctor) doctor of laws
JOBS—Job Opportunities in the Business Sector
JIT—just in time
Jpn.—Japan or Japanese where necessary to abbreviate
Jr.—junior
Judge Adv. Gen.—Judge Advocate General
lat.—latitude
LC—Library of Congress
LCD—liquid crystal display
lc.—lowercase
L.Ed.—Lawyer's edition (U.S. Supreme Court Reports)
LGBTQ—Lesbian, Gay, Bisexual, Transgender, and Questioning
liq.—liquid
lf.—lightface
LF—low frequency
LL.B.—bachelor of laws
LL.D.—doctor of laws
loc. cit.—(loco citato) in the place cited
log (no period)—logarithm
long.—longitude
loran (no periods)—long-range navigation
lox (no periods)—liquid oxygen
LPG—liquefied petroleum gas
Ltd.—limited
Lt. Gov.—lieutenant governor
M—money supply: M1, M2, etc.
M.—monsieur; MM., messieurs
m.—(meridies) noon
M—more
MAC—Military Airlift Command
MARAD—Maritime Administration
MC—Member of Congress (emcee, master of ceremonies)
M.D.—doctor of medicine
MDAP—Mutual Defense Assistance Program
Medi-Cal—Medicaid California

memo—memorandum
MF—medium frequency; microfiche
MFN—most favored nation
MIA—missing in action (plural MIAs)
MIRV—multiple independently targetable reentry vehicle
Misc. Doc. (with number)—miscellaneous document
Mlle.—mademoiselle
MMAR—Materials Management Acquisition Regulation
Mme.—madam
Mmes.—mesdames
mo.—month
MOS—military occupational specialty
M.P.—Member of Parliament
MP—military police
Mr.—mister (plural Messrs.)
MRI—magnetic resonance imaging
Mrs.—mistress
Ms.—feminine title (plural Mses.)
M.S.—master of science
MS.—MSS., manuscript, manuscripts
MSC—Military Sealift Command
Msgr.—monsignor
m.s.l.—mean sea level
MTN—multilateral trade negotiations
N—north
NA—not available; not applicable
NACo.—National Association of Counties
NAFTA—North American Free Trade Agreement
NAS—National Academy of Sciences
NASA—National Aeronautics and Space Administration
NATO—North Atlantic Treaty Organization
NCUA—National Credit Union Administration
NE—northeast
n.e.c.—not elsewhere classified
n.e.s.—not elsewhere specified
net wt.—net weight
N.F.—National Formulary
NFC—National Finance Center
NIH—National Institutes of Health
NIST—National Institute of Standards and Technology
NGA—National Geospatial-Intelligence Agency
n.l.—natural log or logarithm
NLRB—National Labor Relations Board
NNTP—Network News Transfer Protocol
NNW—north-northwest
No.—Nos., number, numbers
NOAA—National Oceanic and Atmospheric Administration
n.o.i.b.n.—not otherwise indexed by name
n.o.p.—not otherwise provided (for)
n.o.s.—not otherwise specified
NPR—National Public Radio
NPS—National Park Service
NRC—Nuclear Regulatory Commission
NS—nuclear ship
NSA—National Security Agency
NSC—National Security Council
NSF—National Science Foundation
n.s.k.—not specified by kind
n.s.p.f.—not specifically provided for
NW—northwest

OAPEC—Organization of Arab Petroleum Exporting Countries
OAS—Organization of American States
OASDHI—Old-Age, Survivors, Disability, and Health Insurance Program
OASI—Old-Age and Survivors Insurance
OD—officer of the day
OD—overdose; Odd, overdosed
O.D.—doctor of optometry
OK—Oked, Oking, Oks
OMB—Office of Management and Budget
Op. Atty. Gen.—Opinions of the Attorney General
op. cit.—(opere citato) in the work cited
OPEC—Organization of Petroleum Exporting Countries
OSD—Office of the Secretary of Defense
PA—public address system; physician assistant
Pac.—Pacific Reporter; P.2d, Pacific Reporter, second series
PAC—political action committee (plural PACs)
PBS—Public Broadcasting Service; Public Buildings Service
PCV—Peace Corps Volunteer
Pet.—Peters (U.S. Supreme Court Reports)
Ph—phenyl
Phar.D.—doctor of pharmacy
Ph.B. or B.Ph.—bachelor of philosophy
Ph.D. or D.Ph.—doctor of philosophy
Ph.G.—graduate in pharmacy
PHS—Public Health Service
PIN—personal identification number
Pl.—place
p.m.—(post meridiem) after noon
P.O. Box (with number)—*but* post office box (in general sense)
POP—Point of Presence; Post Office Protocol
POW—prisoner of war (plural POWs)
Private Res. (with number)—private resolution
Prof.—professor
pro tem—(pro tempore) temporarily
P.S.—(post scriptum) postscript; public school (with number)
PTA—parent-teachers' association
PTSD—post-traumatic stress disorder
Public Res. (with number)—public resolution
PX—post exchange
QT—on the quiet
R.—Rs., range, ranges
racon—radar beacon
radar—radio detection and ranging
R&D—research and development
rato—rocket-assisted takeoff
Rd.—road
RDT&E—research, development, testing, and evaluation
Rev.—reverend
Rev. Stat.—Revised Statutes
RF—radio frequency
R.F.D.—rural free delivery
RGB—red, green, blue
Rh—Rhesus (blood factor)
RIF—reduction(s) in force; RIFed, RIFing, RIFs

R.N.—registered nurse
ROTC—Reserve Officers' Training Corps
RR—railroad
RRB—Railroad Retirement Board
RSS—Really Simple Syndication
Rt. Rev.—right reverend
Ry.—railway
S—south
S.—Senate bill (with number)
SAE—Society of Automotive Engineers
S&L(s)—savings and loan(s)
SALT—strategic arms limitation talks
SAR—Sons of the American Revolution
SBA—Small Business Administration
sc.—(scilicet) namely (see also ss)
s.c.—small caps
S. Con. Res. (with number)—Senate concurrent resolution
s.d.—(sine die) without date
S. Doc. (with number)—Senate document
SE—southeast
SEATO—Southeast Asia Treaty Organization
SEC—Securities and Exchange Commission
sec—secant
sech—hyperbolic secant
2d—second
SEO—Search Engine Optimization
SHF—superhigh frequency
shoran—short range (radio)
SI—Systeme International d'Unités
sic—thus
sin—sine
sinh—hyperbolic sine
S.J. Res. (with number)—Senate joint resolution
sonar—sound, navigation, and ranging (no period)
SOP—standard operating procedure
SOS—wireless distress signal
SP—shore patrol
SPA—simplified purchase agreement
SPAR—Coast Guard Women's Reserve (*s*emper *p*aratus—*a*lways *r*eady)
sp. gr.—specific gravity
Sq.—square (street)
Sr.—senior
S. Rept. (with number)—Senate report
S. Res. (with number)—Senate resolution
SS—steamship
ss—(scilicet) namely (in law) (see also sc.)
SSA—Social Security Administration
SSE—south-southeast
SSS—Selective Service System
St.—Ste., SS., Saint, Sainte, Saints
St.—street
Stat.—Statutes at Large
STEAM—Science, Technology, Engineering, Art and Mathematics
STEM—Science, Technology, Engineering and Mathematics
STP—standard temperature and pressure
Sup. Ct.—Supreme Court Reporter
Supp. Rev. Stat.—Supplement to the Revised Statutes
Supt.—superintendent
Surg.—surgeon
Surg. Gen.—Surgeon General
SW—southwest

S.W.2d—Southwestern Reporter, second series
SWAT—special weapons and tactics (team)
T.—Tps., township, townships
tan—tangent
tanh—hyperbolic tangent
TB—tuberculosis
T.D.—Treasury Decisions
TDY—temporary duty
Ter.—terrace
3d—third
t.m.—true mean
TNT—trinitrotoluol
TPP—Trans-Pacific Partnership
TV—television
TVA—Tennessee Valley Authority
uc.—uppercase
UHF—ultrahigh frequency
U.N.—United Nations
UNESCO—United Nations Educational, Scientific, and Cultural Organization
UNCHR—United Nations High Commissioner for Refugees
UNICEF—United Nations Children's Fund
U.S.—U.S. Supreme Court Reports
U.S.A.—United States of America
USA—U.S. Army
USAF—U.S. Air Force
USAID—U.S. Agency for International Development
U.S.C.—United States Code
U.S.C.A.—United States Code Annotated
USCCR—U.S. Commission on Civil Rights
U.S.C. Supp.—United States Code Supplement
USCG—U.S. Coast Guard
USDA—U.S. Department of Agriculture
USES—U.S. Employment Service
U.S. 61—U.S. No. 61, U.S. Highway No. 61
USGS—U.S. Geological Survey
USMC—U.S. Marine Corps
USN—U.S. Navy
USNR—U.S. Navy Reserve
U.S.P.—United States Pharmacopeia
USPS—U.S. Postal Service
U.S.S.—U.S. Senate
v. or vs.—(versus) against
VA—Department of Veterans Affairs
VAT—value added tax
VCR—video cassette recorder
VHF—very high frequency
VIP—very important person
viz—(videlicet) namely
VLF—very low frequency
VTR—video tape recording
W—west
w.a.e.—when actually employed
Wall.—Wallace (U.S. Supreme Court Reports)
wf—wrong font
Wheat.—Wheaton (U.S. Supreme Court Reports)
WHO—World Health Organization
WIPO—World Intellectual Property Organization
WNW—west-northwest
w.o.p.—without pay
Yale L.J.—Yale Law Journal
ZIP Code—Zone Improvement Plan Code (Postal Service)
ZIP+4—9-digit ZIP Code

Standard letter symbols for units of measure

9.62. The same form is used for singular and plural senses.

A—ampere
Å—angstrom
a—are
a—atto (prefix, one-quintillionth)
aA—attoampere
abs—absolute (temperature and gravity)
ac—alternating current
AF—audiofrequency
Ah—ampere-hour
A/m—ampere per meter
AM—amplitude modulation
asb—apostilb
At—ampere-turn
at—atmosphere, technical
atm—atmosphere
at wt—atomic weight
au—astronomical units
avdp—avoirdupois
b—barn
B—bel
b—bit
bbl—barrel
bbl/d—barrel per day
Bd—baud
bd. ft.—board foot (obsolete); use fbm
Bé—Baumé
Bev (obsolete); see GeV
Bhn—Brinell hardness number
bhp—brake horsepower
bm—board measure
bp—boiling point
Btu—British thermal unit
bu—bushel
c—¢, ct; cent(s)
c—centi (prefix, one-hundredth)
C—coulomb
°C—degree Celsius
cal—calorie (also: cal_{IT}, International Table; cal_{th}—thermochemical)
cd/in²—candela per square inch
cd/m²—candela per square meter
cg—centigram
cd•h—candela-hour
Ci—curie
cL—centiliter
cm—centimeter
c/m—cycles per minute
cm²—square centimeter
cm³—cubic centimeter
cmil—circular mil
cp—candlepower
cP—centipoise
cSt—centistokes
cwt—hundredweight
D—darcy
d—day
d—deci (prefix, one-tenth)
d—pence
da—deka (prefix, 10)
dag—dekagram
daL—dekaliter
dam—dekameter
dam²—square dekameter
dam³—cubic dekameter
dB—decibel
dBu—decibel unit
dc—direct current
dg—decigram
dL—deciliter
dm—decimeter
dm²—square decimeter
dm³—cubic decimeter
dol—dollar
doz—dozen
dr—dram
dwt—deadweight tons
dwt—pennyweight
dyn—dyne
EHF—extremely high frequency
emf—electromotive force
emu—electromagnetic unit

erg—erg
esu—electrostatic unit
eV—electronvolt
°F—degree Fahrenheit
F—farad
f—femto (prefix, one-quadrillionth)
fbm—board foot; board foot measure
fc—footcandle
fL—footlambert
fm—fentometer
FM—frequency modulation
ft—foot
ft^2—square foot
ft^3—cubic foot
ftH_2O—conventional foot of water
ft•lb—foot-pound
ft•lbf—foot-pound force
ft/min—foot per minute
ft^2/min—square foot per minute
ft^3/min—cubic foot per minute
ft-pdl—foot poundal
ft/s—foot per second
ft^2/s—square foot per second
ft^3/s—cubic foot per second
ft/s^2—foot per second squared
ft/s^3—foot per second cubed
G—gauss
G—giga (prefix, 1 billion)
g—gram; acceleration of gravity
Gal—gal cm/s^2
gal—gallon
gal/min—gallons per minute
gal/s—gallons per second
GB—gigabyte
Gb—gilbert
g/cm^3—gram per cubic centimeter
GeV—gigaelectronvolt
GHz—gigahertz (gigacycle per second)
gr—grain; gross
h—hecto (prefix, 100)
H—henry
h—hour
ha—hectare
HF—high frequency
hg—hectogram
hL—hectoliter
hm—hectometer
hm^2—square hectometer
hm^3—cubic hectometer
hp—horsepower
hph—horsepower-hour
Hz—hertz (cycles per second)
id—inside diameter
ihp—indicated horsepower
in—inch
in^2—square inch
in^3—cubic inch
in/h—inch per hour
inH_2O—conventional inch of water
inHg—conventional inch of mercury
in-lb—inch-pound
in/s—inch per second
J—joule
J/K—joule per kelvin
K—kayser
K—kelvin (use without degree symbol)
k—kilo (prefix, 1,000)
k—thousand (7k=7,000)
kc—kilocycle; see also kHz (kilohertz), kilocycles per second
kcal—kilocalorie
keV—kiloelectronvolt
kG—kilogauss
kg—kilogram
kgf—kilogram-force
kHz—kilohertz (kilocycles per second)
kL—kiloliter
klbf—kilopound-force
km—kilometer
km^2—square kilometer
km^3—cubic kilometer
km/h—kilometer per hour
kn—knot (speed)
kΩ—kilohm
kt—kiloton; carat
kV—kilovolt
kVA—kilovoltampere
kvar—kilovar

kW—kilowatt
kWh—kilowatthour
L—lambert
L—liter
lb—pound
lb ap—apothecary pound
lb—avdp, avoirdupois pound
lbf—pound-force
lbf/ft—pound-force foot
lbf/ft^2—pound-force per square foot
lbf/ft^3—pound-force per cubic foot
lbf/in^2—pound-force per square inch (see psi)
lb/ft—pound per foot
lb/ft^2—pound per square foot
lb/ft^3—pound per cubic foot
lct—long calcined ton
ldt—long dry ton
LF—low frequency
lin ft—linear foot
l/m—lines per minute
lm—lumen
lm/ft^2—lumen per square foot
lm/m^2—lumen per square meter
lm•s—lumen second
lm/W—lumen per watt
l/s—lines per second
L/s—liter per second
lx—lux
M—mega (prefix, 1 million)
M—million (3 M=3 million)
m—meter
m—milli (prefix, one-thousandth)
M1—monetary aggregate
m^2—square meter
m^3—cubic meter
μ—micro (prefix, one-millionth)
μm—micrometer
mA—milliampere
μA—microampere
MB—megabyte
mbar—millibar
μbar—microbar
Mc—megacycle; see also MHz (megahertz), megacycles per second
mc—millicycle; see also mHz (millihertz), millicycles per second
mD—millidarcy
meq—milliquivalent
MeV—megaelectronvolts
mF—millifarad
μF—microfarad
mG—milligauss
mg—milligram
μg—microgram
Mgal/d—million gallons per day
mH—millihenry
μH—microhenry
MHz—megahertz
mHz—millihertz
mi—mile (statute)
mi^2—square mile
mi/gal—mile(s) per gallon
mi/h—mile(s) per hour
mil—mil
min—minute (time)
μin—microinch
mL—milliliter
mm—millimeter
mm^2—square millimeter
mm^3—cubic millimeter
μm^2—square micrometer
μm^3—cubic micrometer
μμ—micromicron (use of compound prefixes obsolete; use pm, picometer)
μμf—micromicrofarad (use of compound prefixes obsolete; use pF)
mmHg—conventional millimeter of mercury
mΩ—megohm
mo—month
mol—mole (unit of substance)

mol wt—molecular weight
mp—melting point
ms—millisecond
μs—microsecond
Mt—megaton
mV—millivolt
μV—microvolt
MW—megawatt
mW—milliwatt
μW—microwatt
MWd/t—megawatt-days per ton
Mx—maxwell
n—nano (prefix, one-billionth)
N—newton
nA—nanoampere
nF—nanofarad
N•m—newton meter
N/m²—newton per square meter
nmi—nautical mile
Np—neper
ns—nanosecond
N•s/m²—newton second per square meter
nt—nit
od—outside diameter
Oe—oersted (use of A/m, amperes per meter, preferred)
oz—ounce (avoirdupois)
p—pico (prefix, one-trillionth)
P—poise
Pa—pascal
pA—picoampere
pct—percent
pdl—poundal
pF—picofarad
pF—water-holding energy
pH—hydrogen-ion concentration
ph—phot; phase
pk—peck
pm—picometer
p/m—parts per million
ps—picosecond
psi—pounds per square inch
pt—pint
pW—picowatt
qt—quart
quad—quadrillion (10^{15})
R—rankine
R—roentgen (measurement of radiation)
°R—degree Rankine
rad—radian
rd—rad (radiation-absorbed dose)
rem—roentgen equivalent man
r/min—revolutions per minute
rms—root mean square
r/s—revolutions per second
s—second (time)
s—shilling
S—siemens
sb—stilb
scp—spherical candlepower
s•ft—second-foot
shp—shaft horsepower
slug—slug
sr—steradian
sSf—standard saybolt fural
sSu—standard saybolt universal
stdft³—standard cubic foot (feet)
Sus—saybolt universal second(s)
T—tera (prefix, 1 trillion)
Tft³—trillion cubic feet
T—tesla
t—tonne (metric ton)
tbsp—tablespoonful
thm—therm
ton—ton
tsp—teaspoonful
Twad—twaddell
u—(unified) atomic mass unit
UHF—ultrahigh frequency
V—volt
VA—voltampere
var—var
VHF—very high frequency
V/m—volt per meter
W—watt
Wb—weber

Wh—watthour
W/(m•K)—watt per meter kelvin
W/sr—watt per steradian
W/(sr•m^2)—watt per steradian square meter
x—unknown quantity (italic)
yd—yard
yd^2—square yard
yd^3—cubic yard
yr—year

Standard Latin abbreviations

9.63. When Latin abbreviations are used, follow this list.

a.—annus, year; ante, before
A.A.C.—anno ante, Christum in the year before Christ
A.A.S.—Academiae Americanae Socius, Fellow of the American Academy [Academy of Arts and Sciences]
A.B.—artium baccalaureus, bachelor of arts
ab init.—ab initio, from the beginning
abs. re.—absente reo, the defendant being absent
A.C.—ante Christum, before Christ
A.D.—anno Domini, in the year of our Lord
a.d.—ante diem, before the day
ad fin.—ad finem, at the end, to one end
ad h.l.—ad hunc locum, to this place, on this passage
ad inf.—ad infinitum, to infinity
ad init.—ad initium, at the beginning
ad int.—ad interim, in the meantime
ad lib.—ad libitum, at pleasure
ad loc.—ad locum, at the place
ad val.—ad valorem, according to
A.I.—anno inventionis, in the year of the discovery
al.—alia, alii, other things, other persons
A.M.—anno mundi, in the year of the world; Annus mirabilis, the wonderful year [1666]
a.m.—ante meridiem, before noon
an.—anno, in the year; ante, before
ann.—annales, annals; anni, years
A.R.S.S.—Antiquariorum Regiae Societatis Socius, Fellow of the Royal Society of Antiquaries
A.U.C.—anno urbis conditae, ab urbe conolita, in [the year from] the building of the City [Rome], 753 B.C.
B.A.—baccalaureus artium, bachelor of arts
B.S. or B. Sc.—baccalaureus scientiae, bachelor of science
C.—centum, a hundred; condemno, I condemn, find guilty
c.—circa, about
cent.—centum, a hundred
cf.—confer, compare
C.M.—chirurgiae magister, master of surgery
coch.—cochlear, a spoon, spoonful
coch. amp.—cochlear amplum, a tablespoonful
coch. mag.—cochlear magnum, a large spoonful
coch. med.—cochlear medium, a dessert spoonful
coch. parv.—cochlear parvum, a teaspoonful
con.—contra, against; conjunx, wife
C.P.S.—custos privati sigilli, keeper of the privy seal
C.S.—custos sigilli, keeper of the seal
cwt.—c. for centum, wt. for weight, hundredweight

D.—Deus, God; Dominus, Lord; d., decretum, a decree; denarius, a penny; da, give
D.D.—divinitatis doctor, doctor of divinity
D.G.—Dei gratia, by the grace of God; Deo gratias, thanks to God
D.N.—Dominus noster, our Lord
D.S. or D. Sc.—doctor scientiae, doctor of science
d.s.p.—decessit sine prole, died without issue
D.V.—Deo volente, God willing
dwt.—d. for denarius, wt. for weight pennyweight
e.g.—exempli gratia, for example
et al.—et alibi, and elsewhere; et alii, or aliae, and others
etc.—et cetera, and others, and so forth
et seq.—et sequentes, and those that follow
et ux.—et uxor, and wife
F.—filius, son
f.—fiat, let it be made; forte, strong
fac.—factum similis, facsimile, an exact copy
fasc.—fasciculus, a bundle
fl.—flores, flowers; floruit, flourished; fluidus, fluid
f.r.—folio recto, right-hand page
F.R.S.—Fraternitatis Regiae Socius, Fellow of the Royal Society
f.v.—folio verso, on the back of the leaf
guttat.—guttatim, by drops
H.—hora, hour
h.a.—hoc anno, in this year; hujus anni, this year's
hab. corp.—habeas corpus, have the body—a writ
h.e.—hic est, this is; hoc est, that is
h.m.—hoc mense, in this month; huius mensis, this month's
h.q.—hoc quaere, look for this
H.R.I.P.—hic requiescat in pace, here rests in peace
H.S.—hic sepultus, here is buried; hic situs, here lies; h.s., hoc sensu, in this sense
H.S.S.—Historiae Societatis Socius, Fellow of the Historical Society
h.t.—hoc tempore, at this time; hoc titulo, in or under this title
I—Idus, the Ides; i., id, that; immortalis, immortal
ib. or ibid.—ibidem, in the same place
id.—idem, the same
i.e.—id est, that is
imp.—imprimatur, sanction, let it be printed
I.N.D.—in nomine Dei, in the name of God
in f.—in fine, at the end
inf.—infra, below
init.—initio, in the beginning
in lim.—in limine, on the threshold, at the outset
in loc.—in loco, in its place
in loc. cit.—in loco citato, in the place cited
in pr.—in principio, in the beginning
in trans.—in transitu, on the way
i.q.—idem quod, the same as
i.q.e.d.—id quod erat demonstrandum, what was to be proved
J.—judex, judge

J.C.D.—juris civilis doctor, doctor of civil law
J.D.—jurum or juris doctor, doctor of laws
J.U.D.—juris utriusque doctor, doctor of both civil and canon law
L.—liber, a book; locus, a place
£—libra, pound; placed before figures thus £10; if l., to be placed after, as 401.

L.A.M.—liberalium artium magister, master of the liberal arts
L.B.—baccalaureus literarum, bachelor of letters
lb.—libra, pound (singular and plural)
L.H.D.—literarum humaniorum doctor, doctor of the more humane letters
Litt. D.—literarum doctor, doctor of letters
LL.B.—legum baccalaureus, bachelor of laws
LL.D.—legum doctor, doctor of laws
LL.M.—legum magister, master of laws
loc. cit.—loco citato, in the place cited
loq.—loquitur, he, or she, speaks
L.S.—locus sigilli, the place of the seal
l.s.c.—loco supra citato, in the place above cited
£ s. d.—librae, solidi, denarii, pounds, shillings, pence
M.—magister, master; manipulus, handful; medicinae, of medicine; m., meridies, noon
M.A.—magister artium, master of arts
M.B.—medicinae baccalaureus, bachelor of medicine
M. Ch.—magister chirurgiae, master of surgery
M.D.—medicinae doctor, doctor of medicine
m.m.—mutatis mutandis, with the necessary changes
m.n.—mutato nomine, the name being changed
MS.—manuscriptum, manuscript; MSS., manuscripta, manuscripts
Mus. B.—musicae baccalaureus, bachelor of music
Mus. D.—musicae doctor, doctor of music
Mus. M.—musicae magister, master of music
N.—Nepos, grandson; nomen, name; nomina, names; noster, our; n., natus, born; nocte, at night
N.B.—nota bene, mark well
ni. pri.—nisi prius, unless before
nob.—nobis, for (or on) our part
nol. pros.—nolle prosequi, will not prosecute
non cul.—non culpabilis, not guilty
n.l.—non licet, it is not permitted; non liquet, it is not clear; non longe, not far
non obs.—non obstante, notwithstanding
non pros.—non prosequitur, he does not prosecute
non seq.—non sequitur, it does not follow logically
O.—octarius, a pint
ob.—obiit, he, or she, died; obiter, incidentally
ob. s.p.—obiit sine prole, died without issue
o.c.—opere citato, in the work cited
op.—opus, work; opera, works
op. cit.—opere citato, in the work cited
P.—papa, pope; pater, father; pontifex, bishop; populus, people; p., partim, in part; per, by, for; pius, holy; pondere, by weight; post, after; primus, first; pro, for
p.a.—or per ann., per annum, yearly; pro anno, for the year
p. ae.—partes aequales, equal parts
pass.—passim, everywhere
percent.—per centum, by the hundred
pil.—pilula, pill
Ph. B.—philosophiae baccalaureus, bachelor of philosophy
P.M.—post mortem, after death
p.m.—post meridiem, afternoon
pro tem.—pro tempore, for the time being
prox.—proximo, in or of the next [month]

P.S.—postscriptum, postscript; P.SS., postscripta, postscripts
q.d.—quasi dicat, as if one should say; quasi dictum, as if said; quasi dixisset, as if he had said
q.e.—quod est, which is
Q.E.D.—quod erat demonstrandum, which was to be demonstrated
Q.E.F.—quod erat faciendum, which was to be done
Q.E.I.—quod erat inveniendum, which was to be found out
q.l.—quantum libet, as much as you please
q. pl.—quantum placet, as much as seems good
q.s.—quantum sufficit, sufficient quantity
q.v.—quantum vis, as much as you will; quem, quam, quod vide, which see; qq. v., quos, quas, or quae vide, which see (plural)
R.—regina, queen; recto, right-hand page; respublica, commonwealth
℞—recipe, take
R.I.P.—requiescat, or requiescant, in pace, may he, she, or they, rest in peace
R.P.D.—rerum politicarum doctor, doctor of political science
R.S.S.—Regiae Societatis Sodalis, Fellow of the Royal Society
S.—sepultus, buried; situs, lies; societas, society; socius or sodalis, fellow; s., semi, half; solidus, shilling
s.a.—sine anno, without date; secundum artem, according to art
S.A.S.—Societatis Antiquariorum Socius, Fellow of the Society of Antiquaries
sc.—scilicet, namely; sculpsit, he, or she, carved or engraved it
S.B. or Sc. B.—scientiae baccalaureus, bachelor of science
S.D. or Sc. D.—scientiae doctor, doctor of science
S.D.—salutem dicit, sends greetings
s.d.—sine die, indefinitely
sec.—secundum, according to
sec. leg.—secundum legem, according to law
sec. nat.—secundum naturam, according to nature, or naturally
sec. reg.—secundum regulam, according to rule
seq.—sequens, sequentes, sequentia, the following
S.H.S.—Societatis Historiae Socius, Fellow of the Historical Society
s.h.v.—sub hac voce or sub hoc verbo, under this word
s.l.a.n.—sine loco, anno, vel nomine, without place, date, or name
s.l.p.—sine legitima prole, without lawful issue
s.m.p.—sine mascula prole, without male issue
s.n.—sine nomine, without name
s.p.—sine prole, without issue
S.P.A.S.—Societatis Philosophiae Americanae Socius, Fellow of the American Philosophical Society
s.p.s.—sine prole superstite, without surviving issue
S.R.S.—Societatis Regiae Socius or Sodalis, Fellow of the Royal Society
ss—scilicet, namely (in law)
S.S.C.—Societas Sanctae Crucis, Society of the Holy Cross
stat.—statim, immediately
S.T.B.—sacrae theologiae baccalaureus, bachelor of sacred theology
S.T.D.—sacrae theologiae doctor, doctor of sacred theology

S.T.P.—sacrae theologiae professor, professor of sacred theology
sub.—subaudi, understand, supply
sup.—supra, above
t. or temp.—tempore, in the time of
tal. qual.—talis qualis, just as they come; average quality
U.J.D.—utriusque juris doctor, doctor of both civil and canon law
ult.—ultimo, last month (may be abbreviated in writing but should be spelled out in printing)
ung.—unguentum, ointment
u.s.—ubi supra, in the place above mentioned
ut dict.—ut dictum, as directed
ut sup.—ut supra, as above
ux.—uxor, wife
v.—versus, against; vide, see; voce, voice, word
v. ——a., vixit ——annos—lived [so many] years
verb. sap.—verbum [satis] sapienti, a word to the wise suffices
v.g.—verbi gratia, for example
viz—videlicet, namely
v.s.—vide supra, see above

Information technology acronyms and initialisms

9.64. Use these forms, if abbreviations are required:

3DES—Triple DES encryption
3DM—Data Driven Decision Making
ABLS—Automated Bid List System
ACES—access certificates for electronic services
ACID—Atomicity, Consistency, Isolation and Durability
ACL—Access Control List
ACP—Access Content Package
AES—advanced Encryption Standard
AI—Artificial Intelligence
AIDC—Automatic identification and capture
AIFF—audio interchange file format
AIO—Asynchronous I/O
AIP—Archival Information Package
AJAX—Asynchronous JavaScript and XML
ALPN—Application-Layer Protocol Negotiation
API—Application Programming Interface
ARK—archival resource key
ARP—address resolution protocol
ASCII—American Standard Code for Information Interchange
ASP—application service provider
ATO—Authority to Operate
AWS—Amazon Web Services
BASE—Basically Available, Soft-State, Eventually Consistent
BDA—Big Data Analytics
BI—Business Intelligence
BLOB —Binary Large OBject
BPEL—business process execution language
BPI—business process information
C&I—Cataloging and Indexing
CA—certificate authority
CAP—Consistency, Availability, Partition tolerance
CBC—Cipher Block Chaining
CD—compact disc
CDM—Copy Data Management
CDN—content delivery network
CDR—critical design review
CD-ROM—compact disc read only memory
CE—content evaluator
CentOS—Community Enterprise Operating System

CERN—(European) Centre for Nuclear Research
CGP—Catalog of U.S. Government Publications
CI—Clustered Index
CIM—Common Interface Model
CISCAT—Center for Internet Security -Configuration Assessment Tool
CISSP—Certified Information Systems Security Professional
CK—Candidate Key
CLOB—Character Large Object
CMS—content management system
CN—Canonical Name
CO—content originator
COG—Continuity of Government
COOP—continuity of operations plan
CP—content processor
CPS—Certificate Practice Statement
CRC—cyclic redundancy checks
CRL—Certificate Revocation List
CRM—Customer Relationship Management
CRUD—Create, Read, Update, and Delete
CSS—Cascading Style Sheets
CSV—comma separated variable
CTE—Common Table Expression
CVS—Concurrent Versioning Services
DaaS—Database as a Service
DBA—Database Administrator
DB—Database
DBMS—database management system
DCL—Data Control Language
DDL—Data Definition Language
DDoS—Distributed Denial of Service
DES—data encryption standard
DHCP—Dynamic Host Control Protocol
DH—Diffie-Hellman (Exchange)
DHE—Diffie-Hellman Ephemeral
DHSL—Distributed Hadoop Storage Layer
DIP—Dissemination Information Package
DMD—Data Management Definition
DMI—desktop management interface
DML—Data Manipulation Language
DMV—Dynamic Management Views
DN—Distinguished Name
DNS—domain name system
DO—digital objects
DOI—Digital Object Identifier
DoS—denial of service
DPI—dots per inch
DR—Disaster Recovery
DSL—digital subscriber line
DSR—deployment system review
DSSL—document style and semantics language
DVD—digital versatile disc
DW—Database Warehouse
E_Port—Expansion port, also known as ISL
EAC—estimate at completion
EAD—encoded archival description
EA—enterprise architecture
EAP—enterprise application platform
EBCDIC—Extended Binary Coded Decimal Interchange Code
ECC—Elliptic Curve Cryptography
ECDHE—Elliptic Curve Diffie-Hellman Key Exchange
EPS—Encapsulated PostScript
ERD—Entity Relationship Diagram
ESXi—Elastic Sky X Integrated
ETL—Extract, Transform, Load
EV—Extended Validation
FBCA—Federal Bridge Certificate Authority
FC-AL—Fibre Channel Arbitrated Loop
FCIA—Fibre Channel Industry Association
FC-IP—Fibre Channel Over IP
FCP—Fibre Channel Protocol
FC-SW—Fibre Channel Switched

FDDI—fiber distributed data interface
FDsys—Federal Digital System
FICC—Federal Identity Credentialing Committee
FIFO—first in first out
FIPNet—Federal Information Preservation Network
FIPS—Federal Information Processing Standard
FISMA—Federal Information Security Management Act of 2002
FK—Foreign Key
FOSI—format output specifi cation instance
FTP—file transfer protocol
GBIC—Gigabit Interface Converter
Gbps—Gigabits per second
GDI—graphical device interface
GGP—gateway-to-gateway protocol
GIF—graphics interchange format
GILS—Government Information Locator Service
GUI—graphical user interface
HBA—Host Bus Adapter
HDFS—Hadoop Distributed File System
HDTV—high definition television
HMAC—key hashed message authentication code
HPC—High-Performance Computing
HSM—hardware security module
HSM—Hierarchical Storage Management
HSTS—HTTP Strict Transport Security
HTML—hypertext markup language
HTTP—hypertext transfer protocol
HTTPS—HyperText Transfer Protocol Secure
Hz—Hertz
Iaas—Infrastructure as a Service
IAM—Identity and Access Management
ICMP—internet control message protocol
IDD—interface design description
IDE—Integrated Development Environment
IDE—Integrated Drive Electronics
IEEE—Institute of Electrical and Electronics Engineers
IETF—Internet Engineering Task Force
iFCP—Internet Fibre Channel Protocol
ILS—Integrated Library System
IOPS—I/O operations per second
IOS—Apple Operating System
IOT—Index Organized Table
IoT—Internet of Things
IP—internet protocol
IPR—internal progress review
IPSEC—internet protocol security
IPS—Intrusion Prevention System
ISAM—Indexed Sequential Access Method
ISL—Inter switch link
ISP—internet service provider
IT—information technology
ITU—International Telecommunications Union
JBOD—Just a bunch of disks
JDBC—Java Database Connectivity
JDF—Job Definition Format
JITS—Just-in-time storage
JPEG—Joint Photographic Experts Group
JS—JavaScript
JSON—JavaScript Object Notation
L_Port—Loop port
LAMP—Linux, Apache, MySQL and PHP
LAN—local area network
LDAP—lightweight directory access protocol
LHC—Large Hadron Collider

LOB—Large Object
LPAR—Logical Partition
LPI—lines per inch
LRU—Last Recently Used (algorithm)
LUN—Logical Unit Number
MAC—message authentication code
MAN—Metropolitan area network
MARC—Machine Readable Cataloging
MDC—Multidimensional Clustering Table
METS—Metadata Encoding and Transmission Standard
MIME—multipurpose internet mail extensions
MIPS—millions of instructions per second
MODS—Metadata Object Descriptive Schema
MOOC—massive online open courses
MP3—MPEG-2 Audio Layer III
MPCF—marginally punched continuous forms
MVC—Model View Controller
MV—Materialized View
NAS—Network Attached Storage
NAT—network address translation
NDIIPP—National Digital Information Infrastructure and Preservation Program
NDLP—National Digital Library Program
NF—Normal Form
NNTP—network news transfer protocol
NOSQL—Not Only Structured Query Language
OAI—Open Archives Initiative
OAI-PMH—Open Archives Initiative Protocol for Metadata Harvesting
OAIS—open archival information system
OCLC—Online Computer Library Center
OCR—optical character recognition
OCSP—Online Certificate Status Protocol
ODBC—Open Database Connectivity
OLAP—Online Analytical Processing
OLTP—online transaction processing
OODBMS—Object-Oriented Database Management System
ORM—Object-Relational Mapping
PAAS—Platform as a service
PDF—Portable Document Format
PGP—Pretty Good Privacy
PHP—PHP Hypertext Preprocessor
PKI—Public Key Cryptography
PK—Primary Key
PL/pgSQL—Procedural Language/ SQL
PL/SQL—Procedural Language/SQL
PNG—portable network graphics
PREMIS—Preservation Metadata: Implementation Strategies
PRONOM—Practical Online Compendium of File Formats
PTR—program tracking report
PURL—persistent uniform resource locator
QoS—Quality of service
QPS—Queries Per Second
RAC—Real Application Clusters (Oracle)
RAID—redundant array of inexpensive disks
RAM—random access memory
RC4—Rivest Cipher 4
RDA—Resource Description and Access
REGEX—Regular Expression
REST—Representational State Transfer
RFC—Request for Comments or Request for Change
RHEL—Red Hat Enterprise Linux
RI—representation information

RMA—reliability, maintainability, availability
RPC—remote procedure call
RPM—RPM Package Manager
RSA—Rivest, Shamir, and Adelman (public key cryptosystem)
RTF—rich text format
RVTM—requirements verification traceability matrix
S4—Simple Scalable Streaming System
SAAS—Software as a Service
SAML—security assertion markup language
SAN—Storage-area network
SASL —Simple Authentication and Security Layer
SASS—Syntactically Awesome Stylesheets
SDD—System Design Diagram
SDD—System Design Document
SDK—Software Development Kit
SDLC—software/system development lifecycle
SDR—system design review
Section 508—Section 508 of the Rehabilitation Act
SFTP—Secure File Transfer Protocol
SGML—standard generalized markup language
SHA—Secure Hash Algorithm
SIP—Submission Information Package
SMTP—simple mail transfer protocol
SNMP—simple network management protocol
SOAP—Simple Object Access Protocol
SOA—Service Oriented Architecture
SQL—Structured Query Language
SQL PL—SQL Procedure Language used for writing stored procedures. Also see PL/SQL
SQL/XML—an extension of the SQL language used for querying XML
SSD—Solid State Drive
SSD—System Security Diagram
SSH—Secure Shell
SSL —Secure Sockets Layer
SSP—system security plan
SSR—software specification review
SUSE—Software und System Entwicklung (Software and Systems Development)
SVN—Subversion
TDES—Triple Data Encryption Standard
TFS—Team Foundation Server
TIFF—tagged image file format
TLS—transport layer security
TPS—Transactions Per Second, a measurement of database performance
UAT—User Acceptance Testing
UDF—User Defined Function
UDP—user datagram protocol
UDT—User Defined Type
UID—Unique Identifier
URL—uniform resource locator
URN—uniform resource name/number
UUID—Universal Unique Identifer
VC—Virtual Center
VDC—Virtual Data Center
VIP—Virtual Internet Protocol
VI—Virtual Interface
VLAN—virtual local area network
VM—Virtual Machine
VMW—Vmware
VPN—virtual private network
VSAN—Virtual Storage Area Network
W3C—World Wide Web Consortium
WAI-ARIA—Worldwide Accessibility Initiative - Accessible Rich Internet Applications
WAIS—wide area information service
WAN—Wide Area Network

WAP—wireless application protocol
WAV—waveform audio format
WCAG—Web Content Accessibility Guidelines
Wi-Fi—wireless fidelity
WIP—work in process
WML—wireless markup language
www—world wide web
WYSIWYG—what you see is what you get
XAML—Extensible Application Markup Language
XDW—Extended Data Warehouse
XMLDsig—xml signature
XMLENC—xml encryption
XML—Extensible Markup Language
XPATH—XML Path Language
XQUERY—XML Query
XSD—XML Schema Definition
XSL—Extensible Stylesheet Language
XSL-FO—XSL Formatting Objects
XSLT—Extensible Stylesheet Language Transformations
YAML—Yet Another Markup Language
YARN —Yet Another Resource Negotiator

10. Signs and Symbols

10.1. The increased use of signs and symbols and their importance in technical and scientific work have emphasized the necessity of standardization on a national basis and of the consistent use of the standard forms.

10.2. Certain symbols are standardized—number symbols (the digits, 0, 1, 2, 3, 4, 5, 6, 7, 8, 9); letter symbols (the letters of the alphabet, a, b, c, d, etc.); and graphic symbols (the mathematical signs +, −, ±, ×, ÷).

10.3. The signs +, −, ±, ×, and ÷, etc., are closed against accompanying figures and symbols. When the × is used to indicate "crossed with" (in plant or animal breeding) or magnification, it will be separated from the accompanying words by a space.

i–vii+1–288 pages
The equation A+B
The result is 4×4
20,000±5,000

Early June × Bright (crossed with)
× 4 (magnification)
miles ÷ gallons

Symbols with figures

10.4. In technical publications the degree mark is used in lieu of the word *degree* following a figure denoting measurement.

10.5. Following a figure, the spelled form is preferred. The percent symbol is used in areas where space will not allow the word *percent* to be used.

In that period the price rose 12, 15, and 19 percent.
not In that period the price rose 12 percent, 15 percent, and 19 percent.

10.6. Any symbol set close up to figures, such as the degree mark, number mark, dollar mark, or cent mark, is used before or after each figure in a group or series.

$5 to $8 price range
5'–7' long, *not* 5–7' long
3¢ to 5¢ (no spaces)
±2 to ±7; 2°±1°
#61 to #64

but
§ 12 (thin space)
¶ 1951 (thin space)
from 15 to 25 percent
45 to 65 °F *not* 45° to 65° F

Letter symbols

10.7. Letter symbols are set in italic (see rule 10.8) or in roman (see rule 9.56) without periods and are capitalized only if so shown in copy, since the capitalized form may have an entirely different meaning.

Equations

10.8. In mathematical equations, use italic for all letter symbols—capitals, lowercase, small capitals, and superiors and inferiors (exponents and subscripts); use roman for figures, including superiors and inferiors.

10.9. If an equation or a mathematical expression needs to be divided, break before +, −, =, etc. However, the equal sign is to clear on the left of other beginning mathematical signs.

10.10. A short equation in text should not be broken at the end of a line. Space out the line so that the equation will begin on the next line; or better, center the equation on a line by itself.

10.11. An equation too long for one line is set flush left, the second half of the equation is set flush right, and the two parts are balanced as nearly as possible.

10.12. Two or more equations in a series are aligned on the equal signs and centered on the longest equation in the group.

10.13. Connecting words of explanation, such as *hence, therefore,* and *similarly,* are set flush left either on the same line with the equation or on a separate line.

10.14. Parentheses, braces, brackets, integral signs, and summation signs should be of the same height as the mathematical expressions they include.

10.15. Inferiors precede superiors if they appear together; but if either inferior or superior is too long, the two are aligned on the left.

Chemical symbols

10.16. The names and symbols listed below are approved by the International Union of Pure and Applied Chemistry. They are set in roman without periods.

Element	Symbol	Atomic No.	Element	Symbol	Atomic No.
Actinium	Ac	89	Mendelevium	Md	101
Aluminum	Al	13	Mercury	Hg	80
Americium	Am	95	Molybdenum	Mo	42
Antimony	Sb	51	Moscovium	Mc	115
Argon	Ar	18	Neodymium	Nd	60
Arsenic	As	33	Neon	Ne	10
Astatine	At	85	Neptunium	Np	93
Barium	Ba	56	Nickel	Ni	28
Berkelium	Bk	97	Nihonium	Nh	113
Beryllium	Be	4	Niobium	Nb	41
Bismuth	Bi	83	Nitrogen	N	7
Bohrium	Bh	107	Nobelium	No	102
Boron	B	5	Oganesson	Og	118
Bromine	Br	35	Osmium	Os	76
Cadmium	Cd	48	Oxygen	O	8
Calcium	Ca	20	Palladium	Pd	46
Californium	Cf	98	Phosphorus	P	15
Carbon	C	6	Platinum	Pt	78
Cerium	Ce	58	Plutonium	Pu	94
Cesium	Cs	55	Polonium	Po	84
Chlorine	Cl	17	Potassium	K	19
Chromium	Cr	24	Praseodymium	Pr	59
Cobalt	Co	27	Promethium	Pm	61
Copernicium	Cn	112	Protactinium	Pa	91
Copper	Cu	29	Radium	Ra	88
Curium	Cm	96	Radon	Rn	86
Darmstadtium	Ds	110	Rhenium	Re	75
Dubnium	Db	105	Rhodium	Rh	45
Dysprosium	Dy	66	Roentgenium	Rg	111
Einsteinium	Es	99	Rubidium	Rb	37
Erbium	Er	68	Ruthenium	Ru	44
Europium	Eu	63	Rutherfordium	Rf	104
Fermium	Fm	100	Samarium	Sm	62
Flerovium	Fl	114	Scandium	Sc	21
Fluorine	F	9	Seaborgium	Sg	106
Francium	Fr	87	Selenium	Se	34
Gadolinium	Gd	64	Silicon	Si	14
Gallium	Ga	31	Silver	Ag	47
Germanium	Ge	32	Sodium	Na	11
Gold	Au	79	Strontium	Sr	38
Hafnium	Hf	72	Sulfur	S	16
Hassium	Hs	108	Tantalum	Ta	73
Helium	He	2	Technetium	Tc	43
Holmium	Ho	67	Tellurium	Te	52
Hydrogen	H	1	Tennessine	Ts	117
Indium	In	49	Terbium	Tb	65
Iodine	I	53	Thallium	Tl	81
Iridium	Ir	77	Thorium	Th	90
Iron	Fe	26	Thulium	Tm	69
Krypton	Kr	36	Tin	Sn	50
Lanthanum	La	57	Titanium	Ti	22
Lawrencium	Lr	103	Tungsten	W	74
Lead	Pb	82	Uranium	U	92
Lithium	Li	3	Vanadium	V	23
Livermorium	Lv	116	Xenon	Xe	54
Lutetium	Lu	71	Ytterbium	Yb	70
Magnesium	Mg	12	Yttrium	Y	39
Manganese	Mn	25	Zinc	Zn	30
Meitnerium	Mt	109	Zirconium	Zr	40

Standardized symbols

10.17. Symbols duly standardized by any national scientific, professional, or technical group are accepted as preferred forms within the field of the group. The issuing office desiring or requiring the use of such standardized symbols should see that copy is prepared accordingly.

Signs and symbols

10.18. The following list contains some signs and symbols frequently used in printing. The forms and style of many symbols vary with the method of reproduction employed. It is important that editors and writers clearly identify signs and symbols when they appear within a manuscript.

ACCENTS

´ acute
˘ breve
¸ cedilla
^ circumflex
¨ dieresis
` grave
¯ macron
~ tilde

ARROWS

→ direction
↖ direction
↱ direction
↶ direction
↷ direction
⬅ bold arrow
⇨ open arrow
⇄ reversible reaction

BULLETS

● solid circle; bullet
• bold center dot
• movable accent

CHEMICAL

‰ salinity
♏ minim
⇅ exchange
↑ gas

CIRCLED SYMBOLS

◷ angle in circle
⦶ circle with parallel rule
Ⓐ triangle in circle
⊙ dot in circle
Ⓐ dot in triangle in circle
⊕ cross in circle
© copyright
① Ceres
② Pallas
③ Juno
④ Vesta

CODE

· No. 1 6 pt. code dot
· No. 2 8 pt. code dot
· No. 3 10 pt. code dot
• No. 4 8 pt. code dot
• No. 4 10 pt. code dot
– No. 1 6 pt. code dash
– No. 2 8 pt. code dash
– No. 3 10 pt. code dash
▬ No. 4 8 pt. code dash
▬ No. 4 10 pt. code dash

COMPASS

° degree
°. degree with period
′ minute
′. minute with period
″ second
″. second with period
″̲ canceled second

DECORATIVE

✚ bold cross
✠ cross patte
■ cross patte
⊠ cross patte
✿ (184 N)
⚿ key
⚘ (206 N)
¶ paragraph

ELECTRICAL

ℛ reluctance
↔ reaction goes both right and left
↕ reaction goes both up and down
⇅ reversible
→ direction of flow; yields
→ direct current
⇆ electrical current
⇆ reversible reaction
⇄ reversible reaction
⇆ alternating current
⇄ alternating current
⇌ reversible reaction beginning at left
⇋ reversible reaction beginning at right
Ω ohm; omega
MΩ megohm; omega
μΩ microohm; mu omega
ω angular frequency, solid angle; omega
Φ magnetic flux; phi
Ψ dielectric flux; electrostatic flux; psi
γ conductivity; gamma

ELECTRICAL—Con.

- ρ resistivity; rho
- Λ equivalent conductivity
- HP horsepower

MATHEMATICAL

- — vinculum (above letters)
- ∺ geometrical proportion
- −: difference, excess
- ‖ parallel
- ‖s parallels
- ∦ not parallels
- | | absolute value
- · multiplied by
- : is to; ratio
- ÷ divided by
- ∴ therefore; hence
- ∵ because
- :: proportion; as
- ≪ is dominated by
- > greater than
- ⊏ greater than
- ≥ greater than or equal to
- ≧ greater than or equal to
- ≷ greater than or less than
- ≯ is not greater than
- < less than
- ⊐ less than
- ≶ less than or greater than
- ≮ is not less than
- ⋖ smaller than
- ≤ less than or equal to
- ≦ less than or equal to
- ≧ or ≥ greater than or equal to
- ⋜ equal to or less than
- ⋜ equal to or less than
- ⋠ is not greater than equal to or less than
- ⋝ equal to or greater than
- ⋡ is not less than equal to or greater than
- ⊥ equilateral
- ⊥ perpendicular to
- ⊢ assertion sign
- ≐ approaches

MATHEMATICAL—Con.

- ≐ approaches a limit
- ⩡ equal angles
- ≠ not equal to
- ≡ identical with
- ≢ not identical with
- 𝍸 score
- ≈ or ≒ nearly equal to
- = equal to
- ∼ difference
- ≃ perspective to
- ≅ congruent to approximately equal
- ≏ difference between
- ≎ geometrically equivalent to
- ⊂ included in
- ⊃ excluded from
- ⊂ is contained in
- ∪ logical sum or union
- ∩ logical product or intersection
- √ radical
- √ root
- ²√ square root
- ∛ cube root
- ∜ fourth root
- ⁵√ fifth root
- ⁶√ sixth root
- π pi
- ε base (2.718) of natural system of logarithms; epsilon
- ε is a member of; dielectric constant; mean error; epsilon
- + plus
- **+** bold plus
- − minus
- **−** bold minus
- / shill(ing); slash; virgule
- ± plus or minus
- ∓ minus or plus
- × multiplied by
- **=** bold equal
- # number
- ℔ per
- % percent
- ∫ integral
- | single bond
- \ single bond
- / single bond

MATHEMATICAL—Con.

- ‖ double bond
- ⑊ double bond
- ⫽ double bond
- ⬡ benzene ring
- ∂ or δ differential; variation
- ∂ Italian differential
- → approaches limit of
- ∼ cycle sine
- ⨚ horizontal integral
- ∮ contour integral
- ∝ variation; varies as
- Π product
- Σ summation of; sum; sigma
- ! or ⌊ factorial product

MEASURE

- ℔ pound
- ʒ dram
- fʒ fluid dram
- ℥ ounce
- f℥ fluid ounce
- O pint

MISCELLANEOUS

- § section
- † dagger
- ‡ double dagger
- ℀ account of
- ℅ care of
- 𝍸 score
- ¶ paragraph
- þ Anglo-Saxon
- ℄ center line
- ☌ conjunction
- ⊥ perpendicular to
- 〃 or " ditto
- ∝ variation
- ℞ recipe
- ⊐ move right
- ⊏ move left
- ○ or ⊙ or ① annual
- ⊙⊙ or ② biennial
- ∈ element of
- ℈ scruple
- ƒ function
- ! exclamation mark
- ⊞ plus in square
- ♃ perennial

MISCELLANEOUS—Con.

ϕ diameter
c̄ mean value of c
∪ mathmodifier
⊂ mathmodifier
⊡ dot in square
◬ dot in triangle
⊠ station mark
@ at

MONEY

¢ cent
¥ yen
£ pound sterling
₥ mills

MUSIC

♮ natural
♭ flat
♯ sharp

PLANETS

☿ Mercury
♀ Venus
⊕ Earth
♂ Mars
♃ Jupiter
♄ Saturn
♅ Uranus
♆ Neptune
☊ dragon's head, ascending node
☋ dragon's tail, descending node
☌ conjunction
☍ opposition
☉ or Sun
Sun's lower limb
Sun's upper limb
⦶ solar corona
⊕ solar halo
◍ Moon
● new Moon
☽ first quarter
◐ first quarter
◖ third quarter
◑ last quarter
☾ last quarter
◑ last quarter
○ full Moon
full Moon
⊖ eclipse of Moon

PLANETS—Con.

lunar halo
lunar corona
⚳ Ceres
⚵ Juno

PUNCTUATION

{ } braces
[ ] brackets
( ) parentheses
⟨ ⟩ square parentheses; angle brackets
¡ inverted exclamation mark
¿ inverted question mark

SEX

♂ or ♂ male
□ male, in charts
♀ female
○ female, in charts
⚥ hermaphrodite

SHAPES

◆ solid diamond
◇ open diamond
○ circle
▲ solid triangle
△ triangle
□ square
■ solid square
▱ parallelogram
▭ rectangle
double rectangle
★ solid star
☆ open star
∟ right angle
∠ angle
√ check
✓ check
ß German ss
ß italic German ss
☛ solid index
☚ solid index
☜ index
☞ index

GEOLOGIC SYSTEMS [1]

Q Quaternary
T Tertiary
K Cretaceous
J Jurassic
TR Triassic
P Permian
P Pennsylvanian
M Mississippian
D Devonian
S Silurian
O Ordovician
Ꞓ Cambrian
pꞒ Precambrian
C Carboniferous

VERTICAL

| 5 unit vertical
| 8 point vertical
| 9 unit vertical

WEATHER

T thunder
thunderstorm; sheet lightning
< sheet lightning
↓ precipitate
◍ rain
← floating ice crystals
↔ ice needles
▲ hail
⊗ sleet
∾ glazed frost
⊔ hoarfrost
V frostwork
✳ snow or sextile
⊠ snow on ground
+ drifting snow (low)
≡ fog
∞ haze
Aurora

ZODIAC

♈ Aries; Ram
♉ Taurus; Bull
♊ Gemini; Twins
♋ Cancer; Crab
♌ Leo; Lion
♍ Virgo; Virgin
♎ Libra; Balance
♏ Scorpio; Scorpion
♐ Sagittarius; Archer
♑ Capricornus; Goat
♒ Aquarius; Water bearer
♓ Pisces; Fishes

[1] Standard letter symbols used by the Geological Survey on geologic maps. Capital letter indicates the system and one or more lowercased letters designate the formation and member where used.

11. Italic

(See also Chapter 9 "Abbreviations and Letter Symbols" and Chapter 16 "Datelines, Addresses, and Signatures")

11.1. Italic is sometimes used to differentiate or to give greater prominence to words, phrases, etc. However, an excessive amount of italic defeats this purpose and should be restricted.

Emphasis, foreign words, and titles of publications

11.2. Italic is not used for mere emphasis, foreign words, or the titles of publications.

11.3. In nonlegal work, *ante, post, infra,* and *supra* are italicized only when part of a legal citation. Otherwise these terms, as well as the abbreviations *id., ibid., op. cit., et seq.,* and other foreign words, phrases, and their abbreviations, are printed in roman.

11.4. When [emphasis in original], [emphasis supplied], [emphasis added], or [emphasis ours] appears in copy, it should not be changed; but "underscore supplied" should be changed to "italic supplied." Therefore, when emphasis in quoted or extracted text is referred to by the foregoing terms, such emphasized text must be reflected and set in italic.

11.5. When copy is submitted with instructions to set "all roman (no italic)," these instructions will not apply to *Ordered, Resolved, Be it enacted,* etc.; titles following signatures or addresses; or the parts of datelines that are always set in italic.

Names of aircraft, vessels, and spacecraft

11.6. The names of aircraft, vessels, and manned spacecraft are italicized unless otherwise indicated. In lists set in columns and in stubs and reading columns of tables consisting entirely of such names, they will be set in roman. Missiles and rockets will be set in caps and lowercase and will not be italicized.

SS *America*; the liner *America*	*Apollo 13*, *Atlantis* (U.S. spaceships)
USS *Los Angeles* (submarine)	*West Virginia* class or type
USS *Wisconsin*	the *Missouri*'s (roman "s") turret
ex-USS *Savannah*	the *U-7*'s (roman "s") deck
USCGS (U.S. Coast and Geodetic Survey) ship *Pathfinder*	*Enola Gay*
	but
CSS *Virginia*	Air Force One (President's plane)
CG cutter *Thetus*	B-50 (type of plane)
the *U-7*	DD-882
destroyer *31*	LST-1155
HMS *Hornet*	MiG; MiG-35
HS (hydrofoil ship) *Denison*	PT-109
MS (motorship) *Richard*	F-22 Raptor
GTS (gas turbine ship) *Alexander*	F-117 Nighthawk (Stealth fighter)
NS (nuclear ship) *Savannah*	A-10 Thunderbolt
MV (motor vessel) *Havtroll*	

11.7. Names of vessels are quoted in matter printed in other than capitals and lowercase roman, even if there is italic type available in the series.

Sinking of the "Lusitania"	SINKING OF THE "LUSITANIA"
Sinking of the "Lusitania"	SINKING OF THE "LUSITANIA"

Names of legal cases

11.8. The names of legal cases are italicized, except for the *v.*, which is always set in lowercase. When requested, the names of such cases may be set in roman with an italic *v.* In matter set in italic, legal cases are set in roman with the *v.* being set roman.

"The Hornet" and "The Hood," 124 F.2d 45	SMITH v. BROWN ET AL. (heading)
Smith v. *Brown et al.*	SMITH v. BROWN ET AL. (heading)
Smith Bros. case (172 App. Div. 149)	*Durham* rule
Smith Bros. case, *supra*	*Brown* decision
Smith Bros. case	*John Doe* v. *Richard Roe*
As cited in *Smith Bros.*	*but* John Doe against Richard Roe, the *Cement* case.

Scientific names

11.9. The scientific names of genera, subgenera, species, and subspecies (varieties) are italicized but are set in roman in italic matter; the names of groups of higher rank than genera (phyla, classes, orders, families, tribes, etc.) are printed in roman.

A.s. perpallidus
Dorothia? sp. (roman "?")
Tsuga canadensis
Cypripedium parviflorum var. *pubescens*
the genera *Quercus* and *Liriodendron*
the family Leguminosae; the family Nessiteras rhombopteryx
Measurements of specimens of Cyanoderma erythroptera neocara

11.10. Quotation marks should be used in place of italic for scientific names appearing in lines set in caps, caps and small caps, or boldface, even if there is italic type available in the series.

Words and letters

11.11. The words *Resolved, Resolved further, Provided, Provided, however, Provided further, And provided further,* and *ordered,* in bills, acts, resolutions, and formal contracts and agreements are italicized; also the words *To be continued, Continued on p. —, Continued from p. —,* and *See* and *see also* (in indexes and tables of contents only).

Resolved, That (resolution)
Resolved by the Senate and House of Representatives of the United States of America in Congress assembled, That
[*To be continued*] (centered; no period)
[*Continued from p. 3*] (centered; no period)
see also Mechanical data (index entry)

11.12. All letters (caps, small caps, lowercase, superiors, and inferiors) used as symbols are italicized. In italic matter, roman letters are used. Chemical symbols (even in italic matter) and certain other standardized symbols are set in roman.

*n*th degree; *x* dollars

$$D \div 0.025V_m^{2.7} = 0.042/G - 1V_m^{2.7}$$

$$5Cu_2S \cdot 2(Cu,Fe,Zn)S \cdot 2Sb_2S_3O_4$$

11.13. Letter designations in mathematical and scientific matter, except chemical symbols, are italicized.

11.14. Letter symbols used in legends to illustrations, drawings, etc., or in text as references to such material, are set in italic without periods and are capitalized if so shown in copy.

11.15. Letters (*a*), (*b*), (*c*), etc., and *a*, *b*, *c*, etc., used to indicate sections or paragraphs, are italicized in general work but not in laws or other legal documents.

11.16. Internet websites and email addresses should be set in roman.

12. Numerals

(See also Chapter 13 "Tabular Work" and Chapter 14 "Leaderwork")

12.1. Most rules for the use of numerals are based on the general principle that the reader comprehends numerals more readily than numerical word expressions, particularly in technical, scientific, or statistical matter. However, for special reasons, numbers are spelled out in certain instances, except in FIC & punc. and Fol. Lit. matter.

12.2. The following rules cover the most common conditions that require a choice between the use of numerals and words. Some of them, however, are based on typographic appearance rather than on the general principle stated above.

12.3. Arabic numerals are preferable to Roman numerals.

Numbers expressed in figures

12.4. A figure is used for a single number of *10* or more with the exception of the first word of the sentence. (See also rules 12.9 and 12.23.)

50 ballots	24 horses	nearly 13 buckets
10 guns	about 40 men	10 times as large

Numbers and numbers in series

12.5. When 2 or more numbers appear in a sentence and 1 of them is *10* or larger, figures are used for each number. (See supporting rule 12.6.)

Each of 15 major commodities (9 metal and 6 nonmetal) was in supply.
but Each of nine major commodities (five metal and four nonmetal) was in supply.
Petroleum came from 16 fields, of which 8 were discovered in 1956.
but Petroleum came from nine fields, of which eight were discovered in 1956.
That man has 3 suits, 2 pairs of shoes, and 12 pairs of socks.
but That man has three suits, two pairs of shoes, and four hats.
Of the 13 engine producers, 6 were farm equipment manufacturers, 6 were principally engaged in the production of other types of machinery, and 1 was not classified in the machinery industry.
but Only nine of these were among the large manufacturing companies, and only three were among the largest concerns.
There were three 6-room houses, five 4-room houses, and three 2-room cottages, and they were built by 20 carpenters. (See rule 12.21.)

There were three six-room houses, five four-room houses, and three two-room cottages, and they were built by nine carpenters.

but If two columns of sums of money add or subtract one into the other and one carries points and ciphers, the other should also carry points and ciphers.

At the hearing, only one Senator and one Congressman testified.

There are four or five things that can be done.

12.6. A unit of measurement, time, or money (as defined in rule 12.9), which is always expressed in figures, does not affect the use of figures for other numerical expressions within a sentence.

Each of the five girls earned 75 cents an hour.

Each of the 15 girls earned 75 cents an hour.

A team of four men ran the 1-mile relay in 3 minutes 20 seconds.

This usually requires from two to five washes and a total time of 2 to 4 hours.

This usually requires 9 to 12 washes and a total time of 2 to 4 hours.

The contractor, one engineer, and one surveyor inspected the 1-mile road.

but There were two six-room houses, three four-room houses, and four two-room cottages, and they were built by nine workers in thirty 5-day weeks. (See rule 12.21.)

12.7. Figures are used for serial numbers.

Bulletin 725	290 U.S. 325
Document 71	Genesis 39:20
pages 352–357	202–512–0724 (telephone number)
lines 5 and 6	the year 2001
paragraph 1	1721–1727 St. Clair Avenue
chapter 2	*but* Letters Patent No. 2,189,463

12.8. A colon preceding figures does not affect their use.

The result was as follows: 12 voted yea, 4 dissented.

The result was as follows: nine voted yea, seven dissented.

Measurement and time

12.9. Units of measurement and time, actual or implied, are expressed in figures.

a. Age:

6 years old	a 3-year-old
52 years 10 months 6 days	at the age of 3 (years implied)

b. Clock time (see also Time):

4:30 p.m.; half past 4
10 o'clock *or* 10 p.m. (*not* 10 o'clock p.m.; 2 p.m. in the afternoon; 10:00 p.m.)
12 p.m. (12 noon)
12 a.m. (12 midnight)
4^h30^m *or* 4.5^h, in scientific work, if so written in copy
0025, 2359 (astronomical and military time)
08:31:04 (stopwatch reading)

c. Dates:

9/11 (referring to the attack on the United States that occurred on September 11, 2001)
June 1985 (*not* June, 1985); June 29, 1985 (*not* June 29th, 1985)
March 6 to April 15, 1990 (*not* March 6, 1990, to April 15, 1990)
May, June, and July 1965 (*but* June and July 1965)
15 April 1951; 15–17 April 1951 (military)
4th of July (*but* Fourth of July, meaning the holiday)
the 1st [day] of the month (*but* the last of April or the first [part] of May, not referring to specific days)
in the year 2000 (*not* 2,000)

In referring to a fiscal year, consecutive years, or a continuous period of 2 years or more, when contracted, the forms 1900–11, 1906–38, 1931–32, 1801–2, 1875–79 are used (*but* upon change of century, 1895–1914 and to avoid multiple ciphers together, 2000–2001). For two or more separate years not representing a continuous period, a comma is used instead of a dash (1875, 1879); if the word *from* precedes the year or the word *inclusive* follows it, the second year is not shortened and the word *to* is used in lieu of the dash (from 1933 to 1936; 1935 to 1936, inclusive).

In dates, *A.D.* precedes the year (A.D. 937); *B.C.* follows the year (254 B.C.); C.E. and B.C.E. follow the year.

d. Decimals: In text a cipher should be supplied before a decimal point if there is no whole unit, and ciphers should be omitted after a decimal point unless they indicate exact measurement.

0.25 inch; 1.25 inches
silver 0.900 fine
specific gravity 0.9547
gauge height 10.0 feet

but .30 caliber (meaning 0.30 inch, bore of small arms); 30 calibers (length)

e. Use spaces to separate groups of three digits in a decimal fraction. (See rule 12.27.)

0.123 456 789; *but* 0.1234

f. Degrees, etc. (spaces omitted):

longitude 77°04'06" E
35°30'; 35°30' N
a polariscopic test of 85°
an angle of 57°
strike N 16° E
dip 47° W *or* 47° N 31° W
25.5' (preferred) *also* 25'.5

but
two degrees of justice; 12 degrees of freedom
32d degree Mason
150 million degrees Fahrenheit
30 Fahrenheit degrees

g. Game scores:

1 up (golf)
3 to 2 (baseball)
7 to 6 (football), etc.
2 all (tie)

h. Market quotations:

4½ percent bonds
Treasury bonds sell at 95
Metropolitan Railroad, 109
Dow Jones average of 18500.76
gold is 109
wheat at 2.30
sugar, .03; *not* 0.03

i. Mathematical expressions:

multiplied by 3
divided by 6
a factor of 2
square root of 4

j. Measurements:

7 meters
about 10 yards
8 by 12 or 8 x 12 inches
8- by 12-inch page
2 feet by 1 foot 8 inches by 1 foot 3 inches
2 by 4 or 2 x 4 (lumber) (*not* 2×4)
1½ miles
6 acres
9 bushels
1 gallon
3 ems
20/20 (vision)
30/30 (rifle)
12-gauge shotgun
2,500 horsepower
15 cubic yards
6-pounder
80 foot-pounds
10s (for yarns and threads)
f/2.5 (lens aperture)
4 by 4 or 4 x 4 truck

but	six bales
tenpenny nail	two dozen
fourfold	one gross
three-ply	zero miles
five votes	seven-story building

k. Money:

\$3.65; \$0.75; 75 cents; 0.5 cent	*but*
\$3 (*not* \$3.00) per 200 pounds	two pennies
75 cents apiece	three quarters
Rs32,25,644 (Indian rupees)	one half
CHF 2.5 (Swiss francs)	six bits, etc.
9 euros or 9€	
65 yen	
₱265	

l. Percentage:

12 percent; 25.5 percent; 0.5 percent (*or* one-half of 1 percent)	50–50 (colloquial expression)
thirty-four one hundredths of 1 percent	5 percentage points
3.65 bonds; 3.65s; 5–20 bonds; 5–20s; 4½s; 3s	a 1,100-percent increase, *or* an 1100-percent increase

m. Proportion:

1 to 4	1:62,500
1–3–5	

n. Time (see also Clock time):

6 hours 8 minutes 20 seconds	*but*
10 years 3 months 29 days	four centuries
7 minutes	three decades
8 days	three quarters (9 months)
4 weeks	statistics of any one year
1 month	in a year or two
3 fiscal years; third fiscal year	four afternoons
1 calendar year	one-half hour
millennium	the eleventh hour
FY 2010	FY10

o. Unit modifiers:

5-day week
8-year-old wine
8-hour day
10-foot pole
½-inch pipe
5-foot-wide entrance
10-million-peso loan

a 5-percent increase
20th-century progress

but
two-story house
five-member board
$20 million airfield

p. Vitamins:

B_{12}, B_T, A_1, etc.

Ordinal numbers

12.10. Except as indicated in rules 12.11 and 12.19, and also for day preceding month, figures are used in text and footnotes to text for serial ordinal numbers beginning with *10th.* In tables, leaderwork, footnotes to tables and leaderwork, and in sidenotes, figures are used at all times. Military units are expressed in figures at all times when not the beginning of a sentence, except *Corps.* (For ordinals in addresses, see rule 12.13.)

29th of May, *but* May 29
First Congress; 102d Congress
ninth century; 21st century
Second Congressional District; 20th Congressional District
seventh region; 17th region
323d Fighter Wing
12th Regiment
9th Naval District
7th Fleet
7th Air Force
7th Task Force

eighth parallel; 38th parallel
fifth ward; 12th ward
ninth birthday; 66th birthday
first grade; 11th grade
1st Army
1st Cavalry Division

but
XII Corps (Army usage)
Court of Appeals for the Tenth Circuit
Seventeenth Decennial Census (title)

12.11. When ordinals appear in juxtaposition and one of them is *10th* or more, figures are used for such ordinal numbers.

This legislation was passed in the 1st session of the 102d Congress.
He served in the 9th and 10th Congresses.

From the 1st to the 92d Congress.
Their children were in 1st, 2d, 3d, and 10th grades.
We read the 8th and 12th chapters.
but The district comprised the first and second precincts.
He represented the first, third, and fourth regions.
The report was the sixth in a series of 14.

12.12. Ordinals and numerals appearing in a sentence are treated according to the separate rules dealing with ordinals and numerals standing alone or in a group. (See rules 12.4, 12.5, and 12.24.)

The fourth group contained three items.
The fourth group contained 12 items.
The 8th and 10th groups contained three and four items, respectively.
The eighth and ninth groups contained 9 and 12 items, respectively.

12.13. Beginning with *10th*, figures are used in text matter for numbered streets, avenues, etc. However, figures are used at all times and *street, avenue,* etc. are abbreviated in sidenotes, tables, leaderwork, and footnotes to tables and leaderwork.

First Street NW.; *also* in parentheses: (Fifth Street) (13th Street); 810 West 12th Street; North First Street; 1021 121st Street; 2031 18th Street North; 711 Fifth Avenue; 518 10th Avenue; 51–35 61st Avenue

Punctuation

12.14. The comma is used in a number containing four or more digits, except in serial numbers, common and decimal fractions, astronomical and military time, and kilocycles and meters of not more than four figures pertaining to radio.

Chemical formulas

12.15. In chemical formulas full-sized figures are used before the symbol or group of symbols to which they relate, and inferior figures are used after the symbol.

$$6PbS \bullet (Ag,Cu)_2S \bullet 2As_2S_3O_4$$

Numbers spelled out

12.16. Spell out numbers at the beginning of a sentence or head. Rephrase a sentence or head to avoid beginning with figures. (See rule 12.25 for related numbers.)

Five years ago . . .; *not* 5 years ago . . .
Five hundred fifty men hired . . .; *not* 550 men hired . . .
"Five-Year Plan Announced"; *not* "5-Year Plan Announced" (head)
The year 2065 seems far off. . .; *not* 2065 seems far off. . .
Workers numbering 207,843 . . .; *not* 207,843 workers . . .
Benefits of $69,603,566 . . .; *not* $69,603,566 worth of benefits . . .

1958 REPORT *change to* THE 1958 REPORT
$3,000 BUDGETED *change to* THE SUM OF $3,000 BUDGETED
4 MILLION JOBLESS *change to* JOBLESS NUMBER 4 MILLION

12.17. In verbatim testimony, hearings, transcripts, and question-and-answer matter, figures are used immediately following Q. and A. or name of interrogator or witness for years (e.g., 2015), sums of money, decimals, street numbers, and for numerical expressions beginning with *101*.

Mr. BIRCH, Junior. 2015 was a good year.
Mr. BELL. $1 per share was the return. Two dollars in 1956 was the alltime high. Two thousand twenty-nine may be another story.
Colonel DAVIS. 92 cents.
Mr. SMITH. 12.8 people.
Mr. JONES. 1240 Pennsylvania Avenue NW, Washington, DC 20004.
Mr. SMITH. Ninety-eight persons.
Q. 101 years? *But* Q. One hundred years?
A. 200 years.
Mr. SMITH. Ten-year average would be how much?

12.18. A spelled-out number should not be repeated in figures, except in legal documents. In such instances use these forms:

five (5) dollars, *not* five dollars (5)
ten dollars ($10), *not* ten ($10) dollars

12.19. Numbers appearing as part of proper names, used in a hypothetical or inexact sense, or mentioned in connection with serious and dignified subjects such as Executive orders, legal proclamations, and in formal writing are spelled out.

Three Rivers, PA, Fifteenmile Creek, etc.
the Thirteen Original States
in the year two thousand eight
the One Hundred Tenth Congress
millions for defense but not one cent for tribute
three score years and ten
Ten Commandments
Air Force One (Presidential plane)
back to square one
behind the eight ball
our policy since day one

12.20. If spelled out, whole numbers should be set in the following form:

two thousand twenty
one thousand eight hundred fifty
one hundred fifty-two thousand three hundred five
eighteen hundred fifty (serial number)

When spelled out, any number containing a fraction or piece of a whole should use the word "and" when stating the fraction or piece:

sixty-two dollars and four cents
ninety-nine and three-tenths degrees
thirty-three and seventy-five one-hundredths shares

12.21. Numbers below *100* preceding a compound modifier containing a figure are spelled out.

two ¾-inch boards
twelve 6-inch guns
two 5-percent discounts
but
120 8-inch boards
three four-room houses

12.22. Indefinite expressions are spelled out.

the seventies; the early seventies; *but* the early 1870s *or* 1970s
in his eighties, *not* his '80's *nor* 80's
between two and three hundred horses (*better* between 200 and 300 horses)
twelvefold; thirteenfold; fortyfold; hundredfold; twentyfold to thirtyfold
midthirties (age, years, money)
a thousand and one reasons
but
1 to 3 million
mid-1971; mid-1970s
40-odd people; nine-odd people
40-plus people
100-odd people
3½-fold; 250-fold; 2.5-fold; 41-fold

Words such as *nearly, about, around, approximately,* etc., do not reflect indefinite expressions.

The bass weighed about 6 pounds.
She was nearly 8 years old.

12.23. Except as indicated in rules 12.5 and 12.9, a number less than *10* is spelled out within a sentence.

six horses	*but*
five wells	3½ cans
eight times as large	2½ times or 2.5 times

12.24. For typographic appearance and easy grasp of large numbers beginning with *million,* the word *million, billion,* or *trillion* is used.

The following are guides to treatment of figures as submitted in copy. If copy reads—

$12,000,000, *change to* $12 million
2,750,000,000 dollars, *change to* $2,750 million
2.7 million dollars, *change to* $2.7 million
2⅜ million dollars, *change to* $2⅜ million
two and one-half million dollars, *change to* $2½ million
a hundred cows, *change to* 100 cows
a thousand dollars, *change to* $1,000
a million and a half, *change to* 1½ million
two thousand million dollars, *change to* $2,000 million
less than a million dollars, *change to* less than $1 million
but $2,700,000, *do not convert* to $2.7 million
also $10 to $20 million; 10 or 20 million; between 10 and 20 million
4 million of assets
amounting to 4 trillion
$1,270,000
$1,270,200,000
$2¾ billion; $2.75 billion; $2,750 million
$500,000 to $1 million

300,000; *not* 300 thousand
$½ billion to $1¼ billion (note full figure with second fraction); $1¼ to $1½ billion
three-quarters of a billion dollars
5 or 10 billion dollars' worth

12.25. Related numbers appearing at the beginning of a sentence, separated by no more than three words, are treated alike.

Fifty or sixty more miles away is snowclad Mount Everest.
Sixty and, quite often, seventy listeners responded.
but Fifty or, in some instances, almost 60 applications were filed.

Fractions

12.26. Mixed fractions are always expressed in figures. Fractions standing alone, however, or if followed by *of a* or *of an*, are generally spelled out. (See also rule 12.28.)

three-fourths of an inch; *not* ¾ inch *nor* ¾ of an inch
one-half inch
one-half of a farm; *not* ½ of a farm
one-fourth inch
seven-tenths of 1 percent
three-quarters of an inch
half an inch
a quarter of an inch
one-tenth portion
one-hundredth
two one-hundredths
one-thousandth
five one-thousandths
thirty-five one-thousandths
but
½ to 1¾ pages
½-inch pipe
½-inch-diameter pipe
3½ cans
2½ times

12.27. Fractions (¼, ½, ¾, ⅜, ⅝, ⅞, 1⁄2954) or full-sized figures with the shilling mark (1/4, 1/2954) may be used only when either is specifically requested. Mixed fractions in full-sized figures are joined with a hyphen (2-2/3). A comma should not be used in any part of a built-up fraction of four or more digits or in decimals. (See rule 12.9e.)

12.28. Fractions are used in a unit modifier.

½-inch pipe; *not* one-half-inch pipe
¼-mile run
⅞-point rise

Roman numerals

12.29. A repeated letter repeats its value; a letter placed after one of greater value adds to it; a letter placed before one of greater value subtracts from it; a dashline over a letter denotes multiplied by 1,000.

Numerals

I	1	XXV	25	LXX	70	D	500
II	2	XXIX	29	LXXV	75	DC	600
III	3	XXX	30	LXXIX	79	DCC	700
IV	4	XXXV	35	LXXX	80	DCCC	800
V	5	XXXIX	39	LXXXV	85	CM	900
VI	6	XL	40	LXXXIX	89	M	1,000
VII	7	XLV	45	XC	90	MD	1,500
VIII	8	XLIX	49	XCV	95	MM	2,000
IX	9	L	50	IC	99	MMM	3,000
X	10	LV	55	C	100	MMMM	
XV	15	LIX	59	CL	150	or $M\overline{V}$	4,000
XIX	19	LX	60	CC	200	$\overline{V}$	5,000
XX	20	LXV	65	CCC	300	$\overline{M}$	1,000,000
		LXIX	69	CD	400		

Dates

MDC	1600	MCMXX	1920	MCMLXX	1970
MDCC	1700	MCMXXX	1930	MCMLXXX	1980
MDCCC	1800	MCMXL	1940	MCMXC	1990
MCM or MDCCCC	1900	MCML	1950	MM	2000
MCMX	1910	MCMLX	1960	MMX	2010

13. Tabular Work

(See also Chapter 9 "Abbreviations and Letter Symbols" and Chapter 14 "Leaderwork")

13.1. The object of a table is to present in a concise and orderly manner information that cannot be presented as clearly in any other way.

13.2. Tabular material should be kept as simple as possible, so that the meaning of the data can be easily grasped by the user.

13.3. Tables shall be set without down (vertical) rules when there is at least an em space between columns, except where: (1) in GPO's judgment down rules are required for clarity; or (2) the agency has indicated on the copy they are to be used. The mere presence of down rules in copy or enclosed sample is not considered a request that down rules be used. The publication dictates the type size used in setting tables. Tabular work in the Congressional Record is set 6 on 7. The balance of congressional tabular work sets 7 on 8. If down rules are used they will be set as hairlines, unless a specific weight is requested.

Abbreviations

13.4. To avoid burdening tabular text, commonly known abbreviations are used in tables. Metric and unit-of-measurement abbreviations are used with figures.

13.5. The names of months (except May, June, and July) when followed by the day are abbreviated.

13.6. The words *street, avenue, place, road, square, boulevard, terrace, drive, court,* and *building,* following name or number, are abbreviated. For numbered streets, avenues, etc., figures are used.

13.7. Abbreviate the words *United States* if preceding the word *Government,* the name of any Government organization, or as an adjective generally.

13.8. Use the abbreviations *RR* and *Ry.* following a name, and *SS, MS,* etc., preceding a name.

13.9. Use *lat.* and *long.* with figures.

13.10. Abbreviate, when followed by figures, the various parts of publications, as *article, part, section,* etc.

13.11. Use, generally, such abbreviations and contractions as *98th Cong., 1st sess., H. Res. 5, H.J. Res. 21, S. Doc. 62, S. Rept. 410, Rev. Stat.,* etc.

13.12. In columns containing names of persons, copy is followed as to abbreviations of given names.

13.13. Periods are not used after abbreviations followed by leaders.

Bearoff or inset

13.14. An en space is used for all bearoffs or insets.

13.15. In a crowded table, when down rules are necessary, the bearoff or inset may be reduced in figure columns.

13.16. Fractions are set flush right to the bearoff or inset of the allotted column width, and not aligned.

13.17. Mathematical signs, parentheses, fractions, and brackets are set with a normal bearoff or inset.

Boxheads

13.18. Periods are omitted after all boxheads, but a dash is used after any boxhead which reads into the matter following.

13.19. Boxheads run crosswise.

13.20. Boxheads are set solid, even in leaded tables.

13.21. Boxheads are centered horizontally and vertically.

Down-rule style (see rule 13.3)

Sex and age	Employed students whose work records were obtained						
	Total		Time of year at beginning work [depth of this box does not influence the depth of box on left]				
			June to August		September to May		Not reported
	Number	Distribution (percent)	Number	Distribution (percent)	Number	Distribution (percent)	
Female (16 to 18)	3,869	45.5	1,415	9.6	2,405	15.8	49

No-down-rule style (preferred)

TABLE 9.—*Mine production of gold, silver, copper, lead, and zinc in 2008*

Class of material	Short tons	Gold (fine ounces)	Silver (fine ounces)	Copper (pounds)	Lead (pounds)	Zinc (pounds)
	Concentrate shipped to smelters and recoverable metals					
Copper	220,346	763	70,357	14,242,346	9,950	6,260
Lead	3,931	392	48,326	72,500	5,044,750	290,980
Zinc	25,159	269	41,078	263,400	581,590	26,441,270
Total:						
2008	249,436	1,424	159,756	14,578,246	5,636,290	26,738,510
2007	367,430	1,789	432,122	10,622,155	13,544,875	11,923,060
	Crude material shipped to smelters					
Dry gold, dry gold-silver ore	134	52	2,839	2,200	....	....
Copper:						
Crude ore	107,270	844	39,861	2,442,882	124,100	2,200
Slag	421	10	165	285,421	....	....
Lead	528	12	1,693	5,950	110,870	300
Mill cleanings (lead-zinc)	31	....	254	1,450	8,100	4,300
Total:						
2008	125,749	919	45,444	30,375,754	249,710	6,890
2007	166,184	1,042	47,176	41,601,845	497,125	26,940

13.22. In referring to quantity of things, the word *Number* in boxheads is spelled if possible.

13.23. Column numbers or letters in parentheses may be set under boxheads and are separated by one line space below the deepest head. (If alignment of parentheses is required within the table, use brackets in boxhead.) These column references align across the table. Units of quantity are set in parentheses within boxheads.

States	Department of Agriculture				Department of Commerce		
	Commodity Credit Corporation, value of commodities donated	Special school milk program[1]	Value of commodities distributed within States	Disaster loans, etc. (payments to assist States in furnishing hay in droughtstriken areas)	Civil Aeronautics Administration—Federal airport program—regular grants	Bureau of Public Roads: Highway construction — Regular grants[2]	Bureau of Public Roads: Highway construction — Emergency grants[3]
	(1)	(2)	(3)	(4)	(5)	(6)	(7)
Alabama	$4,730,154	$1,520,362	$7,970,875	....	$79,284	$1,176,401	$247,515
Alaska	393,484	269,274	591,487	....	297,266	12,366,106	472,749
Arizona	4,545,983	823,136	6,512,639	....	127,749	9,317,853	....

13.24. Leaders may be supplied in a column consisting entirely of symbols or years or dates or any combination of these.

Centerheads, flush entries, and subentries

13.25. Heads follow the style of the tables as to the use of figures and abbreviations.

13.26. Punctuation is omitted after centerheads. Flush entries and subentries over subordinate items are followed by a colon (single subentry to run in, preserving the colon), but a dash is used instead of a colon when the entry reads into the matter below.

25	Miscellaneous: Powerplant equipment	$245,040.37
26	Roads, railroads, and bridges	275,900.34
	Total	520,940.71
	TRANSMISSION PLANT	
42	Structures and improvements	26,253.53
43	Station equipment	966,164.41
	Total	992,417.94
	GENERAL PLANT	
	General plant:	
	Norris	753,248.97
	Other	15,335.81
	Total	768,584.78
	Grand total	2,281,943.43

13.27. In reading columns if the centerhead clears the reading matter below by at least an em, the space is omitted; if it clears by less than an em, a space is used. If an overrun, rule, etc., in another column, or in the same column, creates a blank space above the head, the extra space is not added.

13.28. Units of quantity and years used as heads in reading and figure columns are set in italic with space above but no space below.

No-down-rule style (preferred)

The rules are used here to aid readability.

2015								
Oct. 1	35.6	15	Jan. 16	45.2	15	May 8	46.5	15
Oct. 31	45.0	15	Feb. 4	50.2	15	May 22	45.1	18
Nov. 14	40.9	18	Feb. 17	43.4	15	June 9	47.1	14
Dec. 24	41.7	15	Mar. 4	45.6	15	June 24	48.2	16
			Mar. 19	42.7	15	July 9	46.6	17
2016			Apr. 2	40.9	15	July 24	45.9	16
Jan. 3	43.9	15	Apr. 28	47.7	13	Aug. 6	46.5	16

Down-rule style (see rule 13.3)

2015								
Oct. 1	35.6	15	Jan. 16	45.2	15	May 8	46.5	15
Oct. 31	45.0	15	Feb. 4	50.2	15	May 22	45.1	18
Nov. 14	40.9	18	Feb. 17	43.4	15	June 9	47.1	14
Dec. 24	41.7	15	Mar. 4	45.6	15	June 24	48.2	16
			Mar. 19	42.7	15	July 9	46.6	17
2016			Apr. 2	40.9	15	July 24	45.9	16
Jan. 3	43.9	15	Apr. 28	47.7	13	Aug. 6	46.5	16

Ciphers

13.29. Where the first number in a column or under a cross rule is wholly a decimal, a cipher is added at the left of its decimal point. A cipher used alone in a money or other decimal column is placed in the unit row and is not followed by a period. The cipher repeats in mixed units before decimals unless the group totals.

January	+26.4	0	0	0	0	0	[1]+$0.7	27.1+	+40.4
February	+66.7	0	0	0	0	0	–.9	65.8+	+98.1
March	+143.1	+2.6	–7.5	0	0	0	+12.4	150.6	+224.1

13.30. In columns containing both dollars and cents, ciphers will be supplied on right of decimal point in the absence of figures.

13.31. Where column consists of single decimal, supply a cipher on the right unless the decimal is a cipher.

0.6
0
3.0
4.2
5.0

13.32. Where column has mixed decimals of two or more places, do not supply ciphers but follow copy.

0.22453
1.263
4
2.60
3.4567
78
12.6
———
102.14423

13.33. Copy is followed in the use of the word *None* or a cipher to indicate *None* in figure columns. If neither one appears in the copy, leaders are inserted, unless a clear (no leaders) is specifically requested.

13.34. In columns of figures under the heading £ *s d,* if a whole number of pounds is given, one cipher is supplied under *s* and one under *d;* if only shillings are given, one cipher is supplied under *d.*

13.35. In columns of figures under *Ft In,* if only feet are given, supply cipher under *In;* if only inches are given, clear under *Ft;* if ciphers are used for *None,* place one cipher under both *Ft* and *In.*

13.36. In any column containing sums of money, the period and ciphers are omitted if the column consists entirely of whole dollars.

Continued heads

13.37. In continued lines an em dash is used between the head and the word (*Continued*) (in italic). No period is carried after a continued line.

13.38. Continued heads over tables will be worded exactly like the table heading. Notes above tables are repeated; footnote references are repeated in boxheads and in continued lines.

Dashes or rules

13.39. Rules are not carried in reading columns or columns consisting of serial or tracing numbers, but are carried through all figure columns.

13.40. Parallel rules are used to cut off figures from other figures below that are added or subtracted; also, generally, above a grand total.

Ditto (do.)

13.41. The abbreviation *do.* is used to indicate that the previous line is being repeated instead of repeating the line, verbatim, over and over. It is used in reading columns only, lowercased and preceded by leaders (6 periods) when there is matter in preceding column. If ditto marks are requested, closing quotes will be used.

13.42. Capitalize *Do.* in the first and last columns. These are indented 1 or 2 ems, depending on the length of the word being repeated, or the width of the column; the situation will determine as it is encountered.

13.43. In mixed columns made up of figure and reading-matter items, *do.* is used only under the latter items.

13.44. *Do.* is not used—

(1) In a figure or symbol column (tracing columns are figure columns);

(2) In the first line under a centerhead in the column in which the centerhead occurs;

(3) Under a line of leaders or a rule;

(4) Under an item italicized or set in boldface type for a specific reason (italic or boldface *do.* is never used; item is repeated);

(5) Under an abbreviated unit of quantity or other abbreviations; or

(6) Under words of three letters or less.

13.45. *Do.* is used, however, under a clear space and under the word *None* in a reading column.

13.46. *Do.* does not apply to a reference mark on the preceding item. The reference mark, if needed, is added to *do.*

13.47. Leaders are not used before *Do.* in the first column or before or after *Do.* in the last column.

13.48. In a first and/or last column 6 ems or less in width, a 1-em space is used before *Do.* In all other columns 6 ems or less in width, six periods are used. Bearoff is not included.

13.49. In a first and/or last column more than 6 ems in width, 2 ems of space are used before *Do.* In all other columns more than 6 ems in width, six periods are used. Bearoff space is not included. If the preceding line is indented, the indention of *Do.* is increased accordingly.

13.50. *Do.* under an indented item in an inside reading column, with or without matter in preceding column, is preceded by six periods which are indented to align with item above.

Dollar mark

13.51. The dollar mark or any other money symbol is placed close to the figure; it is used only at the head of the table and under cross rules when the same unit of value applies to the entire column.

13.52. In columns containing mixed amounts (as money, tons, gallons, etc.), the dollar mark, pound mark, peso mark, or other symbol, as required, is repeated before each sum of money.

13.53. If several sums of money are grouped together, they are separated from the nonmoney group by a parallel rule, and the symbol is placed on the first figure of the separated group only.

	1958	1967
Water supply available (gallons)	4,000,000	3,000,000
Wheat production (bushels)	9,000,000	8,000,000
Operations:		
Water-dispatching operations	$442,496	$396,800
Malaria control	571,040	426,600
Plant protection	134,971	58,320
Total	1,148,507	881,720
Number of plants	642	525
Percent of budget	96.8	78.8

NOTE.—Preliminary figures.
Source: U.S. Department of Commerce, Bureau of the Census.

13.54. In a double money column, dollar marks are used in the first group of figures only; en dashes are aligned.

$7–$9
10–12
314–316
1,014–1,016

13.55. The dollar mark is omitted from a first item consisting of a cipher.

0	*but* $0.12
$300	13.43
500	15.07
700	23.18

13.56. The dollar mark should be repeated in stub or reading columns.

0 to $0.99 ....
$1 to $24 ....
$25 to $49 ....
$50 to $74 ....

Figure columns

13.57. Figures align on the right, with an en space bearoff. There is no bearoff on leaders.

13.58. In a crowded table the bearoff may be reduced in figure columns only. It is preferable to retain the bearoff.

13.59. Figures in parentheses align.

13.60. In double rows of figures in a single column, connected by a dash, a plus, or minus sign, and in dates appearing in the form 9–4–08, the dashes or signs can be aligned.

13.61. Plus or minus signs at the left of figures are placed against the figures regardless of alignment; plus and minus signs at the right of figures are cleared.

13.62. Words and Roman numerals in figure columns are aligned on the right with the figures, without periods.

Median value of livestock	$224	$62	....
Median value of machinery	$54	Small	....
Median value of furniture	$211	$100	....
Possessing automobiles (percent)	25	17	....
Median age (years)	....	....	5.5
Median value	....	....	$144
Fraternal membership:			
Men	....	IV	486
Women	....	....	None

13.63. Figures (including decimal and common fractions) expressing mixed units of quantity (feet, dollars, etc.) and figures in parentheses are aligned on the right.

13.64. Decimal points are aligned except in columns containing numbers that refer to mixed units (such as pounds, dollars, and percentage) and have irregular decimals.

Footnotes and references

13.65. Footnotes to tables are numbered independently from footnotes to text unless requested by committee or department.

13.66. Superior figures are used for footnote references, beginning with 1 in each table.

13.67. If figures might lead to ambiguity (for example, in connection with a chemical formula), asterisks, daggers, or italic superior letters, etc., may be used.

13.68. When items carry several reference marks, the superior-figure reference precedes an asterisk, dagger, or similar character used for reference. These, in the same sequence, precede mathematical signs. A thin space is used to bear off an asterisk, dagger, or similar character.

13.69. Footnote references are repeated in boxheads or in continued lines over tables.

13.70. References to footnotes are numbered consecutively across the page from left to right.

13.71. Footnote references are placed at the right in reading columns and symbol columns, and at the left in figure columns (also at the left of such words as *None* in figure columns), and are separated by a thin space.

13.72. Two or more footnote references occurring together are separated by spaces, not commas.

13.73. In a figure column, a footnote reference standing alone is set in parentheses and flushed right. In a reading column, it is set at the left in parentheses and is followed by leaders, but in the last column it is followed by a period, as if it were a word. In a symbol column it is set at the left and cleared.

13.74. Numbered footnotes are placed immediately beneath the table. If a sign or letter reference in the heading of a table is to be followed, it is not changed to become the first numbered reference mark. The footnote to it precedes all other footnotes. The remaining footnotes in a table will follow this sequence: footnotes (numbers, letters, or symbols); NOTE.—; then Source:.

13.75. For better makeup or appearance, footnotes may be placed at the end of a lengthy table. A line reading "Footnotes at end of table." is supplied.

13.76. If the footnotes to both table and text fall together at the bottom of a page, the footnotes to the table are placed above the footnotes to the text, and the two groups are separated by a 50-point rule flush left; but if there are footnotes to the text and none to the table, the 50-point rule is retained.

13.77. Footnotes to cut-in and indented tables and tables in rules are set full measure, except when footnotes are short, they can be set in 1 em under indented table.

13.78. Footnotes are set as paragraphs, but two or more short footnotes should be combined into one line, separated by not less than 2 ems.

13.79. The footnotes and notes to tables are set solid.

13.80. Footnotes and notes to tables and boxheads are set the same size, but not smaller than 6 point, unless specified otherwise.

13.81. Footnotes to tables follow tabular style in the use of abbreviations, figures, etc.

13.82. In footnotes, numbers are expressed in figures, even at the beginning of a note or sentence.

13.83. If a footnote consists entirely or partly of a table or leaderwork, it should always be preceded by introductory matter carrying the reference number; if necessary, the copy preparer should add an introductory line, such as "[1] See the following table:".

13.84. An explanatory paragraph without specific reference but belonging to the table rather than to the text follows the footnotes, if any, and is separated from them or from the table by space.

Fractions

13.85. All fractions are set flush right to the bearoff.

Total length	40¾	41	0.42	43	44	0.455	46	47	48	½ in.
Sleeve length	10⅝	10	10	10	11	11	11	11	11	1 in.
Armhole length	8⅝	8½	9	9½	9½	10	10½	10½	11	1 in.
Sleeve cuff length (if cuff is used).	5½	5½	5½	5 7/12	5½	5 7/12	5½	5½	5½	Maximum.
Neck opening	26½	26	27 17/32	28 15/32	28	29 17/32	30	30	31	2 in.
Waist:										
7, 8, 9, 10 cut	23½	24	25½	27 15/32	28	29½	31	32	33½	6 pct.
11, 12, 14 cut	22½	23½	25	26½	27½	29	30½	31½	33	6 pct.

13.86. Fractions standing alone are expressed in figures, even at the beginning of a line, but should be spelled out at the beginning of a footnote.

Headnotes

13.87. Headnotes should be set lowercase, but not smaller than 6 point, bracketed, and period omitted at end, even if the statement is a complete sentence; but periods should not be omitted internally if required by sentence structure.

13.88. Headnotes are repeated under continued heads but the word *Continued* is not added to the headnote.

Indentions and overruns

Subentries

13.89. The indention of subentries is determined by the width of the stub or reading column. Subentries in columns more than 15 ems wide are indented in 2-em units; in columns 15 ems or less, with short entry lines and few overruns, 2-em indentions are also used. All overruns are indented 1 em more.

13.90. Subentries in columns of 15 ems or less are indented in 1-em units. Overruns are indented 1 additional em space.

Total, mean, and average lines

13.91. All total (also mean and average) lines are indented 3 ems. In very narrow stub columns, total lines may be reduced to 1- or 2-em indentions, depending on length of line.

13.92. Where overrun of item above conflicts, the total line is indented 1 em more. Runovers of total lines are also indented 1 additional em space.

13.93. It is not necessary to maintain uniform indention of the word *Total* throughout the same table. The word *Total* is supplied when not in copy.

Wide stub column—subentries 2 ems	Total, all banks	National banks	Non-national banks	Building associations
ASSETS				
Loans and discounts:				
Loans to banks	$74,518	$1,267,493	$947,289	$135,619
Commercial and industrial loans	2,753,456	450,916	211,597	18,949
Total (total lines generally indent 3 ems)	2,827,974	718,409	1,158,886	154,568
Real estate loans:				
Secured by farmland	12,532	29,854	186,228	19,044
Secured by residential property other than rural and farm	1,011,856	167,765	1,554,084	3,172,837
Total (indent 1 em more to avoid conflict with line above)	1,024,388	194,619	1,740,312	3,191,881
Securities:				
U.S. Government obligations:				
Direct obligations:				
U.S. savings bonds	1,149,764	3,285,721	2,361,796	23,506
Nonmarketable bonds (including investment series A-1965)	242,500	490,677	732,689	167,735
Total (indent 1 em more than runover above)	1,392,264	3,776,398	3,094,485	191,241

Italic

13.94. Names of vessels and aircraft (except in columns consisting entirely of such names), titles of legal cases (except *v.* for *versus*), and certain scientific terms are set in italic. The word "Total" and headings in the column do not affect the application of this rule. In gothic typefaces without italic, quotes are allowed.

13.95. Set "See" and "See also" in roman.

Leaders

13.96. Leaders run across the entire table except that they are omitted from a last reading column.

13.97. The style of leadering is guided by two rules: (1) tables with a single reading column leader from the bottom line, or (2) tables with any combination of more than one reading or symbol column leader from the top line.

13.98. If leadering from the top line, overruns end with a period.

13.99. A column of dates is regarded as a reading column only if leaders are added; in all other cases it is treated as a figure column.

13.100. In tables with tracing figures on left and right of page, leader from top line.

Numerals in tables

13.101. Figures, ordinals, and fractions are used in all parts of a table, except fractions that will be spelled out at the beginning of a footnote.

Parallel and divide tables

13.102. Parallel tables are set in pairs of pages; beginning on a left-hand page and running across to facing right-hand page, leader from the top line.

13.103. Heads and headnotes center across the pair of pages, with 2-em hanging indention for three or more lines when combined measure exceeds 30 picas in width. Two-line heads are set across the pair of pages. A single-line head or headnote is divided evenly, each part set flush right and left, respectively. Words are not divided between pages.

13.104. Boxheads and horizontal rules align across both pages.

13.105. Boxheads are not divided but are repeated, with *Continued* added.

13.106. Tracing figures are carried through from the outside columns of both pages and are set to "leader from the top line."

13.107. In divide tables that are made up parallel, with stub column repeated, the head and headnote repeat on each succeeding page, with *Continued* added to the head only.

13.108. Tables with tracing figures or stub, or both, repeating on the left of odd pages, are divide tables and not parallel tables. Over such tables the heads are repeated, with *Continued* added.

Reading columns

13.109. Figures or combinations of figures and letters used to form a reading column align on left and are followed by leaders. *Do.* is not used under such items.

13.110. The en dash is not to be used for *to* in a reading column; if both occur, change to *to* throughout.

13.111. Cut-in items following a colon are indented 2 ems.

13.112. A single entry under a colon line should be run in; retain the colon.

13.113. Numerical terms, including numbered streets, avenues, etc., are expressed in figures, even at the beginning of an item.

Symbol columns

13.114. A column consisting entirely of letters, letters and figures, symbols, or signs, or any combination of these, is called a symbol column. It should be set flush left and cleared, except when it takes the place of the stub, it should then be leadered. No closing period is used when such column is the last column. Blank lines in a last column are cleared. *Do.* is not used in a symbol column.

Symbol	Typical commercial designation	Army product symbol	Filing order symbol	General description	Specification symbol
GM(2)	Gasoline and diesel engine oil, SAE10 and SAE10W grades.	OR10	A	Fuel, grease, chassis, or soap base.	G.&D.
CG	Ball and roller bearing grease.	41-X-59	N	Extreme pressure	BR
CW[1]	Wheel-bearing grease............	OE20[2]	X	......do	WBG[3]
	Grease not typified	....	....	Further tests being conducted.	
G090	Universal gear lubricant	S.&T.	B	Water-pump grease ...	80D

13.115. Columns composed of both symbols and figures are treated as figure columns and are set flush right. In case of blank lines in a last column, leaders will be used as in figure columns.

Symbol or catalog number	Typical commercial designation	Symbol or product number	Symbol or filling order symbol	General description	Symbol or specification number
WBD	Chassis grease, cup grease, under pressure.	961	A	Especially adapted to very cold climates.	1359
14L88	Water-pump bearing grease	SWA	352	Under moderate pressure...	....
5190	Exposed gear chain lubricant	12L	N	High-speed use.....................	AE10
	E.P. hypoid lubricant	863	X	For experimental use only..	NXL
376	Special grade for marine use	....	468	Free flowing in any weather	749

Tables without rules

13.116. It is preferable to set all tables alike; that is, without either down rules or cross rules and with roman boxheads. When so indicated on copy, by ordering agency, tabular matter may be set without rules, with italic boxheads.

13.117. Column heads over figure columns in 6- or 8-point leaderwork are set in 6-point italic.

13.118. Horizontal rules (spanner) used between a spread or upper level column heading carried over two or more lower level column headings are set continuous and without break, from left to right, between the two levels of such headings.

TABLE 9.—*Changes in fixed assets and related allowances*

	Fixed assets					
	Balance June 30, 2008 (table 9–a)	*Investment*		*Operations*		*Balance June 30, 2008*
		Current additions	*Adjustments*	*Transfers*	*Retirements*	
Supporting and general facilities:						
Transportation and utilities:						
Panama Railroad	$12,123,197	$306	....	($539)	($284,358)	$11,838,606
Motor Transportation Division	2,242,999	122,597	....	2,143	(147,561)	2,220,178
Steamship line	13,653,989	10,247	....	....	....	13,664,236
Power system	19,364,373	366,311	....	(342)	(290,174)	19,440,168
Communication system	2,739,012	151,819	($113,261)	....	(26,100)	2,751,470
Water system and hydroelectric facilities	10,590,820	104,039	....	1,661	(48,920)	10,647,600
Total, transportation and utilities	60,714,390	755,319	(113,261)	2,923	(797,113)	60,562,258
Employee service and facilities:						
Commissary Division	7,012,701	105,952	(130,891)	21,777	(36,418)	6,973,121
Service centers	3,684,670	29,086	....	530	(230,276)	3,484,010
Housing Division	35,729,465	(10,336)	....	(485,548)	(937,916)	34,295,665
Total employee service and facilities	46,426,836	124,702	(130,891)	(463,241)	(1,204,610)	44,752,796
Grand total	107,141,236	880,021	(244,152)	(466,164)	(2,001,723)	105,315,054

13.119. More than one figure column, also illustrating use of dollar mark, rule, bearoff, etc.

For property purchased from—			
Central Pipeline Distributing Co.:			
Capital stock issued recorded amount		$75,000	
Undetermined consideration recorded		341	
Pan American Bonded Pipeline Co.: Recorded money outlay		3,476	
M.J. Mitchell: Recorded money outlay		730	
R. Lacy, Inc., and Lynch Refining Co.:			
Recorded money outlay	$157,000		
Note issued	100,000		
Subtotal	257,000		
Less value of oil in lines and salvaged construction material	26,555	230,445	$309,992
For construction, improvements, and replacements, recorded money outlay			522
For construction work in progress, recorded money outlay			933,605
Total			1,244,119

	Quantity (million cubic feet)	*Value at point of consumption*
Use:		
Residential	34,842	$21,218,778
Commercial	14,404	5,257,468
Industrial:		
Field (drilling, pumping, etc.)	144,052	10,419,000
All other industrial:		
Fuel for petroleum refineries	96,702	....
Other, including electric utility plants	346,704	61,440,000
Total	636,704	98,335,246

	Estimated		
	2004	*2008*	*Change*
General account:			
Receipts	$64,800	$69,800	+$5,000
Expenditures	(70,300)	(67,100)	(-3,200)
Net improvement, 2008 over 2004			1,800
Deduct 2004 deficit			1,500
Net surplus, estimated for 2008			300

[In U.S.-dollar equivalent]

Balance with the Treasury Department July 1, 2008		$165,367,704.85
Receipts:		
Collections	$564,944,502.99	
Return from agency accounts of currencies advanced for liquidation of obligations incurred prior to July 1, 2007	4,450,577.07	
Total receipts		569,395,080.06
Total available		734,762,784.91

Units of quantity

13.120. Units of quantity in stub columns are set in lowercase in plural form and placed in parentheses.

Coke (short tons)	4,468,437	[1] 25,526,646	5,080,403	[2] 29,519,871
Diatomite	([123])	([1])	([1])	([123])
Emery (pounds)	765	6,828	1,046	9,349
Feldspar (crude) (long tons)	([1])	([1])	([1])	([1])
Ferroalloys (short tons)	183,465	[2] 18,388,766	259,303	[2] 30,719,756

13.121. Units of quantity and other words as headings over figure columns are used at the beginning of a table or at the head of a continued page or continued column in a double-up table.

13.122. Over figure columns, units of quantity and other words used as headings, and the abbreviations *a.m.* and *p.m.*, if not included in the boxheads, are set in italic and are placed immediately above the figures, without periods other than abbreviating periods. In congressional work (gothic), or at any time when italic is not available, these units should be placed in the boxheads in parentheses. Any well-known abbreviation will be used to save an overrun, but if one unit of quantity is abbreviated, all in the same table will be abbreviated. If units change in a column, the new units are set in italic with space above and no space below. The space is placed both above and below only when there is no italic available.

Quoted tabular work

13.123. When a table is part of quoted matter, quotation marks will open on each centerhead and each footnote paragraph, and, if table is end of quoted matter, quotation marks close at end of footnotes. If there are no footnotes and the table is the end of the quotation, quotation marks close at end of last item.

14. Leaderwork

(See also Chapter 9 "Abbreviations and Letter Symbols" and Chapter 13 "Tabular Work")

14.1. Leaderwork is a simple form of tabular work without boxheads or rules and is separated from text by 4 points of space above and below in solid matter or 6 points of space in leaded matter. It consists of a reading (stub) column and a figure column, leadered from the bottom line. It may also consist of two reading columns, aligning on the top line. In general, leaderwork (except indexes and tables of contents, which are set the same style as text) is governed by the same rules of style as tabular work. Unless otherwise indicated, leaderwork is set in 8 point. The period is omitted immediately before leaders.

Bearoff or inset

14.2. No bearoff or inset is required at the right in a single reading column.

Columns

14.3. A figure column is at least an en quad wider than the largest group of figures but not less than 3 ems in single columns or 2 ems in double-up columns. Total rules are to be the full width of all figure columns.

	Pounds
Year: 2000	655,939
Fiscal year:	
2009	368,233
2010	100,000
Total	1,124,172

14.4. Where both columns are reading columns, they are separated by an em space.

Particulars	*Artist*
To the French Government:	
The entire collection of French paintings on loan, with the exception of Mlle. DuBourg (Mme. Fantin-Latour).	Degas.
Avant la Course	Do.
To Col. Axel H. Oxholm, Washington, DC:	
Martha Washington, George Washington, and Thomas Jefferson.	Attributed to Jonathan E. Earl, Los Angeles, CA.
Roses	Renoir.
Do	Forain.
Roses in a Chinese Vase and Sculpture by Maillol	Vuillard.
Maternity	Gauguin.

Continued heads

14.5. The use of continued heads in leaderwork is not necessary.

Ditto (do.)

14.6. The abbreviation *do.* is indented and capitalized in the stub. It is capitalized and cleared (no leaders) in the last reading column (see above).

Dollar mark and ciphers

14.7. In a column containing mixed amounts (as money, tons, gallons, etc.) the figures are aligned on the right, and the dollar mark or other symbol is repeated before each sum of money. If several sums of money are grouped and added or subtracted to make a total, they are separated from the nonmoney group by a parallel rule, and the symbol is placed on the first figure of the separated group only.

14.8. If two columns of sums of money add or subtract one into the other and one carries points and ciphers, the other should also carry points and ciphers.

Flush items and subheads

14.9. Flush items clear the figure column.

14.10. Subheads are centered in full measure.

Footnotes

14.11. Footnotes to leaderwork follow the style of footnotes to tables.

14.12. Footnote references begin with 1 in each leadered grouping, and footnotes are placed at the end, separated from it by 4 points of space. Separate notes from matter following by not less than 6 points of space.

14.13. If the leaderwork runs over from one page to another, the footnotes will be placed at the bottom of the leadered material.[1]

Units of quantity

14.14. Units of quantity or other words over a stub or figure column are set italic.

14.15. The following example shows the style to be observed where there is a short colon line at left. In case of only one subentry, run in with colon line and preserve the colon.

	Tons
Baltimore & Ohio RR:	
Freight carried:	
May..........	50,000
June..........	52,000
Coal carried	90,000
Dixie RR: Freight carried Jan. 1, 1999, including freight carried by all its subsidiaries..........	[1]2,000

[1]Livestock not included.

14.16. If there is no colon line, the style is as follows:

	Tons
Freight carried by the Dixie RR and the Baltimore & Ohio RR in May..........	71,500

14.17. Explanatory matter is set in 6 point under leaders (note omission of period):

....	....	....
(Name)	(Address)	(Position)

[1] If footnotes to leaderwork and text fall at bottom of page, leaderwork footnotes are placed above text footnotes. The two groups are separated by a 50-point rule.

14.18. In blank forms, leaders used in place of complete words to be supplied are preceded and followed by a space.

On this .... day of .... 20 ....

14.19. In half measure doubled up, units of quantity are aligned across the page.

	Inches		*Inches*
Seedlings:			
Black locust	27	Osage-orange	20
Honey locust	16	Catalpa	16
Green ash	7	Black walnut	10

14.20. Mixed units of quantity and amounts and words in a figure column are set as follows:

Capital invested	$8,000
Value of implements and stock	$3,000
Land under cultivation (acres)	128.6
Orchard (acres)	21.4
Forest land (square miles)	50
Livestock:	
Horses:	
Number	8
Value	$1,500
Cows:	
Number	18
Estimated weekly production of butter per milk cow (pounds)	7½
Hogs:	
Number	46
Loss from cholera	None

15. Footnotes, Indexes, Contents, and Outlines

Footnotes and reference marks

15.1. Text footnotes follow the style of the text with the exception of those things noted in Chapter 9 "Abbreviations and Letter Symbols." Footnotes appearing in tabular material follow the guidelines set forth in Chapter 13 "Tabular Work."

15.2. In a publication divided into chapters, sections, or articles, each beginning a new page, text footnotes begin with 1 in each such division. In a publication without such divisional grouping, footnotes are numbered consecutively from 1 to 99, and then begin with 1 again. However, in supplemental sections, such as appendixes and bibliographies, which are not parts of the publication proper, footnotes begin with 1.

15.3. Copy preparers must see that references and footnotes are plainly marked.

15.4. If a reference is repeated on another page, it should carry the original footnote; but to avoid repetition of a long note, the copy preparer may use the words "See footnote 3 (6, 10, etc.) on p.—." instead of repeating the entire footnote.

15.5. Unless the copy is otherwise marked: (1) footnotes to 12-point text are set in 8 point; (2) footnotes to 11-point text are set in 8 point, except in Supreme Court reports, in which they are set in 9 point; (3) footnotes to 10- and 8-point text are set in 7 point.

15.6. Footnotes are set as paragraphs at the bottom of the page and are separated from the text by a 50-point rule, set flush left, with no less than 2 points of space above and below the rule.

15.7. Footnotes to indented matter (other than excerpt footnotes) are set full measure.

15.8. To achieve faithful reproduction of indented excerpt material (particularly legal work) containing original footnotes, these footnotes are also indented and placed at the bottom of the excerpt, separated by 6 points of space. No side dash is used. Reference numbers are not changed to fit the numbering sequence of text footnotes.

15.9. Footnotes must always begin on the page where they are referenced. If the entire footnote will not fit on the page where it is cited, it will be continued at the bottom of the next page.[1]

15.10. Footnotes to charts, graphs, and other illustrations should be placed immediately beneath such illustrative material.

15.11. A cutoff rule is not required between a chart or graph and its footnotes.

15.12. For reference marks use: (1) roman superior figures, (2) italic superior letters, and (3) symbols. Superior figures (preferred), letters, and symbols are separated from the words to which they apply by thin spaces, unless immediately preceded by periods or commas.

15.13. Where reference figures might lead to ambiguity (for example, in matter containing exponents), asterisks, daggers, etc., or italic superior letters may be used.

15.14. When symbols or signs are used for footnote reference marks, their sequence should be (*) asterisk, (†) dagger, (‡) double dagger, and (§) section mark. Should more symbols be needed, these may be doubled or tripled, but for simplicity and greater readability, it is preferable to extend the assortment by adding other single-character symbols.

15.15. Symbols with established meanings, such as the percent sign (%) and the number mark (#), are likely to cause confusion and should not be used for reference marks.

15.16. To avoid possible confusion with numerals and letters frequently occurring in charts and graphs, it is preferable in such instances to use symbols as reference marks.

---

[1]When a footnote breaks from an odd (right-hand) page to an even (left-hand) page, the word (*Continued*) is set inside parentheses in italic below the last line of the footnote where the break occurs.

A 50-point rule is used above each part of the footnote.

When a footnote break occurs on facing pages, i.e., from an even page to an odd page, the (*Continued*) line is not set, but the 50-point rule is duplicated.

15.17. When items carry several reference marks, the superior-figure reference precedes an asterisk, dagger, or similar character used for reference.

15.18. A superior reference mark follows all punctuation marks except a dash, but it falls inside a closing parenthesis or bracket if applying only to matter within the parentheses or brackets.

15.19. Two or more superior footnote references occurring together are separated by thin spaces.

Indexes and tables of contents

15.20. Indexes and tables of contents are set in the same style as the text, except that *See* and *see also* are set in italic.

15.21. Where a word occurs in an index page column, either alone or with a figure, it is set flush on the right. If the word extends back into the leaders, it is preceded by an en space.

Page
Explanatory diagram.......... Frontispiece
General instructions.......... VIII
Capitalization (*see also* Abbreviations).......... 16
Correct imposition (diagram).......... Facing 34
Legends. (*See* Miscellaneous rules.)
Appendixes A, B, C, and D, maps, illustrations,
    and excerpts.......... In supplemental volume

15.22. For better appearance, Roman numerals should be set in small caps in the figure columns of tables of contents and indexes.

15.23. In indexes set with leaders, if the page numbers will not fit in the leader line, the first number only is set in that line and the other numbers are overrun. If the entry makes three or more lines and the last line of figures is not full, do not use a period at the end.

If page folios overrun due to an excessive amount of figures
    use this form 220,
224, 227, 230, 240

And this way when overrun folios make two or more lines 220,
224–225, 230–240, 245, 246, 250–255, 258, 300, 320, 330, 350,
360, 370, 380, 390, 400, 410–500, 510, 520, 530, 540, 550, 560,
570, 580, 590, 600–620, 630, 640, 650

(For examples of item indentions in a reading column of indexes, see the index in this MANUAL.)

15.24. Overrun page numbers are indented 3½ ems in measures not over 20 picas and 7 ems in wider measures, more than one line being used if necessary. These indentions are increased as necessary to not less than 2 ems more than the line immediately above or below.

15.25. When copy specifies that all overs are to be a certain number of ems, the runovers of the figure column shall be held in 2 ems more than the specified indention.

15.26. Examples of block-type indexes:

Example 1

Medical officer, radiological defense, 3
Medicolegal dosage, 44
Military Liaison Committee, 4
Monitoring, 58
  Air, 62
  Personnel, 59
    Civilian, 60
    Military, 59
  Sea, 61
  Ship, 61
Monitors, radiological defense, 3

Example 2

Brazil—Continued
  Exchange restrictions—Continued
    Williams mission (*see also* Williams, John H., special mission), exchange control situation, 586–588
  Trade agreement with United States, proposed:
    Draft text, 558–567
    Proposals for:
      Inclusion of all clauses, 531

15.27. In index entries the following forms are used:

Brown, A.H., Jr. (*not* Brown, Jr., A.H.)
Brown, A.H., & Sons (*not* Brown & Sons, A.H.)
Brown, A.H., Co. (*not* Brown Co., A.H.)
Brown, A.H., & Sons Co. (*not* Brown & Sons Co., A.H.)

15.28. In a table of contents, where *chapter, plate,* or *figure* is followed by a number and period, an en space is used after the period. The periods are aligned on the right.

Chapter		Page
I.	Introduction	I
II.	Summary	1
VI.	Conclusions	7

15.29. Subheads in indexes and tables of contents are centered in the full measure.

15.30. In contents using two sizes of lightface type, or a combination of boldface and lightface type, all leaders and page numbers will be set in lightface roman type. Contents set entirely in boldface will use boldface page numbers. All page numbers will be set in the predominant size.

	Page
PART I. MAINTENANCE OF PEACE AND SECURITY	5
Disarmament	6
Peaceful Uses of Atomic Energy	7

	Page
Part I. Maintenance of Peace and Security	5
Disarmament	6
Peaceful Uses of Atomic Energy	7

	Page
Part I. Maintenance of Peace and Security	**5**
Disarmament	**6**
Peaceful Uses of Atomic Energy	**7**

Outlines

15.31. Outlines vary in appearance because there is no one set style to follow in designing them. The width of the measure, the number of levels required for the indentions, and the labeling concept selected to identify each new level all contribute to its individuality.

The following sample outline demonstrates a very basic and structured arrangement. It uses the enumerators listed in rule 8.112 to identify each new indented level.

The enumerators for the first four levels are followed by a period and a fixed amount of space. The enumerators for the second four levels are set in parentheses and followed by the same amount of fixed space.

Each new level indents 2 ems more than the preceding level, and data that runs over to the next line aligns with the first word following the enumerator.

Outline example:

I. Balancing a checkbook
    A. Open your check register
        1. Verify all check numbers
            a. Verify no check numbers were duplicated
            b. Verify no check numbers were skipped
    B. Open your bank statement
        1. Put canceled checks in sequence
        2. Compare amounts on checks to those in register
            a. Correct any mistakes in register
            b. Indicate those check numbers cashed
                (1) Mark off check number on the statement
                    (a) Verify amount of check
                        (i) Highlight discrepancies on statement
                            (aa) Enter figures on back
                        (ii) Enter missing check numbers on back with amounts
                            (aa) Identify missing check numbers in register
                            (bb) Verify those check numbers were not cashed previously

16. Datelines, Addresses, and Signatures

16.1. The general principle involved in the typography of datelines, addresses, and signatures is that they should be set to stand out clearly from the body of the letter or paper that they accompany. This is accomplished by using caps and small caps and italic, as set forth below. Other typographic details are designed to ensure uniformity and good appearance. Street addresses and ZIP Code numbers are not to be used. In certain lists that carry ZIP Code numbers, regular spacing will be used preceding the ZIP Code. Certain general instructions apply alike to datelines, addresses, and signatures.

General instructions

16.2. Principal words in datelines, addresses, and titles accompanying signatures are capitalized.

16.3. *Mr., Mrs., Miss, Ms.*, and all other titles preceding a name, and *Esq., Jr., Sr.*, and *2d* following a name in address and signature lines, are set in roman caps and lowercase if the name is in caps and small caps or caps and lowercase; if the name is in caps, they are set in caps and small caps, if small caps are available—otherwise in caps and lowercase.

Spacing

16.4. At least 2 points of space should appear between dateline and text or address, address and text, text and signature, or signature and address.

Datelines

16.5. Datelines at the beginning of a letter or paper are set at the right side of the page, the originating office in caps and small caps, the address and date in italic; if the originating office is not given, the address is set in caps and small caps and the date in italic; if only the date is given, it is set in caps and small caps. Such datelines are indented from the right 1 em for a single line; 3 ems and 1 em, successively, for two lines; or 5 ems, 3 ems, and 1 em, successively, for three lines. In measures 30 picas or wider, these indentions are increased by 1 em.

The White House,□□□
Washington, DC, January 1, 2016.□
The White House, *July 30, 2016.*□

Treasury Department,□□□□□
Office of the Treasurer,□□□
Washington, DC, January 1, 2016.□

Treasury Department, *July 30, 2016.*□

Department of Commerce,□□□
July 30, 2016.□

Fairfax County, VA.□

Office of John Smith & Co.,□□□
New York, NY, June 6, 2016.□

Washington, *May 20, 2016—10 a.m.*□

Thursday, May 5, 2016—2 p.m.□

January 24, 2016.□

Washington, *November 28, 2016.*□□□
[Received December 5, 2016].□

On Board USS "Connecticut,"□□□
January 22, 2016.□

16.6. Congressional hearings:

THURSDAY, NOVEMBER 19, 2015[1]

House of Representatives,□□□□□□□
Committee on the Judiciary,□□□□□
Subcommittee on Immigration□□□
and Border Security,□□□
Washington, DC.□

U.S. Senate,□□□□□
Committee on Armed Services,□□□
Washington, DC.□

Congress of the United States,□□□□□
Joint Committee on Printing,□□□
Washington, DC.□

[1] Normally, dates in House hearings on appropriation bills are set on the right in 10-point caps and small caps.

16.7. Datelines at the end of a letter or paper, either above or below signatures, are set on left in caps and small caps for the address and italic for the date. When the word *dated* is used, dateline is set in roman caps and lowercase.

□May 7, 2016.
□Roanoke, VA.
□Roanoke, VA, *July 1, 2016.*
□Dated July 1, 2016.
□Dated Albany, March 13, 2016.

16.8. Datelines in newspaper extracts are set at the beginning of the paragraph, the address in caps and small caps and the date in roman caps and lowercase, followed by a period and a 1-em dash.

□Aboard USS *Ronald Reagan* April 3, 2016.—
□New York, NY, August 21, 2016.—A message received here from . . . .

Addresses

16.9. Addresses are set flush left at the beginning of a letter or paper in congressional work (or at end in formal usage).

16.10. At beginning or at end:

To Smith & Jones and
□Brown & Green, Esqs.,
Attorneys for Claimant.
(Attention of Mr. Green.)

Hon. Patty Murray,
U.S. Senate.

Hon. Nancy Pelosi,
U.S. House of Representatives. (Collective address.)

The President,
The White House.

16.11. A long title following an address is set in italic caps and lowercase, the first line flush left and right, overruns indented 2 ems to clear a following 1-em paragraph indention.

Hon. Mike Rounds,
Chairman, Subcommittee on Superfund, Waste Management,
□□*and Regulatory Oversight, U.S. Senate, Washington, DC.*

16.12. The name or title forming the first line of the address is set in caps and small caps, but *Mr., Mrs.*, or other title preceding a name, and *Esq., Jr., Sr.*, or *2d* following a name, are set in roman caps and lowercase; the matter following is set in italic. The words *U.S. Army* or *U.S. Navy* immediately following a name are set in roman caps and lowercase in the same line as the name.

Lt. Gen. TODD T. SEMONITE, U.S. Army,
Chief of Engineers.

CHIEF OF ENGINEERS, U.S. ARMY. (Full title, all caps and small caps.)

Lt. Gen. TODD T. SEMONITE,
Chief of Engineers, U.S. Army,
Washington, DC.

Hon. KAREN L. HAAS,
Clerk of the House of Representatives.

Hon. RICHARD J. DURBIN,
U.S. Senator, Washington, DC.

Hon. CORY GARDNER,
Russell Senate Office Building, Washington, DC.

The COMMITTEE ON APPROPRIATIONS,
House of Representatives.

16.13. General (or collective) addresses are set in italic caps and lowercase, flush left, with overruns indented 2 ems and ending with a colon, except when followed by a salutation, in which case a period is used.

16.14. Examples of general addresses when not followed by salutation (note the use of colon at end of italic line):

To the Officers and Members of the Daughters of the American
□□*Revolution, Washington, DC:*

To the American Diplomatic and Consular Officers:

To Whom It May Concern:

Collectors of Customs:

To the Congress of the United States:

16.15. Example of general address when followed by salutation (note the use of period at end of italic line):

Senate and House of Representatives.
□GENTLEMEN: You are hereby * * *.

16.16. Examples illustrating other types of addresses:

To the EDITOR:

To JOHN L. NELSON, *Greeting:*

To JOHN L. NELSON, *Birmingham, AL, Greeting:*

To the CLERK OF THE HOUSE OF REPRESENTATIVES:

CHIEF OF ENGINEERS
(Through the Division Engineer).
□MY DEAR SIR: I have the honor . . . .
□MR. REED: I have the honor . . . .
□DEAR MR. REED: I have the honor . . . .

Lt. (jg.) JOHN SMITH,
Navy Department:
□The care shown by you . . . .

STATE OF NEW YORK,
County of New York, ss:
□Before me this day appeared . . . .

DISTRICT OF COLUMBIA, *ss:*
□Before me this day appeared . . . .

Envelope addresses

U.S. House of Representatives
Committee on Education and the Workforce
2176 Rayburn House Office Building
Washington, DC 20515

Signatures

16.17. Signatures, preceded by an em dash, are sometimes run in with the last line of text.

16.18. Signatures are set at the right side of the page. They are indented 1 em for a single line; 3 ems and 1 em, successively, for two lines; and 5 ems, 3 ems, and 1 em, successively, for three lines. In measures 30 picas or wider, these indentions are increased by 1 em.

16.19. The name or names are set in caps and small caps; *Mr., Mrs.,* and all other titles preceding a name, and *Esq., Jr., Sr.,* and *2d* following a name, are set in roman caps and lowercase; the title following name is set in italic. Signatures as they appear in copy must be followed in regard to abbreviations.

16.20. If name and title make more than half a line, they are set as two lines.

16.21. Two to eight independent signatures, with or without titles, are aligned on the left, at approximately the center of the measure.

Robert E. Schwenk.
Queen E. Hughes.
Erica N. Prophet.
Andre Rodgers,
Commander, U.S. Navy (Retired).□
William H. Coughlin, *Chairman.*

16.22. More than eight signatures, with or without titles, are set full measure, roman caps and lowercase, run in, indented 5 and 7 ems in measures of 26½ picas or wider; in measures less than 26½ picas, indent 2 and 3 ems.

□□□□□Brown, Shipley & Co.; Denniston, Cross & Co.; Fruhling &
□□□□□□□Groschen, Attorneys; C.J. Hambro & Sons; Hardy,
□□□□□□□Nathan & Co.; Heilbut, Symons & Co.; Harrison Bros. &
□□□□□□□Co., by George Harrison; Hoare, Miller & Co.; Thomas
□□□□□□□Eaton Co.

16.23. The punctuation of closing phrases is governed by the sense. A detached complimentary close is made a new paragraph.

16.24. Examples of various kinds of signatures:

United States Improvement Co.,
(By) John Smith, *Secretary.*

Texarkana Textile Merchants &
Manufacturers' Association,
John L. Jones, *Secretary.*

Texarkana Textile Merchants &
Manufacturers' Association,
Joanne Wilder,
Board Member and Secretary.□

John W. Smith□□□
(And 25 others).□

John Smith,□□□□□
Lieutenant Governor□□□
(For the Governor of Maine).□

North American Ice Co.,
Sylvia Rooney, *Secretary.*
John [his thumbmark] Smith.□

Nita M. Lowey,
Barbara Comstock,
Managers on the Part of the House.□

Chris Coons,
Amy Klobuchar,
Managers on the Part of the Senate.□

□I am, very respectfully, yours,
(Signed)□Fred C. Kleinschmidt,□□□
Assistant Clerk, Court of Claims.□

□On behalf of the Philadelphia Chamber of Commerce:
Geo. W. Philips.
Saml. Campbell.

□I have the honor to be,
□□□Very respectfully, your obedient servant,
(Signed)□ John R. King
(Typed)□ John R. King,
Secretary.□

or

(S)□ John R. King
John R. King,
Secretary.□

□Attest:
Richard Roe, *Notary Public.*□

□By the Governor:
Nathaniel Cox, *Secretary of State.*□

□Approved.
John Smith, *Governor.*□

□By the President:
John Kerry, *Secretary of State.*□

□Respectfully submitted.
Mary Farrell, *U.S. Indian Agent.*□

□□□Yours truly,
Capt. James Staley, Jr.,□□□
Superintendent.□

□□□Respectfully yours,
Mrs. Betty Sheffield.□

□□□Very respectfully,
Ron Golden, *U.S. Indian Agent.*□

16.25. In quoted matter:

□□□“Very respectfully,

“Todd S. Gilbert.
“Paul Hartman.
“Dolores Hicks.
“Albert H. Jones.
“Joan C. Nugent.
“Brandon Proctor.”

16.26. Examples of various kinds of datelines, addresses, and signatures:

Re weather reports submitted by the International Advisory Committee of
□□the Weather Council.

Mr. Fred Upton,
Chairman, House Committee on Energy and Commerce,
Washington, DC.

□Dear Mr. Upton: We have been in contact with your office, etc.

Dr. Louis W. Uccellini,□□□□□
Executive Director,□□□
National Weather Service.□

Lincoln Park, MI, *February 15, 2016.*□

Re Romeo O. Umanos, Susanna M. Umanos, case No. S–254, U.S.
□□Citizenship and Immigration Services, application pending.

Hon. John Cornyn,
Chairman, Subcommittee on the Constitution,
Committee on the Judiciary, Washington, DC.

□Dear Mr. Cornyn: You have for some time . . . .
□□□Sincerely yours,

Edward Pultorak,□□□
Architectural Designer.□

Hon. Trey Gowdy,
Chairman, Subcommittee on Immigration and Border Security
□□*of the Committee on the Judiciary, House of Representatives,*
□□*Washington, DC.*

□Dear Mr. Gowdy: You have for some time . . . .

U.S. Department of □□□□□
Commerce,□□□□□
National Weather Service,□□□
Washington, March 3, 2016.□

Hon. Gene Green,
House of Representatives,
Washington, DC.
□Dear Mr. Green: We will be glad to
give you any further information.
□□□Sincerely yours,
F.W. Reichelderfer,□□□
Chief of Service.□

New York, NY, *February 8, 2016.*□

To: All supervisory employees of production plants, northern and
□□eastern divisions, New York State.
From: Production manager.
Subject: Regulations concerning vacations, health and welfare plans,
□□and wage contract negotiations.
□It has come to our attention that the time . . . .

Washington, DC, *May 16, 2016.*□

The Honorable the Secretary of the Navy.
□Dear Mr. Secretary: This is in response to your letter . . . .
□□□Very sincerely yours,

[seal]□Barack Obama.□

East Lansing, MI, *June 10, 2016.*□

To Whom It May Concern:

□I have known Kyu Yawp Lee for 7 years and am glad to testify as to his fine character. He has been employed . . . .

□Wishing you success in your difficult and highly important job, we are,

□□□Sincerely yours,

Agostino J. Gonino.

Louise M. Gonino.

U.S. Department of Veterans Affairs,□□□□□□□

Office of the Secretary of□□□□□

Veterans Affairs,□□□

Washington, DC.□

Hon. Charles E. Grassley,

Chairman, Committee on the Judiciary,

U.S. Senate, Washington, DC.

□Dear Senator Grassley: Further reference is made to your reply . . . .

□□□Sincerely yours,

Gordon M. Mansfield,□□□□□□□

Deputy Secretary□□□□□

(For and in the absence of□□□

James B. Peake, Secretary).□

Washington, DC, *September 16, 2016.*□

Mr. William E. Jones, Jr.,

Special Assistant to the Attorney General, Attorney for Howard
□□*Sutherland, Director, Office of Alien Property.*

□Dear Mr. Jones: In reply to your letter . . . .

□□□Yours truly,

(Signed)□Thomas E. Rhodes,□□□

Special Assistant to the Attorney General.□

□P.S.—A special word of thanks to you from J.R. Brown for your fine
□□help.

T.E.R.□

Tokyo, Japan, *November 13, 2016.*□
U.S. Department of Homeland Security,
U.S. Citizenship and Naturalization Services,
Detroit, MI.
□Gentlemen: This letter will testify to the personal character . . . .
□□□Very truly yours,
Mrs. Grace C. Lohr,□□□□□
Inspector General Section, HQ, AFFE,□□□
APO 343, San Francisco, CA.□

16.27. The word *seal* appearing with the signature of a notary or of an organized body, such as a company, is spaced 1 em from the signature. The word *seal* is to be set in small caps and bracketed.

[seal]□Richard Roe,□□□
Notary Public.□

[seal]□J.M. Wilber.□

[seal]□Bartlett, Robins & Co.□

16.28. Presidential proclamations after May 23, 1967, do not utilize the seal except when they pertain to treaties, conventions, protocols, or other international agreements. Copy will be followed literally with respect to the inclusion of and between elements of numerical expressions.

In 1872, the Congress established Yellowstone National Park—the first park of its kind anywhere in the world. Decades later, the passage of the Antiquities Act in 1906 created our first national historic preservation policy. Under this new authority, and heavily inspired by his time in nature with conservationist John Muir, President Theodore Roosevelt set aside 18 new monuments and landmarks, adding to the scattered collection of existing parks throughout our country. One decade later, in order to provide the leadership necessary for maintaining our growing system of parks, the Congress passed monumental legislation—which President Woodrow Wilson signed on August 25, 1916—to create the National Park Service (NPS). . . .

* * * * * * *

Now, Therefore, I, Barack Obama, President of the United States of America, by virtue of the authority vested in me by the Constitution and the laws of the United States, do hereby proclaim August 25, 2016, as the 100th Anniversary of the National Park Service. I invite all Americans to observe this day with appropriate programs, ceremonies, and activities that recognize the National Park Service for maintaining and protecting our public lands for the continued benefit and enjoyment of all Americans.

IN WITNESS WHEREOF, I have hereunto set my hand this twenty-second day of August, in the year of our Lord two thousand sixteen, and of the Independence of the United States of America the two hundred and forty-first.

BARACK OBAMA.□

17. Useful Tables

This chapter contains useful tables presented in GPO style. The tables display various design features most frequently used in Government publications and can be considered examples of GPO style.

U.S. Presidents and Vice Presidents

President	Years	Vice President	Years
George Washington	(1789–1797)	John Adams	(1789–1797)
John Adams	(1797–1801)	Thomas Jefferson	(1797–1801)
Thomas Jefferson	(1801–1809)	Aaron Burr	(1801–1805)
		George Clinton	(1805–1809)
James Madison	(1809–1817)	George Clinton	(1809–1812)
		Vacant	(1812–1813)
		Elbridge Gerry	(1813–1814)
		Vacant	(1814–1817)
James Monroe	(1817–1825)	Daniel D. Tompkins	(1817–1825)
John Quincy Adams	(1825–1829)	John C. Calhoun	(1825–1829)
Andrew Jackson	(1829–1837)	John C. Calhoun	(1829–1832)
		Vacant	(1832–1833)
		Martin Van Buren	(1833–1837)
Martin Van Buren	(1837–1841)	Richard M. Johnson	(1837–1841)
William Henry Harrison	(1841)	John Tyler	(1841)
John Tyler	(1841–1845)	Vacant	(1841–1845)
James K. Polk	(1845–1849)	George M. Dallas	(1845–1849)
Zachary Taylor	(1849–1850)	Millard Fillmore	(1849–1850)
Millard Fillmore	(1850–1853)	Vacant	(1850–1853)
Franklin Pierce	(1853–1857)	William R. King	(1853)
		Vacant	(1853–1857)
James Buchanan	(1857–1861)	John C. Breckinridge	(1857–1861)
Abraham Lincoln	(1861–1865)	Hannibal Hamlin	(1861–1865)
		Andrew Johnson	(1865)
Andrew Johnson	(1865–1869)	Vacant	(1865–1869)
Ulysses S. Grant	(1869–1877)	Schuyler Colfax	(1869–1873)
		Henry Wilson	(1873–1875)
		Vacant	(1875–1877)
Rutherford B. Hayes	(1877–1881)	William A. Wheeler	(1877–1881)
James A. Garfield	(1881)	Chester A. Arthur	(1881)
Chester A. Arthur	(1881–1885)	Vacant	(1881–1885)
Grover Cleveland	(1885–1889)	Thomas A. Hendricks	(1885)
		Vacant	(1885–1889)
Benjamin Harrison	(1889–1893)	Levi P. Morton	(1889–1893)
Grover Cleveland	(1893–1897)	Adlai E. Stevenson	(1893–1897)
William McKinley	(1897–1901)	Garret A. Hobart	(1897–1901)
		Theodore Roosevelt	(1901)
Theodore Roosevelt	(1901–1909)	Vacant	(1901–1905)
		Charles W. Fairbanks	(1905–1909)
William H. Taft	(1909–1913)	James S. Sherman	(1909–1912)
		Vacant	(1912–1913)
Woodrow Wilson	(1913–1921)	Thomas R. Marshall	(1913–1921)
Warren G. Harding	(1921–1923)	Calvin Coolidge	(1921–1923)
Calvin Coolidge	(1923–1929)	Vacant	(1923–1925)
		Charles G. Dawes	(1925–1929)
Herbert Hoover	(1929–1933)	Charles Curtis	(1929–1933)
Franklin D. Roosevelt	(1933–1945)	John Nance Garner	(1933–1941)
		Henry A. Wallace	(1941–1945)
		Harry S. Truman	(1945)
Harry S. Truman	(1945–1953)	Vacant	(1945–1949)
		Alben W. Barkley	(1949–1953)
Dwight D. Eisenhower	(1953–1961)	Richard M. Nixon	(1953–1961)

U.S. Presidents and Vice Presidents—Continued

President	Years	Vice President	Years
John F. Kennedy	(1961–1963)	Lyndon B. Johnson	(1961–1963)
Lyndon B. Johnson	(1963–1969)	Vacant	(1963–1965)
		Hubert H. Humphrey	(1965–1969)
Richard M. Nixon	(1969–1974)	Spiro T. Agnew	(1969–1973)
		Gerald R. Ford	(1973–1974)
Gerald R. Ford	(1974–1977)	Nelson A. Rockefeller	(1974–1977)
James Earl "Jimmy" Carter	(1977–1981)	Walter F. Mondale	(1977–1981)
Ronald Reagan	(1981–1989)	George H.W. Bush	(1981–1989)
George H.W. Bush	(1989–1993)	J. Danforth Quayle	(1989–1993)
William J. Clinton	(1993–2001)	Albert Gore, Jr.	(1993–2001)
George W. Bush	(2001–2009)	Richard B. Cheney	(2001–2009)
Barack Obama	(2009–)	Joseph R. Biden, Jr.	(2009–)

State Populations and Their Capitals

[As of July 1, 2015 Census estimates]

State, capital	State population	State, capital	State population
Alabama, Montgomery	4,858,979	Montana, Helena	1,032,949
Alaska, Juneau	738,432	Nebraska, Lincoln	1,896,190
Arizona, Phoenix	6,828,065	Nevada, Carson City	2,890,845
Arkansas, Little Rock	2,978,204	New Hampshire, Concord	1,330,608
California, Sacramento	39,144,818	New Jersey, Trenton	8,958,013
Colorado, Denver	5,456,574	New Mexico, Santa Fe	2,085,109
Connecticut, Hartford	3,590,886	New York, Albany	19,795,791
Delaware, Dover	945,934	North Carolina, Raleigh	10,042,802
District of Columbia, Washington	672,228	North Dakota, Bismarck	756,927
Florida, Tallahassee	20,271,272	Ohio, Columbus	11,613,423
Georgia, Atlanta	10,214,860	Oklahoma, Oklahoma City	3,911,338
Hawaii, Honolulu	1,431,603	Oregon, Salem	4,028,977
Idaho, Boise	1,654,930	Pennsylvania, Harrisburg	12,802,503
Illinois, Springfield	12,859,995	Rhode Island, Providence	1,056,298
Indiana, Indianapolis	6,619,680	South Carolina, Columbia	4,896,146
Iowa, Des Moines	3,123,899	South Dakota, Pierre	858,469
Kansas, Topeka	2,911,641	Tennessee, Nashville	6,600,299
Kentucky, Frankfort	4,425,092	Texas, Austin	27,469,114
Louisiana, Baton Rouge	4,670,724	Utah, Salt Lake City	2,995,919
Maine, Augusta	1,329,328	Vermont, Montpelier	626,042
Maryland, Annapolis	6,006,401	Virginia, Richmond	8,382,993
Massachusetts, Boston	6,794,422	Washington, Olympia	7,170,351
Michigan, Lansing	9,922,576	West Virginia, Charleston	1,844,128
Minnesota, St. Paul	5,489,594	Wisconsin, Madison	5,771,337
Mississippi, Jackson	2,992,333	Wyoming, Cheyenne	586,107
Missouri, Jefferson City	6,083,672		

Principal Foreign Countries as of October 2016

Country	UN member	Capital	Chief of state	Legislative body	Government type
Afghanistan	Yes	Kabul	President	National Assembly of House of People, House of Elders	Islamic Republic.
Albania	do	Tirana (Tirane)	do	Assembly (unicameral)	Emerging Democracy.
Algeria	do	Algiers	do	National People's Assembly, Council of Nations	Republic.
Andorra	do	Andorra la Vella	Executive Council President	General Council of the Valleys (unicameral)	Parliamentary Democracy.
Angola	do	Luanda	President	National Assembly (unicameral)	Republic: multiparty presidential regime.
Antigua and Barbuda	do	Saint John's	Queen (represented by Governor General)	Parliament (bicameral)	Constitutional Monarchy with a parliamentary system of government.
Argentina	do	Buenos Aires	President	National Congress (bicameral)	Republic.
Armenia	do	Yerevan	do	National Assembly (Parliament)	Do.
Australia	do	Canberra	Queen (represented by Governor General)	Federal Parliament (bicameral)	Federal Parliamentary Democracy.
Austria	do	Vienna	President	Federal Assembly (bicameral)	Federal Republic.
Azerbaijan	do	Baku (Baki, Baky)	do	National Assembly (unicameral)	Republic.
Bahamas, The	do	Nassau	Queen (represented by Governor General)	Parliament (bicameral)	Constitutional Parliamentary Democracy.
Bahrain	do	Manama	King	Legislature (bicameral)	Constitutional Monarchy.
Bangladesh	do	Dhaka	President	National Parliament (unicameral)	Parliamentary Democracy.
Barbados	do	Bridgetown	Queen (represented by Governor General)	Parliament (bicameral)	Do.
Belarus	do	Minsk	President	National Assembly (bicameral)	Republic in name, although in fact a dictatorship.
Belgium	do	Brussels	King	Parliament (bicameral)	Federal Parliamentary Democracy under a Constitutional Monarchy.
Belize	do	Belmopan	Queen (represented by Governor General)	National Assembly (bicameral)	Parliamentary Democracy.

Principal Foreign Countries as of October 2016—Continued

Country	UN member	Capital	Chief of state	Legislative body	Government type
Benin	Yes	Porto-Novo	President	National Assembly (unicameral)	Republic.
Bhutan	do	Thimphu	King	Parliament (bicameral)	In transition to Constitutional Monarchy; special treaty relationship with India.
Bolivia	do	La Paz (administrative) Sucre (legislative/judiciary)	President	National Congress (bicameral)	Republic.
Bosnia and Herzegovina	do	Sarajevo	Chairman of the Presidency	Parliamentary Assembly (bicameral)	Emerging Federal Democratic Republic.
Botswana	do	Gaborone	President	Parliament (bicameral)	Parliamentary Republic.
Brazil	do	Brasilia	do	National Congress (bicameral)	Federal Republic.
Brunei	do	Bandar Seri	Sultan and Prime Minister	Legislative Council	Constitutional Sultanate.
Bulgaria	do	Sofia	President	National Assembly (unicameral)	Parliamentary Democracy.
Burkina Faso	do	Ouagadougou	do	do	Parliamentary Republic.
Burma (Myanmar)[1]	do	Rangoon Nay Pyi Taw (administrative)	Chairman of the State Peace and Development Council SPDC)	People's Assembly (unicameral)	Military Junta.
Burundi	do	Bujumbura	President	Parliament (bicameral)	Republic.
Cabo Verde[2]	do	Praia	President	National Assembly (unicameral)	Republic.
Cambodia	do	Phnom Penh	King	National Assembly (bicameral)	Multiparty Democracy under a Constitutional Monarchy.
Cameroon	do	Yaoundé	President	National Assembly (unicameral)	Republic; Multiparty Presidential Regime.
Canada	do	Ottawa	Queen (represented by Governor General)	Parliament (bicameral)	Constitutional Monarchy that is also a Parliamentary Democracy and a Federation
Central African Republic	do	Bangui	do	do	Do.
Chad	do	N'Djamena	do	do	Do.

Chile	do	Santiago	President	National Congress (bicameral)	Do.
China [3]	do	Beijing	do	National People's Congress (unicameral)	Communist State.
Colombia	do	Bogotá	do	Congress (bicameral)	Republic, Executive Branch dominates government structure.
Comoros	do	Moroni	do	Assembly of the Union (unicameral)	Republic.
Congo, Democratic Republic of the [4]	do	Kinshasa	do	Legislature (bicameral)	Do.
Congo, Republic of the [4]	do	Brazzaville	do	Parliament (bicameral)	Do.
Costa Rica	do	San José	do	Legislative Assembly (unicameral)	Democratic Republic.
Côte d'Ivoire, Republic of	do	Yamoussoukro	do	National Assembly (bicameral)	Republic; multiparty presidency
Croatia	do	Zagreb	do	Assembly (unicameral)	Presidential/Parliamentary Democracy.
Cuba	do	Havana	do	National Assembly of People's Power (unicameral)	Communist State.
Cyprus	do	Nicosia	do	House of Representatives (unicameral).	Republic.
Czechia [5]	do	Prague	do	Parliament (bicameral)	Parliamentary Democracy.
Denmark	do	Copenhagen	Queen	People's Assembly (unicameral)	Constitutional Monarchy.
Djibouti	do	Djibouti	President	Chamber of Deputies (unicameral)	Republic.
Dominica	do	Roseau	do	House of Assembly (unicameral)	Parliamentary Democracy.
Dominican Republic	do	Santo Domingo	do	National Congress (bicameral)	Democratic Republic.
Ecuador	do	Quito	President	National Congress (unicameral)	Republic.
Egypt	do	Cairo	do	People's Assembly (bicameral)	Do.
El Salvador	do	San Salvador	do	Legislative Assembly (unicameral)	Do.
Equatorial Guinea	do	Malabo	do	House of People's Representatives (unicameral)	Do.
Eritrea	do	Asmara	do	National Assembly (unicameral)	Transitional Government.
Estonia	do	Tallinn	do	Parliament (unicameral)	Parliamentary Republic.
Ethiopia	do	Addis Ababa	do	Parliament (bicameral)	Federal Republic.

Principal Foreign Countries as of October 2016—Continued

Country	UN member	Capital	Chief of state	Legislative body	Government type
Fiji	Yes	Suva	President	do	Republic.
Finland	do	Helsinki	do	Parliament (unicameral)	Do.
France	do	Paris	do	Parliament (bicameral)	Do.
Gabon	do	Libreville	do	Legislature (bicameral)	Republic; Multiparty Presidential Regime.
Gambia, The	do	Banjul	do	National Assembly (unicameral)	Republic.
Georgia	do	Tbilisi	do	Parliament (unicameral, also known as Supreme Council)	Do.
Germany	do	Berlin	do	Parliament (bicameral)	Federal Republic.
Ghana	do	Accra	do	Parliament (unicameral)	Constitutional Democracy.
Greece	do	Athens	do	do	Parliamentary Republic.
Grenada	do	Saint George's	Queen (represented by Governor General)	Parliament (bicameral)	Parliamentary Democracy.
Guatemala	do	Guatemala City	President	Congress of the Republic (unicameral).	Constitutional Democratic Republic.
Guinea	do	Conakry	do	People's National Assembly (unicameral)	Republic.
Guinea-Bissau	do	Bissau	do	National People's Asssembly (unicameral)	Do.
Guyana	do	Georgetown	do	National Assembly (unicameral)	Do.
Haiti	do	Port-au-Prince	do	National Assembly (bicameral)	Do.
Holy See (Vatican City)	No	Vatican City	Pope	Pontifical Commission for the State of Vatican City (unicameral)	Ecclesiastical.
Honduras	Yes	Tegucigalpa	President	National Congress (unicameral)	Democratic Constitutional Republic.
Hungary	do	Budapest	do	National Assembly (unicameral)	Parliamentary Democracy.
Iceland	do	Reykjavik	do	Parliament (unicameral)	Constitutional Republic.
India	do	New Delhi	do	Parliament (bicameral)	Federal Republic.
Indonesia	do	Jakarta	do	House of Representatives	Republic.

Iran	do	Tehran	Supreme Leader	Islamic Consultative Assembly (unicameral)	Theocratic Republic.
Iraq	do	Baghdad	President	Council of Representatives	Parliamentary Democracy.
Ireland	do	Dublin	do	Parliament (bicameral)	Republic, Parliamentary Democracy.
Israel	do	Jerusalem[6]	do	Knesset (unicameral)	Parliamentary Democracy.
Italy	do	Rome	do	Parliament (bicameral)	Republic.
Jamaica	do	Kingston	Queen (represented by Governor General)	Parliament (bicameral)	Constitutional Parliamentary Democracy.
Japan	do	Tokyo	Emperor	Diet (bicameral)	Constitutional Monarchy with a Parliamentary Government.
Jordan	do	Amman	King	National Assembly (bicameral)	Constitutional Monarchy.
Kazakhstan	do	Astana	President	Parliament (bicameral)	Republic, Authoritarian Presidential rule, with little power outside the Executive Branch.
Kenya	do	Nairobi	do	National Assembly (unicameral)	Republic.
Kiribati	do	Tarawa	do	House of Parliament (unicameral)	Do.
Korea, North	do	Pyongyang	Premier	Supreme People's Assembly (unicameral)	Communist State one-man dictatorship.
Korea, South	do	Seoul	President	National Assembly (unicameral)	Republic.
Kosovo	No	Pristina (Prishtine)	do	Kosovo Assembly of the Provisional Government (unicameral)	Do.
Kuwait	Yes	Kuwait City	Amir	National Assembly (unicameral)	Constitutional Emirate.
Kyrgyzstan	do	Bishkek	President	Supreme Council (unicameral)	Republic.
Laos	do	Vientiane	do	National Assembly (unicameral)	Communist State.
Latvia	do	Riga	do	Parliament (unicameral)	Parliamentary Democracy.
Lebanon	do	Beirut	do	National Assembly (unicameral)	Republic.
Lesotho	do	Maseru	King	Parliament (bicameral)	Parliamentary Constitutional Monarchy.
Liberia	do	Monrovia	President	National Assembly (bicameral)	Republic.
Libya	do	Tripoli	Chairman, Presidential Council	Council of Deputies (unicameral)	In transition.
Liechtenstein	do	Vaduz	Prince	Parliament or Landtag (unicameral)	Constitutional Monarchy.

Principal Foreign Countries as of October 2016—Continued

Country	UN member	Capital	Chief of state	Legislative body	Government type
Lithuania	Yes	Vilnius	President	Parliament or Seimas (unicameral)	Parliamentary Democracy.
Luxembourg	do	Luxembourg	Grand Duke	Chamber of Deputies (unicameral)	Constitutional Monarchy.
Macedonia, Republic of [7]	do	Skopje	President	Assembly or Sobranie (unicameral)	Parliamentary Republic.
Madagascar	do	Antananarivo	do	Legislature (bicameral)	Republic.
Malawi	do	Lilongwe	do	National Assembly (unicameral)	Multiparty Democracy.
Malaysia	do	Kuala Lumpur	Paramount Ruler	Parliament (bicameral)	Constitutional Monarchy.
Maldives	do	Male	President	People's Council (unicameral)	Republic.
Mali	do	Bamako	do	National Assembly (unicameral)	Do.
Malta	do	Valletta	do	House of Representatives (unicameral).	Do.
Marshall Islands	do	Majuro	do	Legislature (unicameral)	Constitutional Government in free association with the U.S.
Mauritania	do	Nouakchott	President	Legislature (bicameral)	Democratic Republic.
Mauritius	do	Port Louis	do	National Assembly (unicameral)	Parliamentary Democracy.
Mexico	do	Mexico City	do	National Congress (bicameral)	Federal Republic.
Micronesia, Federated States of	do	Palikir	do	Congress (unicameral)	Constitutional Government in free association with the U.S.
Moldova, Republic of	do	Chisinau	do	Parliament (unicameral)	Republic.
Monaco	do	Monaco	Prince	National Council (unicameral)	Constitutional Monarchy.
Mongolia	do	Ulaanbaatar	President	State Great Hural (unicameral)	Mixed Parliamentary/Presidential.
Montenegro	do	Podgorica	do	Assembly (unicameral)	Republic.
Morocco	do	Rabat	King	Parliament (bicameral)	Constitutional Monarchy.
Mozambique	do	Maputo	President	Assembly of the Republic (unicameral)	Republic.
Namibia	do	Windhoek	do	Legislature (bicameral)	Do.
Nauru	do	No official capital; government offices in Yaren District	do	Parliament (unicameral)	Do.

Nepal	do	Kathmandu	Prime Minister	330 seat Interim Parliament	Constitutional Monarchy.
Netherlands	do	Amsterdam The Hague (seat of government)	Queen	States General (bicameral)	Do.
New Zealand	do	Wellington	do	House of Representatives (unicameral)	Parliamentary Democracy.
Nicaragua	do	Managua	President	National Assembly (unicameral)	Republic.
Niger	do	Niamey	do	do	Do.
Nigeria	do	Abuja	do	National Assembly (bicameral)	Federal Republic.
Norway	do	Oslo	King	Parliament (Storting), (modified unicameral)[8]	Constitutional Monarchy.
Oman	do	Muscat	Sultan and Prime Minister	Majlis Oman (bicameral)	Monarchy.
Pakistan	do	Islamabad	President	Parliament (bicameral)	Federal Republic.
Palau	do	Ngerulmud	do	National Congress (bicameral)	Constitutional Government in free association with the U.S.
Panama	do	Panama City	do	National Assembly (unicameral)	Constitutional Democracy.
Papua New Guinea	do	Port Moresby	Queen	National Parliament (unicameral)	Constitutional Parliamentary Democracy.
Paraguay	do	Asunción	President	Congress (bicameral)	Constitutional Republic.
Peru	do	Lima	do	Congress of the Republic of Peru (unicameral)	Do.
Philippines	do	Manila	do	Congress (bicameral)	Republic.
Poland	do	Warsaw	do	National Assembly (bicameral)	Do.
Portugal	do	Lisbon	do	Assembly of the Republic (unicameral)	Parliamentary Democracy.
Qatar	do	Doha	Amir	Advisory Council (unicameral)	Emirate.
Romania	do	Bucharest	President	Parliament (bicameral)	Republic.
Russia	do	Moscow	do	Federal Assembly (bicameral)	Federation.
Rwanda	do	Kigali	do	Parliament (bicameral)	Republic; presidential, multiparty system.
Saint Kitts and Nevis	do	Basseterre	Queen	National Assembly (unicameral)	Parliamentary Democracy.
Saint Lucia	do	Castries	Queen	Parliament (bicameral)	Parliamentary Democracy.

Principal Foreign Countries as of October 2016—Continued

Country	UN member	Capital	Chief of state	Legislative body	Government type
Saint Vincent and the Grenadines	Yes	Kingstown	do	House of Assembly (unicameral)	Do.
Samoa	do	Apia	Chief of State	Legislative Assembly (unicameral)	Do.
San Marino	do	San Marino	Co-Chiefs of State (Captains Regent)	Grand and General Council (unicameral)	Republic.
Sao Tome and Principe	do	São Tomé	President	National Assembly (unicameral)	Do.
Saudi Arabia	do	Riyadh	King and Prime Minister	Consultative Council	Monarchy.
Senegal	do	Dakar	President	Parliament (bicameral)	Republic.
Serbia	do	Belgrade	do	National Assembly (unicameral)	Do.
Seychelles	do	Victoria	do	do	Do.
Sierra Leone	do	Freetown	do	Parliament (unicameral)	Constitutional Democracy.
Singapore	do	Singapore	do	do	Parliamentary Republic.
Slovakia	do	Bratislava	do	National Council (unicameral)	Parliamentary Democracy.
Slovenia	do	Ljubljana	do	Parliament (bicameral)	Parliamentary Republic.
Solomon Islands	do	Honiara	Queen	National Parliament (unicameral)	Parliamentary Democracy.
Somalia	do	Mogadishu	Transitional Federal President	National Assembly (unicameral)	No permanent National Government; transitional Parliamentary Federal Government.
South Africa	do	Pretoria (administrative) Cape Town (legislative) Bloemfontein (judiciary)	President	Parliament (bicameral)	Republic.
South Sudan, Republic of[9]	do	Juba	President	National Legislature (bicameral)	Presidential Republic.
Spain	do	Madrid	King	General Courts or National Assembly (bicameral)	Parliamentary Monarchy.

Sri Lanka	do	Colombo Sri Jayewardenepura Kotte (legislative)	President	Parliament (unicameral)	Republic.
Sudan	do	Khartoum	do	National Legislature (bicameral)	Government of National Unity (GNU).
Suriname	do	Paramaribo	do	National Assembly (unicameral)	Constitutional Democracy.
Swaziland	do	Mbabane (administrative) Lobamba (legislative)	King	Parliament (bicameral)	Monarchy.
Sweden	do	Stockholm	King	Parliament (unicameral)	Constitutional Monarchy.
Switzerland	do	Bern	President	Federal Assembly (bicameral)	Formally a Confederation but similar in structure to a Federal Republic.
Syria	do	Damascus	do	People's Council (unicameral)	Republic under an authoritarian military-dominated regime.
Tajikistan	do	Dushanbe	do	Supreme Assembly (bicameral)	Republic.
Tanzania	do	Dar es Salaam Dodoma (legislative)	do	National Assembly (unicameral)	Republic.
Thailand	do	Bangkok	King	National Assembly (bicameral)	Constitutional Monarchy.
Timor-Leste	do	Dili	President	National Parliament (unicameral)	Republic.
Togo	do	Lomé	President	National Assembly (unicameral)	Republic under transition to multiparty democratic rule.
Tonga	do	Nuku'alofa	King	Legislative Assembly (unicameral)	Constitutional Monarchy.
Trinidad and Tobago	do	Port-of-Spain	President	Parliament (bicameral)	Parliamentary Democracy.
Tunisia	do	Tunis	do	Chamber of Deputies and the Chamber of Advisors (bicameral)	Republic.
Turkey	do	Ankara	do	Grand National Assembly of Turkey (unicameral)	Republican Parliamentary Democracy
Turkmenistan	do	Ashgabat (Ashkhabad)	do	Two Parliamentary Bodies: People's Council and a National Assembly	Republic; Authoritarian Presidential rule, with little power outside the executive branch.
Tuvalu	do	Funafuti	Queen	Parliament (also called House of Assembly; unicameral)	Constitutional Monarchy with a Parliamentary Democracy.
Uganda	do	Kampala	President	National Assembly (unicameral)	Republic.

Principal Foreign Countries as of October 2016—Continued

Country	UN member	Capital	Chief of state	Legislative body	Government type
Ukraine	Yes	Kyiv (Kiev)	do	Supreme Council (unicameral)	Do.
United Arab Emirates	do	Abu Dhabi	do	Federal National Council (FNC) (unicameral)	Federation with specified powers delegated to the UAE federal government and other powers reserved to member emirates
United Kingdom	do	London	Queen	Parliament (bicameral)	Constitutional Monarchy.
Uruguay	do	Montevideo	President	General Assembly (bicameral)	Constitutional Republic.
Uzbekistan	do	Tashkent	do	Supreme Assembly (bicameral)	Republic; authoritarian presidential rule, with little power outside the executive branch.
Vanuatu	do	Port-Vila (on Efate)	do	Parliament (unicameral)	Parliamentary Republic.
Venezuela	do	Caracas	do	National Assembly (unicameral)	Federal Republic.
Vietnam	do	Hanoi	do	do	Communist State.
Yemen	do	Sanaa	do	Legislature (bicameral)	Republic.
Zambia	do	Lusaka	do	National Assembly (unicameral)	Do.
Zimbabwe	do	Harare	Executive President	Parliament (bicameral)	Parliamentary Democracy.

[1] Since 1989, the military authorities in Burma have promoted the name Myanmar as a conventional name for their state; this decision was not approved by any sitting legislature in Burma, and the U.S. Government did not adopt the name, which is a derivative of the Burmese short-form name Myanma Naingngandaw.

[2] In a diplomatic note sent on November 27, 2013, the Embassy of Cape Verde requested that the U.S. Government change the name of the country from "Cape Verde" to "Cabo Verde". The U.S. Board on Geographic Names approved the change on December 9, 2013.

[3] With the establishment of diplomatic relations with China on January 1, 1979, the U.S. Government recognized the People's Republic of China as the sole legal government of China and acknowledged the Chinese position that there is only one China and that Taiwan is part of China.

[4] "Congo" is the official short-form name for both the Democratic Republic of the Congo and the Republic of the Congo. To distinguish one from the other, see capital names.

[5] Following U.N. and U.S. State Department notification, the Czech Republic officially changed its English short-form name to Czechia as of July 1, 2016.

[6] In 1950, the Israel Parliament proclaimed Jerusalem as the capital. The United States does not recognize Jerusalem as the capital and the U.S. Embassy continues to be located in Tel Aviv.

[7] In November 2004, the United States recognized the country under its consitutional name: the Republic of Macedonia.

[8] No accurate English equivalents.

[9] The United States recognized South Sudan as a sovereign, independent state on July 9, 2011 following its secession from Sudan.

Source: World Factbook, Central Intelligence Agency, https://www.cia.gov/library/publications/resources/the-world-factbook/index.html and the U.S. Department of State.

Demonyms: Names of Nationalities

[Demonym is a name given to a people or inhabitants of a place.]

Country	Demonym*
Afghanistan	Afghan.
Albania	Albanian.
Algeria	Algerian.
American Samoa	American Samoan.
Andorra	Andorran.
Angola	Angolan.
Anguilla	Anguillan.
Antigua and Barbuda	Antiguan, Barbudan.
Argentina	Argentine.
Armenia	Armenian.
Aruba	Aruban.
Australia	Australian.
Austria	Austrian.
Azerbaijan	Azerbaijani.
The Bahamas	Bahamian.
Bahrain	Bahraini.
Bangladesh	Bangladeshi.
Barbados	Barbadian or Bajan.
Belarus	Belarusian.
Belgium	Belgian.
Belize	Belizean.
Benin	Beninese (singular and plural).
Bermuda	Bermudian.
Bhutan	Bhutanese (singular and plural).
Bolivia	Bolivian.
Bosnia and Herzegovina	Bosnian, Herzegovinian.
Botswana	Motswana (singular), Batswana (plural).
Brazil	Brazilian.
British Virgin Islands	British Virgin Islander.
Brunei	Bruneian.
Bulgaria	Bulgarian.
Burkina Faso	Burkinabe (singular and plural).
Burma (Myanmar[1])	Burmese (singular and plural).
Burundi	Burundian.
Cabo Verde	Cabo Verdean.
Cambodia	Cambodian.
Cameroon	Cameroonian.
Canada	Canadian.
Cayman Islands	Caymanian.
Central African Republic	Central African.
Chad	Chadian.
Chile	Chilean.
China	Chinese (singular and plural).
Christmas Island	Christmas Islander.
Cocos (Keeling) Islands	Cocos Islander.
Colombia	Colombian.
Comoros	Comoran.
Congo, Democratic Republic of the.	Congolese (singular and plural).
Congo, Republic of the	Congolese (singular and plural).
Cook Islands	Cook Islander.
Costa Rica	Costa Rican.
Côte d'Ivoire	Ivorian.
Croatia	Croat or Croatian.
Cuba	Cuban.
Curacao	Curacaoan.
Cyprus	Cypriot.
Czechia	Czech.
Denmark	Dane.
Djibouti	Djiboutian.
Dominica	Dominican.
Dominican Republic	Dominican.
Ecuador	Ecuadorian.
Egypt	Egyptian.
El Salvador	Salvadoran.
Equatorial Guinea	Equatorial Guinean or Equatoguinean.
Eritrea	Eritrean.
Estonia	Estonian.
Ethiopia	Ethiopian.
Falkland Islands	Falkland Islander.
Faroe Islands	Faroese (singular and plural).
Fiji	Fijian.
Finland	Finn.
France	French, Frenchman (men), or Frenchwoman (women).
French Polynesia	French Polynesian.
Gabon	Gabonese (singular and plural).
The Gambia	Gambian.
Georgia	Georgian.
Germany	German.
Ghana	Ghanaian.
Gibraltar	Gibraltarian.
Greece	Greek.
Greenland	Greenlander.
Grenada	Grenadian.
Guam	Guamanian.
Guatemala	Guatemalan.
Guernsey	Channel Islander.
Guinea	Guinean.
Guinea-Bissau	Bissau-Guinean.
Guyana	Guyanese (singular and plural).
Haiti	Haitian.
Honduras	Honduran.
Hong Kong	Chinese/Hong Konger.
Hungary	Hungarian.
Iceland	Icelander.
India	Indian.
Indonesia	Indonesian.
Iran	Iranian.
Iraq	Iraqi.
Ireland	Irishman (men), Irishwoman (women), Irish (collective plural).
Israel	Israeli.
Italy	Italian.
Jamaica	Jamaican.

Demonyms: Names of Nationalities—Continued

[Demonym is a name given to a people or inhabitants of a place.]

Country	Demonym*
Japan	Japanese (singular and plural).
Jersey	Channel Islander.
Jordan	Jordanian.
Kazakhstan	Kazakhstani.
Kenya	Kenyan.
Kiribati	I-Kiribati (singular and plural).
Korea, North	Korean.
Korea, South	Korean.
Kosovo	Kosovar (Albanian), Kosovski (Serbian).
Kuwait	Kuwaiti.
Kyrgyzstan	Kyrgyzstani.
Laos	Lao or Laotian.
Latvia	Latvian.
Lebanon	Lebanese (singular and plural).
Lesotho	Mosotho (singular), Basotho (plural).
Liberia	Liberian.
Libya	Libyan.
Liechtenstein	Liechtensteiner.
Lithuania	Lithuanian.
Luxembourg	Luxembourger.
Macau	Chinese (singular and plural).
Macedonia	Macedonian.
Madagascar	Malagasy (singular and plural).
Malawi	Malawian.
Malaysia	Malaysian.
Maldives	Maldivian.
Mali	Malian.
Malta	Maltese (singular and plural).
Marshall Islands	Marshallese (singular and plural).
Mauritania	Mauritanian.
Mauritius	Mauritian.
Mexico	Mexican.
Micronesia, Federated States of.	Micronesian.
Moldova	Moldovan.
Monaco	Monegasque or Monacan.
Mongolia	Mongolian.
Montenegro	Montenegrin.
Montserrat	Montserratian.
Morocco	Moroccan.
Mozambique	Mozambican.
Namibia	Namibian.
Nauru	Nauruan.
Nepal	Nepali (singular and plural).
Netherlands	Dutchman (men), Dutchwoman (women), Dutch (collective).
Netherlands Antilles	Dutch Antillean.
New Caledonia	New Caledonian.
New Zealand	New Zealander.
Nicaragua	Nicaraguan.
Niger	Nigerien.
Nigeria	Nigerian.
Niue	Niuean.
Norfolk Island	Norfolk Islander.
Norway	Norwegian.
Oman	Omani.
Pakistan	Pakistani.
Palau	Palauan.
Panama	Panamanian.
Papua New Guinea	Papua New Guinean.
Paraguay	Paraguayan.
Peru	Peruvian.
Philippines	Filipino.
Pitcairn Islands	Pitcairn Islander.
Poland	Pole.
Portugal	Portuguese (singular and plural).
Qatar	Qatari.
Romania	Romanian.
Russia	Russian.
Rwanda	Rwandan.
Saint Helena	Saint Helenian.
Saint Kitts and Nevis	Kittian, Nevisian.
Saint Lucia	Saint Lucian.
Saint Pierre and Miquelon	French, Frenchman (men), or Frenchwoman (women).
Saint Vincent and the Grenadines.	Saint Vincentian or Vincentian.
Samoa	Samoan.
San Marino	Sammarinese (singular and plural).
Sao Tome and Principe	Sao Tomean.
Saudi Arabia	Saudi, Saudi Arabian.
Senegal	Senegalese (singular and plural).
Serbia	Serb.
Seychelles	Seychellois (singular and plural).
Sierra Leone	Sierra Leonean.
Singapore	Singaporean.
Slovakia	Slovak.
Slovenia	Slovene.
Solomon Islands	Solomon Islander.
Somalia	Somali.
South Africa	South African.
South Sudan	South Sudanese.
Spain	Spaniard.
Sri Lanka	Sri Lankan.
Sudan	Sudanese (singular and plural).
Suriname	Surinamer.
Swaziland	Swazi.
Sweden	Swede.
Switzerland	Swiss (singular and plural).

Demonyms: Names of Nationalities—Continued

[Demonym is a name given to a people or inhabitants of a place.]

Country	Demonym*	Country	Demonym*
Syria	Syrian.	United Arab Emirates	Emirati.
Taiwan	Taiwan (singular and plural).	United Kingdom	Briton, British (collective plural).
Tajikistan	Tajikistani.	United States	American.
Tanzania	Tanzanian.	Uruguay	Uruguayan.
Thailand	Thai (singular and plural).	Uzbekistan	Uzbekistani.
Timor-Leste	Timorese (singular and plural).	Vanuatu	Ni-Vanuatu (singular and plural).
Togo	Togolese (singular and plural).	Venezuela	Venezuelan.
Tokelau	Tokelauan.	Vietnam	Vietnamese (singular and plural).
Tonga	Tongan.	Virgin Islands	Virgin Islander.
Trinidad and Tobago	Trinidadian, Tobagonian.	Wallis and Futuna	Wallisian, Futunan, or Wallis and Futuna Islander.
Tunisia	Tunisian.	Western Sahara	Sahrawi, Sahraoui.
Turkey	Turk.	Yemen	Yemeni.
Turkmenistan	Turkmen.	Zambia	Zambian.
Tuvalu	Tuvaluan.	Zimbabwe	Zimbabwean.
Uganda	Ugandan.		
Ukraine	Ukrainian.		

[1] Since 1989 the military authorities in Burma have promoted the name Myanmar as a conventional name for their state; this decision was not approved by any sitting legislature in Burma, and the U.S. Government did not adopt the name, which is a derivative of the Burmese short-form name Myanma Naingngandaw.

*NOTE.—Plural references add *s* unless otherwise indicated.

Source: Information courtesy of World Factbook as of September 2016; for more information see https://www.cia.gov/library/publications/resources/the-world-factbook/fields/2110.html.

Currency

[As of July 2016]

Country	Currency	Alphabetic code
Afghanistan	Afghani	AFN
Åland Islands	Euro	EUR
Albania	Lek	ALL
Algeria	Algerian dinar	DZD
American Samoa	U.S. dollar	USD
Andorra	Euro	EUR
Angola	Kwanza	AOA
Anguilla	East Caribbean dollar	XCD
Antarctica	No universal currency	
Antigua and Barbuda	East Caribbean dollar	XCD
Argentina	Argentine peso	ARS
Armenia	Armenian dram	AMD
Aruba	Aruban florin	AWG
Australia	Australian dollar	AUD
Austria	Euro	EUR
Azerbaijan	Azerbaijanian manat	AZN
Bahamas (The)	Bahamian dollar	BSD
Bahrain	Bahraini dinar	BHD
Bangladesh	Taka	BDT
Barbados	Barbados dollar	BBD
Belarus	Belarusian ruble	BYN
Belarus	Belarusian ruble	BYR
Belgium	Euro	EUR
Belize	Belize dollar	BZD

Currency—Continued

[As of July 2016]

Country	Currency	Alphabetic code
Benin	CFA franc BCEAO	XOF
Bermuda	Bermudian dollar	BMD
Bhutan	Indian rupee	INR
Bhutan	Ngultrum	BTN
Bolivia (Plurinational State of)	Boliviano	BOB
Bolivia (Plurinational State of)	Mvdol	BOV
Bonaire, Sint Eustatius and Saba	U.S. dollar	USD
Bosnia and Herzegovina	Convertible mark	BAM
Botswana	Pula	BWP
Bouvet Island	Norwegian krone	NOK
Brazil	Brazilian real	BRL
British Indian Ocean Territory (The)	U.S. dollar	USD
Brunei Darussalam	Brunei dollar	BND
Bulgaria	Bulgarian lev	BGN
Burkina Faso	CFA franc BCEAO	XOF
Burundi	Burundi franc	BIF
Cabo Verde	Cabo Verde escudo	CVE
Cambodia	Riel	KHR
Cameroon	CFA franc BEAC	XAF
Canada	Canadian dollar	CAD
Cayman Islands (The)	Cayman Islands dollar	KYD
Central African Republic (The)	CFA franc BEAC	XAF
Chad	CFA franc BEAC	XAF
Chile	Chilean peso	CLP
Chile	Unidad de Fomento	CLF
China	Yuan renminbi	CNY
Christmas Island	Australian dollar	AUD
Cocos (Keeling) Islands (The)	Australian dollar	AUD
Colombia	Colombian peso	COP
Colombia	Unidad de Valor real	COU
Comoros (The)	Comoro franc	KMF
Congo (The Democratic Republic of the)	Congolese franc	CDF
Congo (The)	CFA franc BEAC	XAF
Cook Islands (The)	New Zealand dollar	NZD
Costa Rica	Costa Rican colon	CRC
Côte d'Ivoire	CFA franc BCEAO	XOF
Croatia	Kuna	HRK
Cuba	Cuban peso	CUP
Cuba	Peso convertible	CUC
Curaçao	Netherlands Antillean guilder	ANG
Cyprus	Euro	EUR
Czech Republic (The)	Czech koruna	CZK
Denmark	Danish krone	DKK
Djibouti	Djibouti franc	DJF
Dominica	East Caribbean dollar	XCD
Dominican Republic (The)	Dominican peso	DOP
Ecuador	U.S. dollar	USD
Egypt	Egyptian pound	EGP
El Salvador	El Salvador colon	SVC
El Salvador	U.S. dollar	USD
Equatorial Guinea	CFA franc BEAC	XAF
Eritrea	Nakfa	ERN
Estonia	Euro	EUR
Ethiopia	Ethiopian birr	ETB
European Union	Euro	EUR
Falkland Islands (The) [Malvinas]	Falkland Islands pound	FKP
Faroe Islands (The)	Danish krone	DKK
Fiji	Fiji dollar	FJD
Finland	Euro	EUR

Currency—Continued

[As of July 2016]

Country	Currency	Alphabetic code
France	Euro	EUR
French Guiana	Euro	EUR
French Polynesia	CFP franc	XPF
French Southern Territories (The)	Euro	EUR
Gabon	CFA franc BEAC	XAF
Gambia (The)	Dalasi	GMD
Georgia	Lari	GEL
Germany	Euro	EUR
Ghana	Ghana cedi	GHS
Gibraltar	Gibraltar pound	GIP
Greece	Euro	EUR
Greenland	Danish krone	DKK
Grenada	East Caribbean dollar	XCD
Guadeloupe	Euro	EUR
Guam	U.S. dollar	USD
Guatemala	Quetzal	GTQ
Guernsey	Pound sterling	GBP
Guinea	Guinea franc	GNF
Guinea-Bissau	CFA franc BCEAO	XOF
Guyana	Guyana dollar	GYD
Haiti	Gourde	HTG
Haiti	U.S. dollar	USD
Heard Island and McDonald Islands	Australian dollar	AUD
Holy See (The)	Euro	EUR
Honduras	Lempira	HNL
Hong Kong	Hong Kong dollar	HKD
Hungary	Forint	HUF
Iceland	Iceland krona	ISK
India	Indian rupee	INR
Indonesia	Rupiah	IDR
International Monetary Fund (IMF)	SDR (Special Drawing Right)	XDR
Iran (Islamic Republic of)	Iranian rial	IRR
Iraq	Iraqi dinar	IQD
Ireland	Euro	EUR
Isle of Man	Pound sterling	GBP
Israel	New Israeli sheqel	ILS
Italy	Euro	EUR
Jamaica	Jamaican dollar	JMD
Japan	Yen	JPY
Jersey	Pound sterling	GBP
Jordan	Jordanian dinar	JOD
Kazakhstan	Tenge	KZT
Kenya	Kenyan shilling	KES
Kiribati	Australian dollar	AUD
Korea (The Democratic People's Republic of)	North Korean won	KPW
Korea (The Republic of)	Won	KRW
Kuwait	Kuwaiti dinar	KWD
Kyrgyzstan	Som	KGS
Lao People's Democratic Republic (The)	Kip	LAK
Latvia	Euro	EUR
Lebanon	Lebanese pound	LBP
Lesotho	Loti	LSL
Lesotho	Rand	ZAR
Liberia	Liberian dollar	LRD
Libya	Libyan dinar	LYD
Liechtenstein	Swiss franc	CHF
Lithuania	Euro	EUR
Luxembourg	Euro	EUR
Macao	Pataca	MOP

Currency—Continued

[As of July 2016]

Country	Currency	Alphabetic code
Macedonia (The Former Yugoslav Republic of)	Denar	MKD
Madagascar	Malagasy ariary	MGA
Malawi	Malawi kwacha	MWK
Malaysia	Malaysian ringgit	MYR
Maldives	Rufiyaa	MVR
Mali	CFA franc BCEAO	XOF
Malta	Euro	EUR
Marshall Islands (The)	U.S. dollar	USD
Martinique	Euro	EUR
Mauritania	Ouguiya	MRO
Mauritius	Mauritius rupee	MUR
Mayotte	Euro	EUR
Member Countries of the African Development Bank Group	ADB Unit of Account	XUA
Mexico	Mexican peso	MXN
Mexico	Mexican Unidad de Inversion (UDI)	MXV
Micronesia (Federated States of)	U.S. dollar	USD
Moldova (The Republic of)	Moldovan leu	MDL
Monaco	Euro	EUR
Mongolia	Tugrik	MNT
Montenegro	Euro	EUR
Montserrat	East Caribbean dollar	XCD
Morocco	Moroccan dirham	MAD
Mozambique	Mozambique metical	MZN
Myanmar	Kyat	MMK
Namibia	Namibia dollar	NAD
Namibia	Rand	ZAR
Nauru	Australian dollar	AUD
Nepal	Nepalese rupee	NPR
Netherlands (The)	Euro	EUR
New Caledonia	CFP franc	XPF
New Zealand	New Zealand dollar	NZD
Nicaragua	Cordoba oro	NIO
Niger (The)	CFA franc BCEAO	XOF
Nigeria	Naira	NGN
Niue	New Zealand dollar	NZD
Norfolk Island	Australian dollar	AUD
Northern Mariana Islands (The)	U.S. dollar	USD
Norway	Norwegian krone	NOK
Oman	Rial omani	OMR
Pakistan	Pakistan rupee	PKR
Palau	U.S. dollar	USD
Palestine, State of	No universal currency	
Panama	Balboa	PAB
Panama	U.S. dollar	USD
Papua New Guinea	Kina	PGK
Paraguay	Guarani	PYG
Peru	Sol	PEN
Philippines (The)	Philippine peso	PHP
Pitcairn	New Zealand dollar	NZD
Poland	Zloty	PLN
Portugal	Euro	EUR
Puerto Rico	U.S. dollar	USD
Qatar	Qatari rial	QAR
Réunion	Euro	EUR
Romania	Romanian leu	RON
Russian Federation (The)	Russian ruble	RUB
Rwanda	Rwanda franc	RWF
Saint Barthélemy	Euro	EUR

Currency—Continued

[As of July 2016]

Country	Currency	Alphabetic code
Saint Helena, Ascension and Tristan Da Cunha	Saint Helena pound	SHP
Saint Kitts and Nevis	East Caribbean dollar	XCD
Saint Lucia	East Caribbean dollar	XCD
Saint Martin (French Part)	Euro	EUR
Saint Pierre and Miquelon	Euro	EUR
Saint Vincent and the Grenadines	East Caribbean dollar	XCD
Samoa	Tala	WST
San Marino	Euro	EUR
Sao Tome and Principe	Dobra	STD
Saudi Arabia	Saudi riyal	SAR
Senegal	CFA franc BCEAO	XOF
Serbia	Serbian dinar	RSD
Seychelles	Seychelles rupee	SCR
Sierra Leone	Leone	SLL
Singapore	Singapore dollar	SGD
Sint Maarten (Dutch Part)	Netherlands Antillean guilder	ANG
Sistema Unitario De Compensacion Regional De Pagos "Sucre"	Sucre	XSU
Slovakia	Euro	EUR
Slovenia	Euro	EUR
Solomon Islands	Solomon Islands dollar	SBD
Somalia	Somali shilling	SOS
South Africa	Rand	ZAR
South Georgia and the South Sandwich Islands	No universal currency	
South Sudan	South Sudanese pound	SSP
Spain	Euro	EUR
Sri Lanka	Sri Lanka rupee	LKR
Sudan (The)	Sudanese pound	SDG
Suriname	Surinam dollar	SRD
Svalbard and Jan Mayen	Norwegian krone	NOK
Swaziland	Lilangeni	SZL
Sweden	Swedish krona	SEK
Switzerland	Swiss franc	CHF
Switzerland	WIR Euro	CHE
Switzerland	WIR franc	CHW
Syrian Arab Republic	Syrian pound	SYP
Taiwan (Province of China)	New Taiwan dollar	TWD
Tajikistan	Somoni	TJS
Tanzania, United Republic of	Tanzanian shilling	TZS
Thailand	Baht	THB
Timor-Leste	U.S. dollar	USD
Togo	CFA franc BCEAO	XOF
Tokelau	New Zealand dollar	NZD
Tonga	Pa'anga	TOP
Trinidad and Tobago	Trinidad and Tobago dollar	TTD
Tunisia	Tunisian dinar	TND
Turkey	Turkish lira	TRY
Turkmenistan	Turkmenistan new manat	TMT
Turks and Caicos Islands (The)	U.S. dollar	USD
Tuvalu	Australian dollar	AUD
Uganda	Uganda shilling	UGX
Ukraine	Hryvnia	UAH
United Arab Emirates (The)	UAE dirham	AED
United Kingdom of Great Britain and Northern Ireland (The)	Pound sterling	GBP
United States Minor Outlying Islands (The)	U.S. dollar	USD
United States of America (The)	U.S. dollar	USD

Currency—Continued

[As of July 2016]

Country	Currency	Alphabetic code
United States of America (The)	U.S. dollar (Next day)	USN
Uruguay	Peso Uruguayo	UYU
Uruguay	Uruguay peso en Unidades Indexadas (URUIURUI)	UYI
Uzbekistan	Uzbekistan sum	UZS
Vanuatu	Vatu	VUV
Venezuela (Bolivarian Republic of)	Bolívar	VEF
Viet Nam	Dong	VND
Virgin Islands (British)	U.S. dollar	USD
Virgin Islands (U.S.)	U.S. dollar	USD
Wallis and Futuna	CFP franc	XPF
Western Sahara	Moroccan dirham	MAD
Yemen	Yemeni rial	YER
Zambia	Zambian kwacha	ZMW
Zimbabwe	Zimbabwe dollar	ZWL

Source: http://www.currency-iso.org/en/home/tables/table-a.1.html.

Metric and U.S. Measures[1]

Length

Metric unit		U.S. unit	
10 millimeters	1 centimeter.	12 inches	1 foot (ft).
10 centimeters	1 decimeter.	3 feet	1 yard.
10 decimeters	1 meter.	22 yards	1 chain.
10 meters	1 dekameter.	10 chains	1 furlong (660 ft).
10 dekameters	1 hectometer.	8 furlongs	1 mile (5,280 ft).
10 hectometers	1 kilometer.	1 nautical mile	1.1508 mile.
1 kilometer	1,000 meters.	1 league	3 nautical miles.

Mass Weight

Metric unit		U.S. unit	
10 milligrams (mg)	1 centigram.	16 ounces	1 pound.
10 centigrams	1 decigram (100 mg).	100 pounds (lbs)	1 hundredweight.
10 decigrams	1 gram (1,000 mg).	2,000 lbs	1 ton.
10 grams (g)	1 dekagram.		
10 dekagrams	1 hectogram (100 g).		
10 hectograms	1 kilogram (1,000 g).		
1,000 kilograms	1 metric ton.		

Volume

Metric unit		U.S. liquid capacity	
10 milliliters	1 centiliter.	3 teaspoons	1 tablespoon.
10 centiliters	1 deciliter.	2 tablespoons	1 fluid ounce (fl oz).
10 deciliters	1 liter.	1 cup	8 fl oz.
1,000 liters	1 cubic meter.	2 cups	1 pint.
		2 pints	1 quart.
		4 quarts	1 gallon.
		42 gallons	1 petroleum barrel.
		U.S. dry measure[2]	
		2 pints	1 quart.
		4 quarts	1 gallon.
		2 gallons	1 peck.
		4 pecks	1 bushel.
		8 bushels	1 quarter.

Temperature Conversion[3]

Celsius	Fahrenheit	Kelvin	Celsius	Fahrenheit	Kelvin
100	212	373.1	0	32	273.1
50	122	323.1	-10	14	263.1
40	104	313.1	-20	-4	253.1
30	86	303.1	-30	-22	243.1
20	68	293.1	-40	-40	233.1
10	50	283.1	-50	-58	223.1
			-273.1	-459.7	0

[1] At this time, only three countries—Burma, Liberia, and the United States—have not significantly transitioned to the International System of Units (SI, or metric system) as their official system of weights and measures.

[2] Dry measurements are mainly used for measuring grain or fresh produce. Do not confuse dry measure for liquid measure, as they are not the same.

[3] The equation for converting temperatures is as follows: °C to °F: multiply by 9, then divide by 5, then add 32; °F to °C: subtract 32, then multiply by 5, then divide by 9.

Common Measures and Their Metric Equivalents

U.S. to metric		Metric to U.S.	
Inch	2.54 centimeters.	Centimeter	0.3937 inch.
Foot	0.3048 meter.	Meter	3.2808 feet.
Yard	0.9144 meter.	Do	1.0936 yards.
Mile	1.6093 kilometers.	Kilometer	0.6214 mile.
Nautical mile	1.852 kilometers.	Do	0.5399 nautical mile.
League	5.556 kilometers.	Do	0.1799 league.
Square inch	6.452 square centimeters.	Square centimeter	0.155 square inch.
Square foot	0.0929 square meter.	Square meter	10.7639 square feet.
Square yard	0.836 square meter.	Do	1.196 square yards.
Acre	0.4047 hectare.	Hectare	2.471 acres.
Square mile	259 hectares.	Do	0.0039 square mile.
Cubic inch	16.39 cubic centimeters.	Cubic centimeter	0.06 cubic inch.
Cubic foot	0.0283 cubic meter.	Cubic meter	35.3146 cubic feet.
Cubic yard	0.7646 cubic meter.	Do	1.3079 cubic yards.
Cord	128 cubic feet.		
Ounce (liquid)	29.574 milliliters.	Milliliter	0.0338 ounce (liquid).
Pint (liquid)	473.176 milliliters.		
Quart (liquid)	946.35 milliliters.	Liter	1.06 quarts (liquid).
Gallon (liquid)	3.79 liters.	Do	0.26 gallon (liquid).
Pint (dry)	550.61 milliliters.		
Quart (dry)	1101 milliliters.	Do	0.91 quart (dry).
Quart, imperial	1137 milliliters.		
Gallon (dry)	4.40 liters.	Do	0.23 gallon (dry).
Gallon, imperial	4.55 liters.		
Peck	8.810 liters.	Do	0.1135 peck.
Peck, imperial	9.092 liters.		
Bushel	35.24 liters.	Do	0.028 bushel.
Bushel, imperial	36.37 liters.		
Grain[1]	64.799 milligrams.		
Ounce[2]	28.35 grams.	Gram	0.04 ounce.
Ounce, troy[3]	31.103 grams.	Do	0.032 troy ounce.
Pound[2]	0.4536 kilogram.	Kilogram	2.20 pounds.
Pound, troy	12 troy ounces.		
Ton, short	907.185 kilograms.		
Do	2,000 pounds.		
Ton, metric	1,000 kilograms.		
Do	2,204.6 pounds.		
Ton, long	1,016.047 kilograms.		
Do	2,240 pounds.		

[1] The grain is used to measure in ballistics and archery; grains were originally used in medicine but have been replaced by milligrams.

[2] Avoirdupois; avoirdupois is the measure of mass of everyday items.

[3] The troy ounce is used in pricing silver, gold, platinum, and other precious metals and gemstones.

Measurement Conversion

Fractional inch	Decimal inches	Milli-meters	Picas	Points	Fractional inch	Decimal inches	Milli-meters	Picas	Points
1/16	.0625	1.587	0p4.5	4.5	7/8	.875	22.225	5p3	63
1/8	.125	3.175	0p9	9	15/16	.9375	23.812	5p7.5	67.5
3/16	.1875	4.762	1p1.5	13.5	1	1	25.4	6	72
1/4	.25	6.35	1p6	18	1 1/4	1.25	31.75	7p6	90
5/16	.3125	7.937	1p10.5	22.5	1 1/2	1.5	38.1	9	108
3/8	.375	9.525	2p3	27	1 3/4	1.75	44.5	10p6	126
7/16	.4375	11.112	2p7.5	31.5	2	2	50.8	12	144
1/2	.5	12.7	3	36	2 1/2	2.5	63.5	15	180
9/16	.5625	14.287	3p4.5	40.5	3	3	76.2	18	216
5/8	.625	15.875	3p9	45	3 1/2	3.5	88.9	21	252
11/16	.6875	17.462	4p1.5	49.5	4	4	100.6	24	288
3/4	.75	19.05	4p6	54	5	5	127	30	360
13/16	.8125	20.637	4p10.5	58.5	6	6	152.4	36	432

18. Geologic Terms and Geographic Divisions

Geologic terms

For capitalization, compounding, and use of quotations in geologic terms, copy is to be followed. Geologic terms quoted verbatim from published material should be left as the original author used them; however, it should be made clear that the usage is that of the original author.

Formal geologic terms are capitalized: Proterozoic Eon, Cambrian Period. Structural terms such as arch, anticline, or uplift are capitalized when preceded by a name: Cincinnati Arch, Cedar Creek Anticline, Ozark Uplift. See Chapter 4 geographic terms for more information.

Divisions of Geologic Time
[Most recent to oldest]

Eon	Era	Period
Phanerozoic	Cenozoic	Quaternary.
		Tertiary (Neogene, Paleogene).
	Mesozoic	Cretaceous.
		Jurassic.
		Triassic.
	Paleozoic	Permian.
		Carboniferous (Pennsylvanian, Mississippian).
		Devonian.
		Silurian.
		Ordovician.
		Cambrian.
Proterozoic	Neoproterozoic	Ediacaran.
		Cryogenian.
		Tonian.
	Mesoproterozoic	Stenian.
		Ectasian.
		Calymmian.
	Paleoproterozoic	Statherian.
		Orosirian.
		Rhyacian.
		Siderian.
Archean	Neoarchean.	
	Mesoarchean.	
	Paleoarchean.	
	Eoarchean.	
Hadean.		

Source: Information courtesy of the U.S. Geological Survey; for graphic see http://pubs.usgs.gov/fs/2007/3015/fs2007-3015.pdf.

Physiographic regions

Physiographic regions are based on terrain texture, rock type, and geologic structure and history. The classification system has three tiers: divisions, which are broken into provinces, and some provinces break further into sections. All names are capitalized, not the class; for graphic see http://tapestry.usgs.gov/physiogr/physio.html.

Physiographic Regions of the Lower 48 United States

Division	Province	Section
Laurentian Upland	Superior Upland.	
Atlantic Plain	Continental Shelf.	
	Coastal Plain	Embayed.
		Sea Island.
		Floridian.
		East Gulf Coastal Plain.
		Mississippi Alluvial Plain.
		West Gulf Coastal Plain.
Appalachian Highlands	Piedmont	Piedmont Upland.
		Piedmont Lowlands.
	Blue Ridge	Northern.
		Southern.
	Valley and Ridge	Tennessee.
		Middle.
		Hudson Valley.
	St. Lawrence Valley	Champlain.
		Northern.
	Appalachian Plateaus	Mohawk.
		Catskill.
		Southern New York.
		Allegheny Mountain.
		Kanawha.
		Cumberland Plateau.
		Cumberland Mountain.
	New England	Seaboard Lowland.
		New England Upland.
		White Mountain.
		Green Mountain.
		Taconic.
	Adirondack.	
Interior Plains	Interior Low Plateaus	Highland Rim.
		Lexington Plain.
		Nashville Basin.
	Central Lowland	Eastern Lake.
		Western Lake.
		Wisconsin Driftless.
		Till Plains.
		Dissected Till Plains.
		Osage Plains.

Division	Province	Section
	Great Plains	Missouri Plateau, glaciated.
		Missouri Plateau, unglaciated.
		Black Hills.
		High Plains.
		Plains Border.
		Colorado Piedmont.
		Raton.
		Pecos Valley.
		Edwards Plateau.
		Central Texas.
Interior Highlands	Ozark Plateaus	Springfield-Salem Plateaus.
		Boston "Mountains."
	Ouachita	Arkansas Valley.
		Ouachita Mountains.
Rocky Mountain System	Southern Rocky Mountains.	
	Wyoming Basin.	
	Middle Rocky Mountains.	
	Northern Rocky Mountains.	
Intermontane Plateaus	Columbia Plateau	Walla Walla Plateau.
		Blue Mountain.
		Payette.
		Snake River Plain.
		Harney.
	Colorado Plateaus	High Plateaus of Utah.
		Uinta Basin.
		Canyon Lands.
		Navajo.
		Grand Canyon.
		Datil.
	Basin and Range	Great Basin.
		Sonoran Desert.
		Salton Trough.
		Mexican Highland.
		Sacramento.
Pacific Mountain System	Cascade-Sierra Mountains	Northern Cascade Mountains.
		Middle Cascade Mountains.
		Southern Cascade Mountains.
		Sierra Nevada.
	Pacific Border	Puget Trough.
		Olympic Mountains.
		Oregon Coast Range.
		Klamath Mountains.
		California Trough.
		California Coast Ranges.
		Los Angeles Ranges.
	Lower California.	

Source: Information courtesy of the U.S. Geological Survey.

Geographic divisions

The Public Land Survey System has a hierarchy of lines. Principal meridians and base lines and their related townships, sections, and subdivisions of sections are incorporated in the description of land conveyed by the Federal Government and others.

The Principal Meridians and Base Lines of the United States [1]

Black Hills Meridian and Base Line. (South Dakota)	New Mexico Principal Meridian and Base Line. (New Mexico-Colorado)
Boise Meridian and Base Line. (Idaho)	Point of Beginning and Geographer's Line. (Ohio)
Chickasaw Meridian and Base Line. (Mississippi-Tennessee)	Principal Meridian and Base Line. (Montana)
Choctaw Meridian and Base Line. (Mississippi)	Salt Lake Meridian and Base Line. (Utah)
Cimarron Meridian and Base Line. (Oklahoma)	San Bernardino Meridian and Base Line. (California-Nevada)
Copper River Meridian and Base Line. (Alaska)	Second Principal Meridian and Base Line. (Illinois-Indiana)
Fairbanks Meridian and Base Line. (Alaska)	Seward Principal Meridian and Base Line. (Alaska)
Fifth Principal Meridian and Base Line. (Arkansas-Iowa-Minnesota-Missouri-North Dakota-South Dakota)	Sixth Principal Meridian and Base Line. (Colorado-Kansas-Nebraska-South Dakota-Wyoming)
First Principal Meridian and Base Line. (Ohio-Indiana)	St. Helena Meridian and Base Line. (Louisiana)
Fourth Principal Meridian and Base Line. (Illinois)	St. Stephens Meridian and Base Line. (Alabama-Mississippi)
Fourth Principal Meridian and Base Line Wisconsin. (Minnesota-Wisconsin)	Tallahassee Meridian and Base Line. (Florida)
Gila and Salt River Meridian and Base Line. (Arizona)	Third Principal Meridian and Base Line. (Illinois)
Humboldt Meridian and Base Line. (California)	Uintah Special Meridian and Base Line. (Utah)
Huntsville Meridian and Base Line. (Alabama-Mississippi)	Umiat Principal Meridian and Base Line. (Alaska)
Indian Meridian and Base Line. (Oklahoma)	Ute Principal Meridian and Base Line. (Colorado)
Kateel River Principal Meridian and Base Line. (Alaska)	Washington Meridian and Base Line. (Mississippi)
Louisiana Meridian and Base Line. (Louisiana-Texas)	Willamette Meridian and Base Line. (Oregon-Washington)
Michigan Meridian and Base Line. (Michigan-Ohio)	Wind River Meridian and Base Line. (Wyoming)
Mount Diablo Meridian and Base Line. (California-Nevada)	
Navajo Meridian and Base Line. (Arizona-New Mexico)	

[1] Information courtesy of the U.S. Department of the Interior, Bureau of Land Management.

Public Land Surveys Having No Initial Point as an Origin for Both Township and Range Numbers[1]

Between the Miamis, north of Symmes Purchase. (Ohio)	Scioto River Base. (Ohio)
Muskingum River Survey. (Ohio)	Twelve-Mile-Square Reserve. (Ohio)
Ohio River Base. (Indiana)	United States Military Survey. (Ohio)
Ohio River Survey. (Ohio)	West of the Great Miami. (Ohio)

[1] Information courtesy of the U.S. Department of the Interior, Bureau of Land Management.

Sources: Manual of Surveying Instructions: For the Survey of the Public Lands of the United States, Bureau of Land Management, 2009, GPO; Initial Points of the Rectangular Survey System, C. Albert White, 1996.

See http://www.blm.gov/wo/st/en/prog/more/cadastralsurvey.html for more information on prinicipal meridians and base lines.

Major Rivers of the World

River	Length (in miles)	River	Length (in miles)
Nile (Africa)	4,160	MacKenzie (Canada)	2,635
Amazon (S. America)	4,000	Mekong (Vietnam)	2,600
Yangtze (China)	3,964	Niger (Africa)	2,590
Yellow (China)	3,395	Yenisey (Russia)	2,543
Ob-Irtysh (Russia)	3,362	Missouri (U.S.)	2,540
Amur (Asia)	2,744	Parana (S. America)	2,485
Lena (Russia)	2,734	Mississippi (U.S.)	2,340
Congo (Africa)	2,718	Murray-Darling (Australia)	2,310

NOTE.—Information compiled from numerous public domain websites; references cite different lengths for the same river depending on origin.

Major Rivers of the United States

River	Length (in miles)	River	Length (in miles)
Missouri	2,540	Ohio	1,310
Mississippi	2,340	Red	1,290
Yukon	1,980	Brazos	1,280
Rio Grande	1,900	Columbia	1,249
St. Lawrence	1,900	Snake	1,040
Arkansas	1,469	Platte	990
Colorado	1,450	Pecos	926
Atchafalaya	1,420	Canadian	906

Source: Information courtesy of the U.S. Geological Survey; see http://water.usgs.gov/edu/riversofworld.html.

States, capitals, and counties

The following includes parishes, boroughs, census divisions, districts, islands, municipalities, and "municipios" of the 50 States, U.S. possessions, and territories. County totals include city counties as defined by the National Association of Counties. See www.naco.org for more information.

ALABAMA (AL) (67 counties)
Capital: Montgomery

Autauga
Baldwin
Barbour
Bibb
Blount
Bullock
Butler
Calhoun
Chambers
Cherokee
Chilton
Choctaw
Clarke
Clay
Cleburne
Coffee
Colbert
Conecuh
Coosa
Covington
Crenshaw
Cullman
Dale
Dallas
DeKalb
Elmore
Escambia
Etowah
Fayette
Franklin
Geneva
Greene
Hale
Henry
Houston
Jackson
Jefferson
Lamar
Lauderdale
Lawrence
Lee
Limestone
Lowndes
Macon
Madison
Marengo
Marion
Marshall
Mobile
Monroe
Montgomery
Morgan
Perry
Pickens
Pike
Randolph
Russell
St. Clair
Shelby
Sumter
Talladega
Tallapoosa
Tuscaloosa
Walker
Washington
Wilcox
Winston

ALASKA (AK) (29 entities: 19 boroughs,* 10 census areas)
Capital: Juneau

Aleutians East*
Aleutians West
Anchorage*
Bethel
Bristol Bay*
Denali*
Dillingham
Fairbanks North Star*
Haines*
Hoonah-Angoon
Juneau*
Kenai Peninsula*
Ketchikan Gateway*
Kodiak Island*
Kusilvak
Lake and Peninsula*
Matanuska-Susitna*
Nome
North Slope*
Northwest Arctic*
Petersburg*
Prince of Wales-Hyder
Sitka*
Skagway*
Southeast Fairbanks
Valdez-Cordova
Wrangell*
Yakutat*
Yukon-Koyukuk

AMERICAN SAMOA (AS) (5 entities: 2 islands,* 3 districts)
Capital: Pago Pago

Eastern
Manu'a
Rose*
Swains*
Western

ARIZONA (AZ) (15 counties)
Capital: Phoenix

Apache	Gila	La Paz	Navajo	Santa Cruz
Cochise	Graham	Maricopa	Pima	Yavapai
Coconino	Greenlee	Mohave	Pinal	Yum

ARKANSAS (AR) (75 counties)
Capital: Little Rock

Arkansas	Craighead	Howard	Miller	Randolph
Ashley	Crawford	Independence	Mississippi	St. Francis
Baxter	Crittenden	Izard	Monroe	Saline
Benton	Cross	Jackson	Montgomery	Scott
Boone	Dallas	Jefferson	Nevada	Searcy
Bradley	Desha	Johnson	Newton	Sebastian
Calhoun	Drew	Lafayette	Ouachita	Sevier
Carroll	Faulkner	Lawrence	Perry	Sharp
Chicot	Franklin	Lee	Phillips	Stone
Clark	Fulton	Lincoln	Pike	Union
Clay	Garland	Little River	Poinsett	Van Buren
Cleburne	Grant	Logan	Polk	Washington
Cleveland	Greene	Lonoke	Pope	White
Columbia	Hempstead	Madison	Prairie	Woodruff
Conway	Hot Spring	Marion	Pulaski	Yell

CALIFORNIA (CA) (58 counties)
Capital: Sacramento

Alameda	Imperial	Modoc	San Diego	Solano
Alpine	Inyo	Mono	San Francisco	Sonoma
Amador	Kern	Monterey	San Joaquin	Stanislaus
Butte	Kings	Napa	San Luis Obispo	Sutter
Calaveras	Lake	Nevada		Tehama
Colusa	Lassen	Orange	San Mateo	Trinity
Contra Costa	Los Angeles	Placer	Santa Barbara	Tulare
Del Norte	Madera	Plumas	Santa Clara	Tuolumne
El Dorado	Marin	Riverside	Santa Cruz	Ventura
Fresno	Mariposa	Sacramento	Shasta	Yolo
Glenn	Mendocino	San Benito	Sierra	Yuba
Humboldt	Merced	San Bernardino	Siskiyou	

COLORADO (CO) (64 counties)
Capital: Denver

Adams
Alamosa
Arapahoe
Archuleta
Baca
Bent
Boulder
Broomfield
Chaffee
Cheyenne
Clear Creek
Conejos
Costilla
Crowley
Custer
Delta
Denver
Dolores
Douglas
Eagle
Elbert
El Paso
Fremont
Garfield
Gilpin
Grand
Gunnison
Hinsdale
Huerfano
Jackson
Jefferson
Kiowa
Kit Carson
Lake
La Plata
Larimer
Las Animas
Lincoln
Logan
Mesa
Mineral
Moffat
Montezuma
Montrose
Morgan
Otero
Ouray
Park
Phillips
Pitkin
Prowers
Pueblo
Rio Blanco
Rio Grande
Routt
Saguache
San Juan
San Miguel
Sedgwick
Summit
Teller
Washington
Weld
Yuma

CONNECTICUT (CT) (8 counties)
Capital: Hartford

Fairfield
Hartford
Litchfield
Middlesex
New Haven
New London
Tolland
Windham

DELAWARE (DE) (3 counties)
Capital: Dover

Kent
New Castle
Sussex

DISTRICT OF COLUMBIA (DC) (single entity)

FEDERATED STATES OF MICRONESIA (FM) (4 States)
Capital: Palikir

Chuuk
Kosrae
Pohnpei
Yap

FLORIDA (FL) (67 counties)
Capital: Tallahassee

Alachua
Baker
Bay
Bradford
Brevard
Broward
Calhoun
Charlotte
Citrus
Clay
Collier
Columbia
DeSoto
Dixie
Duval
Escambia
Flagler
Franklin
Gadsden
Gilchrist
Glades
Gulf
Hamilton
Hardee
Hendry
Hernando
Highlands
Hillsborough
Holmes
Indian River
Jackson
Jefferson
Lafayette
Lake
Lee

Leon
Levy
Liberty
Madison
Manatee
Marion
Martin
Miami-Dade
Monroe
Nassau
Okaloosa
Okeechobee
Orange
Osceola
Palm Beach
Pasco
Pinellas
Polk
Putnam
St. Johns
St. Lucie
Santa Rosa
Sarasota
Seminole
Sumter
Suwannee
Taylor
Union
Volusia
Wakulla
Walton
Washington

GEORGIA (GA) (159 counties)
Capital: Atlanta

Appling
Atkinson
Bacon
Baker
Baldwin
Banks
Barrow
Bartow
Ben Hill
Berrien
Bibb
Bleckley
Brantley
Brooks
Bryan
Bulloch
Burke
Butts
Calhoun
Camden
Candler
Carroll
Catoosa
Charlton
Chatham
Chattahoochee
Chattooga
Cherokee
Clarke
Clay
Clayton
Clinch
Cobb
Coffee
Colquitt
Columbia
Cook
Coweta
Crawford
Crisp
Dade
Dawson
Decatur
DeKalb
Dodge
Dooly
Dougherty
Douglas
Early
Echols
Effingham
Elbert
Emanuel
Evans
Fannin
Fayette
Floyd
Forsyth
Franklin
Fulton
Gilmer
Glascock
Glynn
Gordon
Grady
Greene
Gwinnett
Habersham
Hall
Hancock
Haralson
Harris
Hart
Heard
Henry
Houston
Irwin
Jackson
Jasper
Jeff Davis
Jefferson
Jenkins
Johnson
Jones
Lamar
Lanier
Laurens
Lee
Liberty
Lincoln
Long
Lowndes
Lumpkin
McDuffie
McIntosh
Macon
Madison
Marion
Meriwether
Miller
Mitchell
Monroe
Montgomery
Morgan
Murray
Muscogee
Newton
Oconee
Oglethorpe
Paulding
Peach
Pickens
Pierce
Pike
Polk
Pulaski
Putnam
Quitman
Rabun
Randolph
Richmond
Rockdale
Schley
Screven
Seminole
Spalding
Stephens
Stewart
Sumter
Talbot
Taliaferro
Tattnall
Taylor
Telfair
Terrell
Thomas
Tift
Toombs
Towns
Treutlen
Troup
Turner
Twiggs
Union
Upson
Walker
Walton
Ware
Warren
Washington
Wayne
Webster
Wheeler
White
Whitfield
Wilcox
Wilkes
Wilkinson
Worth

GUAM (GU) (single entity)
Capital: Agana

HAWAII (HI) (4 counties)
Capital: Honolulu

Hawaii
Honolulu
Kalawao
Kauai
Maui

IDAHO (ID) (44 counties)
Capital: Boise

Ada
Adams
Bannock
Bear Lake
Benewah
Bingham
Blaine
Boise
Bonner
Bonneville
Boundary
Butte
Camas
Canyon
Caribou
Cassia
Clark
Clearwater
Custer
Elmore
Franklin
Fremont
Gem
Gooding
Idaho
Jefferson
Jerome
Kootenai
Latah
Lemhi
Lewis
Lincoln
Madison
Minidoka
Nez Perce
Oneida
Owyhee
Payette
Power
Shoshone
Teton
Twin Falls
Valley
Washington

ILLINOIS (IL) (102 counties)
Capital: Springfield

Adams
Alexander
Bond
Boone
Brown
Bureau
Calhoun
Carroll
Cass
Champaign
Christian
Clark
Clay
Clinton
Coles
Cook
Crawford
Cumberland
DeKalb
De Witt
Douglas
DuPage
Edgar
Edwards
Effingham
Fayette
Ford
Franklin
Fulton
Gallatin
Greene
Grundy
Hamilton
Hancock
Hardin
Henderson
Henry
Iroquois
Jackson
Jasper
Jefferson
Jersey
Jo Daviess
Johnson
Kane
Kankakee
Kendall
Knox
Lake
LaSalle
Lawrence
Lee
Livingston
Logan
McDonough
McHenry
McLean
Macon
Macoupin
Madison
Marion
Marshall
Mason
Massac
Menard
Mercer
Monroe
Montgomery
Morgan
Moultrie
Ogle
Peoria
Perry
Piatt
Pike
Pope
Pulaski
Putnam
Randolph
Richland
Rock Island
St. Clair
Saline
Sangamon
Schuyler
Scott
Shelby
Stark
Stephenson
Tazewell
Union
Vermilion
Wabash
Warren
Washington
Wayne
White
Whiteside
Will
Williamson
Winnebago
Woodford

INDIANA (IN) (92 counties)
Capital: Indianapolis

Adams
Allen
Bartholomew
Benton
Blackford
Boone
Brown
Carroll
Cass
Clark
Clay
Clinton
Crawford
Daviess
Dearborn
Decatur
DeKalb
Delaware
Dubois
Elkhart
Fayette
Floyd
Fountain
Franklin
Fulton
Gibson
Grant
Greene
Hamilton
Hancock
Harrison
Hendricks
Henry
Howard
Huntington
Jackson
Jasper
Jay
Jefferson
Jennings
Johnson
Knox
Kosciusko
LaGrange
Lake
LaPorte
Lawrence
Madison
Marion
Marshall
Martin
Miami
Monroe
Montgomery
Morgan
Newton
Noble
Ohio
Orange
Owen
Parke
Perry
Pike
Porter
Posey
Pulaski
Putnam
Randolph
Ripley
Rush
St. Joseph
Scott
Shelby
Spencer
Starke
Steuben
Sullivan
Switzerland
Tippecanoe
Tipton
Union
Vanderburgh
Vermillion
Vigo
Wabash
Warren
Warrick
Washington
Wayne
Wells
White
Whitley

IOWA (IA) (99 counties)
Capital: Des Moines

Adair
Adams
Allamakee
Appanoose
Audubon
Benton
Black Hawk
Boone
Bremer
Buchanan
Buena Vista
Butler
Calhoun
Carroll
Cass
Cedar
Cerro Gordo
Cherokee
Chickasaw
Clarke
Clay
Clayton
Clinton
Crawford
Dallas
Davis
Decatur
Delaware
Des Moines
Dickinson
Dubuque
Emmet
Fayette
Floyd
Franklin
Fremont
Greene
Grundy
Guthrie
Hamilton
Hancock
Hardin
Harrison
Henry
Howard
Humboldt
Ida
Iowa
Jackson
Jasper
Jefferson
Johnson
Jones
Keokuk
Kossuth
Lee
Linn
Louisa
Lucas
Lyon
Madison
Mahaska
Marion
Marshall
Mills
Mitchell
Monona
Monroe
Montgomery
Muscatine
O'Brien
Osceola
Page
Palo Alto
Plymouth
Pocahontas
Polk
Pottawattamie
Poweshiek
Ringgold
Sac
Scott
Shelby
Sioux
Story
Tama
Taylor
Union
Van Buren
Wapello
Warren
Washington
Wayne
Webster
Winnebago
Winneshiek
Woodbury
Worth
Wright

KANSAS (KS) (105 counties)
Capital: Topeka

Allen
Anderson
Atchison
Barber
Barton
Bourbon
Brown
Butler
Chase
Chautauqua
Cherokee
Cheyenne
Clark
Clay
Cloud
Coffey
Comanche
Cowley
Crawford
Decatur
Dickinson
Doniphan
Douglas
Edwards
Elk
Ellis
Ellsworth
Finney
Ford
Franklin
Geary
Gove
Graham
Grant
Gray
Greeley
Greenwood
Hamilton
Harper
Harvey
Haskell
Hodgeman
Jackson
Jefferson
Jewell
Johnson
Kearny
Kingman
Kiowa
Labette
Lane
Leavenworth
Lincoln
Linn
Logan
Lyon
McPherson
Marion
Marshall
Meade
Miami
Mitchell
Montgomery
Morris
Morton
Nemaha
Neosho
Ness
Norton
Osage
Osborne
Ottawa
Pawnee
Phillips
Pottawatomie
Pratt
Rawlins
Reno
Republic
Rice
Riley
Rooks
Rush
Russell
Saline
Scott
Sedgwick
Seward
Shawnee
Sheridan
Sherman
Smith
Stafford
Stanton
Stevens
Sumner
Thomas
Trego
Wabaunsee
Wallace
Washington
Wichita
Wilson
Woodson
Wyandotte

KENTUCKY (KY) (120 counties)
Capital: Frankfort

Adair
Allen
Anderson
Ballard
Barren
Bath
Bell
Boone
Bourbon
Boyd
Boyle
Bracken
Breathitt
Breckinridge
Bullitt
Butler
Caldwell
Calloway
Campbell
Carlisle
Carroll
Carter
Casey
Christian
Clark
Clay
Clinton
Crittenden
Cumberland
Daviess
Edmonson
Elliott
Estill
Fayette
Fleming
Floyd
Franklin
Fulton
Gallatin
Garrard
Grant
Graves
Grayson
Green
Greenup
Hancock
Hardin
Harlan
Harrison
Hart
Henderson
Henry
Hickman
Hopkins
Jackson
Jefferson
Jessamine
Johnson
Kenton
Knott
Knox
Larue
Laurel
Lawrence
Lee
Leslie
Letcher
Lewis
Lincoln
Livingston
Logan
Lyon
McCracken
McCreary
McLean
Madison
Magoffin
Marion
Marshall
Martin

Mason
Meade
Menifee
Mercer
Metcalfe
Monroe
Montgomery
Morgan
Muhlenberg
Nelson
Nicholas
Ohio
Oldham
Owen
Owsley
Pendleton
Perry
Pike
Powell
Pulaski
Robertson
Rockcastle
Rowan
Russell
Scott
Shelby
Simpson
Spencer
Taylor
Todd
Trigg
Trimble
Union
Warren
Washington
Wayne
Webster
Whitley
Wolfe
Woodford

LOUISIANA (LA) (64 parishes)
Capital: Baton Rouge

Acadia
Allen
Ascension
Assumption
Avoyelles
Beauregard
Bienville
Bossier
Caddo
Calcasieu
Caldwell
Cameron
Catahoula
Claiborne
Concordia
De Soto
East Baton Rouge
East Carroll
East Feliciana
Evangeline
Franklin
Grant
Iberia
Iberville
Jackson
Jefferson
Jefferson Davis
Lafayette
Lafourche
La Salle
Lincoln
Livingston
Madison
Morehouse
Natchitoches
Orleans
Ouachita
Plaquemines
Pointe Coupee
Rapides
Red River
Richland
Sabine
St. Bernard
St. Charles
St. Helena
St. James
St. John the Baptist
St. Landry
St. Martin
St. Mary
St. Tammany
Tangipahoa
Tensas
Terrebonne
Union
Vermilion
Vernon
Washington
Webster
West Baton Rouge
West Carroll
West Feliciana
Winn

MAINE (ME) (16 counties)
Capital: Augusta

Androscoggin
Aroostook
Cumberland
Franklin
Hancock
Kennebec
Knox
Lincoln
Oxford
Penobscot
Piscataquis
Sagadahoc
Somerset
Waldo
Washington
York

MARSHALL ISLANDS (MH) (33 municipalities)
Capital: Majuro

Ailinginae
Ailinglaplap
Ailuk
Arno
Aur
Bikar
Bikini
Bokak
Ebon
Enewetak
Erikub
Jabat
Jaluit
Jemo
Kili
Kwajalein
Lae
Lib
Likiep
Majuro
Maloelap
Mejit
Mili
Namorik
Namu
Rongelap
Rongrik
Toke
Ujae
Ujelang
Utirik
Wotho
Wotje

MARYLAND (MD) (24 counties)
Capital: Annapolis

Allegany
Anne Arundel
Baltimore
Calvert
Caroline
Carroll
Cecil
Charles
Dorchester
Frederick
Garrett
Harford
Howard
Kent
Montgomery
Prince George's
Queen Anne's
St. Mary's
Somerset
Talbot
Washington
Wicomico
Worcester
Baltimore city

MASSACHUSETTS (MA) (14 counties)
Capital: Boston

Barnstable
Berkshire
Bristol
Dukes
Essex
Franklin
Hampden
Hampshire
Middlesex
Nantucket
Norfolk
Plymouth
Suffolk
Worcester

MICHIGAN (MI) (83 counties)
Capital: Lansing

Alcona
Alger
Allegan
Alpena
Antrim
Arenac
Baraga
Barry
Bay
Benzie
Berrien
Branch
Calhoun
Cass
Charlevoix
Cheboygan
Chippewa
Clare
Clinton
Crawford
Delta
Dickinson
Eaton
Emmet
Genesee
Gladwin
Gogebic
Grand Traverse
Gratiot
Hillsdale
Houghton
Huron
Ingham
Ionia
Iosco
Iron
Isabella
Jackson
Kalamazoo
Kalkaska
Kent
Keweenaw
Lake
Lapeer
Leelanau
Lenawee
Livingston
Luce
Mackinac
Macomb
Manistee
Marquette
Mason
Mecosta
Menominee
Midland
Missaukee
Monroe
Montcalm
Montmorency
Muskegon
Newaygo
Oakland
Oceana
Ogemaw
Ontonagon
Osceola
Oscoda
Otsego
Ottawa
Presque Isle
Roscommon
Saginaw
St. Clair
St. Joseph
Sanilac
Schoolcraft
Shiawassee
Tuscola
Van Buren
Washtenaw
Wayne
Wexford

MINNESOTA (MN) (87 counties)
Capital: St. Paul

Aitkin
Anoka
Becker
Beltrami
Benton
Big Stone
Blue Earth
Brown
Carlton
Carver
Cass
Chippewa
Chisago
Clay
Clearwater
Cook
Cottonwood
Crow Wing
Dakota
Dodge
Douglas
Faribault
Fillmore
Freeborn
Goodhue
Grant
Hennepin
Houston
Hubbard
Isanti
Itasca
Jackson
Kanabec
Kandiyohi
Kittson

Koochiching
Lac qui Parle
Lake
Lake of the Woods
Le Sueur
Lincoln
Lyon
McLeod
Mahnomen
Marshall
Martin
Meeker
Mille Lacs
Morrison
Mower
Murray
Nicollet
Nobles
Norman
Olmsted
Otter Tail
Pennington
Pine
Pipestone
Polk
Pope
Ramsey
Red Lake
Redwood
Renville
Rice
Rock
Roseau
St. Louis
Scott
Sherburne
Sibley
Stearns
Steele
Stevens
Swift
Todd
Traverse
Wabasha
Wadena
Waseca
Washington
Watonwan
Wilkin
Winona
Wright
Yellow Medicine

MISSISSIPPI (MS) (82 counties)
Capital: Jackson

Adams
Alcorn
Amite
Attala
Benton
Bolivar
Calhoun
Carroll
Chickasaw
Choctaw
Claiborne
Clarke
Clay
Coahoma
Copiah
Covington
DeSoto
Forrest
Franklin
George
Greene
Grenada
Hancock
Harrison
Hinds
Holmes
Humphreys
Issaquena
Itawamba
Jackson
Jasper
Jefferson
Jefferson Davis
Jones
Kemper
Lafayette
Lamar
Lauderdale
Lawrence
Leake
Lee
Leflore
Lincoln
Lowndes
Madison
Marion
Marshall
Monroe
Montgomery
Neshoba
Newton
Noxubee
Oktibbeha
Panola
Pearl River
Perry
Pike
Pontotoc
Prentiss
Quitman
Rankin
Scott
Sharkey
Simpson
Smith
Stone
Sunflower
Tallahatchie
Tate
Tippah
Tishomingo
Tunica
Union
Walthall
Warren
Washington
Wayne
Webster
Wilkinson
Winston
Yalobusha
Yazoo

MISSOURI (MO) (115 counties)
Capital: Jefferson City

Adair
Andrew
Atchison
Audrain
Barry
Barton
Bates
Benton
Bollinger
Boone
Buchanan
Butler
Caldwell
Callaway
Camden
Cape Girardeau
Carroll
Carter
Cass
Cedar
Chariton
Christian
Clark
Clay
Clinton
Cole
Cooper
Crawford
Dade
Dallas
Daviess
DeKalb
Dent
Douglas
Dunklin
Franklin
Gasconade
Gentry
Greene
Grundy
Harrison
Henry
Hickory
Holt
Howard

Howell
Iron
Jackson
Jasper
Jefferson
Johnson
Knox
Laclede
Lafayette
Lawrence
Lewis
Lincoln
Linn
Livingston
McDonald
Macon
Madison
Maries
Marion
Mercer
Miller
Mississippi
Moniteau
Monroe
Montgomery
Morgan
New Madrid
Newton
Nodaway
Oregon
Osage
Ozark
Pemiscot
Perry
Pettis
Phelps
Pike
Platte
Polk
Pulaski
Putnam
Ralls
Randolph
Ray
Reynolds
Ripley
St. Charles
St. Clair
Ste. Genevieve
St. Francois
St. Louis
Saline
Schuyler
Scotland
Scott
Shannon
Shelby
Stoddard
Stone
Sullivan
Taney
Texas
Vernon
Warren
Washington
Wayne
Webster
Worth
Wright
St. Louis City

MONTANA (MT) (56 counties)
Capital: Helena

Beaverhead
Big Horn
Blaine
Broadwater
Carbon
Carter
Cascade
Chouteau
Custer
Daniels
Dawson
Deer Lodge
Fallon
Fergus
Flathead
Gallatin
Garfield
Glacier
Golden Valley
Granite
Hill
Jefferson
Judith Basin
Lake
Lewis and Clark
Liberty
Lincoln
McCone
Madison
Meagher
Mineral
Missoula
Musselshell
Park
Petroleum
Phillips
Pondera
Powder River
Powell
Prairie
Ravalli
Richland
Roosevelt
Rosebud
Sanders
Sheridan
Silver Bow
Stillwater
Sweet Grass
Teton
Toole
Treasure
Valley
Wheatland
Wibaux
Yellowstone
Yellowstone National Park

NEBRASKA (NE) (93 counties)
Capital: Lincoln

Adams
Antelope
Arthur
Banner
Blaine
Boone
Box Butte
Boyd
Brown
Buffalo
Burt
Butler
Cass
Cedar
Chase
Cherry
Cheyenne
Clay
Colfax
Cuming
Custer
Dakota
Dawes
Dawson
Deuel
Dixon
Dodge
Douglas
Dundy
Fillmore
Franklin
Frontier
Furnas
Gage
Garden
Garfield
Gosper
Grant
Greeley
Hall
Hamilton
Harlan
Hayes
Hitchcock
Holt
Hooker
Howard
Jefferson
Johnson
Kearney
Keith
Keya Paha
Kimball
Knox
Lancaster

Lincoln	Nemaha	Polk	Seward	Valley
Logan	Nuckolls	Red Willow	Sheridan	Washington
Loup	Otoe	Richardson	Sherman	Wayne
McPherson	Pawnee	Rock	Sioux	Webster
Madison	Perkins	Saline	Stanton	Wheeler
Merrick	Phelps	Sarpy	Thayer	York
Morrill	Pierce	Saunders	Thomas	
Nance	Platte	Scotts Bluff	Thurston	

NEVADA (NV) (17 counties)
Capital: Carson City

Churchill	Esmeralda	Lincoln	Pershing	Carson City City
Clark	Eureka	Lyon	Storey	
Douglas	Humboldt	Mineral	Washoe	
Elko	Lander	Nye	White Pine	

NEW HAMPSHIRE (NH) (10 counties)
Capital: Concord

Belknap	Cheshire	Grafton	Merrimack	Strafford
Carroll	Coos	Hillsborough	Rockingham	Sullivan

NEW JERSEY (NJ) (21 counties)
Capital: Trenton

Atlantic	Cumberland	Mercer	Passaic	Warren
Bergen	Essex	Middlesex	Salem	
Burlington	Gloucester	Monmouth	Somerset	
Camden	Hudson	Morris	Sussex	
Cape May	Hunterdon	Ocean	Union	

NEW MEXICO (NM) (33 counties)
Capital: Santa Fe

Bernalillo	Dona Ana	Lincoln	Rio Arriba	Socorro
Catron	Eddy	Los Alamos	Roosevelt	Taos
Chaves	Grant	Luna	Sandoval	Torrance
Cibola	Guadalupe	McKinley	San Juan	Union
Colfax	Harding	Mora	San Miguel	Valencia
Curry	Hidalgo	Otero	Santa Fe	
De Baca	Lea	Quay	Sierra	

NEW YORK (NY) (62 counties)
Capital: Albany

Albany
Allegany
Bronx
Broome
Cattaraugus
Cayuga
Chautauqua
Chemung
Chenango
Clinton
Columbia
Cortland
Delaware
Dutchess
Erie
Essex
Franklin
Fulton
Genesee
Greene
Hamilton
Herkimer
Jefferson
Kings
Lewis
Livingston
Madison
Monroe
Montgomery
Nassau
New York
Niagara
Oneida
Onondaga
Ontario
Orange
Orleans
Oswego
Otsego
Putnam
Queens
Rensselaer
Richmond
Rockland
St. Lawrence
Saratoga
Schenectady
Schoharie
Schuyler
Seneca
Steuben
Suffolk
Sullivan
Tioga
Tompkins
Ulster
Warren
Washington
Wayne
Westchester
Wyoming
Yates

NORTH CAROLINA (NC) (100 counties)
Capital: Raleigh

Alamance
Alexander
Alleghany
Anson
Ashe
Avery
Beaufort
Bertie
Bladen
Brunswick
Buncombe
Burke
Cabarrus
Caldwell
Camden
Carteret
Caswell
Catawba
Chatham
Cherokee
Chowan
Clay
Cleveland
Columbus
Craven
Cumberland
Currituck
Dare
Davidson
Davie
Duplin
Durham
Edgecombe
Forsyth
Franklin
Gaston
Gates
Graham
Granville
Greene
Guilford
Halifax
Harnett
Haywood
Henderson
Hertford
Hoke
Hyde
Iredell
Jackson
Johnston
Jones
Lee
Lenoir
Lincoln
McDowell
Macon
Madison
Martin
Mecklenburg
Mitchell
Montgomery
Moore
Nash
New Hanover
Northampton
Onslow
Orange
Pamlico
Pasquotank
Pender
Perquimans
Person
Pitt
Polk
Randolph
Richmond
Robeson
Rockingham
Rowan
Rutherford
Sampson
Scotland
Stanly
Stokes
Surry
Swain
Transylvania
Tyrrell
Union
Vance
Wake
Warren
Washington
Watauga
Wayne
Wilkes
Wilson
Yadkin
Yancey

NORTH DAKOTA (ND) (53 counties)
Capital: Bismarck

Adams
Barnes
Benson
Billings
Bottineau
Bowman
Burke
Burleigh
Cass
Cavalier
Dickey
Divide
Dunn
Eddy
Emmons
Foster
Golden Valley
Grand Forks
Grant
Griggs
Hettinger
Kidder
LaMoure
Logan
McHenry
McIntosh
McKenzie
McLean
Mercer
Morton
Mountrail
Nelson
Oliver
Pembina
Pierce
Ramsey
Ransom
Renville
Richland
Rolette
Sargent
Sheridan
Sioux
Slope
Stark
Steele
Stutsman
Towner
Traill
Walsh
Ward
Wells
Williams

NORTHERN MARIANA ISLANDS (MP) (4 municipalities)
Capital: Saipan

Northern Islands
Rota
Saipan
Tinian

OHIO (OH) (88 counties)
Capital: Columbus

Adams
Allen
Ashland
Ashtabula
Athens
Auglaize
Belmont
Brown
Butler
Carroll
Champaign
Clark
Clermont
Clinton
Columbiana
Coshocton
Crawford
Cuyahoga
Darke
Defiance
Delaware
Erie
Fairfield
Fayette
Franklin
Fulton
Gallia
Geauga
Greene
Guernsey
Hamilton
Hancock
Hardin
Harrison
Henry
Highland
Hocking
Holmes
Huron
Jackson
Jefferson
Knox
Lake
Lawrence
Licking
Logan
Lorain
Lucas
Madison
Mahoning
Marion
Medina
Meigs
Mercer
Miami
Monroe
Montgomery
Morgan
Morrow
Muskingum
Noble
Ottawa
Paulding
Perry
Pickaway
Pike
Portage
Preble
Putnam
Richland
Ross
Sandusky
Scioto
Seneca
Shelby
Stark
Summit
Trumbull
Tuscarawas
Union
Van Wert
Vinton
Warren
Washington
Wayne
Williams
Wood
Wyandot

OKLAHOMA (OK) (77 counties)
Capital: Oklahoma City

Adair	Cotton	Jackson	Mayes	Roger Mills
Alfalfa	Craig	Jefferson	Murray	Rogers
Atoka	Creek	Johnston	Muskogee	Seminole
Beaver	Custer	Kay	Noble	Sequoyah
Beckham	Delaware	Kingfisher	Nowata	Stephens
Blaine	Dewey	Kiowa	Okfuskee	Texas
Bryan	Ellis	Latimer	Oklahoma	Tillman
Caddo	Garfield	Le Flore	Okmulgee	Tulsa
Canadian	Garvin	Lincoln	Osage	Wagoner
Carter	Grady	Logan	Ottawa	Washington
Cherokee	Grant	Love	Pawnee	Washita
Choctaw	Greer	McClain	Payne	Woods
Cimarron	Harmon	McCurtain	Pittsburg	Woodward
Cleveland	Harper	McIntosh	Pontotoc	
Coal	Haskell	Major	Pottawatomie	
Comanche	Hughes	Marshall	Pushmataha	

OREGON (OR) (36 counties)
Capital: Salem

Baker	Deschutes	Josephine	Morrow	Wasco
Benton	Douglas	Klamath	Multnomah	Washington
Clackamas	Gilliam	Lake	Polk	Wheeler
Clatsop	Grant	Lane	Sherman	Yamhill
Columbia	Harney	Lincoln	Tillamook	
Coos	Hood River	Linn	Umatilla	
Crook	Jackson	Malheur	Union	
Curry	Jefferson	Marion	Wallowa	

PALAU (PW) (16 States)
Capital: Melekeok

Aimeliik	Kayangel	Ngarchelong	Ngeremlengui
Airai	Koror	Ngardmau	Ngiwal
Angaur	Melekeok	Ngatpang	Peleliu
Hatohobei	Ngaraard	Ngchesar	Sonsorol

PENNSYLVANIA (PA) (67 counties)
Capital: Harrisburg

Adams	Beaver	Blair	Butler	Carbon
Allegheny	Bedford	Bradford	Cambria	Centre
Armstrong	Berks	Bucks	Cameron	Chester

Clarion
Clearfield
Clinton
Columbia
Crawford
Cumberland
Dauphin
Delaware
Elk
Erie
Fayette
Forest
Franklin
Fulton
Greene
Huntingdon
Indiana
Jefferson
Juniata
Lackawanna
Lancaster
Lawrence
Lebanon
Lehigh
Luzerne
Lycoming
McKean
Mercer
Mifflin
Monroe
Montgomery
Montour
Northampton
Northumberland
Perry
Philadelphia
Pike
Potter
Schuylkill
Snyder
Somerset
Sullivan
Susquehanna
Tioga
Union
Venango
Warren
Washington
Wayne
Westmoreland
Wyoming
York

PUERTO RICO (PR) (78 municipios)
Capital: San Juan

Adjuntas
Aguada
Aguadilla
Aguas Buenas
Aibonito
Añasco
Arecibo
Arroyo
Barceloneta
Barranquitas
Bayamón
Cabo Rojo
Caguas
Camuy
Canóvanas
Carolina
Cataño
Cayey
Ceiba
Ciales
Cidra
Coamo
Comerío
Corozal
Culebra
Dorado
Fajardo
Florida
Guánica
Guayama
Guayanilla
Guaynabo
Gurabo
Hatillo
Hormigueros
Humacao
Isabela
Jayuya
Juana Díaz
Juncos
Lajas
Lares
Las Marías
Las Piedras
Loíza
Luquillo
Manatí
Maricao
Maunabo
Mayagüez
Moca
Morovis
Naguabo
Naranjito
Orocovis
Patillas
Peñuelas
Ponce
Quebradillas
Rincón
Río Grande
Sabana Grande
Salinas
San Germán
San Juan
San Lorenzo
San Sebastián
Santa Isabel
Toa Alta
Toa Baja
Trujillo Alto
Utuado
Vega Alta
Vega Baja
Vieques
Villalba
Yabucoa
Yauco

RHODE ISLAND (RI) (5 counties)
Capital: Providence

Bristol
Kent
Newport
Providence
Washington

SOUTH CAROLINA (SC) (46 counties)
Capital: Columbia

Abbeville
Aiken
Allendale
Anderson
Bamberg
Barnwell
Beaufort
Berkeley
Calhoun
Charleston
Cherokee
Chester
Chesterfield
Clarendon
Colleton
Darlington
Dillon
Dorchester
Edgefield
Fairfield
Florence
Georgetown
Greenville
Greenwood
Hampton
Horry
Jasper
Kershaw
Lancaster
Laurens

Lee
Lexington
McCormick
Marion
Marlboro
Newberry
Oconee
Orangeburg
Pickens
Richland
Saluda
Spartanburg
Sumter
Union
Williamsburg
York

SOUTH DAKOTA (SD) (66 counties)
Capital: Pierre

Aurora
Beadle
Bennett
Bon Homme
Brookings
Brown
Brule
Buffalo
Butte
Campbell
Charles Mix
Clark
Clay
Codington
Corson
Custer
Davison
Day
Deuel
Dewey
Douglas
Edmunds
Fall River
Faulk
Grant
Gregory
Haakon
Hamlin
Hand
Hanson
Harding
Hughes
Hutchinson
Hyde
Jackson
Jerauld
Jones
Kingsbury
Lake
Lawrence
Lincoln
Lyman
McCook
McPherson
Marshall
Meade
Mellette
Miner
Minnehaha
Moody
Pennington
Perkins
Potter
Roberts
Sanborn
Shannon
Spink
Stanley
Sully
Todd
Tripp
Turner
Union
Walworth
Yankton
Ziebach

TENNESSEE (TN) (95 counties)
Capital: Nashville

Anderson
Bedford
Benton
Bledsoe
Blount
Bradley
Campbell
Cannon
Carroll
Carter
Cheatham
Chester
Claiborne
Clay
Cocke
Coffee
Crockett
Cumberland
Davidson
Decatur
DeKalb
Dickson
Dyer
Fayette
Fentress
Franklin
Gibson
Giles
Grainger
Greene
Grundy
Hamblen
Hamilton
Hancock
Hardeman
Hardin
Hawkins
Haywood
Henderson
Henry
Hickman
Houston
Humphreys
Jackson
Jefferson
Johnson
Knox
Lake
Lauderdale
Lawrence
Lewis
Lincoln
Loudon
McMinn
McNairy
Macon
Madison
Marion
Marshall
Maury
Meigs
Monroe
Montgomery
Moore
Morgan
Obion
Overton
Perry
Pickett
Polk
Putnam
Rhea
Roane
Robertson
Rutherford
Scott
Sequatchie
Sevier
Shelby
Smith
Stewart
Sullivan
Sumner
Tipton
Trousdale
Unicoi
Union
Van Buren
Warren
Washington
Wayne
Weakley
White
Williamson
Wilson

TEXAS (TX) (254 counties)
Capital: Austin

Anderson	Coke	Freestone	Jasper	Matagorda
Andrews	Coleman	Frio	Jeff Davis	Maverick
Angelina	Collin	Gaines	Jefferson	Medina
Aransas	Collingsworth	Galveston	Jim Hogg	Menard
Archer	Colorado	Garza	Jim Wells	Midland
Armstrong	Comal	Gillespie	Johnson	Milam
Atascosa	Comanche	Glasscock	Jones	Mills
Austin	Concho	Goliad	Karnes	Mitchell
Bailey	Cooke	Gonzales	Kaufman	Montague
Bandera	Coryell	Gray	Kendall	Montgomery
Bastrop	Cottle	Grayson	Kenedy	Moore
Baylor	Crane	Gregg	Kent	Morris
Bee	Crockett	Grimes	Kerr	Motley
Bell	Crosby	Guadalupe	Kimble	Nacogdoches
Bexar	Culberson	Hale	King	Navarro
Blanco	Dallam	Hall	Kinney	Newton
Borden	Dallas	Hamilton	Kleberg	Nolan
Bosque	Dawson	Hansford	Knox	Nueces
Bowie	Deaf Smith	Hardeman	Lamar	Ochiltree
Brazoria	Delta	Hardin	Lamb	Oldham
Brazos	Denton	Harris	Lampasas	Orange
Brewster	DeWitt	Harrison	La Salle	Palo Pinto
Briscoe	Dickens	Hartley	Lavaca	Panola
Brooks	Dimmit	Haskell	Lee	Parker
Brown	Donley	Hays	Leon	Parmer
Burleson	Duval	Hemphill	Liberty	Pecos
Burnet	Eastland	Henderson	Limestone	Polk
Caldwell	Ector	Hidalgo	Lipscomb	Potter
Calhoun	Edwards	Hill	Live Oak	Presidio
Callahan	Ellis	Hockley	Llano	Rains
Cameron	El Paso	Hood	Loving	Randall
Camp	Erath	Hopkins	Lubbock	Reagan
Carson	Falls	Houston	Lynn	Real
Cass	Fannin	Howard	McCulloch	Red River
Castro	Fayette	Hudspeth	McLennan	Reeves
Chambers	Fisher	Hunt	McMullen	Refugio
Cherokee	Floyd	Hutchinson	Madison	Roberts
Childress	Foard	Irion	Marion	Robertson
Clay	Fort Bend	Jack	Martin	Rockwall
Cochran	Franklin	Jackson	Mason	Runnels

Rusk
Sabine
San Augustine
San Jacinto
San Patricio
San Saba
Schleicher
Scurry
Shackelford
Shelby
Sherman
Smith
Somervell
Starr
Stephens
Sterling
Stonewall
Sutton
Swisher
Tarrant
Taylor
Terrell
Terry
Throckmorton
Titus
Tom Green
Travis
Trinity
Tyler
Upshur
Upton
Uvalde
Val Verde
Van Zandt
Victoria
Walker
Waller
Ward
Washington
Webb
Wharton
Wheeler
Wichita
Wilbarger
Willacy
Williamson
Wilson
Winkler
Wise
Wood
Yoakum
Young
Zapata
Zavala

UTAH (UT) (29 counties)
Capital: Salt Lake City

Beaver
Box Elder
Cache
Carbon
Daggett
Davis
Duchesne
Emery
Garfield
Grand
Iron
Juab
Kane
Millard
Morgan
Piute
Rich
Salt Lake
San Juan
Sanpete
Sevier
Summit
Tooele
Uintah
Utah
Wasatch
Washington
Wayne
Weber

VERMONT (VT) (14 counties)
Capital: Montpelier

Addison
Bennington
Caledonia
Chittenden
Essex
Franklin
Grand Isle
Lamoille
Orange
Orleans
Rutland
Washington
Windham
Windsor

VIRGIN ISLANDS (VI) (3 islands)
Capital: Charlotte Amalie

St. Croix
St. John
St. Thomas

VIRGINIA (VA) (95 counties)
Capital: Richmond

Accomack
Albemarle
Alleghany
Amelia
Amherst
Appomattox
Arlington
Augusta
Bath
Bedford
Bland
Botetourt
Brunswick
Buchanan
Buckingham
Campbell
Caroline
Carroll
Charles City
Charlotte
Chesterfield
Clarke
Craig
Culpeper
Cumberland
Dickenson
Dinwiddie
Essex
Fairfax
Fauquier
Floyd
Fluvanna
Franklin
Frederick
Giles
Gloucester
Goochland
Grayson
Greene
Greensville
Halifax
Hanover
Henrico
Henry
Highland

Isle of Wight
James City
King and Queen
King George
King William
Lancaster
Lee
Loudoun
Louisa
Lunenburg
Madison
Mathews
Mecklenburg
Middlesex
Montgomery
Nelson
New Kent
Northampton
Northumberland
Nottoway
Orange
Page
Patrick
Pittsylvania
Powhatan
Prince Edward
Prince George
Prince William
Pulaski
Rappahannock
Richmond
Roanoke
Rockbridge
Rockingham
Russell
Scott
Shenandoah
Smyth
Southampton
Spotsylvania
Stafford
Surry
Sussex
Tazewell
Warren
Washington
Westmoreland
Wise
Wythe
York

WASHINGTON (WA) (39 counties)
Capital: Olympia

Adams
Asotin
Benton
Chelan
Clallam
Clark
Columbia
Cowlitz
Douglas
Ferry
Franklin
Garfield
Grant
Grays Harbor
Island
Jefferson
King
Kitsap
Kittitas
Klickitat
Lewis
Lincoln
Mason
Okanogan
Pacific
Pend Oreille
Pierce
San Juan
Skagit
Skamania
Snohomish
Spokane
Stevens
Thurston
Wahkiakum
Walla Walla
Whatcom
Whitman
Yakima

WEST VIRGINIA (WV) (55 counties)
Capital: Charleston

Barbour
Berkeley
Boone
Braxton
Brooke
Cabell
Calhoun
Clay
Doddridge
Fayette
Gilmer
Grant
Greenbrier
Hampshire
Hancock
Hardy
Harrison
Jackson
Jefferson
Kanawha
Lewis
Lincoln
Logan
McDowell
Marion
Marshall
Mason
Mercer
Mineral
Mingo
Monongalia
Monroe
Morgan
Nicholas
Ohio
Pendleton
Pleasants
Pocahontas
Preston
Putnam
Raleigh
Randolph
Ritchie
Roane
Summers
Taylor
Tucker
Tyler
Upshur
Wayne
Webster
Wetzel
Wirt
Wood
Wyoming

WISCONSIN (WI) (72 counties)
Capital: Madison

Adams	Douglas	Kewaunee	Ozaukee	Taylor
Ashland	Dunn	La Crosse	Pepin	Trempealeau
Barron	Eau Claire	Lafayette	Pierce	Vernon
Bayfield	Florence	Langlade	Polk	Vilas
Brown	Fond du Lac	Lincoln	Portage	Walworth
Buffalo	Forest	Manitowoc	Price	Washburn
Burnett	Grant	Marathon	Racine	Washington
Calumet	Green	Marinette	Richland	Waukesha
Chippewa	Green Lake	Marquette	Rock	Waupaca
Clark	Iowa	Menominee	Rusk	Waushara
Columbia	Iron	Milwaukee	St. Croix	Winnebago
Crawford	Jackson	Monroe	Sauk	Wood
Dane	Jefferson	Oconto	Sawyer	
Dodge	Juneau	Oneida	Shawano	
Door	Kenosha	Outagamie	Sheboygan	

WYOMING (WY) (23 counties)
Capital: Cheyenne

Albany	Crook	Laramie	Platte	Uinta
Big Horn	Fremont	Lincoln	Sheridan	Washakie
Campbell	Goshen	Natrona	Sublette	Weston
Carbon	Hot Springs	Niobrara	Sweetwater	
Converse	Johnson	Park	Teton	

Common misspellings

Geographers and cartographers omit the possessive apostrophe in placenames; however, apostrophes appearing in legally constituted names of counties should not be changed.

The names of the following counties are often misspelled and/or confused:

Allegany in Maryland and New York
Alleghany in North Carolina and Virginia
Allegheny in Pennsylvania
Andrew in Missouri
Andrews in Texas
Aransas in Texas
Arkansas in Arkansas
Barber in Kansas
Barbour in Alabama and West Virginia
Brevard in Florida
Broward in Florida
Brooke in West Virginia
Brooks in Georgia and Texas
Bulloch in Georgia
Bullock in Alabama
Burnet in Texas
Burnett in Wisconsin
Cheboygan in Michigan
Sheboygan in Wisconsin
Clarke in Alabama, Georgia, Iowa, Mississippi, and Virginia
Clark in all other States

Coffee in Alabama, Georgia, and Tennessee
Coffey in Kansas
Coal in Oklahoma
Cole in Missouri
Coles in Illinois
Cook in Illinois and Minnesota
Cooke in Texas
Davidson in North Carolina and Tennessee
Davie in North Carolina
Daviess in Indiana, Kentucky, and Missouri
Davis in Iowa and Utah
Davison in South Dakota
DeKalb all one word
Dickenson in Virginia
Dickinson in Iowa, Kansas, and Michigan
Dickson in Tennessee
Forrest in Mississippi
Forest in all other States
Glascock in Georgia
Glasscock in Texas
Green in Kentucky and Wisconsin
Greene in all other States
Harford in Maryland
Hartford in Connecticut
Huntingdon in Pennsylvania
Huntington in Indiana
Johnston in North Carolina and Oklahoma
Johnson in all other States
Kanabec in Minnesota
Kennebec in Maine
Kearney in Nebraska
Kearny in Kansas
Kenedy in Texas
Linn in Iowa, Kansas, Missouri, and Oregon
Lynn in Texas
Loudon in Tennessee
Loudoun in Virginia
Manatee in Florida
Manistee in Michigan
Merced in California
Mercer in all other States
Morton in Kansas
Norton in Kansas
Muscogee in Georgia
Muskogee in Oklahoma
Park in Colorado and Montana
Parke in Indiana
Pottawatomie in Kansas and Oklahoma
Pottawattamie in Iowa
Prince George in Virginia
Prince George's in Maryland
Sanders in Montana
Saunders in Nebraska
Smyth in Virginia
Smith in all other States
Stafford in Virginia
Strafford in New Hampshire
Stanley in South Dakota
Stanly in North Carolina
Stark in Illinois, North Dakota, and Ohio
Starke in Indiana
Stephens in Georgia, Oklahoma, and Texas
Stevens in Kansas, Minnesota, and Washington
Storey in Nevada
Story in Iowa
Terrell in Georgia and Texas
Tyrrell in North Carolina
Tooele in Utah
Toole in Montana
Vermillion in Indiana
Vermilion in all other States
Woods in Oklahoma
Wood in all other States
Wyandot in Ohio
Wyandotte in Kansas

19. Congressional Record

Code of laws of the United States and rules for publication of the Congressional Record

Title 44, Section 901. Congressional Record: Arrangement, style, contents, and indexes.—The Joint Committee on Printing shall control the arrangement and style of the Congressional Record, and while providing that it shall be substantially a verbatim report of proceedings, shall take all needed action for the reduction of unnecessary bulk. It shall provide for the publication of an index of the Congressional Record semimonthly during and at the close of sessions of Congress.

Title 44, Section 904. Congressional Record: Maps, diagrams, illustrations.—Maps, diagrams, or illustrations may not be inserted in the Record without the approval of the Joint Committee on Printing.

General rules

The rules governing document work (FIC & punc.) apply to the Congressional Record, except as may be noted herein. The same general style should be followed in the permanent (bound) Record as is used in the daily Record. It is important to be familiar with the exceptions and the forms peculiar to the Record.

Much of the data printed in the Congressional Record is forwarded to GPO using the captured keystrokes of the floor reporters. Element identifier codes are programmatically inserted, and galley output is accomplished without manual intervention. It is not cost-effective to prepare the accompanying manuscript as per the GPO Style Manual, and it is too time-consuming to update and change the data once it is already in type form. Therefore, the Record is to be FIC & punc. Because of its volume, it is not necessary to stamp the manuscript FIC & punc. However, Record style will be followed, as stated in the following rules:

Daily and permanent Record texts are set in 8-point type on a 9-point body. Extracts are set in 7-point type on an 8-point body.

An F-dash will be used preceding 8-point cap lines in the proceedings of the Senate and House.

All 7-point extracts and poetry will carry 2 points of space above and below unless heads appear, which generate their own space.

All extracts are set 7 point unless otherwise ordered by the Joint Committee on Printing.

Except as noted below, all communications from the President must be set in 8 point, but if such communications contain extracts, etc., the extracts are set in 7 point.

An address of the President delivered outside of Congress or referred to as an extract is set in 7 point.

A letter from the President to the Senate is set in 7 point when any form of treaty is enclosed that is to be printed in the Record in connection therewith. The letter is set in 7 point whether the treaty follows or precedes it or is separated from it by intervening matter.

In all quoted amendments and excerpts of bills and in reprinting bills, the style and manuscript as printed in the bill will be followed.

Except where otherwise directed, profanity, obscene wording, or extreme vulgarisms are to be deleted and a 3-em dash substituted.

Floor-approved statements in a foreign language, will be printed following their English translation.

Extreme caution must be used in making corrections in manuscript, and no important change will be made without proper authorization.

Observe the lists of names of Senators, Representatives, and Delegates, committees of both Houses, and duplicate names. Changes caused by death, resignation, or otherwise must be noted. There is no excuse for error in the spelling of names of Senators, Representatives, or department officials. In case of doubt, the Congressional Directory will be the authority.

Datelines should be followed on Extensions of Remarks. If any question arises as to the proper date to be used, a supervisor must be consulted.

Indented matter in leaderwork will be 1 em only.

Do not write queries on proofs.

Capitalization

(See also Chapter 3 "Capitalization Rules")

If the name of the Congressional Record is mentioned, it must be set in caps and small caps and never abbreviated, even when appearing in citations, except in extract matter, then cap/lowercase.

The name of a Senator or a Representative preceding his or her direct remarks is set in caps and is followed by a period with equal spacing to be used.

The name of a Senator or a Representative used in connection with a bill or other paper—that is, in an adjectival sense—is lowercased, as the Engel bill, the Fish amendment, etc.; but UDALL's amendment, etc.

The names of Members and Members-elect of both Houses of the Congress, including those of the Vice President and Speaker, will be printed in caps and small caps if mention is made of them, except in extract matter.

Deceased Members' names will be set in caps and small caps in eulogies only on the first day the House or Senate is in session following the death of a Member, in a speech carrying date when the Member was eulogized, or on memorial day in the Senate and House. Eulogy day in one House will be treated the same in the other.

Certificates of Senators-elect of a succeeding Congress are usually presented to the current Congress, and in such cases the names of the Senators-elect must be in caps and small caps.

Names of Members of Congress must be set in caps and lowercase in votes, in lists set in columns, in the list of standing and select committees, in contested-election cases, in lists of pairs, and in all parts of tabular matter (head, body, and footnotes).

Observe that the names of all persons not certified Members of Congress are to be set in caps and lowercase; that is, names of secretaries, clerks, messengers, and others.

Names of proposed Federal boards, commissions, services, etc., are capitalized.

Capitalize principal words and quote after each of the following terms: *address, album, article, book, caption, chapter heading, editorial, essay, heading, headline, motion picture* or *play* (including TV or radio program), *paper, poem, report, song, subheading, subject, theme,* etc. Also, following the word *entitled*, except with reference to bill titles which are treated as follows: "A bill (or an act) transferring certain functions of the Price Administrator to the Petroleum Administrator for War," etc.

Figures

Follow the manuscript as to the use of numerals. Dollar amounts in Record manuscript are to be followed.

Figures appearing in manuscript as "20 billion 428 million 125 thousand dollars" should be followed.

Tabular matter and leaderwork

Record tables may be set either one or three columns in width, as follows:

One-column table: 14 picas (168 points).

Three-column table: 43½ picas (522 points). Footnote(s) will be set 43½ picas.

All short footnotes should be run in with 2 ems between each.

Italic

Italic, boldface, caps, or small caps shall not be used for emphasis; nor shall unusual indentions be used. This does not apply to literally reproduced quotations from historical, legal, or official documents. If italic other than restricted herein is desired, the words should be underscored and "Fol. ital." written on each folio. Do not construe this to apply to *"Provided," "Provided further," "Ordered," "Resolved," "Be it enacted,"* etc.

Names of vessels must be set in italic, except in headings, where they will be quoted.

The prayer delivered in either House must be set in 8-point roman. If prefaced or followed by a quotation from the Bible, such quotation must be set in 8-point italic. Extracts from the Bible or other literature contained in the body of the prayer will be set in 8-point roman and quoted.

When general or passing mention is made of a case in 8 point, the title is set in roman, as Smith Bros. case. When a specific citation is indicated and reference follows, use italic for title, as *Smith Bros.* case (172 App. Div. 149).

In 8-point manuscript, titles of cases are always set in italic if followed by references. In 7 point, manuscript is followed.

In 8-point matter, when only the title of a case is given, set in roman, as United States versus 12 Diamond Rings.

When *versus* is used in other than legal phrases and for the purposes of showing contrast, it is not abbreviated or set in italic, as "airplanes versus battleships."

Miscellaneous

Do not quote any communication carrying date and signature. However, a letter (or other communication) bearing both date and signature that appears within a letter shall be quoted.

Do not put quotation marks on centerheads in 7-point extracts unless centerheads belong to original matter.

In newspaper extracts, insert place and date at beginning of paragraph. Use caps and small caps for name of place and roman lowercase for spelled-out date. Connect date and extract by a period and an em dash. If date and place are credited in a bracket line above extract, they need not be used again at the beginning of the paragraph.

Each *Whereas* in a preamble must begin a new paragraph. The *Therefore be it* must be preceded by a colon and be run in with the last *Whereas. Be it* will run in with the word *Therefore, but* it must not be supplied when not in manuscript. Note the following:

Whereas it has been deemed advisable to, etc.: Therefore be it

Resolved, That the committee, etc.

In the titles of legal cases, manuscript is followed as to spelling, abbreviations, and use of figures.

Use single punctuation in citations of cases and statutes:

United States v. *12 Diamond Rings* (124 U.S. 329; R.S. p. 310, sec. 1748).

Indent asterisk lines 2 ems on each side. Use five asterisks.

If a title is used as part of the name of an organization, vessel, etc., spell; thus, General Ulysses S. Grant Post No. 76, Grand Army of the Republic.

The order of subdivision of the Constitution of the United States is as follows: article I, section 2, clause 3.

If an exhibit appears at the end of a speech, the head *Exhibit* is set in 7-point caps and small caps.

In extracts containing votes the names must be run in, as Mr. Smith of Texas, AuCoin, and Clay, etc.

In a Senator's or a Representative's remarks, when amendments, sections, etc., are referred to by number, follow the manuscript.

In text references to Senate and House reports and in executive and miscellaneous documents, follow the manuscript.

In headings and text references to resolutions and memorials, follow the manuscript.

In gross or en gros

When a bill comes to final action, in the presentment of amendments collectively for a vote, either the term "*in gross*" or the French equivalent "*en gros*" may be used.

Examples of Congressional Record

USE OF CAPS AND SMALL CAPS

[Note the use of parentheses and brackets in the following examples. Each will be used as submitted, as long as they are consistent throughout.]

Mr. THUNE. (Name all caps when a Member or visitor addresses Senate or House.)

On motion by [or of] Mr. Franken, it was, etc.

The VICE PRESIDENT resumed the chair.

The PRESIDING OFFICER (Mr. Blunt). Is there objection?

The SPEAKER called the House to order.

Mr. Hudson's amendment was adopted.

Mr. FARR. Madam Speaker, I yield to Mr. Hoyer.

Mr. HOYER said: If not paired, I would vote "no" on this bill.

A Member. And debate it afterward.

Several Senators. I object.

But: Several Senators addressed the Chair.

Mr. COATS, Mr. DONNELLY (and others). Let it be read.

The Acting Secretary. In line 11, after the word "*Provided*", it is proposed, etc.

Mrs. CAPPS was recognized, and yielded her time to Mr. CÁRDENAS.

[When two Members from the same State have the same surname, full name is used.]

On motion of Ms. LINDA T. SÁNCHEZ of California . . .

On motion of Ms. LORETTA SANCHEZ of California . . .

Mr. DESANTIS and Mr. MARIO DIAZ-BALART of Florida rose to a point of order.

The CHAIRMAN appointed Mr. POE and Mr. ISRAEL as conferees.

[Extracts that consist of colloquies will use caps and small caps for names of persons speaking, as shown below:]

Mr. DEFAZIO. I think this bill is so well understood that no time will be required for its discussion.

Ms. NORTON. Does this bill come from the Committee on Armed Services?

The SPEAKER. It does.

SPECIAL ORDERS GRANTED

By unanimous consent, permission to address the House, following the legislative and any special orders heretofore entered, was granted to:

Mr. HOYER, for 1 hour, on Wednesday, February 2.

Mr. ENGEL (at the request of Mr. HOYER), for 1 hour, on February 2.

(The following Members (at the request of Mr. KING of New York) and to revise and extend their remarks and include therein extraneous matter:)

Mrs. COMSTOCK, for 5 minutes, today.

Mr. HOLDING, for 5 minutes, today.

Mr. COFFMAN, for 60 minutes, today.

[Note the following double action:]

(Mr. HOYER asked and was given permission to extend his remarks at this point in the RECORD and to include extraneous matter.)

(Mr. HOYER addressed the House. His remarks will appear hereafter in the Extensions of Remarks.)

The SPEAKER pro tempore. Under a previous order of the House, the gentleman from Nebraska (Mr. FORTENBERRY) is recognized for 5 minutes.

(Mr. FORTENBERRY addressed the House. His remarks will appear hereafter in the Extensions of Remarks.)

PUNCTUATION

Mr. REID. Mr. President, I call up my amendment which is identified as "unprinted amendment No. 1296," and ask that it be stated.

The bill was reported to the Senate as amended, and the amendment was concurred in.

The bill was reported to the Senate without amendment, ordered to be engrossed for a third reading, read the third time, and passed.

The bill was ordered to be engrossed for a third reading, read the third time, and passed.

[Use this form when title of bill is given:]

The bill was ordered to be engrossed and read the third time, was read the third time, and passed.

The title was amended so as to read: "A bill for the relief of Maude S. Burman."

A motion to reconsider was laid on the table. [House.]

[Use this form when title of bill is not given:]

The bill was ordered to be engrossed and read a third time, was read the third time, and passed, and a motion to reconsider was laid on the table. [House.]

The bill was ordered to be engrossed and read a third time, and passed.

The amendments were ordered to be engrossed and the bill to be read a third time.

The amendment was agreed to, and the bill as amended was ordered to be engrossed and read a third time; and being engrossed, it was accordingly read the third time and passed.

There was no objection, and, by unanimous consent, the Senate proceeded . . .

The question was taken, and the motion was agreed to.

The question being taken, the motion was agreed to.

Ordered to lie on the table and to be printed.

Ms. EDWARDS. Mr. Chairman, I move to strike the requisite number of words.

(Ms. EDWARDS asked and was given permission to revise and extend her remarks.)

[Note use of interrogation mark in the following:]

Mr. NELSON. Mr. President, what does this mean?—

We have never received a dollar of this amount.

POM–376. A resolution adopted by the House of Representatives of the State of Rhode Island expressing its opposition to federal proposals to authorize increases in the size or weight of commercial motor vehicles; to the Committee on Commerce, Science, and Transportation.

House Resolution No. 8296

Whereas, The State of Rhode Island is committed to protecting the safety of motorists on its highways and to protecting taxpayers' investment in our highway infrastructure; and

Whereas, The General Assembly of the State of Rhode Island and Providence Plantations resolved jointly to urge the Congress of the United States to . . .

Resolved, That this House of Representatives of the State of Rhode Island and Providence Plantations hereby reaffirms its opposition to proposals, at all levels of government, that would authorize increases in the size and weight of commercial motor vehicles because of the impact that these increases would have on highway infrastructure, especially bridges; and be it further

Resolved, That the Secretary of State be and he hereby is authorized and directed to transmit duly certified copies of this resolution to the President and Vice President of the United States, the Speaker of the United States House of Representatives, the Majority Leader of the United States Senate and the Rhode Island Delegation to the Congress of the United States.

[Note use of italic in title of cases:]

. . . This is the occasion America did not have to consider what other options might guarantee maternal safety while protecting the unborn. This is our national opportunity to reconsider *Roe* v. *Wade*, 410 U.S. 113 (1973).

Roe against Wade and its companion case, *Doe* v. *Bolton*, 410 U.S. 179 (1973), granted abortion the elevated status of a fundamental constitutional right and invalidated almost all effective restrictions on abortion throughout the 9 months of pregnancy . . . .

PARENTHESES AND BRACKETS

[The use of parentheses and brackets will be followed as submitted for acronyms, symbols, or abbreviations.]

This legislation would exempt certain defined Central Intelligence Agency [CIA] operational files from the search and review process of the Freedom of Information Act [FOIA], thus permitting the Agency to respond much more quickly to those FOIA requests which are at all likely to result in the release of information.

Mr. HUFFMAN. Madam Speaker, I now yield 5 minutes to the gentleman from Indiana (Mr. Higgins).

(Mr. BUTTERFIELD asked and was given permission to revise and extend his remarks in the Record.)

Ms. MOORE. There is no "may not" about it. Here is the form in which they are printed.

Mr. DOYLE. I am in hopes we shall be able to secure a vote on the bill tonight.

["Vote! Vote!"]

Mr. HICE. The Chair rather gets me on that question. [Laughter.] I did not rise. [Cries of "Vote! Vote!"]

Mrs. CAPPS [one of the tellers]. I do not desire to press the point that no quorum has voted.

The CHAIRMAN [after a pause]. If no gentleman claims the floor, the Clerk will proceed with the reading of the bill.

Mr. HURD of Texas. Then he is endeavoring to restrict the liberty of the individual in the disbursement of his own money. [Applause on the Republican side.]

Mr. ELLISON. Mr. Speaker, I desire to ask unanimous consent that the time of the gentleman——[Cries of "Regular Order!"]

[Laughter.]

The SPEAKER. Is there objection to the consideration of this bill at this time? [After a pause.] There is no objection.

The CHAIRMAN [rapping with his gavel]. Debate is exhausted.

Mr. HURT of Virginia. Patrick Henry said:

> Ceasar had his Brutus, Charles I his Cromwell, and George III——
>
> [here he was interrupted by cries of "Treason, Treason"]
>
> and George III may profit by their example. If this be treason, let us make the most of it!

(Mr. MILLER of Florida addressed the Committee [or House]. His remarks will appear hereafter in the Extensions of Remarks.)

[Names of Senators or Representatives appearing in remarks of other Members of Congress should be enclosed in brackets, except in listing of tellers or when some title other than "Mr." is used, as in the following examples:]

Mr. SCHUMER. Mr. President, I thank my friend from Rhode Island [Senator WHITEHOUSE] for that magnificent exchange of correspondence between the Hebrew congregation of Newport, RI, and President Washington.

May I say that Senator WHITEHOUSE, in his own bearing and substance, lives out the promise of religious freedom that our first President gave to all Americans.

Perhaps I should say I say that as one of the descendants of the Stock of Abraham who is privileged to be a Member of the Senate today. I thank Senator WHITEHOUSE. I thank Senator MORAN.

I am going to take the liberty, if I may, to speak for a few minutes while we are waiting for either Senator MURKOWSKI, Senators WARNER or MENENDEZ, who are going to read documents before I conclude.

[In Senate manuscript a Senator is referred to as "the Senator from —— [Mr. ——]." Do not supply name and brackets if name does not appear in manuscript.]

[Note that brackets are used only when *Mr.*, etc., appears in manuscript.]

[See also use of *Mr., Mrs., Miss, Ms.* in explanation of votes under "Pairs."]

VOTING IN THE HOUSE AND IN COMMITTEE OF THE WHOLE

[Note that a dash is used only when a comma is necessary to separate the ayes and noes. If only the ayes or the noes are given, no punctuation is to be used. If the word *and* is used to connect the ayes and noes, as *ayes 52 and noes 65,* or *52 ayes and 65 noes,* the dash is omitted after the word *were* or *being.*]

On the question of ordering the yeas and nays there were 18 ayes and 88 noes.

The House divided; and there were—ayes 52, noes 65.

So (no further count being called for) the amendment of Mr. SCOTT of Virginia was not agreed to.

So (two-thirds having voted in favor thereof) the rules were suspended, and the bill was passed.

So (two-thirds not having voted in favor thereof) the motion was rejected.

The CHAIRMAN. The gentleman raises the point of no quorum. The Chair will count. [After counting.]

Two hundred and seventeen present, a quorum. The noes have it, and the amendment is rejected.

The question being taken on the motion of Mr. HOYER to suspend the rules and pass the bill, it was agreed to (two-thirds voting in favor thereof).

So (the affirmative not being one-fifth of the whole vote) the yeas and nays were not ordered.

The question was taken by a viva voice vote, and the Speaker announced that two-thirds appeared to have voted in the affirmative and [after a pause] that the bill was passed.

The yeas and nays were ordered, there being 43 in the affirmative, more than one-fifth of the last vote.

The question being taken on Mr. SHELBY's motion, there were—ayes 18, noes 35.

The question being taken on concurring in the amendments of the Senate, there were—ayes 101, noes 5.

The question was taken; and on a division [demanded by Mr. HOYER] there were—ayes 17, noes 29.

Mr. HOYER. Mr. Chairman, I demand a recorded vote, and pending that, I make the point of order that a quorum is not present.

The CHAIRMAN. Evidently a quorum is not present.

The Chair announces that pursuant to clause 2, rule XXIII, he will vacate proceedings under the call when a quorum of the Committee appears.

Members will record their presence by electronic device.

The call was taken by electronic device.

☐ 1715

[The above box followed by a four-digit number indicates floor time in the House (5:15 p.m.)]

QUORUM CALL VACATED

The CHAIRMAN. One hundred Members have appeared. A quorum of the Committee of the Whole is present. Pursuant to rule XXIII, clause 2, further proceedings under the call shall be considered as vacated.

The Committee will resume its business.

The pending business is the demand of the gentleman from Minnesota [Mr. PAULSEN] for a recorded vote.

A recorded vote was refused.

So the amendment to the amendment offered as a substitute for the amendment was rejected.

The CHAIRMAN. The question is on the amendment offered by the gentleman from Pennsylvania [Mr. MEEHAN] as a substitute for the amendment offered by the gentlewoman from South Dakota [Mrs. NOEM].

The question was taken; and the Chairman announced that the noes appeared to have it.

RECORDED VOTE

Mr. MEEHAN. Mr. Chairman, I demand a recorded vote.

A recorded vote was ordered.

The vote was taken by electronic device, and there were—ayes 228, noes 188, answered "present" 1, not voting 47, as follows

[Roll No. 509]

AYES—228

Abraham	Ellmers (NC)	Huelskamp
Babin	Farenthold	Sensenbrenner
Brooks (AL)	Fincher	Walker
Brooks (IN)	Garrett	Westerman
Chabot	Goodlatte	Yoho
Curbelo (FL)	Hartzler	Zeldin

NOES—188

Adams	Matsui	Takano
Bonamici	McCollum	Van Hollen
DeGette	O'Rourke	Vargas
Deutch	Ryan (OH)	Veasey
Hastings	Sarbanes	Wilson (FL)
Langevin	Schakowsky	Yarmuth

ANSWERED "PRESENT"—1

Fleming

NOT VOTING—17

Bishop (UT)	Lipinski	Price (NC)
Duckworth	McKinley	Reichert
Gohmert	Nugent	Ross
Graves (LA)	Palazzo	Valadao

□ 1311

Mr. RYAN of Wisconsin changed his vote from "aye" to "no."

Ms. WASSERMAN SCHULTZ, Ms. ESHOO, and Ms. ROS-LEHTINEN changed their vote from "no" to "aye."

[The Speaker's vote is recorded only in the "Ayes" or "Noes." It is never recorded as "not voting."]

[If the Speaker votes, his name is not used, but at the end of the "yeas" or "nays," according to his vote, insert: "The Speaker."]

So the amendment offered as a substitute for the amendment was agreed to.

The result of the vote was announced as above recorded.

VOTING BY YEAS AND NAYS

Senate

QUORUM CALL

The clerk will call the roll.

The assistant legislative clerk proceeded to call the roll, and the following Senators entered the Chamber and answered to their names:

[Quorum No. 42]

Alexander	Murkowski	Tillis
Feinstein	Nelson	Udall
Grassley	Paul	Vitter
Hatch	Sullivan	Warner
Heinrich	Tester	Whitehouse
Kaine	Thune	Wicker

The PRESIDING OFFICER [Mr. SASSE]. A quorum is not present.

Mr. REID. Mr. President, I move that the Sergeant at Arms be instructed to require the attendance of absent Senators, and I ask for the yeas and nays on the motion.

THE PRESIDING OFFICER. Is there a sufficient second? There is a sufficient second.

The yeas and nays were ordered.

The PRESIDING OFFICER. The question is on agreeing to the motion of the Senator from Nevada. On this question the yeas and nays have been ordered, and the clerk will call the roll.

The Assistant legislative clerk called the roll.

Mr. DURBIN. I announce that the Senator from Ohio (Mr. BROWN), the Senator from Massachusetts (Mr. MARKEY), the Senator from Illinois (Mr. KIRK), the Senator from Arkansas (Mr. BOOZMAN), and the Senator from Montana (Mr. TESTER) are necessarily absent.

Mr. CORNYN. The following Senators are necessarily absent: the Senator from Minnesota (Mr. FRANKLIN), the Senator from Nevada (Mr. HELLER), the Senator from South Carolina (Mr. GRAHAM), the Senator from New Hampshire (Mrs. SHAHEEN), the Senator from Arizona (Mr. MCCAIN), the Senator from Alaska (Ms. MURKOWSKI), the Senator from South Dakota (Mr. THUNE), the Senator from Louisiana (Mr. VITTER), and the Senator from Mississippi (Mr. WICKER).

Further, if present and voting, the Senator from Minnesota (Ms. KLOBUCHAR) would have voted "yea."

The result was announced—yeas 52, nays 40, as follows:

[Rollcall Vote No. 163 Leg.]

YEAS—76

Baldwin	Heitkamp	Pryor
Begich	Hirono	Reed
Bennet	Johnson (SD)	Reid
Blumenthal	Kaine	Rockefeller
Booker	Klobuchar	Sanders
Boxer	Landrieu	Schatz
Brown	Leahy	Schumer
Cantwell	Levin	Shaheen
Cardin	Manchin	Stabenow
Carper	Markey	Tester
Casey	McCaskill	Udall (CO)
Coons	Menendez	Udall (NM)
Durbin	Merkley	Walsh
Feinstein	Mikulski	Warner
Franken	Murphy	Warren
Gillibrand	Murray	Whitehouse
Hagan	Nelson	Wyden
Heinrich		

NAYS—10

Alexander	Flake	Murkowski
Ayotte	Graham	Paul
Boozman	Grassley	Portman
Burr	Heller	Risch
Coats	Hoeven	Rubio
Coburn	Inhofe	Scott
Cochran	Isakson	Sessions
Collins	Johanns	Shelby
Corker	Johnson (WI)	Thune
Cornyn	King	Toomey
Crapo	Kirk	Vitter
Cruz	Lee	Wicker
Enzi	McCain	
Fischer	McConnell	

NOT VOTING—14

Barrasso	Donnelly	Moran
Blunt	Harkin	Roberts
Chambliss	Hatch	

So the motion was agreed to.

PAIRS

[The word *with* must always be used in pairs in the House, not *and*; and manuscript must be altered to conform thereto, as Mr. Smith with Mr. Jones—*not* Mr. Smith and Mr. Jones. Note use of lowercase for names in list of pairs in House.]

The Clerk announced the following pairs:

On this vote:

Mr. Abraham for, with Mr. Aderholt against.

Until further notice:

Mr. Barr with Mrs. Beatty.

Mrs. Capps with Mr. Calvert.

Ms. Maxine Waters of California with Mr. Sean Patrick Maloney of New York.

Mr. Ackerman with Mr. Young of Alaska.

Mr. HANNA of New York, Mrs. BUSTOS, Messrs. FOSTER, HILL, and ISRAEL changed their votes from "nay" to "yea."

So the bill was passed.

The result of the vote was announced as above recorded.

A motion to reconsider was laid on the table.

Mr. BARR. Mr. Speaker, I voted, but, being paired with the gentlelady from Minnesota, Mrs. BEATTY, I withdraw my vote.

Ms. MAXINE WATERS of California. Mr. Speaker, I have a pair with the gentleman from New York, Mr. SEAN PATRICK MALONEY of New York, who, if present, would have voted "yea." I voted "nay." I withdraw my vote and vote "present."

[In House pairs do not use brackets when members are referred to by name. In Senate pairs observe the following use of brackets:]

Mr. DAWES (when his name was called). I am paired on this question with the senior Senator from Massachusetts [Mr. MARKEY]. If he were here, I should vote "yea."

CALL OF THE HOUSE

Mr. PALLONE. Ms. Speaker, I move a call of the House.

A call of the House was ordered.

The call was taken by electronic device and the following Members responded to their names:

[Roll No. 41]

Abraham	Garamendi	Tiberi
Aguilar	Hurd (TX)	Tipton
Brady (PA)	Hurt (VA)	Tonko
Brady (TX)	Neugebauer	Torres
Davis, Rodney	Perlmutter	Yoho
DeFazio	Ros-Lehtinen	Young (AK)

[No reference will be made of the names of those not voting.]

FORMS OF TITLES

[Always in roman lowercase, flush and hang 1 em, if more than two lines.]

H.J. RES. 2

Joint resolution authorizing the Secretary of the Treasury to issue to the public 2 per centum bonds or certificates, etc.

Resolved by the Senate and House of Representatives of the United States of America in Congress assembled, That the . . .

H.R. 4487

A bill to authorize the Rock Island and Southwestern Railway Company to construct a bridge, etc.

Be it enacted by the Senate and House of Representatives of the United States of America in Congress assembled, That it shall be lawful for the Rock Island and Southwestern Railway Company, a corporation organized under the general incorporation, etc.

ADDRESSES AND SIGNATURES

[No line spacing, street addresses, or ZIP Code numbers are to be used in communications in the Record.]

The Honorable the Secretary of the
□□Navy.
□Dear Mr. Secretary: This is in response to your letter, etc.
□□□Very sincerely yours,
George W. Bush.□

Columbia, MO,□□□
January 17, 2016.□

Hon. Claire McCaskill,
Cannon House Office Building,
Washington, DC.
□The President's farm message of today . . . farmers and prevent the spread of this depression to every part of our country.
Missouri Farmers
Association,
F.V. Heinkel, *President.*

January 20, 2016.□

Hon. Jacob J. Lew,
The Secretary of the Treasury, Department
□□*of the Treasury, Washington, DC.*
□Dear Mr. Secretary: Mindful of the tremendous workload, etc.
I would appreciate your comment on the foregoing proposal.
Your proposal seems to be in the best interest of all concerned.
□□□Sincerely yours,
John P. Sarbanes,□□□
Member of Congress.□□

Alexandria, MN,□□□
November 10, 2016.□

Hon. Amy Klobuchar,
Senate Office Building,
Washington, DC.
□We oppose the nomination of John Smith for Secretary of Agriculture because he resists family farms.
Raymond Wagner.□
□Brandon, MN.

January 17, 1972.□

Re resignation from committee.
Hon. Carl Albert,
The Speaker, U.S. House of Representa-
□□*tives, U.S. Capitol, Washington, DC.*
□Dear Mr. Speaker: Having changed my politics from Republican to Democrat, etc.
□With my best wishes.
□□□Sincerely,
Vincent J. Dellay.□

U.S. Senate,□□□□□
President pro tempore,□□□
Washington, DC, March 17, 2016.□

To the Senate:
□Being temporarily absent from the Senate, I appoint Hon. Rob Portman, a Senator from the State of Montana, to perform the duties of the Chair during my absence.
Orrin G. Hatch,□□□
President pro tempore.□

DESIGNATION OF SPEAKER PRO TEMPORE

□The SPEAKER pro tempore laid before the House the following communication from the Speaker:

Washington, DC,□□□
June 17, 2016.□

□I hereby appoint the Honorable Ken Buck to act as Speaker pro tempore on this day.
Paul D. Ryan,□□□
Speaker of the House of Representatives.□

□□The International Union, United□□□
□□□Automobile, Aerospace and Agri-□□□
□□□cultural Implement Workers of□□□
□□□America,
Detroit, MI, March 25, 2016.□

To the Senate of the United States.
To the United States House of Representa-
□□*tives.*
□Honorable Sirs: April 7, 2016, being the 60th anniversary of the modification, etc.

[Two to eight independent signatures, with or without titles, are aligned on the left.]

To the Honorable Senate and House of
□□*Representatives of the United States of*
□□*America Now Assembled at Washington,*
□□*DC:*
□The undersigned, officers of the Navy of the United States, respectfully show unto

your honorable bodies the following information, etc.

JAMES G. GREEN.
W.H. SOUTHERLAND.
THOMAS HARRISON.
F.F. FLETCHER.
ROBERT WHELAN.
C.C. WILSON.

☐Respectfully submitted,
KARL F. FELLER,
International President.☐
THOMAS RUSCH,
Director of Organization.☐
ARTHUR GILDEA,
Secretary-Treasurer.☐
JOSEPH E. BRADY,
Director of Legislation.☐

[More than eight signatures, with or without titles, are set full measure, caps and lowercase, run in, indented 2 and 3 ems, as follows:]

Gene H. Rosenblum, Cochairman; Paul H. Ray, Cochairman; Cynthia Asplund, James Pedersen, George Doty, Thomas St. Martin; Joan O'Neill; Lloyd Moosebrugger; Sam Kaplan; Ronald Nemer; Dean Potter; Philip Archer; Thomas McDonough; Mrs. Lloyd Moosebrugger; Minnesota Young Democratic Civil Rights Committee.

JOHN SMITH,☐☐☐☐☐
Lieutenant Governor☐☐☐
(For the Governor of Maine).☐

TEXARKANA TEXTILE
MERCHANTS &
MANUFACTURERS'
ASSOCIATION,
JOHN L. JONES,
Secretary.

CREDITS

[From the Wall Street Journal, Oct. 31, 2007]

SURVEILLANCE SANITY

(By Benjamin Civiletti, Dick Thornburgh and William Webster)

Following the terrorist attacks of Sept. 11, 2001, President Bush authorized the National Security Agency to target al Qaeda communications into and out of the country. Mr. Bush concluded that this was essential for protecting the country, that using the Foreign Intelligence Surveillance Act would not permit the necessary speed and agility, and that he had the constitutional power to authorize such surveillance without court orders to defend the country.

Since the program became public in 2006, Congress has been asserting appropriate oversight. Few of those who learned the details of the program have criticized its necessity. Instead, critics argued that if the president found FISA inadequate, he should have gone to Congress and gotten the changes necessary to allow the program to proceed under court orders. That process is now underway. The administration has brought the program under FISA, and the Senate Intelligence Committee recently reported out a bill with a strong bipartisan majority of 13–2, that would make the changes to FISA needed for the program to continue. This bill is now being considered by the Senate Judiciary Committee.

POETRY

[If poetry is quoted, each stanza should start with quotation marks, but only the last stanza should end with them. The lines of the poem should align on the left, those that rhyme taking the same indention. Poems are flush left; overs 3 ems; 2 points of space between stanzas, and 2 points of space above and below.]

CASEY AT THE BAT

The outlook wasn't brilliant for the Mudville nine that day:
The score stood four to two, with but one inning more to play.
And then when Cooney died at first, and Barrows did the same,
A pall-like silence fell upon the patrons of the game.

A straggling few got up to go in deep despair.
The rest clung to that hope which springs eternal in the human breast;
They thought, if only Casey could get but a whack at that—
We'd put up even money now, with Casey at the bat.

But Flynn preceded Casey, as did also Jimmy Blake,
And the former was a hoodoo and the latter was a cake;
So upon that stricken multitude grim melancholy sat,
For there seemed but little chance of Casey's getting to the bat.

But Flynn let drive a single, to the wonderment of all,
And Blake, the much despised, tore the cover off the ball;
And when the dust had lifted, and the men saw what had occurred,
There was Jimmy safe at second and Flynn a-hugging third.

Then from five thousand throats and more there rose a lusty yell;
It rumbled through the valley, it rattled in the dell;
It pounded on the mountain and recoiled upon the flat,
For Casey, mighty Casey, was advancing to the bat.

There was ease in Casey's manner as he stepped into his place;
There was pride in Casey's bearing and a smile lit Casey's face.
And when, responding to the cheers, he lightly doffed his hat,
No stranger in the crowd could doubt 'twas Casey at the bat.

Ten thousand eyes were on him as he rubbed his hands with dirt;
Five thousand tongues applauded when he wiped them on his shirt.
Then while the writhing pitcher ground the ball into his hip,
Defiance gleamed in Casey's eye, a sneer curled Casey's lip.

And now the leather-covered sphere came hurtling through the air,
And Casey stood a-watching it in haughty grandeur there.
Close by the sturdy batsman the ball unheeded sped—
"That ain't my style," said Casey. "Strike one," the umpire said.

From the benches, black with people, there went up a muffled roar,
Like the beating of the storm-waves on a stern and distant shore.
"Kill him! Kill the umpire!" shouted someone on the stand;
And it's likely they'd a-killed him had not Casey raised his hand.

With a smile of Christian charity great Casey's visage shone;
He stilled the rising tumult; he bade the game go on;
He signaled to the pitcher, and once more the dun sphere flew;
But Casey still ignored it, and the umpire said, "Strike two."

"Fraud!" cried the maddened thousands, and echo answered fraud;
But one scornful look from Casey and the audience was awed.
They saw his face grow stern and cold, they saw his muscles strain,
And they knew that Casey wouldn't let that ball go by again.

The sneer is gone from Casey's lip, his teeth are clenched in hate;
He pounds with cruel violence his bat upon the plate.
And now the pitcher holds the ball, and now he lets it go,
And now the air is shattered by the force of Casey's blow.

Oh, somewhere in this favored land the sun is shining bright;
The band is playing somewhere, and somewhere hearts are light,
And somewhere men are laughing, and somewhere children shout;
But there is no joy in Mudville—mighty Casey has struck out.

—Ernest Lawrence Thayer.

EXTRACTS

[Extracts must be set in 7 point unless ordered otherwise by the Joint Committee on Printing. This does not refer to a casual quotation of a few words or a quotation that would not make more than 3 lines of 7-point type. The beginning of the 7-point extract must start with a true paragraph; 8-point type following is always a paragraph.]

On February 29, Sue Payton, who is the Air Force's Assistant Secretary for Acquisition, said at a DOD news briefing:

We have been extremely open and transparent. We have had a very thorough review of what we're doing. We've got it nailed.

A week later, she told the House Appropriations Subcommittee on Defense:

The Air Force followed a carefully structured source selection process,—

They what?

designed to provide transparency, maintain integrity, and ensure a fair competition.

And throughout the last 4 months, Air Force officials have insisted that they selected the cheapest plane that best met their criteria and that they made no mistakes.

[Note, as above, that following an excerpt, the 8 point must begin with a paragraph.]

[An address of the President delivered outside of Congress or referred to as an extract will be set in 7 point.]

SCHEME OF TEXT HEADINGS

[In 8-point, heads are 8-point caps. After the cap head, all sub heads are 7-point small caps, regardless of any perceived hierarchy.

[In 7-point, the progression is as follows (in descending order):

7-point caps and small caps.

7-point small caps.

7-point italic lowercase.

7-point roman caps and lowercase.

7-point roman lowercase.]

USE OF DOUBLE HEADS

This is something which has been entirely overlooked by the . . .

ANALYSIS OF SPECIFIC PROVISIONS OF THE COMMITTEE BILL

AMENDMENTS CHANGING THE INTERSTATE COMMERCE PROVISIONS OF THE ACE

As the law stands today, it applies only to an employee who . . .

EXECUTIVE PROGRAM

ESTATE TAX CONVENTION WITH CANADA

AMENDMENTS SUBMITTED

RECIPROCAL TRADE AGREEMENTS

WARREN AMENDMENT NO. 1194

HEADS USED IN EXTENSIONS OF REMARKS

VA ACCOUNTABILITY FIRST AND APPEALS MODERNIZATION ACT OF 2016

SPEECH OF

HON. CHRIS VAN HOLLEN

OF MARYLAND

IN THE HOUSE OF REPRESENTATIVES

Tuesday, September 13, 2016

The House in Committee of the Whole House on the state of the Union had under consideration the bill (H.R. 5620) to amend title 38, United States Code, to provide for the removal or demotion of employees of the Department of Veterans Affairs based on performance or misconduct, and for other purposes:

[The words "Speech of" are to be used only when on manuscript and is an indication that that particular Extension of Remarks is to be inserted in the proceedings of the bound Record of the date used in the heading.]

MISSING CHILDREN

HON. ORRIN G. HATCH

OF UTAH

IN THE SENATE OF THE UNITED STATES

Wednesday, February 3, 1999

Mr. HATCH. Mr. President, I rise before this distinguished assembly to focus additional attention on the tragedy of missing children. The Department of Health and Human Services has estimated that approximately 1.3 million children disappear each year. A significant number do not leave of their own accord. . . .

CONGRESSIONAL PROCEEDINGS

SENATE

TUESDAY, JULY 12, 2016

(Legislative day of Monday, July 11, 2016)[1]

The Senate met at 9:30 a.m., on the expiration of the recess, and was called to order by the Honorable LISA MERKOWSKI, a Senator from the State of Alaska.

[Above line to be used only when Senate had been in recess.]

The Senate met at 9:30 a.m., and was called to order by the Honorable JAMES LANKFORD, a Senator from the State of Oklahoma.

[Note.—Entire prayer set in 8 point.]

PRAYER

The Chaplain, Dr. Barry C. Black, offered the following prayer:

Let us pray.

Our Father in heaven, we thank You for the beautiful differences in the human family, for its varied shapes and sizes, its features and colors, its abilities and talents. Deliver us from the forces that would destroy our unity by eliminating our diversity.

Bless the Members of this body. Help them in their debates to distinguish between substance and semantics, between rhetoric and reality. Free them from personal and partisan preoccupations that would defeat their aspirations and deprive Americans of just and equitable solutions. May our lawmakers avoid the works of darkness and put on Your armor of light.

We pray in Your holy Name. Amen.

PLEDGE OF ALLEGIANCE

The Presiding Officer led the Pledge of Allegiance, as follows:

I pledge allegiance to the Flag of the United States of America, and to the Republic for which it stands, one nation under God, indivisible, with liberty and justice for all.

APPOINTMENT OF ACTING PRESIDENT PRO TEMPORE

The PRESIDING OFFICER. The clerk will please read a communication to the Senate from the President pro tempore (Mr. HATCH).

The legislative clerk read the following letter:

U.S. SENATE,
PRESIDENT PRO TEMPORE,
Washington, DC, September 26, 2016.

To the Senate:

Under the provisions of rule I, section 3, of the Standing Rules of the Senate, I hereby appoint the Honorable JONI ERNST, a Senator from the State of Iowa, to perform the duties of the Chair.

ORRIN G. HATCH,
President pro tempore.

Mrs. ERNST thereupon assumed the chair as Acting President pro tempore.

RECOGNITION OF THE MAJORITY LEADER

The ACTING PRESIDENT pro tempore. The majority leader is recognized.

SCHEDULE

Mr. McCONNELL. Mr. President, following my remarks and those of Senator REID, there will be a period of morning business for 1 hour, with Senators permitted to speak therein for up to 10 minutes each. The majority will control the first 30 minutes;

[1] To be used only when the Senate had been in recess.

the Republicans will control the second 30 minutes.

Following morning business, the Senate will resume consideration of the motion to proceed to S. 3044, the Consumer-First Energy Act. The first 4 hours of debate will be equally divided and controlled in 30-minute alternating blocks of time, with the majority controlling the first 30 minutes and Republicans controlling the next 30 minutes.

Upon conclusion of the controlled time, Senators will be permitted to speak for up to 10 minutes each.

As a reminder, yesterday, I filed cloture on the motion to proceed to S. 3101, the Medicare Improvements for Patients and Providers Act. That cloture vote will occur tomorrow morning.

RESERVATION OF LEADER TIME

The ACTING PRESIDENT pro tempore. Under the previous order, the leadership time is reserved.

MORNING BUSINESS

The ACTING PRESIDENT pro tempore. Under the previous order, the Senate will proceed to a period of morning business for up to 1 hour, with Senators permitted to speak therein for up to 10 minutes each, with the time equally divided and controlled between the two leaders or their designees, with the majority controlling the first half and the Republicans controlling the final half.

Ms. BALDWIN. Mr. President, I ask unanimous consent that the order for the quorum call be rescinded.

The PRESIDING OFFICER. Without objection, it is so ordered.

CONCLUSION OF MORNING BUSINESS

The PRESIDING OFFICER. Morning business is now closed.

LEGISLATIVE BRANCH APPROPRIATIONS ACT, 2017—MOTION TO PROCEED

The PRESIDING OFFICER. Under the previous order, the Senate will resume consideration of the motion to proceed to H.R. 5325, which the clerk will report.

The senior assistant legislative clerk read as follows:

Motion to proceed to Calendar No. 516, H.R. 5325, a bill making appropriations for the Legislative Branch for the fiscal year ending September 30, 2017, and for other purposes.

The PRESIDING OFFICER. The assistant Democratic leader.

ZIKA VIRUS FUNDING

Mr. DURBIN. Mr. President, I can still recall the first briefing I had as a Member of Congress on something called HIV/AIDS. . . .

LEGISLATIVE BRANCH APPROPRIATIONS ACT, 2017—MOTION TO PROCEED—Continued

---

[Note the use of bullets signifying that which was not spoken on the floor.]

ADDITIONAL STATEMENTS

TRIBUTE TO GEORGE TAKEI

• Ms. HIRONO. Mr. President, "Oh Myyy!" My friend George Takei is being honored with the National Asian Pacific American Bar Association's NAPABA, Inspire Award. In addition to his many contributions to the arts, George has been on the forefront for decades, fighting for those who don't have a voice. . . .•

MESSAGES FROM THE PRESIDENT

Messages from the President of the United States were communicated to the Senate by Mr. Pate, one of his secretaries.

EXECUTIVE MESSAGES REFERRED

As in executive session the Presiding Officer laid before the Senate messages from the President of the United States submitting sundry nominations which were referred to the appropriate committees.

(The nominations received today are printed at the end of the Senate proceedings.)

REPORT OF THE VETO OF S. 2040, THE JUSTICE AGAINST SPONSORS OF TERRORISM ACT, RECEIVED DURING ADJOURNMENT OF THE SENATE ON SEPTEMBER 23, 2016—PM 56

The PRESIDING OFFICER laid before the Senate the following message from the President of the United States which was ordered to be printed in the RECORD, spread in full upon the Journal and held at the desk:

To the Senate of the United States:

I am returning herewith without my approval S. 2040, the "Justice Against Sponsors of Terrorism Act" (JASTA) . . . .

The JASTA, however, does not contribute to these goals, does not enhance the safety of Americans from terrorist attacks, and undermines core U.S. interests. For these reasons, I must veto the bill.

BARACK OBAMA.

THE WHITE HOUSE, *September 23, 2016.*

[The above to be 8 point.]

[When communications from the President contain extracts, etc., such extracts must be in 7 point.]

MESSAGES FROM THE HOUSE

At 12:21 p.m., a message from the House of Representatives, delivered by Mr. Novotny, one of its reading clerks, announced that the House has passed the following bill, with an amendement and an amendment to the title, in which it requests the concurrence of the Senate:

S. 253. An act to amend the Communications Act of 1934 to consolidate the reporting obligations of the Federal Communications Commission in order to improve congressional oversight and reduce reporting burdens.

ENROLLED BILLS SIGNED

At 10:05 a.m., a message from the House of Representatives, delivered by Mr. Novotny, one of its reading clerks, announced that the Speaker has signed the following enrolled bill:

H.R. 5325. An act making continuing appropriations for fiscal year 2017, and for other purposes. The enrolled bill was subsequently signed by the President pro tempore (Mr. HATCH).

The President pro tempore (Mr. HATCH) announced that on today, September 29, 2016, he signed the following enrolled bills, which were previously signed by the Speaker of the House:

S. 1878. An act to extend the pediatric priority review voucher program.

S. 2683. An act to include disabled veteran leave in the personnel management system of the Federal Aviation Administration.

At 12:56 p.m., a message from the House of Representatives, delivered by Mr. Novotny, one of its reading clerks, announced that the House has passed the following bill, in which it requests the concurrence of the Senate:

H.R. 5303. An act to provide for improvements to the rivers and harbors of the United States, to provide for the conservation and development of water and related resources, and for other purposes.

MEASURES REFERRED

The following bills were read the first and the second times by unanimous consent, and referred as indicated:

H.R. 5065. An act to direct the Administrator of the Transportation Security Administration to notify air carriers and security screening personnel of the Transportation Security Administration of such Administration's guidelines regarding permitting baby formula, breast milk, purified deionized water, and juice on airplanes, and for other purposes, to the Committee on Commerce, Science, and Transportation.

MEASURES PLACED ON THE CALENDAR

The following bill was read the second time, and placed on the calendar:

S. 3326. A bill to give States the authority to provide temporary access to affordable private health insurance options outside of Obamacare exchanges.

MEASURES READ THE FIRST TIME

The following bill was read the first time:

H.R. 954. An act to amend the Internal Revenue Code of 1986 to exempt from the individual mandate certain individuals who had coverage under a terminated qualified health plan funded through the Consumer Operated and Oriented Plan (CO-OP) program.

ENROLLED BILL PRESENTED

The Secretary of the Senate reported that on September 12, 2016, she had presented to the President of the United States the following enrolled bill:

S. 2040. An act to deter terrorism, provide justice for victims, and for other purposes.

EXECUTIVE AND OTHER COMMUNICATIONS

The following communications were laid before the Senate, together with accompanying papers, reports, and documents, and were referred as indicated:

EC–7000. A communication from the Secretary of the Commodity Futures Trading Commission, transmitting, pursuant to law, the report of a rule entitled "System Safeguards Testing Requirements for Derivatives Clearing Organizations" (RIN3038–AE29) received in the Office of the President of the Senate on September 21, 2016; to the Committee on. . . .

REPORT ON CLASSIFIED INFORMATION (S. DOC. NO. 107)

Mr. WARNER. Mr. President, the Committee on Armed Services of the Senate has recently requested the Office of Public Relations of the Department of the Navy to submit to it a report on classified information. The Department of the Navy has complied with the request, and I now present the report and ask that it be published as a Senate document.

The VICE PRESIDENT. Without objection, the report will be printed as a document as requested by the Senator from Virginia.

[Note the insertion of S. Doc. No. — in cases where papers are ordered to be printed as a document. To be inserted only when ordered to be printed or its equivalent is in manuscript.]

Third reading and passage of a bill.

MISSOURI RIVER BRIDGE NEAR ST. CHARLES, MO

The bill (S. 4174) to extend the times for commencing and completing the construction of a bridge across the Missouri River at or near St. Charles, MO, was considered, ordered to be engrossed for a third reading, read the third time, and passed, as follows:

S. 4174

Be it enacted by the Senate and House of Representatives of the United States of America in Congress assembled, That the times for commencing and completing the construction of the bridge across the Missouri River, etc.

GOVERNMENT OF THE TERRITORY OF HAWAII

The Senate proceeded to consider the bill (S. 1881) to amend an act entitled "An act to provide a government for the Territory of Hawaii," approved April 30, 1900, as amended, to establish a Hawaiian Homes Commission, and for other purposes, which had been reported from the Committee on Interior and Insular Affairs with amendments.

The first amendment was, on page 4 line 22, to strike out "Keaaupaha" and insert "Keaaukaha".

The amendment was agreed to.

The next amendment was, on page 6, line 19, after the figure "(1)", to insert "by further authorization of Congress and", so as to make the paragraph read:

(1) by further authorization of Congress and for a period of five years after the first meeting of the Hawaiian Homes Commission only those lands situated on the island of Molokaki, etc.

The Amendment was agreed to.

The bill was ordered to be engrossed for a third reading, read the third time, and passed.

Forms of amendments

The joint resolution (S.J. Res. 4) requesting the President to negotiate a treaty or treaties for the protection of salmon in retrain parts of the Pacific Ocean was announced as next in order.

Mr. INHOFE. Mr. President, I have just had an opportunity to examine this joint resolution. I offer this amendment.

The PRESIDING OFFICER. The Secretary will state the amendment offered by the Senator from Arizona.

The READING CLERK. On page 1, line 11, it is proposed to strike out the words "both within and", so as to make the joint resolution read:

Resolved by the Senate and House of Representatives of the United States of America in Congress assembled, That the President of the United States be, and he is hereby, requested to negotiate on behalf of the United States, as promptly as is practicable, etc.

Mr. McCONNELL. Mr. President, I observe in the report of the bill by the chairman of the Foreign Relations Committee that it is reported as a Senate joint resolution. I ask for a modification of it so that it will be a Senate resolution instead of a Senate joint resolution.

The LEGISLATIVE CLERK. It is proposed to strike out "S.J. Res. 4" and insert "S. Res. 85".

The PRESIDING OFFICER. Is there objection to the modification? The Chair hears one and it will be so modified.

Mr. INHOFE. Would it not be necessary to change the resolving clause also? The resolving clause reads:

Resolved by the Senate and House of Representatives of the United States of America in Congress assembled,

The amendment was agreed to.

[Note use of words, figures, and punctuation in the following example. Follow manuscript.]

The next amendment was, on page 34, in line 9, under the heading "Employees' Compensation Commission", before the word "assistants", to strike out "five" and insert "three"; in line 10, after the word "clerks" and before the words "of class 3", to strike out "seven" and insert "five"; in line 11, before the words "of class 2", to strike out "twelve" and insert "nine"; in the same line, before the words "of class 1", to strike out "twenty-seven" and insert "twenty"; in line 12, before the words "at $1.000 each", to strike out "three" and insert "two"; and in line 18, to strike out "$124,940" and insert "$102,590", so as to read:

EMPLOYEE'S COMPENSATION COMMISSION

Salaries: Three Commissioners at $4,000 each; secretary, $2,750; attorney, $4,000; chief statistician, $3,000; chief of accounts, $2,500; accountant, $2,250; claim examiners—chief $2,250, assistant $2,000, assistant $1,800, three assistants at $1,600 each; special agents—two at $1,800 each, two at $1,600 each; clerks—five of class 3, nine of class 2, twenty of class 1, two at $1,000 each; in all $102,590.

Mr. UDALL submitted an amendment intended to be proposed by him to the sundry civil appropriation bill, which was ordered to lie on the table and to be printed, as follows:

Add a new section, as follows: "*That the President of the Senate appoint three Members of the Senate; and the Speaker of the House three Members of the House.*"

The Senate resumed the consideration of the bill (H.R. 4075) to limit the immigration of aliens into the United States.

[An executive session usually being open, the following precedes the recess or adjournment heading:]

REPORT ON THE STATE OF THE UNION DELIVERED TO A JOINT SESSION OF CONGRESS ON JANUARY 12, 2016—PM 36

The PRESIDING OFFICER laid before the Senate the following message from the President of the United States which was ordered to lie on the table.

To the Congress of the United States:

Mr. Speaker, Mr. Vice President, Members of Congress, my fellow Americans:

Tonight marks the eighth year I've come here to report on the State of the Union. And for this final one, I'm going to try to make it shorter. I know some of you are antsy to get back to Iowa. I also understand that because it's an election season, expectations for what we'll achieve this year are low. Still, Mr. Speaker, I appreciate the constructive approach you and the other leaders took at the end of last year to pass a budget and make tax cuts permanent for working families. So I hope we can work together this year on bipartisan priorities like criminal justice reform, and helping people who are battling prescription drug abuse. We just might surprise the cynics agains.

But tonight, I want to go easy on the traditional list of proposals for the year ahead. Don't worry, I've got plenty, from helping students learn to write computer code to personalizing medical treatments for patients. And I'll keep pushing for progress on the work that still needs doing. Fixing a broken immigration system. Protecting our kids from gun violence. Equal pay for equal work, paid leave, raising the minimum wage. All these things still matter to hardworking families; they are still the right thing to do; and I will not let up until they get done. . . .

That's the America I know. That's the country we love. Clear-eyed. Bighearted. Optimistic that unarmed truth and unconditional love will have the final word. That's what makes me so hopeful about our future. Because of you. I believe in you. That's why I stand here confident that the State of our Union is strong.

Thank you, God bless you, and God bless the United States of America.

BARACK OBAMA. ☐

THE WHITE HOUSE, *January 12, 2016.*

To the Senate of the United States:

To the end that I may receive the advice and consent of the Senate to ratification, I transmit herewith a treaty of arbitration and conciliation between the United States and Switzerland, signed at Washington on March 17, 1952.

HARRY S. TRUMAN. ☐

THE WHITE HOUSE, *March 17, 1952.*

[A letter from the President to the Senate is set in 7-point type when any form of treaty is encloses that is to be printed in the Record in connection therewith. The letter is set in 7-point type whether the treaty follows or precedes it or separated from it by intervening matter.]

RECESS UNTIL TOMORROW AT 10:30 A.M.

Mr. McCONNELL. Mr. President, I know of no further business to come before the Senate. I move, in accordance with the order previously entered, that the Senate stand in recess until the hour of 10:30 a.m. tomorrow.

The motion was agreed to and, at 7:34 p.m., the Senate recessed until Wednesday, June 5, 2016, at 10:30 a.m.

[After the recess or adjournment the following may appear:]

NOMINATIONS

Executive Nominations received by the Senate.

[Under the heads *Nominations, Confirmations, Withdrawal,* and *Rejection,* the following scheme for subheads is to be followed:

[Heads indicating service, or branch or department of Government and subheads

indicating subdivision or type of service—7-point small caps.]

[Subheads indicating new rank of appointee—7-point italic initial cap.

[Text is set in 5-point caps.

[Note: Nominations will be set first name, middle name (or first middle initial), and last name throughout followed by period. Asterisks, if any, precede names as in executive nominations.]

Executive nominations received by the Senate:

NATIONAL FOUNDATION ON
THE ARTS AND THE HUMANITIES

JANE MARIE DOGGETT, OF MONTANA, TO BE A MEMBER OF THE NATIONAL COUNCIL ON THE HUMANITIES FOR A TERM EXPIRING JANUARY 26, 2022, VICE CATHY M. DAVIDSON, TERM EXPIRED.

STATE JUSTICE INSTITUTE

WILFREDO MARTINEZ, OF FLORIDA, TO BE A MEMBER OF THE BOARD OF DIRECTORS OF THE STATE JUSTICE INSTITUTE FOR A TERM EXPIRING SEPTEMBER 17, 2019. (REAPPOINTMENT)

IN THE NAVY

THE FOLLOWING NAMED OFFICER FOR APPOINTMENT IN THE UNITED STATES NAVY TO THE GRADE INDICATED WHILE ASSIGNED TO A POSITION OF IMPORTANCE AND RESPONSIBILITY UNDER TITLE 10, U.S.C., SECTION 601:

To be vice admiral

VICE ADMIN. DIXON R. SMITH

CONFIRMATIONS

Executive nominations confirmed by the Senate September 28, 2016:

IN THE AIR FORCE

THE FOLLOWING NAMED OFFICER FOR APPOINTMENT IN THE UNITED STATES AIR FORCE TO THE GRADE INDICATED UNDER TITLE 10, U.S.C., SECTION 624:

To be brigadier general

COL. KENNETH P. EKMAN

To be brigadier general

COL. ALFRED F. ABRAMSON III

COL. PETER B. ANDRYSIAK, JR.

COL. ROBERT W. BENNETT, JR.

HOUSE OF REPRESENTATIVES

FRIDAY, SEPTEMBER 9, 2016

[When the Speaker is in the Chair, follow this style.]

The House met at noon.

The Chaplain, the Reverend Patrick J. Conroy, offered the following prayer:

Merciful God, we give You thanks for giving us another day.

In this year of post-9/11, we pray that the children of this generation and their children's children may never have to experience another day like the one that flooded our TV screens so many years ago.

Protect and guide this Nation to a new security, built upon human integrity and communal solidarity with all who love freedom and human dignity, while respecting the lives and beliefs of others.

Empower the Members of Congress and governments around the world to establish just laws and seek the common good that will lead to ways of equity and peace.

May all that is done this day be for Your greater honor and glory.

Amen.

[When the Speaker is not in the Chair, follow this style.]

The House met at 12:30 and was called to order by the Speaker pro tempore (Mr. BOST).

DESIGNATION OF SPEAKER PRO TEMPORE

The SPEAKER pro tempore laid before the House the following communication from the Speaker:

WASHINGTON, DC,
June 17, 2016.

I hereby appoint the Honorable MIKE BOST to act as Speaker pro tempore on this day.

PAUL D. RYAN,
Speaker of the House of Representatives.

PRAYER[1]

The Chaplain, the Reverend Patrick J. Conroy, offered the following prayer:

We give You thanks, O God, for giving us another day. In the wake of a great American holiday, we ask Your special blessing on American workers, those fortunate to have jobs during these difficult economic times and those desiring work. May they know and be confident of the nobility and sacredness of their labor.

As the Members of the people's House return to the Capitol, call them, as well, with Your gentling voice of collegiality.

When a sense of alienation shadows all of our souls, we find our differences difficult to bear; we move away from each other. Insofar as this spirit of alienation has descended upon this House, help each Member to overcome unnecessary divisions that hamper productive work on behalf of our Nation.

Bring them to a deeper level of awareness of Your spirit, and make us one Nation. Give the Members listening hearts, ready and willing to respond to Your spirit living in each one.

And may all that is done be for Your greater honor and glory.

Amen.

THE JOURNAL

The SPEAKER pro tempore. The Chair has examined the Journal of the last day's proceedings and announces to the House his approval thereof.

Pursuant to clause 1, rule I, the Journal stands approved.

[1] Head is not used when the Speaker is in the chair. See preceding example.

PLEDGE OF ALLEGIANCE

The SPEAKER pro tempore. Will the gentleman from Iowa (Mr. BLUM) come forward and lead the House in the Pledge of Allegiance.

Mr. BLUM led the Pledge of Allegiance as follows:

I pledge allegiance to the Flag of the United States of America, and to the Republic for which it stands, one nation under God, indivisible, with liberty and justice for all.

SWEARING IN OF THE HONORABLE WARREN DAVIDSON, OF OHIO, AS A MEMBER OF THE HOUSE

Ms. KAPTUR. Mr. Speaker, I ask unanimous consent that the gentleman from Ohio, the Honorable WARREN DAVIDSON, be permitted to take the oath of office today.

His certificate of election has not arrived, but there is no contest and no question has been raised with regard to his election.

The SPEAKER. Is there objection to the request of the gentlewoman from Ohio?

There was no objection.

The SPEAKER. Will Representative-elect DAVIDSON and the members of the Ohio delegation present themselves in the well.

All Members will rise and the Representative-elect will please raise his right hand.

Mr. DAVIDSON appeared at the bar of the House and took the oath of office, as follows:

Do you solemnly swear that you will support and defend the Constitution of the United States against all enemies, foreign and domestic; that you will bear true faith and allegiance to the same; that you take this obligation freely, without any mental reservation or purpose of evasion; and that you will well and faithfully discharge the duties of the office on which you are about to enter, so help you God

The SPEAKER. Congratulations. You are now a Member of the 114th Congress.

WELCOMING THE HONORABLE WARREN DAVIDSON TO THE HOUSE OF REPRESENTATIVES

[Welcoming speeches follow.]

[Initial speech of new Representative follows.]

ANNOUNCEMENT BY THE SPEAKER

The SPEAKER. Under clause 5(d) of rule XX, the Chair announces to the House that, in light of the administration of the oath of office to the gentleman from Ohio (Mr. DAVIDSON), the whole number of the House is 435.

OATH OF OFFICE OF MEMBERS

The oath of office required by the sixth article of the Constitution of the United States, and as provided by section 2 of the act of May 13, 1884 (23 Stat. 22), to be administered to Members, Resident Commissioner, and Delegates or the House of Representatives, the text of which is carried in 5 U.S.C. 3331:

> "I, AB, do solemnly swear (or affirm) that I will support and defend the Constitution of the united States against all enemies, foreign and domestic; that you will bear true faith and allegiance to the same; that you take this obligation freely, without and mental reservation or purpose of evasion; and that you will well and faithfully discharge the duties of the office on which you are about to enter, so help you God.

has been subscribed to in person and filed in duplicate with the Clerk of the House of Representatives by the following Member of the 110th Congress, pursuant to Public Law 412 of the 80th Congress entitled "An act to amend section 30 of the Revised Statues of the United States" (2 U.S.C. 25, approved February 18, 1948:

WARREN DAVIDSON, 8th District of Ohio.

MESSAGE FROM THE SENATE

A message from the Senate by Ms. Curtis, one of its clerks, announced that the Senate concurs in the amendment of the House to the bill (S. 2146) "An Act to authorize the Administrator of the Environmental Protection Agency to accept, as part of a settlement, diesel emission reduction Supplemental Environmental Projects, and for other purposes."

[Above usage occurs when there is only one bill referenced. For more than one bill, use the following style.]

MESSAGE FROM THE SENATE

A message from the Senate by Ms. Curtis, one of its clerks, announced that the Senate has passed without amendment a bill of the House of the following titles:

H.R. 3969. An act to designate the Department of Veterans Affairs community-based Outpatient clinic in Laughlin, Nevada, as the "Master Chief Petty Officer Jesse Dean VA Clinic".

[Observe that bills from the Senate to the House read *An act*. If the manuscript should read *A bill*, change to *An act* in conformity with this rule, and place number first. Note also the following forms:]

PRESIDENTIAL ALLOWANCE MODERNIZATION ACT OF 2016—VETO MESSAGE FROM THE PRESIDENT OF THE UNITED STATES (H. DOC. NO. 114–155)

The SPEAKER pro tempore laid before the House the following veto message from the President of the United States:

To the House of Representatives:

II am returning herewith without my approval H.R. 1777, the "Presidential Allowance Modernization Act of 2016," which would amend the Former Presidents Act of 1958.

I agree with H.R. 1777's goal of reforming the pensions and allowances provided to former Presidents so as to reduce unnecessary costs to taxpayers. But if implemented as drafted, the bill would have unintended consequences. It would impose onerous and unreasonable burdens on the offices of former Presidents, including by requiring the General Services Administration to immediately terminate salaries and benefits of office employees and to remove furnishings and equipment from offices. It would withdraw the General Services Administration's ability to administer leases and negatively impact operations, with unanticipated implications for the protection and security of former Presidents.

My Administration will work with the authors of the bill and other leaders in the Congress, in consultation with the offices of former Presidents, to explore the best ways to achieve these goals going forward. If the Congress returns the bill having appropriately addressed these concerns, I will sign it. For now, I must veto the bill.

BARACK OBAMA.

THE WHITE HOUSE, *July 22, 2016.*

The SPEAKER pro tempore. The objections of the President will be spread at large upon the Journal, and the veto message and the bill will be printed as a House document.

Without objection, further consideration of the veto message and the bill, H.R. 1777, is postponed until the legislative day of September 23, 2016.

There was no objection.

[Debate and vote follow.]

MESSAGE FROM THE PRESIDENT

A message in writing from the President of the United States was communicated to the House by Mr. Sherman Williams, one of his secretaries, who also informed the House that on the following dates the

President approved and signed bills of the House and Senate of the following titles:

On July 1, 1996:

H.R. 3029. An act to designate the United States courthouse in Washington, District of Columbia, as the "E. Barrett Prettyman United States Courthouse."

On July 2, 1996:

H.R. 2803. An act to amend the anti-car theft provisions of title 49, United States Code, to increase the utility of motor vehicle title information to the State and Federal law enforcement officials, and for other purposes.

On July 3, 1996:

H.R. 3525, An act amend title 18, United States Code, to clarify the Federal jurisdiction over offenses relating to damage to religious property. . . .

[Observe that bills coming from the President take the form of *An act*. This rule must be followed invariably, even if the manuscript reads *A bill*.]

MOURNING THE LOSS OF SHIMON PERES

(Mr. CICILLINE asked and was given permission to address the House for 1 minute.)

Mr. CICILLINE. Mr. Speaker, I rise to express my deep sadness on the passing of former Israeli President and Prime Minister Shimon Peres. Shimon Peres was devoted to the cause of the Jewish state and worked tirelessly to achieve a lasting peace in the Middle East.

He was the founding father of the State of Israel and remained, throughout his life, one of its greatest champions. He was the central architect of the Oslo Accords and was respected around the world for his strong leadership as Prime Minister and President of Israel. His example should be an inspiration to us all, as he fought so long for peace.

My thoughts are with his family and friends as well as the people of Israel, who have lost a beloved leader.

MRS. VIRGINIA THRIFT

Mr. GOSAR. Ms. Speaker, by direction of the Committee on House Administration, I offer a privileged resolution (H. Res. 321) and ask for its immediate consideration.

The Clerk read as follows:

H. RES. 321

Resolved, That there shall be paid out of the contingent fund of the House to Mrs. Virginia Thrift, widow of Chester R. Thrift, late an employee of the House, an amount equal to six months' salary compensation at the rate he was receiving at the time of his death, and an additional amount not to exceed $250 to defray funeral expenses of the said Chester R. Thrift.

The Resolution was agreed to.

A motion to reconsider was laid on the table.

BILLS PRESENTED TO THE PRESIDENT

Karen L. Haas, Clerk of the House, reported that on February 23, 2016, she presented to the President of the United States, for his approval, the following bill:

H.R. 644. To reauthorize trade facilitation and trade enforcement functions and activities, and for other purposes.

ENROLLED BILLS SIGNED

Ms. Lorraine C. Miller, Clerk of the House, reported and found truly enrolled bills of the House of the following titles, which were thereupon signed by the Speaker:

H.R. 430. An act to designate the United States bankruptcy courthouse located at 271 Cadman Plaza East in Brooklyn, New York, as the "Conrad B. Duberstein United States Bankruptcy Courthouse".

H.R. 781. An act to redesignate Lock and Dam No. 5 of the McClellan-Kerr Arkansas River Navigation System near Redfield, Arkansas, authorized by the Rivers and Harbors Act approved July 24, 1946, as the "Colonel Charles D. Maynard Lock and Dam".

H.R. 1019. An act to designate the United States customhouse building located at 31 Gonzalez Clemente Avenue in Mayagüez, Puerto Rico, as the "Rafael Martinez Nadal United States Customhouse Building".

PRIVATE CALENDAR

The SPEAKER pro tempore (Mrs. BLACK). This is the day for the call of the Private Calendar.

The Clerk will call the bill on the calendar.

CORINA DE CHALUP TURCINOVIC

The Clerk called called the bill (H.R. 306) for the relief of Corina de Chalup Turcinovic.

There being no objection, the Clerk read the bill as follows:

H.R. 306

Be it enacted by the Senate and House of Representatives of the United States of America in Congress assembled,

SECTION 1. PERMANENT RESIDENT STATUS FOR CORINA DE CHALUP TURCINOVIC.

(a) IN GENERAL.—Notwithstanding subsections (a) and (b) of section 201 of the Immigration and Nationality Act, Corina de Chalup Turcinovic shall be eligible for issuance of an immigrant visa or for adjustment of status to that of an alien lawfully admitted for permanent residence upon filing an application for issuance of an immigrant visa under section 204 of such Act or for adjustment of status to lawful permanent resident. . . .

(e) DENIAL OF PREFERENTIAL IMMIGRATION TREATMENT FOR CERTAIN RELATIVES.—The natural parents, brothers, and sisters of Corina de Chalup Turcinovic shall not, by virtue of such relationship, be accorded any right, privilege, or status under the Immigration and Nationality Act.

The bill was ordered to be engrossed and read a third time, was read the third time, and passed, and a motion to reconsider was laid on the table.

The SPEAKER pro tempore. This concludes the call of the Private Calendar.

SENATE BILLS REFERRED

Bills of the Senate of the following titles were taken from the Speaker's table and, under the rule, referred as follows:

S. 1479. An act to amend the Comprehensive Environmental Response, Compensation, and Liability Act of 1980 to modify provisions relating to grants, and for other purposes; to the Committee on Energy and Commerce; in addition, to the Committee on Transportation and Infrastructure for a period to be subsequently determined by the Speaker, in each case for consideration of such provisions as fall with the jurisdiction of the committee concerned.

S. 2829. An act to amend and enhance certain maritime programs of the Department of Transportation, and for other purposes; to the Committee on Armed Services; in addition, to the Committee on Transportation and Infrastructure; to the Committee on Natural Resources; to the Committee on Veterans' Affairs; to the Committee on the Judiciary; and to the Committee on Oversight and Government Reform for a period to be subsequently determined by the Speaker, in each case for consideration of such provisions as fall within the jurisdiction of the committee concerned.

[In the reference of Senate acts to House committees the name of the committee will be repeated after the act, though there may be several acts referred to the same committee.]

COMMITTEE OF THE WHOLE HOUSE ON THE STATE OF THE UNION

WATER RESOURCES DEVELOPMENT ACT OF 2016

The SPEAKER pro tempore. Pursuant to House Resolution 897 and rule XVIII, the Chair declares the House in the Committee of the Whole House on the state of the Union for the further consideration of the bill, H.R. 5303.

Will the gentleman from Illinois (Mr. HULTGREN) kindly take the chair.

☐ 1535

IN THE COMMITTEE OF THE WHOLE

Accordingly, the House resolved itself into the Committee of the Whole House on the state of the Union for the further consideration of the bill (H.R. 5303) to provide for improvements to the rivers and harbors of the United States, to provide for the conservation and development of water and related resources, and for other purposes, with Mr. HULTGREN (Acting Chair) in the chair.

The Clerk read the title of the bill.

The Acting CHAIR. When the Committee of the Whole rose earlier today, amendment No. 10 printed in House Report 114–790 offered by the gentleman from Louisiana (Mr. GRAVES) had been disposed of.

Pursuant to House Resolution 897, no further amendment to the amendment in the nature of a substitute referred to in House Resolution 892 shall be in order except those printed in House Report 114–794.

Each such further amendment shall be considered only in the order printed in the report, may be offered only by a Member designated in the report, shall be considered as read, shall be debatable for the time specified in the report equally divided and controlled by the proponent and an opponent, shall not be subject to amendment, and shall not be subject to a demand for division of the question.

AMENDMENT NO. 1 OFFERED BY MR. BYRNE

The Acting CHAIR. It is now in order to consider amendment No. 1 printed in House Report 114–794.

Mr. BYRNE. Mr. Chairman, I have an amendment at the desk.

The Acting CHAIR. The Clerk will designate the amendment.

The text of the amendment is as follows:

At the end of title I, add the following:

SEC. 11. GULF COAST OYSTER BED RECOVERY ASSESSMENT. . . .

(Voting occurs)

The amendment was agreed to.

The Acting CHAIR. Under the rule, the Committee rises.

Accordingly, the Committee rose; and the Speaker pro tempore (Mr. YODER) having assumed the chair, Mr. EMMER of Minnesota, Acting Chair of the Committee of the Whole House on the state of the Union, reported that that Committee, having had under consideration the bill (H.R. 5303) to provide for improvements to the rivers and harbors of the United States, to provide for the conservation and development of water and related resources, and for other purposes, and, pursuant to House Resolution 897, he reported the bill back to the House with an amendment adopted in the Committee of the Whole.

The SPEAKER pro tempore. Under the rule, the previous question is ordered.

Is a separate vote demanded on any amendment to the amendment reported from the Committee of the Whole?

If not, the question is on the amendment in the nature of a substitute, as amended.

The amendment was agreed to.

The SPEAKER pro tempore. The question is on the engrossment and third reading of the bill.

The bill was ordered to be engrossed and read a third time, and was read the third time.

So the bill was passed.

The result of the vote was announced as above recorded.

A motion to reconsider was laid on the table.

CONFERENCE REPORT AND STATEMENT

Conference reports and statements to be set in 7 point.

Use 3-point space before and after conference report and statement.

In the House the names of Members are to be first.

Follow manuscript literally in the report. Observe the form *Amendments numbered 1, 2, 3, etc.*, and, when the amendment is to make an independent paragraph, the phrase *And the Senate* [or *House*] *agree to the same* will be a paragraph by itself; otherwise it will be run in after the amendment with a semicolon. Examples of each are given in the report following.

In the statement change *numbered* to *No.*, as *amendment No. 1*, but do not supply *No.* or *amendment* if omitted in manuscript; otherwise regular style will prevail.

CONFERENCE REPORT (H. REPT. 114–669)

The committee of conference on the disagreeing votes of the two Houses on the amendments of the House do the bill (S. 524), to authorize the Attorney General to award grants to address the national epidemics of prescription opioid abuse and heroin use, having met, after full and free conference, have agreed to recommend and do recommend to their respective Houses as follows:

That the Senate recede from its disagreement to the amendment of the House to the text of the bill and agree to the same with an amendment as follows:

In lieu of the matter proposed to be inserted by the House amendment, insert the following:

SECTION 1. SHORT TITLE; TABLE OF CONTENTS.

(a) SHORT TITLE.–This act may be cited as the "Comprehensive Addiction and Recovery Act of 2016".

(b) TABLE OF CONTENTS.–The table of contents for this Act is as follows:

Sec. 1. Short title; table of contents.

Title 1–PREVENTION AND EDUCATION

Sec. 101. Task force on pain management.

Sec. 102. Awareness campaigns. . . .

In lieu of the matter proposed to be inserted by the House amendment to the title of the bill, insert the following: "An Act to authorize the Attorney General and Secretary of Health and Human Services to award grants to address the prescription opioid abuse and heroin use crisis, and for other purposes.".

And the House agree to the same.

For consideration of the Senate bill and the House amendments, and modifications committed to conference:

FRED UPTON,
JOSEPH R. PITTS,
LEONARD LANCE,
BRETT GUTHRIE,
ADAM KINZINGER,
LARRY BUCSHON,
SUSAN W. BROOKS,
BOB GOODLATTE,
F. JAMES SENSENBRENNER, JR.,
LAMAR SMITH,
TOM MARINO,
DOUG COLLINS,
DAVID A. TROTT,
MIKE BISHOP,
KEVIN MCCARTHY,

From the Committee on Education and the Workforce, for consideration of title VII of the House amendment, and modifications committed to conference:

LOU BARLETTA,
EARL L. "BUDDY" CARTER,

From the Committee on Veterans' Affairs, for consideration of title III of the House amendment, and modifications committed to conference:

GUS M. BILIRAKIS,
JACKIE WALORSKI,

From the Committee on Ways and Means, for consideration of sec. 705 of the Senate bill, and sec. 804 of the House amendment, and modifications committed to conference:

PATRICK MEEHAN,
ROBERT J. DOLD,

Managers on the Part of the House.
CHUCK GRASSLEY,
LAMAR ALEXANDER,
ORRIN G. HATCH,
JEFF SESSIONS,
Managers on the Part of the Senate.

JOINT EXPLANATORY STATEMENT OF THE COMMITTEE OF CONFERENCE

The managers on the part of the House and the Senate at the conference on the disagreeing votes of the two Houses on the amendments of the House to the bill (S. 524), to authorize the Attorney General to award grants to address the national epidemics of prescription opioid abuse and heroin use, submit the following joint statement to the House and the Senate in explanation of the effect of the action agreed upon by the managers and recommended in the accompanying conference report:

The House amendment to the text of the bill struck all of the Senate bill after the enacting clause and inserted a substitute text.

The Senate recedes from its disagreement to the amendment of the House with an amendment that is a substitute for the Senate bill and the House amendment. . . .

CONSTITUTIONAL STATEMENT OF AUTHORITY

Congress has the power to enact this legislation pursuant to the following: Article I, Section 8, Clause 3 of the United States Constitution.

For consideration of the Senate bill and the House amendments, and modifications committed to conference:
FRED UPTON,
JOSEPH R. PITTS,
LEONARD LANCE,
BRETT GUTHRIE,
ADAM KINZINGER,
LARRY BUCSHON,
SUSAN W. BROOKS,
BOB GOODLATTE,
F. JAMES SENSENBRENNER, JR.,
LAMAR SMITH,
TOM MARINO,
DOUG COLLINS,
DAVID A. TROTT,
MIKE BISHOP,
KEVIN MCCARTHY,

From the Committee on Education and the Workforce, for consideration of title VII of the House amendment, and modifications committed to conference:
LOU BARLETTA,
EARL L. "BUDDY" CARTER,

From the Committee on Veterans' Affairs, for consideration of title III of the House amendment, and modifications committed to conference:
GUS M. BILIRAKIS,
JACKIE WALORSKI,

From the Committee on Ways and Means, for consideration of sec. 705 of the Senate bill, and sec. 804 of the House amendment, and modifications committed to conference:
PATRICK MEEHAN,
ROBERT J. DOLD,
Managers on the Part of the House.
CHUCK GRASSLEY,
LAMAR ALEXANDER,
ORRIN G. HATCH,
JEFF SESSIONS,
Managers on the Part of the Senate.

Amendments

[As figures are used in bills to express sums of money, dates, paragraph numbers, etc., amendments involving such expressions must be set in figures thus: Strike out "$840" and insert "$1,000", etc. for other enumerations, etc., follow the manuscript as the data is picked up from the bill and used for the Record and then picked up from the Record and used for the report.]

EMANUEL F. LENKERSDORF

The Clerk called the bill (H.R. 2520) for the relief of Emanuel F. Lenkersdorf.

There being no objection, the Clerk read the bill as follows:

H.R. 2520

Be it enacted by the Senate and House of Representatives of the United States of America in Congress assembled, That for the purposes of the Immigration and Nationality Act, Emanuel F. Lenkersdorf shall be held and considered to have been lawfully admitted to the United States for permanent residence as of the date of the enactment of this Act, upon payment of the required visa fee. Upon the granting of permanent residence to such alien as provided for in this Act, the Secretary of State shall instruct the proper officer to deduct one number from the total number of immigrant visas and conditional entries which are made available to natives of the country of the alien's birth under paragraphs (1) through (8) of section 203(a) of the Immigration and Nationality Act.

With the following committee amendment:

On page 2, strike lines 4 through 6 and insert in lieu thereof: "which are made available to natives of the country of the alien's birth under section 203(a) of the Immigration and Nationality Act or, if applicable, from the total number of such visas which are made available to such natives under section 202(3) of such Act.".

The committee amendment was agreed to.

The bill was ordered to be engrossed and read a third time, was read the third time, and passed, and a motion to reconsider was laid on the table.

CONTESTED ELECTION, CARTER AGAINST LeCOMPTE—MESSAGE FROM THE CLERK OF THE HOUSE OF REPRESENTATIVES (H. DOC. NO. 235)

The SPEAKER laid before the House the following message from the Clerk of the House of Representatives, which was read and, with the accompanying papers, referred to the Committee on House Administration:

JULY 29, 2008.

The Honorable the SPEAKER,
House of Representatives.

SIR: *I have the honor to lay before the House of Representatives the contest for a seat in the House of Representatives from the Fourth Congressional District of the State of Iowa, Steven V. Carter against Karl M. LeCompte, notice of which has been filed in the office of the Clerk of the House; and also transmit herewith original testimony, papers, and documents relating thereto.*

LEAVE OF ABSENCE

By unanimous consent, leave of absence was granted to:

Mr. CONYERS (at the request of Mr. HOYER) for today on account of personal business.

Mr. ENGEL (at the request of Mr. HOYER) for today on account of a codel flight delay.

Mr. GENE GREEN of Texas (at the request of Mr. HOYER) for today on account of a doctor's appointment.

SPECIAL ORDERS GRANTED

By unanimous consent, permission to address the House, following the legislative program and any special orders heretofore entered, was granted to:

(The following Members (at the request of Ms. HAHN) to revise and extend their remarks and include extraneous material:)

Ms. HAHN, for 5 minutes, today.

Mr. DEFAZIO, for 5 minutes, today.

Ms. KAPTUR, for 5 minutes, today.

Mr. SIMPSON, for 5 minutes, today.

(The following Members (at the request of Mr. SMITH of Nebraska) to revise and extend their remarks and include extraneous material:)

Mr. POE, for 5 minutes, June 20, 23 and 24.

Mr. JONES of North Carolina, for 5 minutes, June 20, 23 and 24.

Mr. BISHOP of Utah, for 5 minutes, today and June 18.

Mr. MCCAUL, for 5 minutes, June 19.

ADJOURNMENT

Mr. FORBES. Mr. Speaker, I move that the House do now adjourn.

The motion was agreed to; accordingly (at 9 o'clock and 56 minutes p.m.), under its previous order, the House adjourned until tomorrow, Wednesday, June 15, 2016, at 9:30 a.m.

RECESS

The SPEAKER pro tempore. Pursuant to clause 12(a) of rule I, the Chair declares the House in recess until 2 p.m. today.

Accordingly (at 12 o'clock and 50 minutes p.m.), the House stood in recess until 2 p.m.

☐ 1400

AFTER RECESS

The recess having expired, the House was called to order by the Speaker pro tempore (Mr. BOST) at 2 p.m.

[Follow manuscript as to expressing time of adjournment as 6 o'clock and 25 minutes p.m., or 6:25 p.m.]

MOTION TO DISCHARGE COMMITTEE

MARCH 17, 2008.

TO THE CLERK OF THE HOUSE OF REPRESENTATIVES:

Pursuant to clause 4 of rule XXVII, I, PERCY J. PRIEST, move to discharge the Committee on Banking and Currency from the consideration of the bill (H.R. 2887) entitled "A bill transferring certain functions of the Price Administrator, with respect to petroleum and petroleum products, to the petroleum Administrator for War," which was referred to said committee March 7, 2008, in support of which motion the undersigned Members of the House of Representatives affix their signatures, to wit:

1. Percy J. Priest.
2. Oren Harris. . . .
217. William E. Hess.
218. James G. Polk.

This motion was entered upon the Journal, entered in the CONGRESSIOAL RECORD with signatures thereto, and referred to the Calendar of Motions To Discharge Committees, February 29, 2008.

House briefs

[The briefs follow at end of day's proceedings, heads and dashes to be used as shown here. This data is supplied from the House and is printed as submitted.]

EXECUTIVE COMMUNICATIONS, ETC.

Under clause 2 of rule XIV, executive communications were taken from the Speaker's table and referred as follows:

6340. A letter from the Congressional Review Coordinator, Animal and Plant Health Inspection Service, Department of Agriculture, transmitting the Department's interim rule—Tuberculosis in Cattle and Bison; State and Zone Designations; California [Docket No.: APHIS-2016-0052] received August 8, 2016, pursuant to 5 U.S.C. 801(a)(1)(A); Public Law 104-121, Sec. 251; (110 Stat. 868); to the Committee on Agriculture.

6341. A letter from the Director, Issuances Staff, Department of Agriculture, transmitting the Department's final rule — Eligibility of Namibia To Export Meat Products to the United States [Docket No.: FSIS-2012-0028] (RIN: 0583-AD51) received July 28, 2016, pursuant to 5 U.S.C. 801(a)(1)(A); Public Law 104-121, Sec. 251; (110 Stat. 868); to the Committee on Agriculture.

[Use the following form if only one communication is submitted—8 point:]

7147. Under clause 8 of rule XII, a letter from the Director, Regulatory Management Division, Environmental Protection Agency, transmitting the Agency's final rule—(Z)-7,8-epoxy-2-methyloctadecane (Disparlure); Exemption from the Requirement of a Tolerance [EPA-HQ-OPP-2007-0596; FRL-8367-7] received June 9, 2016, pursuant to 5 U.S.C. 801(a)(1)(A), was taken from the Speaker's table, referred to the Committee on Agriculture, and ordered to be printed.

REPORTS OF COMMITTEES ON PUBLIC BILLS AND RESOLUTIONS

Under clause 2 of rule XIV, executive communications were taken from the Speaker's table and referred as follows:

6340. A letter from the Congressional Review Coordinator, Animal and Plant Health Inspection Service, Department of Agriculture, transmitting the Department's interim rule—Tuberculosis in Cattle and Bison; State and Zone Designations; California [Docket No.: APHIS-2016-0052] received August 8, 2016, pursuant to 5 U.S.C. 801(a)(1)(A); Public Law 104-121, Sec. 251; (110 Stat. 868); to the Committee on Agriculture.

REPORTS OF COMMITTEES ON PUBLIC BILLS AND RESOLUTIONS

Under clause 2 of rule XIII, reports of committees were delivered to the

Clerk for printing and reference to the proper calendar, as follows:

Mr. GOODLATTE: Committee on the Judiciary. H.R. 5578. A bill to establish certain rights for sexual assault survivors, and for other purposes (Rept. 114–707, Pt. 1). Referred to the Committee of the Whole House on the state of the Union.

Mr. MILLER of Florida: Committee on Veterans' Affairs. H.R. 3286. A bill to encourage effective, voluntary private sector investments to recruit, employ, and retain men and women who have served in the United States military with annual presidential awards to private sector employers recognizing such efforts, and for other purposes; with an amendment (Rept. 114–708). Referred to the Committee of the Whole House on the state of the Union.

[Use above form also when only one report is submitted.]

PUBLIC BILLS AND RESOLUTIONS

Under clause 2 of rule XII, public bills and resolutions of the following titles were introduced and severally referred, as follows:

By Mr. SHADEGG:

H.R. 6274. A bill to provide an equivalent to habeas corpus protection for persons held under military authority under that part of Cuba leased to the United States; to the Committee on the Judiciary, and in addition to the Committee on Armed Services, for a period to be subsequently determined by the Speaker, in each case for consideration of such provisions as fall within the jurisdiction of the committee concerned.

By Mr. ROYCE (for himself, Mr. ZELDIN, Ms. ROS-LEHTINEN, Mr. NUNES, Mr. MEADOWS, Mr. THORNBERRY, Mr. SESSIONS, Mr. DONOVAN, Mr. MCCAUL, Mr. DENT, Mr. CHAFFETZ, Mr. CONAWAY, Mr. ROHRABACHER, Mr. RIBBLE, Mr. TROTT, Mr. YOUNG of Iowa, Mr. DESJARLAIS, Mr. COOK, Mr. PITTENGER, Mr. DESANTIS, Mr. DUFFY, Mr. STIVERS, Mr. FITZPATRICK, Mr. YOHO, Mr. ROTHFUS, Mr. CHABOT, and Mr. WILLIAMS):

H.R. 5931. A bill to provide for the prohibition on cash payments to the Government of Iran, and for other purposes; to the Committee on Foreign Affairs.

By Ms. DUCKWORTH (for herself and Mr. ZELDIN):

H.R. 5932. A bill to amend title 38, United States Code, to eliminate copayments by the Department of Veterans Affairs for medicines relating to preventive health services, and for other purposes; to the Committee on Veterans' Affairs.

[Use the following form when only one bill or resolution is submitted:]

Under clause 2 of rule XII:

Mr. FATTAH (for himself and Mr. WOLF): introduced a bill (H.R. 5158) to provide for the sealing or expungement of records relating to Federal nonviolent criminal offenses, and for other purposes; which was referred to the Committee on the Judiciary, and in addition to the Committees on Agriculture, and Ways and Means, for a period to be subsequently determined by the Speaker, in each case for consideration of such provisions as fall within the jurisdiction of the committee concerned.

MEMORIALS

Under clause 3 of rule XII, memorials were presented and referred as follows:

[Use the following form when submitted by the Speaker if *By the Speaker* is not in manuscript:]

296. The SPEAKER presented a memorial of the Senate of the State of California, relative to Senate Joint Resolution 26, calling upon the President of the United States to encourage the Secretary of the United States Department of Health and Human Services to adopt policies to repeal the current discriminatory donor suitability policies of the United States Food and Drug Administration (FDA) regarding blood donations by men who have had sex with another man and, instead, direct the FDA to develop science-based policies such as criteria based on risky behavior in lieu of sexual orientation; to the Committee on Energy and Commerce.

297. Also, a memorial of the Senate of the State of California, relative to Senate Joint Resolution 29, declaring unnecessary and unexplained increases in pharmaceutical pricing is a harm to our health care system that will no longer be tolerated because the system cannot sustain it; to the Committee on Energy and Commerce.

MEMORIALS

Under clause 3 of rule XII,

[Use the following form when only one memorial is submitted:]

326. The SPEAKER presented a memorial of the Legislature of the State of Louisiana, relative to Senate Concurrent Resolution No. 51 memorializing the Congress of the United States to establish a grant program to assist the seafood industry in St. Tammany, St. Bernard, Orleans, and Plaquemines parishes; to the Committee on Financial Services.

PRIVATE BILLS AND RESOLUTIONS

Under clause 3 of rule XII, private bills and resolutions of the following titles were introduced and severally referred, as follows:

By Mr. GROTHMAN:

H.R. 808. A bill to authorize the President to award the Medal of Honor to James Megellas, formerly of Fond du Lac, Wisconsin, and currently of Colleyville, Texas, for acts of valor on January 28, 1945, during the Battle of the Bulge in World War II; to the Committee on Armed Services.

By Mr. UPTON:

H.R. 809. A bill for the relief of Ibrahim Parlak; to the Committee on the Judiciary.

[Use the following form when only one bill or resolution is submitted:]

Under clause 3 of rule XII,

Mr. HUFFMAN introduced a bill (H.R. 6296) For the relief of Yeganeh Salehi Rezaian; which was referred to the Committee on the Judiciary.

ADDITIONAL SPONSORS

Under clause 7 of rule XII, sponsors were added to public bills and resolutions, as follows:

H.R. 27: Mr. Renacci.

H.R. 169: Mr. Reichert.

H.R. 213: Mrs. Beatty and Mr. Connolly,

H.R. 265: Ms. McCollum,

H.R. 297: Ms. Roybal-Allard, Ms. Kelly of Illinois, Mr. Farr, Ms. Eddie Bernice Johnson of Texas, Mr. Ryan of Ohio, and Ms. Wilson of Florida.

[Note.—Set sponsors caps and Members caps and lower case.]

DISCHARGE PETITIONS

Under clause 2 of rule XV, the following discharge petitions were filed:

Petition 8, March 12, 2014, by Mr. BRADLEY S. SCHNEIDER on House Resolution 490, was signed by the following Members: Bradley S. Schneider, Steny H. Hoyer, James E. Clyburn, Sam Farr, Sanford D. Bishop, Jr., Joseph Crowley, Terri A. Sewell, Eddie Bernice Johnson, Adam B. Schiff, Sander M. Levin, Sheila Jackson Lee, Nydia M. Vela´zquez, Rube´n Hinojosa, Zoe Lofgren, Janice D. Schakowsky, . . .

DISCHARGE PETITIONS—ADDITIONS OR DELETIONS

The following Members added their names to the following discharge petitions:

Petition 1 by Ms. DELAURO on the bill (H.R. 377): Katherine M. Clark.

Petition 9 by Mr. GARCIA on the bill (H.R. 15): Rosa L. DeLauro, David Scott, William L. Enyart, Bennie G. Thompson, John Conyers Jr., Allyson Y. Schwartz, Eliot L. Engel, Brad Sherman, Suzan K. DelBene, Donald M. Payne Jr., Carolyn McCarthy, Theodore E. Deutch, John B. Larson, Henry A. Waxman, Emanuel Cleaver, G.K. Butterfield, Andre´ Carson, William R. Keating, Terri A. Sewell, and Tim Ryan.

The following Member's name was deleted from the following discharge petition:

Petition 1 by Ms. DELAURO on H.R. 377: Edward J. Markey.

PETITIONS, ETC.

Under clause 3 of rule XII, petitions and papers were laid on the Clerk's desk and referred as follows:

19. The SPEAKER presented a petition of the City Commission of the City of Lauderhill, FL, relative to Resolution No. 15R-07-161, condemning the Dominican Republic's impending mass deportation of Haitian immigrants; to the Committee on Foreign Affairs.

20. Also, a petition of the Oakland County Board of Commissioners, Oakland County, MI, relative to Miscellaneous Resolution No. 15154, objecting to the development of a nuclear waste repository in close proximity to the Great Lakes; to the Committee on Foreign Affairs.

[Use the following form when only one petition is submitted:]

Under clause 1 of rule XXII,

139. The SPEAKER presented a petition of the Council of the District of Columbia, relative to the Council-adopted resolution entitled, "National Park Service-Georgetown Branch Rail Right-of-Way Acquisition Resolution of 1990"; which was referred to the Committee on the District of Columbia.

AMENDMENTS

Under clause 8 of rule XVIII, proposed amendments were submitted as follows:

H.R. 5303

OFFERED BY: MR. KILDEE

AMENDMENT NO.: Add at the end the following:

TITLE V—DRINKING WATER

SEC. 501. DRINKING WATER INFRASTRUCTURE.

(a) DEFINITIONS.—In this section: . . . .

CONGRESSIONAL RECORD INDEX

General instructions

Set in 7 point on 8 point, Record measure (168 points, 14 picas).

Cap lines or italic lines are set flush left.

Entries are indented 1 em, with overs 2 ems.

Bill introductions are to be identified as to sponsor or cosponsor.

Bullet following page number in index identifies unspoken material.

Pages are identified as S (Senate), H (House), and E (Extensions).

Pages in bound Record index are entered numerically, without S, H, or E prefixes.

Abbreviations and acronyms—

(for use on notation of content line)

Abbreviations

Streets: St.; Ave.; Ct.; Dr.; Blvd.; Rd.; Sq.; Ter.
Names: Jr.; Sr.; II (etc.)
Businesses: Co.; Corp. (includes all Federal corporations); Inc.; Ltd.; Bros.
States: See rule 9.13.

Dept. of Agriculture	Sec. of Agriculture.
Dept. of Commerce	Sec. of Commerce.
Dept. of Defense	Sec. of Defense.
Dept. of Education	Sec. of Education.
Dept. of Energy	Sec. of Energy.
Dept. of Health and Human Services	Sec. of Health and . . .
Dept. of Homeland Security	Sec. of Homeland Security
Dept. of Housing and Urban Development	Sec. of Housing and . . .
Dept. of the Interior	Sec. of the Interior.
Dept. of Justice	Attorney General.
Dept. of Labor	Sec. of Labor.
Dept. of State	Sec. of State.
Dept. of Transportation	Sec. of Transportation.
Dept. of the Treasury	Sec. of the Treasury.
Dept. of Veterans Affairs	Sec. of Veterans Affairs.

Acronyms

Agency for International Development	AID
Acquired immunodeficiency syndrome	AIDS
American Association of Retired Persons	AARP
American Bar Association	ABA
American Civil Liberties Union	ACLU
American Federation of Labor and Congress of Industrial Organizations	AFL–CIO
American Medical Association	AMA
British Broadcasting Corp	BBC
Bureau of Alcohol, Tobacco, Firearms and Explosives	ATF
Bureau of Indian Affairs	BIA
Bureau of Land Management	BLM
Bureau of Labor Statistics	BLS
Cable News Network	CNN
Cable Satellite Public Affairs Network	C–SPAN
Central Intelligence Agency	CIA
Civil Service Retirement System	CSRS
Civilian Health and Medical Program of the Uniformed Services	CHAMPUS
Commodity Credit Corp	CCC
Commodity Futures Trading Commission	CFTC
Comprehensive Environmental Response, Compensation and Liability Act	CERCLA
Congressional Budget Office	CBO
Consolidated Omnibus Budget Reconciliation Act	COBRA
Consumer Product Safety Commission	CPSC
Daughters of the American Revolution	DAR
Deoxyribonucleic acid	DNA
Disabled American Veterans	DAV
Drug Enforcement Administration	DEA
Employee Retirement Income Security Act	ERISA
Environmental Protection Agency	EPA
Equal Employment Opportunity Commission	EEOC
Export-Import Bank of the United States	EXIM Bank
Federal Aviation Administration	FAA
Federal Bureau of Investigation	FBI
Federal Communications Commission	FCC
Federal Crop Insurance Corp	FCIC
Federal Deposit Insurance Corp	FDIC
Federal Election Commission	FEC
Federal Emergency Management Agency	FEMA
Federal Employee Retirement System	FERS
Federal Energy Regulatory Commission	FERC
Federal Housing Administration	FHA
Federal Insurance Contributions Act	FICA

Federal National Mortgage Association	Fannie Mae
Federal Reserve System	FRS
Federal Trade Commission	FTC
Food and Drug Administration	FDA
General Agreement on Tariffs and Trade	GATT
General Services Administration	GSA
Government Accountability Office	GAO
Government Publishing Office	GPO
Gross national product	GNP
Health maintenance organization(s)	HMO(s)
Human immunodeficiency virus	HIV
Internal Revenue Service	IRS
International Business Machines Corp.	IBM
International Monetary Fund	IMF
International Trade Commission	ITC
Legal Services Corp.	LSC
Low-Income Home Energy Assistance Program	LIHEAP
Missing in action	MIA(s)
National Aeronautics and Space Administration	NASA
National Association for the Advancement of Colored People	NAACP
National Broadcasting Co.	NBC
National Collegiate Athletic Association	NCAA
National Institute of Standards and Technology	NIST
National Institutes of Health	NIH
National Labor Relations Board	NLRB
National Oceanic and Atmospheric Administration	NOAA
National Railroad Passenger Corp.	Amtrak
National Rifle Association	NRA
National Security Council	NSC
National Science Foundation	NSF
National Transportation Safety Board	NTSB
North American Free Trade Agreement	NAFTA
North Atlantic Treaty Organization	NATO
Nuclear Regulatory Commission	NRC
Occupational Safety and Health Administration	OSHA
Office of Management and Budget	OMB
Office of Personnel Management	OPM
Organization of American States	OAS
Organization of Petroleum Exporting Countries	OPEC
Overseas Private Investment Corp.	OPIC
Palestine Liberation Organization	PLO
Parent-Teachers Association	PTA
Prisoner of war	POW

Public Broadcasting Service	PBS
Racketeer Influenced Corrupt Organization Act	RICO
Reserve Officers' Training Corps	ROTC
Securities and Exchange Commission	SEC
Small Business Administration	SBA
Social Security Administration	SSA
Supplemental security income	SSI
Tennessee Valley Authority	TVA
Trans-Pacific Partnership	TPP
United Auto Workers	UAW
United Nations	U.N.
United Nations Children's Fund	UNICEF
United Nations Educational, Scientific, and Cultural Organization	UNESCO
Veterans of Foreign Wars	VFW
Voice of America	VOA
Women, Infants, and Children Program	WIC
World Health Organization	WHO
Young Men's Christian Association	YMCA
Young Women's Christian Association	YWCA

Spacing

Biweekly Record index folioed in upper right and left corner; no extra spacing.

Bound Record index folioed in upper right and left corner; no extra spacing.

History of Bills folioed in upper right and left corner using H.B. numbers; no extra spacing.

Bound History of Bills folioed in lower right and left corner, first folio numerically higher than the last folio of index; no extra spacing.

Capitalization

Capitalize principal words after these formats:

Addresses
Analyses
Appendices
Articles and editorials
Biographies
Book reviews
Booklets
Brochures
Conference reports
Descriptions
Documents
Essays
Essays: Voice of Democracy
Eulogies

Explanations
Factsheets
Forewords
Histories
Homilies
Hymns
Memorandums
Messages
Oaths of office
Pamphlets
Papers
Platforms
Poems
Prayers
Prayers by visitors
Prefaces
Press releases
Proclamations
Reports
Report filed
Resolutions of ratification
Résumés
Sermons
Songs
Statements
Studies
Summaries
Surveys
Synopses
Testimonies
Transcripts
Treaties

Lowercase after these formats:

Advertisements
Affidavits
Agenda
Agreements
Amendments
Announcements
Appointments
Awards
Bills and resolutions
Bills and resolutions cosponsored
Bills and resolutions introduced
Bills and resolutions relative to
Briefs
Briefings
Broadcasts
Bulletins
Certificates of election
Chronologies
Citations
Civilian
Cloture motions
Colloquies
Commentaries
Comments
Communications from
Communiques
Comparisons
Cost estimates
Court decisions
Court documents
Declarations
Dedications
Definitions
Descriptions
Designated acting Presidents pro tempore
Designated acting Speaker pro tempore
Digests
Dispatches
Examples
Excerpts
Executive orders
Financial statements
Granted
Granted in the House
Granted in the Senate
Guidelines
Hearings
Inscriptions
Interviews
Introductions

Invocations
Journals
Letters
Lists
Meetings
Military
Motions
Newsletters
Notices
Obituaries
Opinion polls
Orders
Outlines
Petitions
Petitions and memorials
Press conferences
Privilege of the floor
Programs
Projects
Proposals
Questionnaires
Questions
Questions and answers
Quotations
Recorded
Regulations
Remarks
Remarks in House
Remarks in House relative to
Remarks in Senate
Remarks in Senate relative to
Resignations
Resolutions by organizations
Results
Reviews
Rollcalls
Rosters
Rules
Rulings of the chair
Schedules
Subpoena notices
Subpoenas
Tables
Tests
Texts of
Transmittals
Tributes
Voting record

Punctuation

Comma precedes folio figures.

If numbers of several bills are given, use this form: (see S. 24, 25); (see H.R. 217, 218), etc.; that is, do not repeat S. or H.R. with each number.

In consecutive numbers (more than two) use an en dash to connect first with last: S46–S48, 518–520.

Quotes are used for book titles.

A 3-em dash is used as a ditto for word or words leading up to colon:

Taxation: capital gains rates
———earned income tax credit
———rates

Roman and italic

Use italic for Members of Congress descriptive data:

COCHRAN, THAD *(a Senator from Mississippi)*;
CONYERS, JOHN, Jr. *(a Representative from Michigan)*.

Names of vessels in italic:

Brooklyn (U.S.S.);
Savannah (vessel);
Columbia (space shuttle).

Flush cap lines

All cap lines are separate entries. They are set flush with overs indented 2 ems:

LEAHY, PATRICK *(a Senator from Vermont)*

YOUNG, DON *(a Representative from Alaska)*

PRESIDENT OF THE UNITED STATES (Barack Obama)

VICE PRESIDENT OF THE UNITED STATES (Joseph R. Biden, Jr.)

COMMITTEE ON FOREIGN AFFAIRS (House)

COMMITTEE ON FOREIGN RELATIONS (Senate)

FARMERS *see* Agriculture

SENATE *related term(s)* Committees of the Senate; Legislative Branch of the Government; Members of Congress; Votes in Senate

DEPARTMENT OF THE INTERIOR *related term(s)* Bureau of Land Management, Bureau of Reclamation

PRESIDENTIAL APPOINTMENTS

VOTES IN HOUSE

VOTES IN SENATE

No. XII

Congressional Record Index

PROCEEDINGS AND DEBATES OF THE *114th* CONGRESS, SECOND SESSION

Vol. 162   JULY 21 TO AUGUST 8, 2016   *Nos. 119 to 132*

NOTE.—For debate and action on bills and resolutions see "History of Bills and Resolutions" at end of Index, under numbers referred to in Index entry.

DATES, ISSUE NUMBERS, AND PAGES INCLUDED IN INDEX XII

July 21	No. 119	S6947–S6980	H6731–H6734	E1507–E1511	D919–D922
July 22	No. 120	S6981–S7088	H6735–H6826	E1513–E1527	D923–D930
July 23	No. 121	S7089–S7201	H6827–H7059	E1529–E1547	D931–D940
July 24	No. 122	S7203–S7434	H7061–H7166	E1549–E1554	D941–D948
July 25	No. 123	S7435–S7485		E1555–E1572	D950–D956
July 26	No. 124	S7487–S7537			D958–D960
July 27	No. 125	S7539			D961–D962
July 28	No. 126	S7541–S7578	H7167–H7169	E1573–E1577	D963–D966
July 29	No. 127	S7579–S7708	H7171–H7330	E1579–E1591	D968–D980
July 30	No. 128	S7709–S7804	H7331–H7631	E1593–E1625	D981–D994
July 31	No. 129	S7805–S7982	H7633–H7707	E1627–E1640	D996–D1008
July 31 (Pt. II)*	No. 129		H7709–H7790		D996–D1008
August 1	No. 130	S7983–S8079	H7791–H7810	E1641–E1703	D1009–D1016
August 5	No. 131	S8081			D1017–D1018
August 8	No. 132	S8083			D1019–D1020

*Continuation of proceedings

NOTE: Elements in brackets which follow page numbers in the Index refer to the dates of the Congressional Record in which those pages may be found. Unspoken material is indicated by a bullet (•).

AARP (ORGANIZATION)

Letters

Evaluate and extend the basic pilot program for employment eligibility confirmation and ensure protection of Social Security beneficiaries, H7592 [30JY]

Press releases

Medicare Trigger Ignores Real Problem-Skyrocketing Health Care Costs, H7125 [24JY]

ABERCROMBIE, NEIL (*a Representative from Hawaii*)

Bills and resolutions cosponsored

Armed Forces: tribute to the 28th Infantry Division (see H. Con. Res. 390), H7308 [29JY]

Bulgaria: independence anniversary (see H. Res. 1383), H7630 [30JY]

Bureau of Prisons: provide stab-resistant personal body armor to all correctional officers and require such officers to wear such armor while on duty (see H.R. 6462), H6734 [21JY]

Diseases: improve and enhance research and programs on cancer survivorship (see H.R. 4450), H7308 [29JY]

Education: strengthen communities through English literacy, civic education, and immigrant integration programs (see H.R. 6617), H7164 [24JY]

Medicare: ensure more timely access to home health services for beneficiaries (see H.R. 6826), H7808 [1AU]

————replace the prescription drug benefit with a revised and simplified program for all beneficiaries (see H.R. 6800), H7807 [1AU]

Motor vehicles: encourage increased production of natural gas vehicles and provide tax incentives for natural gas vehicle infrastructure (see H.R. 6570), H7630 [30JY]

Palladio, Andrea: anniversary of birth (see H. Con. Res. 407), H7788 [31JY]

Power resources: open Outer Continental shelf areas to oil and gas leasing, curb excessive energy speculation, and require Strategic Petroleum Reserve sale and acquisitions of certain fuels (see H.R. 6670), H7628 [30JY]

————provide a comprehensive plan for greater energy independence (see H.R. 6709), H7785 [31JY]

U.S. Public Service Academy: establish (see H.R. 1671), H7789 [31JY]

Yunus, Muhammad: award Congressional Gold Medal (see H.R. 1801), H7629 [30JY]

Remarks

Pearl Harbor, HI: anniversary of the Pearl Harbor Naval Shipyard (H. Res. 1139), H6773, H6774 [22JY]

ABORTION

Remarks in House

China, People's Republic of: mandatory abortion and sterilization policies, H7344, H7345 [30JY]

Supreme Court: anniversary of Roe v. Wade decision, H7283 [29JY], H7611 [30JY], H7776 [31JY], E1545 [23JY], E1701 [1AU]

U.S. Leadership Against HIV/AIDS, Tuberculosis, and Malaria Act: prohibit use of funds for any organization or program which supports or participates in the management of coerced abortions or involuntary sterilization, H7116 [24JY]

In history of bills, sequence is: Senate bills, Senate joint resolutions, Senate concurrent resolutions, and Senate resolutions; then House bills, House joint resolutions, House concurrent resolutions, and House resolutions: S. 14, S.J. Res. 7, S. Con. Res. 26, S. Res. 5, H.R. 980, H.J. Res. 9, H. Con. Res. 16, and H. Res. 50.

History of Bills and Resolutions

DATES, ISSUE NUMBERS AND BILLS INTRODUCED IN INDEX VIII

May 12	No. 77	S.	3001–3009	....	S. Con. Res. 82	S. Res. 558–560
		H.R.	6021–6024	....	....	....
May 13	No. 78	S.	3010–3014	S.J. Res. 32	....	S. Res. 561–563
		H.R.	6025–6046	....	H. Con. Res. 348	H. Res. 1187–1193
May 19	No. 82	S.	3030–3034	....	....	S. Res. 569–570
		H.R.	6083–6084	....	H. Con. Res. 354	H. Res. 1208–1209
May 21	No. 84	S.	3045–3047	S.J. Res. 33	S. Con. Res. 83	S. Res. 572–573
		H.R.	6104–6122	H.J. Res. 86–87	H. Con. Res. 360	H. Res. 1217–1219
May 22	No. 85	S.	3048–3073	S.J. Res. 34–36	S. Con. Res. 84–85	S. Res. 574–579
		H.R.	6123–6166	H.J. Res. 88–89	H. Con. Res. 361–365	H. Res. 1220–1232

Bills receiving legislative action during this Index period numerically precede new bills introduced.

SENATE BILLS

S. 11—A bill to provide liability protection to volunteer pilot nonprofit organizations that fly for public benefit and to the pilots and staff of such nonprofit organizations, and for other purposes; to the Committee on the Judiciary.
Cosponsors added, S4621 [21MY]

S. 2062—A bill to amend the Native American Housing Assistance and Self-Determination Act of 1996 to reauthorize that Act, and for other purposes; to the Committee on Indian Affairs.
Committee on Banking, Housing, and Urban Affairs discharged, S814 [8FE]
Amendments, S850 [11FE], S4836, S4839, S4844 [22MY]
Passed Senate amended, S4839 [22MY]

SENATE JOINT RESOLUTIONS

S.J. Res. 17—A joint resolution directing the United States to initiate international discussions and take necessary steps with other Nations to negotiate an agreement for managing migratory and transboundary fish stocks in the Arctic Ocean; to the Committee on Foreign Relations.
Debated, H4067 [19MY]
Text, H4067 [19MY]
Rules suspended. Passed House, H4402 [21MY]
Message from the House, S4790 [22MY]

S.J. Res. 28—A joint resolution disapproving the rule submitted by the Federal Communications Commission with respect to broadcast media ownership; to the Committee on Commerce, Science, and Transportation.
By Mr. DORGAN (for himself, Ms. Snowe, Mr. Kerry, Ms. Collins, Mr. Dodd, Mr. Obama, Mr. Harkin, Mrs. Clinton, Ms. Cantwell, Mr. Biden, Mr. Reed, Mrs. Feinstein, Mr. Sanders, Mr. Tester, and Mr. Stevens), S1597 [5MR]
Cosponsors added, S1704 [6MR], S1878 [11MR], S2136 [13MR], S2233 [31MR], S2348 [2AP], S2947 [10AP], S3081 [16AP], S3700 [1MY]
Reported (S. Rept. 110–334), S3975 [8MY]
Passed Senate amended, S4267 [15MY]
Text, S4270 [15MY]
Message from the Senate, H4065 [19MY]
Held at the desk, H4065 [19MY]

SENATE CONCURRENT RESOLUTIONS

S. Con. Res. 82—A concurrent resolution supporting the Local Radio Freedom Act; to the Committee on Commerce, Science, and Transportation.
By Mrs. LINCOLN (for herself, Mr. Wicker, Mr. Brownback, Mr. Allard, Mr. Nelson of Nebraska, Ms. Murkowski, and Mr. Webb), S4029 [12MY]

S. Con. Res. 85—A concurrent resolution authorizing the use of the rotunda of the Capitol to honor Frank W. Buckles, the last surviving United States veteran of the First World War.
By Mr. SPECTER (for himself, Mr. Byrd, Mrs. Dole, Mr. McCain, Mr. Warner, Mr. Lieberman, Mr. Rockefeller, and Mr. Burr), S4793 [22MY]

S. Con. Res. 85—Continued
Text, S4810, S4848 [22MY]
Agreed to in the Senate, S4848 [22MY]

SENATE RESOLUTIONS

S. Res. 496—A resolution honoring the 60th anniversary of the commencement of the carving of the Crazy Horse Memorial; to the Committee on the Judiciary.
By Mr. THUNE (for himself and Mr. Johnson), S2346 [2AP]
Text, S2362 [2AP], S4427 [20MY]
Committee discharged. Agreed to in the Senate, S4427 [20MY]

S. Res. 562—A resolution honoring Concerns of Police Survivors as the organization begins its 25th year of service to family members of law enforcement officers killed in the line of duty.
By Ms. MURKOWSKI (for herself, Mr. Biden, Mr. Brown, Mr. Menendez, Ms. Mikulski, Mr. Craig, Mr. Whitehouse, Mr. Baucus, Mr. Dodd, Mrs. Feinstein, Mr. Inouye, Mr. Lautenberg, Mrs. Lincoln, Mr. Nelson of Florida, Mr. Pryor, Mr. Smith, Ms. Stabenow, Mr. Stevens, Mr. Tester, and Mr. Thune), S4106 [13MY]
Text, S4114, S4121 [13MY]
Agreed to in the Senate, S4120 [13MY]

HOUSE BILLS

H.R. 158—A bill to direct the Secretary of the Treasury to mint coins in commemoration of the battlefields of the Revolutionary War and the War of 1812, and for other purposes; to the Committee on Financial Services.
Cosponsors added, H3108 [6MY], H4061 [15MY]

H.R. 503—A bill to amend the Horse Protection Act to prohibit the shipping, transporting, moving, delivering, receiving, possessing, purchasing, selling, or donation of horses and other equines to be slaughtered for human consumption, and for other purposes; to the Committees on Energy and Commerce; Agriculture.
By Ms. SCHAKOWSKY (for herself, Mr. Whitfield, Mr. Rahall, Mr. Spratt, Mr. Gallegly, Mr. Markey, Mr. Pallone, Mr. Nadler, Mr. Van Hollen, Ms. McCollum of Minnesota, Ms. Bordallo, Ms. Schwartz, Mr. Ackerman, Mr. Doyle, Ms. Lee, Mr. Cleaver, Mr. Serrano, Ms. Berkley, Mr. Shays, Mr. Jones of North Carolina, Mr. McCotter, Mr. Cummings, Ms. DeLauro, Mr. George Miller of California, Mr. Grijalva, Mrs. Capps, Ms. Bean, Ms. Matsui, Mr. King of New York, Mr. Burton of Indiana, Mr. Kildee, Ms. Kaptur, Mr. Dicks, Mr. Berman, Ms. Hirono, Mr. Chandler, Mr. Gerlach, Mr. Tierney, Mr. Bishop of New York, Mr. Frank of Massachusetts, Mr. Lynch, Mr. Kirk, Mr. Campbell of California, Mr. Wilson of South Carolina, Ms. Jackson-Lee of Texas, Mr. Sherman, Mr. LaTourette, Mr. Larson of Connecticut, Mr. Israel, Ms. Woolsey, Mr. Brown of South Carolina, Ms. Eddie Bernice Johnson of Texas, Mr. Moore of Kansas, Mr. Moran of Virginia, Mr. McNulty, Mrs. Maloney of New York, Mr. Inslee, Mr. Wolf, Ms. Carson, Mr. Weiner, Mr. Ruppersberger, Mr. Smith of New Jersey, and Mr. Linder), H670 [17JA]
Cosponsors added, H1055 [30JA], H1153 [31JA], H1565 [13FE], H1668 [14FE], H1896 [16FE], H2165 [5MR], H2621 [15MR], H2821 [21MR], H3279 [28MR], H3363 [29MR], H3476 [17AP], H3724 [20AP], H4553 [7MY], H5054 [15MY], H5927 [24MY], H6181 [7JN], H6439, H6476 [14JN], H6828 [20JN], H7202 [26JN], H8121 [18JY], H8821 [27JY], H9656 [2AU], H10696 [20SE], H11028 [27SE]

H.R. 4841—A bill to approve, ratify, and confirm the settlement agreement entered into to resolve claims by the Soboba Band of Luiseno Indians relating to alleged interences with the water resources of the Tribe, to authorize and direct the Secretary of the Interior to execute and perform the Settlement Agreement and related waivers, and for other purposes; to the Committee on Natural Resources.
Cosponsors added, H390 [22JA], H480 [28JA], H558 [29JA]
Reported with amendment (H. Rept. 110–649), H4059 [15MY]
Debated, H4075 [19MY]
Text, H4075 [19MY]
Rules suspended. Passed House amended, H4401 [21MY]
Message from the House, S4790 [22MY]
Passed Senate, S7197 [23JY]

H.R. 6081—A bill to amend the Internal Revenue Code of 1986 to provide benefits for military personnel, and for other purposes; to the Committee on Ways and Means.
By Mr. RANGEL (for himself, Mr. Stark, Mr. McDermott, Mr. Lewis of Georgia, Mr. Neal of Massachusetts, Mr. Pomeroy, Mrs. Jones of Ohio, Mr. Larson of Connecticut, Mr. Emanuel, Mr. Blumenauer, Mr. Kind, Ms. Berkley, Mr. Crowley, Mr. Van Hollen, Mr. Meek of Florida, Mr. Altmire, Mrs. Boyda of Kansas, Mr. Cohen, Ms. DeLauro, Mr. Ellsworth, Mr. Loebsack, Ms. Tsongas, Mr. Welch of Vermont, Mr. Walz of Minnesota, Mr. Arcuri, Ms. Shea-Porter, Mr. Becerra, Mrs. Davis of California, and Mr. Doggett), H4064 [16MY]
Cosponsors added, H4151 [19MY]
Debated, H4160 [20MY]
Text, H4160 [20MY]
Rules suspended. Passed House amended, H4187 [20MY]
Message from the House, S4617 [21MY]
Passed Senate, S4772 [22MY]
Message from the Senate, H4821 [22MY]

H.R. 6166—A bill to impose certain limitations on the receipt of out-of-State municipal solid waste, and for other purposes; to the Committee on Energy and Commerce.
By Mr. WITTMAN of Virginia (for himself, Mr. Wolf, Mr. Moran of Virginia, and Mr. Donnelly),

20. Reports and Hearings

The data for these publications arrives at GPO from many different sources. Congressional committee staff members are responsible for gathering the information printed in these publications.

Report language is compiled and submitted along with the bill language to the clerks of the respective Houses. The clerks assign the report numbers, etc., and forward this information to GPO for typesetting and printing. In many instances the reports are camera-ready copy, needing only insertion of the assigned report number.

Likewise, hearings are also compiled by committee staff members. The data or captured keystrokes as submitted by the various reporting services are forwarded to GPO where the element identifier codes are programmatically inserted and galley or page output is accomplished without manual intervention. It is not cost effective to prepare the manuscript as per the GPO STYLE MANUAL as it is too time-consuming to update and change the data once it is already in type form. Therefore, these publications are to be FIC & punc., unless specifically requested otherwise by the committee. It is not necessary to stamp the copy. However, style as stated in the following rules will be followed.

Style and format of congressional reports

Below are rules that should be followed for the makeup of congressional numbered reports. In either Senate or House reports, follow bill style in extracts from bills. Report numbers run consecutively from first to second session:

1. All excerpts to be set in 10-point type, cut in 2 ems on each side, except as noted in paragraph 3 below. For ellipses in cut-in matter, lines of five asterisks are used.

2. Contempt proceedings to be considered as excerpts.

3. The following are to be set in 10-point type, but not cut in:

(a) Letters that are readily identified as such by salutation and signature.

(b) Appendixes and/or exhibits that have a heading readily identifying them as such; and

(c) Matter printed in compliance with the Ramseyer rule.[1]

4. All leaderwork and lists of more than six items to be set in 8-point type.

5. All tabular work to be set in 7-point gothic type.

6. An amendment in the nature of a substitute to be set in 8-point type, but quotations from such amendment later in the report to be treated as excerpts, but set full measure (see paragraph 10 below).

7. Any committee print having a report head indicated on original copy to be set in report type and style.

8. Committee prints not having a report head indicated on original copy to be set in committee print style; that is, excerpts to be set in 8 point, full measure.

9. If a committee print set as indicated in paragraph 8 is later submitted as a report or included in a report, and the type is available for pickup, such type shall be picked up and used as is in the report.

10. On matter that is cut in on the left only for purposes of breakdown, no space is used above and below, but on all matter that is cut in on both sides, 4 points are used above and below. Because of the indentions and the limited number of element identifiers, do not squeeze bills that are submitted as excerpts.

11. In reports of immigration cases, set memorandums in full measure unless preceded or followed directly by committee language. Memorandums are indented on both sides if followed by such language. Preparers should indicate the proper indention on copy.

12. Order of printing (Senate reports only): (1) Report, (2) minority or additional views, (3) the Cordon rule,[2] (4) appendix (if any).

---

[1] If a House report contains the "Changes in Existing Law" section (in compliance with the Ramseyer rule), all main heads within that report should be set in caps and small caps, with secondary heads set in all small caps.

[2] If a Senate report contains the "Changes in Existing Law" section (in compliance with the Cordon rule) with potential changes in law indicated, all main heads within that report should be set in caps and small caps, with secondary heads set in all small caps. However, if the "Changes in Existing Law" section consists of only an explanatory paragraph, all main heads within that report should be set in all small caps.

13. Minority or additional views will begin a new page with 10-point cap heading. In Senate reports, "Changes in Existing Law" begins a new page if following "views." In conference reports, "Joint Explanatory Statement" begins a new odd page.

14. Minority or additional views are printed only if they have been signed by the authoring congressperson.

[Sample of excerpt]

In *Palmer v. Mass.*, decided in 1939, which involved the reorganization of the New Haven Railroad, the Supreme Court said:

> The judicial processes in bankruptcy proceedings under section 77 are, as it were, brigaded with the administrative processes of the Commission.

[Sample of an excerpt with an added excerpt]

The Interstate Commerce Commission in its report dated February 29, 1956, which is attached hereto and made a part hereof, states that it has no objection to the enactment of S. 3025, and states, in part, as follows:

> The proposed amendment, however, should be considered together with the provisions of section 959(b), title 28, United States Code, which reads as follows:
>
> "A trustee, receiver, or manager appointed in any cause pending in any court of the United States," etc.

[Sample of amendment]

On page 6, line 3, strike the words "and the service", strike all of lines 4, 5, and 6, and insert in lieu thereof the following:

> and, notwithstanding any other provision of law, the service credit authorized by this clause 3 of rule XIII of the Rule of the House of Representatives, change shall not—

(A) be included in establishing eligibility for voluntary or involuntary retirement or separation from the service, under any provision of law;

[Sample of amendment]

The amendments are indicated in the bill as reported and are as follows:

On page 2, line 15, change the period to a colon and add the following:

Provided, That such approaches shall include only those necessary portions of streets, avenues, and boulevards, etc.

On page 3, line 12, after "operated", insert "free of tolls".

[Sample of amendment in the nature of a substitute]

The amendment is as follows:

Strike all after the enacting clause and insert the following:

That the second paragraph under the heading "National Park Service" in the Act of July 31, 1953 (67 Stat. 261, 271), is amended to read as follows: "The Secretary of the Interior shall hereafter report in detail all proposed awards of concessions leases and contracts involving a gross annual business of $100,000 or more, or of more than five years in duration, including renewals thereof, sixty days before such awards are made, to the President of the Senate and Speaker of the House of Representatives for transmission to the appropriate committees."

[Sample of letter inserted in report]

The Department of Defense recommends enactment of the proposed legislation and the Office of Management and Budget interposes no objection as indicated by the following attached letter, which is hereby made a part of this report:

MARCH 21, 2008.

Hon. NANCY PELOSI,
Speaker of the House of Representatives,
Washington, DC.

MY DEAR MADAM SPEAKER: There is forwarded herewith a draft of legislation to amend section 303 of the Career Compensation Act.

* * * * * * *

Sincerely yours,

DOUGLAS A. BROOK,□□□□□
Assistant Secretary of the Navy□□□
(Financial Management).□

[Sample of cut-in for purposes of breakdown; no spacing above or below]

Under uniform regulations prescribed by the Secretaries concerned, a member of the uniformed services who—

(1) is retired for physical disability or placed upon the temporary disability retired list; or

(2) is retired with pay for any other reason, or is discharged with severance pay, immediately following at least eight years of continuous active duty (no single break therein of more than ninety days);

may select his home for the purposes of the travel and transportation allowances payable under this subsection, etc.

[Sample of leaderwork]

Among the 73 vessels mentioned above, 42 are classified as major combatant ships (aircraft carriers through escort vessels), in the following types:

Forrestal-class aircraft carriers	4
Destroyers	10
* * * * * * *	
Guided-missile submarine	1
Total	42

[Sample of sectional analysis]

SECTIONAL ANALYSIS

Section 1. Increase of 1 year in constructive service for promotion purposes

The principal purpose of the various subsections of section 1 is to provide a 1-year increase for medical and dental officers in . . .

* * * * * * *

Subsection 101(a) is in effect a restatement of the existing law

This subsection authorizes the President to make regular appointments in the grade of first lieutenant through . . .

* * * * * * *

[Sample of amendment under Ramseyer rule]

CHANGES IN EXISTING LAW

In compliance with clause 3 of rule XII of the Rules of the House of Representatives, changes in existing law made by the bill, as introduced, are shown as follows (existing law proposed to be omitted is enclosed in black brackets, new matter is printed in italic, existing law in which no change is proposed is shown in roman):

EXPORT CONTROL ACT OF 1949

* * * * * * *

TERMINATION DATE

SEC. 12. The authority granted herein shall terminate on June 30, **[**1956**]** *1959*, or upon any prior date which the Congress by concurrent resolution or the President may designate.

[The following examples are for sample purposes only]
[Sample of "Report" Skeleton]

114TH CONGRESS *2d Session*	HOUSE OF REPRESENTATIVES	REPORT 114–716

PROVIDING FOR STABILITY OF TITLE TO CERTAIN LANDS IN THE STATE OF LOUISIANA, AND FOR OTHER PURPOSES [1]

SEPTEMBER 6, 2016.—Committed to the Committee of the Whole House on the State of the Union and ordered to be printed [2]

Mr. BISHOP of Utah, from the Committee on Natural Resources, submitted the following

R E P O R T

together with

DISSENTING VIEWS

[To accompany H.R. 3342]

[Including cost estimate of the Congressional Budget Office]

The Committee on Natural Resources, to whom was referred the bill (H.R. 3342) to provide for stability of title to certain lands in the State of Louisiana, and for other purposes, having considered the same, report favorably thereon without amendment and recommend that the bill do pass. [3]

PURPOSE OF THE BILL [4]

The purpose of H.R. 3342 is to provide for the stability of title to certain lands in the State of Louisiana.

BACKGROUND AND NEED FOR LEGISLATION

In 1842, the U.S. government completed a survey of lands in Louisiana that included the area surrounding Lake Bistineau. Using the results of this survey, Louisiana delineated its ownership of lands under the Equal Footing Doctrine and transferred 7,000 acres of land around Lake Bistineau to the Commissioners of the Bossier Levee District in 1901. Three years later, the Commissioners of the Bossier Levee District conveyed this land to private ownership.

59–006

[1] If title makes more than three lines in 10-point caps, set in 8-point caps.

[2] Must be set as indicated in copy. If illustrations accompany copy and are not ordered to be printed, do not add *with illustrations*. Return copy to Production Manager.

[3] If the wording in this paragraph is prepared in the singular form, follow.

[4] For *Senate Committee on Finance* and *House Committee on Ways and Means*, heads are set in bold caps.

[Sample of "Report" Skeleton]

Calendar No. 584 [1]

114TH CONGRESS *2d Session*	SENATE	REPORT 114–312

JOHN MUIR NATIONAL HISTORIC SITE EXPANSION ACT

AUGUST 30, 2016.—Ordered to be printed

Filed, under authority of the order of the Senate of July 14, 2016 [2]

Ms. MURKOWSKI, from the Committee on Energy and Natural Resources, submitted the following

R E P O R T

[To accompany H.R. 1289]

The Committee on Energy and Natural Resources, to which was referred the bill (H.R. 1289) to authorize the Secretary of the Interior to acquire approximately 44 acres of land in Martinez, California, and for other purposes, having considered the same, reports favorably thereon without amendment and recommends that the bill do pass.

PURPOSE

The purpose of H.R. 1289 is to acquire approximately 44 acres of land in Martinez, California.

BACKGROUND AND NEED

The John Muir National Historic Site was established by Congress in 1964 (Public Law 88–547) and is located in the San Francisco Bay Area, in Martinez, California. The historic site preserves the 14-room Italianate Victorian mansion where the naturalist and writer John Muir lived, as well as a nearby 325-acre tract of native oak woodlands and grasslands historically owned by the Muir family.

The legislation would authorize the Department of the Interior to acquire by donation approximately 44 acres for inclusion in the John Muir National Historic Site. The 44 acres includes adjacent lands from John Swett's historic estate, who was also a farmer, friend, and neighbor of John Muir in the Alhambra Valley hills. Securing this property would benefit the Muir site as it will help pro-

59–010

[1] Use this type and form only on Senate reports. There is only one calendar in the Senate.
[2] Style for filed line, if present.

[Sample of "Report" Skeleton]

114TH CONGRESS *2d Session*	HOUSE OF REPRESENTATIVES	REPORT 114–724

PROVIDING[1] FOR CONSIDERATION OF THE BILL (H.R. 5063) TO LIMIT DONATIONS MADE PURSUANT TO SETTLEMENT AGREEMENTS TO WHICH THE UNITED STATES IS A PARTY, AND FOR OTHER PURPOSES[2]

SEPTEMBER 6, 2016.—Referred to the House Calendar and ordered to be printed

Mr. COLLINS of Georgia, from the Committee on Rules, submitted the following

R E P O R T

[To accompany H. Res. 843]

The Committee on Rules, having had under consideration House Resolution 843, by a record vote of 9 to 2, report the same to the House with the recommendation that the resolution be adopted.

SUMMARY OF PROVISIONS OF THE RESOLUTION

The resolution provides for consideration of H.R. 5063, the Stop Settlement Slush Funds Act of 2016, under a structured rule. The resolution waives all points of order against consideration of the bill. The resolution provides one hour of general debate equally divided and controlled by the chair and ranking minority member of the Committee on the Judiciary. The resolution makes in order as original text for the purpose of amendment the amendment in the nature of a substitute recommended by the Committee on the Judiciary now printed in the bill and provides that it shall be considered as read. The resolution waives all points of order against that amendment in the nature of a substitute. The resolution makes in order only those further amendments printed in this report. Each such amendment may be offered only in the order printed in this report, may be offered only by a Member designated in this report, shall be considered as read, shall be debatable for the time specified in this report equally divided and controlled by the proponent and an opponent, shall not be subject to amendment, and shall not be subject to a demand for division of the question in the House or in the Committee of the Whole. The resolution waives all points of order against the amendments printed in this report. The resolution provides one motion to recommit with or without instructions.

59–008

[1] If copy reads "To make" change to "Making", "To provide" change to "Providing", "To amend" change to "Amending".

[2] Sample of 8-point head.

114TH CONGRESS
1st Session } HOUSE OF REPRESENTATIVES { REPORT
114–376

TRADE FACILITATION AND TRADE ENFORCEMENT ACT OF 2015

DECEMBER 9, 2015.—Ordered to be printed

Mr. BRADY of Texas, from the committee of conference, submitted the following

CONFERENCE REPORT

[To accompany H.R. 644]

The committee of conference on the disagreeing votes of the two Houses on the amendment of the House to the amendment of the Senate to the bill (H.R. 644), to reauthorize trade facilitation and trade enforcement functions and activities, and for other purposes, having met, after full and free conference, have agreed to recommend and do recommend to their respective Houses as follows:

That the Senate recede from its disagreement to the amendment of the House to the amendment of the Senate and agree to the same with an amendment as follows:

In lieu of the matter proposed to be inserted by the House amendment, insert the following:

SECTION 1. SHORT TITLE; TABLE OF CONTENTS.

(a) SHORT TITLE.—This Act may be cited as the "Trade Facilitation and Trade Enforcement Act of 2015".

(b) TABLE OF CONTENTS.—The table of contents for this Act is follows:

97–818

JOINT EXPLANATORY STATEMENT OF THE COMMITTEE OF CONFERENCE

The managers on the part of the House and the Senate at the conference on the disagreeing votes of the two Houses on the amendment of the House to the amendment of the Senate to the bill (H.R. 644), to reauthorize trade facilitation and trade enforcement functions and activities, and for other purposes, submit the following joint statement to the House and the Senate in explanation of the effect of the action agreed upon by the managers and recommended in the accompanying conference report:

The Senate amendment struck all of the House bill after the enacting clause and inserted a substitute text.

The House amendment struck all of the Senate amendment after the enacting clause and inserted a substitute text.

The Senate recedes from its disagreement to the amendment of the House with an amendment that is a substitute for the House amendment and the Senate amendment. The differences between the Senate amendment, the House amendment, and the substitute agreed to in conference are noted below, except for clerical corrections, conforming changes made necessary by agreements reached by the conferees, and minor drafting and clarifying changes.

DIVISION A—TRADE FACILITATION AND TRADE ENFORCEMENT ACT OF 2015

TITLE I—TRADE FACILITATION AND TRADE ENFORCEMENT

SECTION 101. IMPROVING PARTNERSHIP PROGRAMS

Present Law

The Customs-Trade Partnership Against Terrorism (C–TPAT), codified in the Security and Accountability for Every Port Act (SAFE Port Act) of 2006 (6 U.S.C. 961 et seq.), is a voluntary trade partnership program in which Customs and Border Protection (CBP) and members of the trade community work together to secure and facilitate the movement of legitimate trade. Companies that are members of C–TPAT are considered low-risk, which expedites cargo clearance based on the company's security profile and compliance history.

House Amendment

Section 101 requires the Commissioner of CBP to work with the private sector and other Federal agencies to ensure that all CBP partnership programs provide trade benefits to participants. This would apply to partnership programs established before enactment of this bill, and any programs established after enactment. It establishes elements for the development and operation of any such partnership programs, which require the Commissioner to: 1) con-

103

EARMARK, LIMITED TAX BENEFITS, AND LIMITED TARIFF BENEFITS

In compliance with clause 9(e), 9(f), and 9(g) of Rule XXI of the Rules of the House of Representatives, the conference report and joint explanatory statement contain no earmarks, limited tax benefits, or limited tariff benefits.

CONSTITUTIONAL STATEMENT OF AUTHORITY

Congress has the power to enact this legislation pursuant to the following: Article I, Section 8, Clause 3 of the United States Constitution.

For consideration of the Senate bill and the House amendments, and modifications committed to conference:

FRED UPTON,
JOSEPH R. PITTS,
LEONARD LANCE,
BRETT GUTHRIE,
ADAM KINZINGER,
LARRY BUCSHON,
SUSAN W. BROOKS,
BOB GOODLATTE,
F. JAMES SENSENBRENNER, Jr.,
LAMAR SMITH,
TOM MARINO,
DOUG COLLINS,
DAVID A. TROTT,
MIKE BISHOP,
KEVIN MCCARTHY,

From the Committee on Education and the Workforce, for consideration of title VII of the House amendment, and modifications committed to conference:

LOU BARLETTA,
EARL L. "BUDDY" CARTER,

From the Committee on Veterans' Affairs, for consideration of title III of the House amendment, and modifications committed to conference:

GUS M. BILIRAKIS,
JACKIE WALORSKI,

From the Committee on Ways and Means, for consideration of sec. 705 of the Senate bill, and sec. 804 of the House amendment, and modifications committed to conference:

PATRICK MEEHAN,
ROBERT J. DOLD,
Managers on the Part of the House.

CHUCK GRASSLEY,
LAMAR ALEXANDER,
ORRIN G. HATCH,
JEFF SESSIONS,
Managers on the Part of the Senate.

○

FINANCIAL SERVICES AND GENERAL GOVERNMENT APPROPRIATIONS FOR 2016

HEARINGS

BEFORE A

SUBCOMMITTEE OF THE

COMMITTEE ON APPROPRIATIONS

HOUSE OF REPRESENTATIVES

ONE HUNDRED FOURTEENTH CONGRESS

FIRST SESSION

SUBCOMMITTEE ON FINANCIAL SERVICES AND GENERAL GOVERNMENT APPROPRIATIONS

ANDER CRENSHAW, Florida, *Chairman*

TOM GRAVES, Georgia
KEVIN YODER, Kansas
STEVE WOMACK, Arkansas
JAIME HERRERA BEUTLER, Washington
MARK E. AMODEI, Nevada
E. SCOTT RIGELL, Virginia

JOSÉ E. SERRANO, New York
MIKE QUIGLEY, Illinois
CHAKA FATTAH, Pennsylvania
SANFORD D. BISHOP, JR., Georgia

NOTE: Under Committee Rules, Mr. Rogers, as Chairman of the Full Committee, and Mrs. Lowey, as Ranking Minority Member of the Full Committee, are authorized to sit as Members of all Subcommittees.

WINNIE CHANG, KELLY HITCHCOCK,
ARIANA SARAR, and AMY CUSHING,
Subcommittee Staff

PART 5

U.S. GOVERNMENT PUBLISHING OFFICE

96–927 WASHINGTON : 2015

COMMITTEE ON APPROPRIATIONS

HAROLD ROGERS, Kentucky, *Chairman*

RODNEY P. FRELINGHUYSEN, New Jersey
ROBERT B. ADERHOLT, Alabama
KAY GRANGER, Texas
MICHAEL K. SIMPSON, Idaho
JOHN ABNEY CULBERSON, Texas
ANDER CRENSHAW, Florida
JOHN R. CARTER, Texas
KEN CALVERT, California
TOM COLE, Oklahoma
MARIO DIAZ-BALART, Florida
CHARLES W. DENT, Pennsylvania
TOM GRAVES, Georgia
KEVIN YODER, Kansas
STEVE WOMACK, Arkansas
JEFF FORTENBERRY, Nebraska
THOMAS J. ROONEY, Florida
CHARLES J. FLEISCHMANN, Tennessee
JAIME HERRERA BEUTLER, Washington
DAVID P. JOYCE, Ohio
DAVID G. VALADAO, California
ANDY HARRIS, Maryland
MARTHA ROBY, Alabama
MARK E. AMODEI, Nevada
CHRIS STEWART, Utah
E. SCOTT RIGELL, Virginia
DAVID W. JOLLY, Florida
DAVID YOUNG, Iowa
EVAN H. JENKINS, West Virginia
STEVEN M. PALAZZO, Mississippi

NITA M. LOWEY, New York
MARCY KAPTUR, Ohio
PETER J. VISCLOSKY, Indiana
JOSÉ E. SERRANO, New York
ROSA L. DELAURO, Connecticut
DAVID E. PRICE, North Carolina
LUCILLE ROYBAL-ALLARD, California
SAM FARR, California
CHAKA FATTAH, Pennsylvania
SANFORD D. BISHOP, JR., Georgia
BARBARA LEE, California
MICHAEL M. HONDA, California
BETTY McCOLLUM, Minnesota
STEVE ISRAEL, New York
TIM RYAN, Ohio
C. A. DUTCH RUPPERSBERGER, Maryland
DEBBIE WASSERMAN SCHULTZ, Florida
HENRY CUELLAR, Texas
CHELLIE PINGREE, Maine
MIKE QUIGLEY, Illinois
DEREK KILMER, Washington

WILLIAM E. SMITH, *Clerk and Staff Director*

(II)

[House Appropriation Hearing sample]

DEPARTMENT OF HOMELAND SECURITY APPROPRIATIONS FOR 2009

TUESDAY, FEBRUARY 26, 2008.

IMMIGRATION ENFORCEMENT: IDENTIFICATION AND REMOVAL OF CRIMINAL ALIENS, STUDENT AND EXCHANGE VISITOR PROGRAM FEE INCREASES

WITNESSES

CATHERYN COTTEN, DIRECTOR, INTERNATIONAL OFFICE, DUKE UNIVERSITY

JULIE L. MYERS, ASSISTANT SECRETARY, U.S. IMMIGRATION AND CUSTOMS ENFORCEMENT [ICE], DEPARTMENT OF HOMELAND SECURITY

Mr. PRICE. Subcommittee will come to order. Good morning, everyone. Today we will be discussing the wide variety of activities carried out by Immigration and Customs Enforcement, or ICE, and we will first focus on the Agency's Student and Exchange Visitor Program.

BALANCING SECURITY AND STUDENT NEEDS

Mr. PRICE. Thank you very much. We will put your entire statement in the record, which of course elaborates on the points you made and goes beyond them. Let me ask you first a rather broad question, and then I will zero in somewhat on the fee increases and the benefits that might accrue from an increased flow of fee revenue.

[Note style for questions and answers]

Question. What percentage of cases presented to prosecutors along the Southwest border are prosecuted? Provide by sector and/or state. What was the prosecution rate of criminals picked up off the street? (Culberson)

Answer. ICE does not track prosecutions, however, ICE works closely with U.S. Attorneys and state and local prosecutors nationwide on a wide variety of cases.

FY2007 SAC office	Criminal arrests	Indictments	Convictions*
El Paso, TX	2,435	1,882	1,704
Phoenix, AZ	1,641	623	770
San Antonio, TX	1,588	1,172	1,155
San Diego, CA	2,318	1,147	1,842
Fiscal Year Total	7,982	4,824	5,471

*Indictments and convictions may be comprised of arrests from previous years.

Mr. CULBERSON. Okay.

[Standard Hearing sample]

ORGANIZATIONAL MEETING ON ADOPTION OF COMMITTEE RULES; CONSIDERATION OF INTERIM REPORT; AND HEARING ON VOTING IN THE HOUSE OF REPRESENTATIVES

THURSDAY, SEPTEMBER 27, 2007

HOUSE OF REPRESENTATIVES,
SELECT COMMITTEE TO INVESTIGATE THE VOTING
IRREGULARITIES OF AUGUST 2, 2007,
Washington, DC.

The committee met, pursuant to call, at 9:11 a.m., in Room H–313, The Capitol, Hon. William D. Delahunt (Chairman of the committee) presiding.

Present: Representatives Delahunt, Davis, Herseth Sandlin, Pence, LaTourette and Hulshof.

The CHAIRMAN. A quorum being present, the select committee will come to order.

Today we are meeting to do three tasks: adopt our committee rules, adopt the internal report, and to hear for the first time—of what we expect to be multiple occasions—from the Office of the House Clerk. We will wait for the gentlelady from South Dakota, who was at her other select committee.

I now recognize myself for 5 minutes to make an opening statement, but before I do, let me note I will then go to Congressman Pence as the Ranking Member. And in subsequent hearings, it would be our hope that just he and I would make opening statements. But on this initial hearing, any member of the panel that wishes to make an opening statement is most welcome.

I would be remiss not to begin by thanking the Chair of the House Rules Committee, Louise Slaughter, and the Ranking Member, David Dreier, for making their hearing room available to the select committee.

I also want to welcome everyone to this initial meeting of the select committee that has been mandated by the House to review roll call No. 814. I would note that none of the Members sought this particular assignment, but each of us appreciates the role and the significance of the House in our unique constitutional order, and recognize that the integrity of the system by which we cast our votes on the House floor is essential to the confidence that the American people have in this institution, aptly described as the people's House.

Index

[Numbers in parentheses refer to rules; **bold** indicates chapter heading]

A

B

C

D

G

H

N

S

T

www.ingramcontent.com/pod-product-compliance
Lightning Source LLC
Chambersburg PA
CBHW072244260726
48659CB00004BA/1014
* 9 7 8 1 9 8 6 4 0 8 0 5 9 *